“Beilby’s scriptural and theologic He does not claim too much for any of the passages but simply shows how those texts that might seem to close the door to Postmortem Opportunity, when considered fully and in context, do not. Beilby’s book has convinced me of the plausibility of a Postmortem Opportunity for salvation for those who have not heard at all or have not heard well. Such a suggestion aligns with what I have found to be true of the character of God and enlivening for Christian mission and discipleship.”

Amy Peeler, associate professor of New Testament at Wheaton College, author of *You Are My Son: The Family of God in the Epistle to the Hebrews*

“Well-anchored in Scripture and Christian orthodoxy, Jim Beilby’s book provides a careful and wise exploration of Postmortem Opportunity. Beilby’s book is honest, humble, judicious, and insightful. Even if readers may disagree at points, Beilby will expand their horizons and offer much important food for thought.”

Paul Copan, Pledger Chair of Philosophy and Ethics at Palm Beach Atlantic University and author of *Loving Wisdom: A Guide to Philosophy and Christian Faith*

“Beilby does an admirable job of working through every dimension of how we should understand the fate of those who have died without hearing the saving message of Christ. This is not just a complex and interesting theological question. The answers have emotional and existential importance to those deeply concerned about the eternal status of loved ones. Beilby skillfully draws on exegetical, philosophical, and theological resources to offer his view of Postmortem Opportunity for salvation, both for the unevangelized and the pseudoevangelized. Throughout, the book offers creative alternatives while avoiding speculative conclusions, all the time insisting on the centrality of salvation in Christ.”

Steve Wilkens, professor of philosophy and ethics at Azusa Pacific University

“Beilby’s defense of the controversial idea of postmortem conversion is biblically engaged, theologically robust, and philosophically sophisticated. It is hard to imagine a better or more thorough treatment of this complex set of issues. Indeed, this book is a model of how philosophical theology ought to be done.”

Jerry L. Walls, professor of philosophy and scholar in residence at Houston Baptist University

POSTMORTEM OPPORTUNITY

A BIBLICAL AND THEOLOGICAL ASSESSMENT OF SALVATION AFTER DEATH

JAMES BEILBY

IVP Academic
An imprint of InterVarsity Press
Downers Grove, Illinois

InterVarsity Press
P.O. Box 1400, Downers Grove, IL 60515-1426
ivpress.com
email@ivpress.com

InterVarsity Press® is the book-publishing division of InterVarsity Christian Fellowship/USA®, a movement of students and faculty active on campus at hundreds of universities, colleges, and schools of nursing in the United States of America, and a member movement of the International Fellowship of Evangelical Students. For information about local and regional activities, visit intervarsity.org.

Cover design and image composite: Cindy Kiple
Interior design: Daniel van Loon
Image: white and orange staircase: © B Knight / Moment Collection / Getty Images

ISBN 978-0-8308-5376-2 (print)
ISBN 978-0-8308-5377-9 (digital)

Printed in the United States of America ♾

InterVarsity Press is committed to ecological stewardship and to the conservation of natural resources in all our operations. This book was printed using sustainably sourced paper.

Library of Congress Cataloging-in-Publication Data
A catalog record for this book is available from the Library of Congress.

P 25 24 23 22 21 20 19 18 17 16 15 14 13 12 11 10 9 8 7 6 5 4 3 2 1
Y 37 36 35 34 33 32 31 30 29 28 27 26 25 24 23 22 21

TO PAUL EDDY

colleague,

coauthor/collaborator,

researcher-than-which-none-better-can-be-conceived-of,

true friend

CONTENTS

PREFACE

The destiny of the unevangelized is one of the perennial questions in Christian theology. In short, it is the question of how we should think about the salvation of those who had no opportunity to respond to the gospel in this life. This book is a defense of a version of the theory of Postmortem Opportunity, or the idea that those who die without a genuine opportunity to hear and respond to the gospel will receive an opportunity after death to do so. The uniqueness of this theory is driven by a pair of commitments: one typically thought as solidly traditional and the other deemed to be "outside-the-box." The defender of Postmortem Opportunity assumes that explicit, conscious, and intentional faith in Jesus Christ is necessary for salvation, but they also make a claim that many have discounted as impossible, theologically liberal, or otherwise problematic: that death is not the end of salvific opportunity and that some might receive their first and only opportunity to hear the gospel and respond to God's salvific offer after death.

My goals for this book are twofold. My first goal is apologetic in nature—that is, I want to provide what I think is a good answer to the question of the destiny of the unevangelized. I have wrestled with this issue for as long as I have thought about theological questions, though I am clearly not the only one to do so. I routinely poll my students at Bethel University regarding the questions they deem to be most pressing or difficult. For the last eight years, the question of the destiny of the unevangelized has never been lower than number two on that list, and it has only been beaten by the problem of evil. The second goal is theological in nature—that is, I seek to explain the theological commitments that underlie the commitment to Postmortem Opportunity.

Engaging these theological questions is not the primary goal of this book, but it is impossible to articulate the theory of Postmortem Opportunity without doing at least some theological spadework. This is because one's understanding of the salvific fate of the unevangelized is closely connected with other significant debates in soteriology, not the least of which is the perennial debate between Calvinists and Arminians on the role of divine and human choice in salvation. But it would be folly to pretend to plumb the depths of that argument. It will have to suffice to explain my perspective and discuss the various ways the debate as a whole affects my claims. As such, the tone of this volume is largely constructive. I do not spend much time deconstructing other answers, either apologetic or theological. When I do engage other answers or views, it is primarily to discuss objections to my view or to explain where my view differs from those alternative theories.

There is one other feature of this volume that is important to mention—namely, its interdisciplinary nature. The theological nature of this book will be immediately apparent. This is because the destiny of the unevangelized is an explicitly soteriological question, but also because a good number of my interlocutors are theologians. The philosophical nature of significant stretches of this book is also fairly obvious. Everything from how I articulate the question of the destiny of the unevangelized to how I argue for my preferred view draws on philosophical insights and methods.[1] The emphasis on theology and philosophy in this volume make sense, for while my academic position and most of my teaching work is in theology, my personal and academic interests have always driven me toward the intersection of theology and philosophy. However, in addition to theology and philosophy, this volume includes a quite a bit of exegetical work and a

[1]In particular, I resonate with an approach to philosophy and theology known as analytic theology. For a helpful discussion of its nature, I recommend Thomas McCall, *An Invitation to Analytic Theology* (Downers Grove, IL: IVP Academic, 2015). For excellent examples of the practice of analytic theology, see Oliver D. Crisp and Michael C. Rea, eds., *Analytic Theology: New Essays in the Philosophy of Theology* (New York: Oxford University Press, 2009).

chapter that addresses historical issues in depth. While I do not claim to be a specialist in biblical or historical theology, I firmly believe that some of the most important, interesting, and pressing theological conundrums—and the destiny of the evangelized question is paramount among them—require robustly interdisciplinary work. So, I have (courageously at best, foolishly at worst) thrown myself into areas in which I am not an expert, hoping that the value of the attempt to speak to this complex issue as a whole will be apparent. However, in doing this, I am swimming against a strong tide. Grand statements about the value of interdisciplinarity are common in the academic world, but the subtle push toward specialization and disciplinary purity is both ubiquitous and powerful.[2]

There are also a number of assumptions made in this volume that will be helpful to be upfront about. My discussion of the destiny of the unevangelized occurs wholly within the Christian tradition. This is not in any way to devalue the perspective of other traditions on this matter. There are non-Christian views of salvation, such as the *karma-moksha-samsura* doctrine in which people are reincarnated until they achieve some sense of "salvation," that might be taken as an answer to the question of the destiny of the unevangelized. However, I am merely seeking to answer the version that arises within my own religious tradition. Not only am I writing from within the Christian tradition, I am trying this stay within an orthodox strand of it, and consequently, I will be assuming the ontological necessity of Jesus Christ for salvation. If anybody is saved, it is only because of the salvific work of Jesus Christ.

Further, I will assume that the individualistic framing of the problem of the destiny of the unevangelized is not insuperably problematic. While I wholeheartedly agree that much of Western Christianity

[2]My experience of this push toward specialization has been that in the eyes of some I have done too much philosophy to be "truly a theologian" and too much theology to be "truly a philosopher."

assumes an individualistic mindset that skews the biblical picture of salvation, the question of the destiny of the unevangelized is as individualized as it is precisely because the unevangelized are, by definition, separated from any ecclesiological context. If one assumes that an ecclesial context is a necessary condition for salvation, then one has defined the unevangelized beyond salvific reach. Not only does this seem unreasonable, I would argue that there is an irreducibly individualistic component of the Christian notion of salvation. To see this, we need a distinction between the result of salvation and the means to salvation. The Christian picture of the result of salvation is undeniably and irreducibly communal. Salvation is union with Christ and being part of the body of Christ; one cannot even talk about the Christian picture of salvation without talking about others: God and neighbors. But the question of the destiny of the unevangelized is not primarily an inquiry into the result of salvation, it is to inquire about the means to salvation and particularly how those who do not possess the means of salvation, who have not heard the gospel of Jesus Christ, can be saved.

Last, I will be assuming that salvation includes an eschatological dimension. In particular, I will be assuming that there is a conscious afterlife for all persons, those who embrace relationship with God and those who do not. Moreover, contrary to those who believe heaven and hell exist as metaphors for aspects of or experiences in this life, I am assuming that heaven and hell exist in a realist sense—they are mind-independent realms of being. This is not to suggest that the point of salvation is wholly eschatological. Salvation is not just a promissory note for entrance to heaven, but a current participation in the life of God. Just as Christ's resurrection was described by Paul as the "firstfruits" (1 Cor 15:20), so it might be said that our experience of God in this life is the firstfruits, not complete or final, but very real and important. The question of the destiny of the unevangelized, however, is by its very nature, a question that is outside the norm. It asks whether those who did not hear the gospel in this life and therefore did not have an opportunity to experience the this-worldly significance of salvation, still have an opportunity to be saved.

The sequence of argument in this book is the following. In chapter one, I describe the problem of the destiny of the unevangelized itself and discuss what sorts of people might fall into the category of "the unevangelized." I argue that the problem is far more complex than most people who have addressed this issue have allowed. In addition to more traditional pictures of the unevangelized, there are a diverse group of people who might be called "pseudoevangelized" that must be reckoned with. After discussing the conceptual relationships between the problem of the destiny of the unevangelized, the problem of evil, and the problem of divine hiddenness, I offer a way of understanding the problem that has structural similarities to the trilemma. This way of understanding the problem of the destiny of the unevangelized also nicely highlights the three major categories of responses to it. I briefly canvas these responses and suggest the possibility of a different sort of answer to the problem of the destiny of the unevangelized: Postmortem Opportunity. In chapter two, I describe Postmortem Opportunity and explain the rationale for it. I also articulate the specific claims of my version of Postmortem Opportunity and apply these claims to the case studies of the unevangelized and pseudoevangelized discussed in the first chapter. In chapter three, I develop a theological argument for the theory of Postmortem Opportunity. In doing so, I first lay out the theological assumptions that undergird my argument. These assumptions are not radical or unheard of, but they are not universally held. The argument itself employs abductive reasoning, a form of argument often called "inference to the best explanation." Chapter four considers two categories of scriptural objections to Postmortem Opportunity: the claim that Scripture rules out Postmortem Opportunity by teaching that death is the end of salvific opportunity, and the claim that Scripture teaches things that imply the falsity of Postmortem Opportunity.

Chapter five addresses the scriptural evidence for Postmortem Opportunity, both indirect and direct. The most difficult set of texts here are the "descent into Hades" texts. While there is some scriptural evidence for Postmortem Opportunity, it is not as strong as the defender of Postmortem Opportunity might hope, and as such, the chapter concludes with a discussion of how to think about theological concepts that are not directly and explicitly taught by Scripture. Chapter six considers the historical objection that the church has decisively rejected Postmortem Opportunity as an orthodox option. I discuss the witness of the early church and seek to explain why the postmortem hope held by some in the early church waned. Chapter seven addresses the primary theological objections to Postmortem Opportunity: the objection that we shouldn't try to answer this question, objections to the problematic implications of Postmortem Opportunity for this life, objections to the eschatological details of Postmortem Opportunity, and difficulties associated with the very concept of the pseudoevangelized. Chapter eight addresses a common and influential wider hope view: Inclusivism. I argue that the combination of Inclusivism and Postmortem Opportunity is significantly preferable to Inclusivism alone. Chapter nine considers the biblical and theological arguments for and against Universalism. I argue that the evidence does not support the belief that all will be saved. The final chapter considers whether the commitment to Postmortem Opportunity requires one to be a Universalist. After arguing that it does not, I discuss what the concept of hell might look like for a defender of Postmortem Opportunity.

Regarding Postmortem Opportunity, I make two claims. The first is that Christians are permitted to believe that God will provide a Postmortem Opportunity to the unevangelized. The language of permission, here, has two senses: (1) epistemological—there is nothing epistemically substandard or irrational about embracing the theory of Postmortem Opportunity—and (2) theological—there is nothing heretical or contrary to the clear teaching of Scripture about Postmortem

Opportunity. My second claim is that, for synergists at least, the theory of Postmortem Opportunity is better than other answers to the question of the destiny of the unevangelized. That being said, the primary burden of this volume is to establish the first of these claims. While I do speak to the second, I do not really do the detailed comparative work necessary to establish it.

ACKNOWLEDGMENTS

There are a large number of people who have contributed to this book in one way or another. In particular, there are a number of authors whose work was especially helpful: John Sanders's *No Other Name* is quite simply the best book available on the question of the destiny of the unevangelized; Clark Pinnock's *A Wideness of God's Mercy* was my introduction to the Postmortem Opportunity view; Millard Erickson's *How Shall They Be Saved?* was an invaluable source of fair, clear objections to my view; Terrence Tiessen's *Who Can Be Saved?* is a magisterial treatment of soteriological questions; Jerry Walls's *Hell: The Logic of Eternal Damnation* provides the best version of Postmortem Opportunity of which I am aware; and finally, Richard Bauckham's *The Fate of the Dead* saved me from making a good number of mistakes in my treatment of the early church.

In addition, a good number of friends have also offered comments on the manuscript of this book or discussed portions of it with me. Their help has been invaluable. They include Greg Boyd, Paul Eddy, Steve Enderlein, Josh Gerth, Juan Hernández, Mike Holmes, Erik Leafblad, Tom McCall, Tim Pawl, Mike Rea, Dan Reid, Tom Schreiner, Mark Strauss, and Jerry Walls. My apologies to anybody I have missed. Thanks is also due to the participants of the Analytic Theology group at the 2019 Evangelical Theology Society: Amy Peeler, Daniel Strange, and Marc Cortez. I have also received valuable assistance from a number of students, most of them my TAs: Anna Anderson, Gabrielle Arland, Sierra Beilby, Kasey Erickson, Allie Fauth, Evan Gosen, Mckenzie Van Loh, and especially John Barclay III, who read and provided comments on the entire manuscript. Thanks is also due to Bethel University, which provided me with a sabbatical in spring 2016 and a course release in January 2017 and 2018. I wish to thank David McNutt and the editorial staff at IVP for their wise counsel and assistance. I also offer my thanks to the staff at the Lino Lakes Caribou Coffee and HammerHeart Brewing Company, where I wrote much of this book.

In addition, I cannot thank my family enough for their love and support. My wife Michelle, and my kids Sierra, Maddie, Zach, and Malia have put up with my early morning writing sessions and with my being distracted by some abstruse aspect of this project at other times during the day. You all bring joy to my life like nothing else in this world.[1] Finally, I wish to thank a person who has been an interlocutor on the issues in this book, a coauthor/coeditor on many other projects, and a treasured friend who has been there for me in times of tears and in times of side-splitting laughter. Paul Eddy, this book is dedicated to you.

[1]I should also acknowledge the attempted contribution of my son, Zach. He thought the title of this book should be *Death? Life, Part 2: Electric Boogaloo*. I am sad to say that I chose a more boring title.

1

THE DESTINY OF THE UNEVANGELIZED

If Christ declares Himself to be the Way of salvation, the Grace and the Truth, and affirms that in Him alone, and only to souls believing in Him, is the way of return to God, what has become of men who lived in the many centuries before Christ came? . . . What, then, has become of such an innumerable multitude of souls, who were in no wise blameworthy, seeing that He in whom alone saving faith can be exercised had not yet favored men with His advent?

PORPHYRY, *AGAINST THE CHRISTIANS*

If Christ is the only way and if there are millions who never hear of him, then any being worthy of the title "God" must have known this fact when he chose to create. And if he did know that millions would never even have an opportunity to be saved, it is impossible to think of God as perfectly loving. As such, even though I am lucky to be among those who hears the gospel, I cannot believe in a God who makes the opportunity to be saved a matter of temporal and geographical luck.

ME, LETTER FROM JUNE 1991

Porphyry's objection is a well-known and succinct statement of what has come to be known as the "problem of the destiny of the unevangelized."[1] The Christian affirmation that salvation is through

[1]Quoted by Augustine in *Epistle 102*, ed. Philip Schaff, *Nicene and Post Nicene Fathers*, Series 1 (1886-1889; repr., Grand Rapids, MI: Eerdmans, 1974), 416 (section 8). Hereafter cited as NPNF. We are forced to rely on Augustine's (and other Christian theologians') quotations of Porphyry

Jesus Christ alone forces the question of how to think about those who lived and died without ever hearing of the gospel of Jesus Christ. Less well-known, but more personally relevant, the second quote is from a letter written to a friend during a crisis of faith I experienced in 1990–1991. The root issue for my crisis of faith was the problem of evil, catalyzed by the death from cancer of my college football coach. But my faith crisis also brought to light and intensified several theological issues I had struggled with as long as I could remember. Paramount among those was the destiny of the unevangelized. Part of my coming back to faith in late 1991 was a belief there might be an answer the question of the destiny of the unevangelized. And since then I have been wrestling with what that answer might look like.

The issue of the destiny of the unevangelized is first and foremost a theological conundrum. The problem finds its origin in the common belief that God desires everyone to be saved. Some see this as a straightforward implication of God's love for humanity. Others point to the scriptural basis for such a claim, including 1 Timothy 2:4, which says that God "wants all people to be saved and to come to a knowledge of the truth" and 2 Peter 3:9, which says that God "is patient with you, not wanting anyone to perish, but everyone to come to repentance." These passages (and others) make it difficult to make sense of the idea that there are many (probably many millions) who seem to never receive an opportunity to hear the gospel of Jesus Christ. There are, of course many different ways to look at these theological issues and, given some of those, this problem is less pressing. Nevertheless, the destiny of the unevangelized represents a genuine theological dilemma for many ways of thinking about God's salvific will and human salvation. While theology is front and center in the issue of the destiny of the unevangelized, apologetics is lurking close by. For many, this issue constitutes a serious challenge to central claims of Christianity: the fact that there are some

because in 435 and 438 CE Theodosius II ordered that all extant copies of *Against the Christians* be burned.

who (apparently) never have an opportunity to respond to the gospel calls into question either God's love or God's justice or both. For others, this issue highlights possible contradictions (or at least conundrums) in Scripture. And, last, as is always the case in theological matters, one's personal experience can intensify the power of this objection—such as when one's ancestors (apparently) never had an opportunity to hear the gospel, or if one's child died before they had the capacity to hear and understand the gospel message.

So the problem of the destiny of the unevangelized, simply stated, is the question of how to think salvific possibilities of those who never hear the gospel. But answering this question is anything but simple. Engaging the question of the destiny of the unevangelized forces one to think about the nature of faith, grace, and salvation; God's will with respect to salvation; beliefs about what happens to people at death; and ultimately the nature of judgment and hell. In other words, the matter of the destiny of the unevangelized is connected with some of the most significant issues in soteriology and eschatology, not to mention some important matters in theology proper, anthropology, pneumatology, and ecclesiology. It is for this reason that I call the destiny of the unevangelized a "theological nexus"—answering this question requires networking together a good number of theological answers.

It is the task of this book to explicate and defend a somewhat nontraditional answer to this problem. The task of this chapter is to introduce the problem itself and then introduce the traditional answers to the problem. But first, we need to address an obviously important question.

WHO ARE THE UNEVANGELIZED?

This is not a *pro forma* introductory question, for one's belief as to who is, in fact, unevangelized has the power to shape their answer to this question, or at least shape their sense of what sorts of answers are possible/impossible or likely/unlikely. For the purposes of concreteness, I will offer a trio of case studies, each of which presses the issue of the problem of the destiny of the unevangelized in a slightly different way.

George. The first category of "unevangelized" are those who never hear the gospel because of geographic or temporal isolation from anyone who could tell them about Jesus. Take for example, a denizen of Upper Mongolia in the ninth century BCE; let's call him George. George exists prior to Jesus and in a part of the world where he will not have access to the special revelation given to the nation of Israel. This does not mean, of course, that George does not receive any revelation. According to Romans 1:20, which says that God has made his essential nature known through his creation, all people, including George, receive general revelation. What is hotly debated is whether general revelation alone can be salvific. For instance, even if George walks out of his hut, looks up at the night sky, and is struck with awe by the majesty and power of God's creation and on the basis of that experience chooses to faithfully trust the "creator of the stars," some will say that he cannot be saved, because he has not heard the gospel of Jesus Christ. In other words, people like George are referred to as "unevangelized" because (it seems) they have been given only general revelation, and general revelation (it is claimed by some) is insufficient for salvation.

There are undoubtedly many "Georges," but the exact number can only be guessed at, and guesses vary widely depending on one's view of human origins. (Do all humans come from two specially and recently created human beings? If not, are only "modern" humans to be counted or do we include various other species—Neanderthals, for instance—with whom modern humans interbred?) Nonetheless, it is plausible that there were hundreds of millions of people who lived before Christ and had no access to the special revelation given to Israel. To that number, we must add those who have lived since the time of Christ, but have never heard his gospel. This number is also up for debate, but since there were approximately 310 million people in 1000 CE,[2] and only an estimated 50 million Christians,[3] it would not be unreasonable to say that there have been tens of billions of people (and maybe a lot more) who have never heard the gospel of Jesus Christ.

Baby Anna. The second category of "unevangelized" are those who, at the time of death, lack the cognitive capacity to grasp the gospel message. Consider the example of an infant named Anna, who dies at the age of six months.[4] Obviously, Anna died well before developing the intellectual capacities to understand and respond to the gospel of Jesus Christ. How should we think about the salvation of babies like Anna?[5] Unfortunately, Scripture is not as helpful on this matter as we might wish. Despite the fact that the word *infant* (in its various forms) occurs nearly one thousand times, there is not a single scriptural text that directly speaks to the salvific status of infants who die before developing the capacity to understand the gospel.[6]

Nonetheless, placing infants in the same category, soteriologically speaking, as George is controversial. Even if it we grant that Scripture does not speak clearly to the salvific status of those who die in infancy, it is undeniable that, throughout history, there have been a range of ways Christian theologians have dealt with the problem of infant salvation.

---

[2]Data from United Nations Department of Economic and Social Affairs, Population Division. Estimates of the population for 1000 CE range from 254 to 345 million.

[3]This commonly cited number is based on "conjecture" by the English historian Sharon Taylor. See his *History of the Anglo-Saxons*, 5th ed., vol. 3 (London: Longman, Rees, Orme, Brown, and Green, 1828), 484.

[4]The name Anna does not refer to any actual person.

[5]It is common to acknowledge that the salvation of infants is a part of the problem of the destiny of the unevangelized. What is less commonly acknowledged is the extent of this problem. One estimate places the number of infants who never have the opportunity to hear the gospel (including embryos that fail to implant, spontaneous abortions, miscarriages, stillbirths, and infants who die before their cognitive capabilities are sufficiently developed) at 350 billion. See Gregory Paul, "Theodicy's Problem: A Statistical Look at the Holocaust of the Children, and the Implications of Natural Evil for the Free Will and Best of All Worlds Hypotheses," *Philosophy & Theology* 19, nos. 1–2 (2007): 127-29.

[6]R. A. Webb, *Theology of Infant Salvation* (Harrisonburg, PA: Sprinkle, 1981 [1907]), 11. See also Millard Erickson, *How Shall They Be Saved? The Destiny of Those Who Do Not Hear of Jesus* (Grand Rapids, MI: Baker, 1996), 236.

Age of accountability. One common solution is to claim that since infants do not have any personal guilt (that is, guilt associated with their own conscious, intentional sin), they do not need faith until they reach what is called the age of accountability. There is no reason, of course, to think that the age of accountability can be specified precisely or is even the same for all children.[7] But, however the idea of the age of accountability is understood, it is pretty clear that there are many who die before being able to understand the gospel. Defenders of the age of accountability have used a number of scriptural texts. Jesus' words in Matthew 19:14, "Let the little children come to me, and do not hinder them, for the kingdom of heaven belongs to such as these" is commonly cited in this context, as is Matthew 18:3 and parallels: "Truly I tell you, unless you change and become like little children, you will never enter the kingdom of heaven." But perhaps the most significant text is David's words to his deceased infant son: "I will go to him, but he will not return to me" (2 Sam 12:23). The hopefulness of David's words, especially considered in juxtaposition to the lack of hope in David's words following the death of his adult son Absalom (2 Sam 18:33), has been taken to teach that infants are saved despite their inability to hear and respond to the gospel.[8] The assumption here is that (1) as a "man after [God's] own heart" (1 Sam 13:14; Acts 13:22), David is of course saved and (2) therefore, "I will go to him" should be understood as "the infant is already in heaven and David will be reunited with him there." The problem with this assumption is that it projects a New Testament understanding of death and the afterlife onto the Old Testament, and the Old Testament is shockingly silent on specifics about the reality of the postmortem world,

---

[7]There is also no reason to assume a very early age to the age of accountability. Recent research on the brain development of children and adolescents shows that the human brain is not fully developed in important respects until a person is in their twenties. There are, of course, layers of difficult issues here and there is much we do not know. Agnosticism on when any given child reaches the age of accountability is the best choice.

[8]R. A. Webb goes so far as to say that "this incident verges very nigh to a dogmatic prooftext for the assertion that all infants dying in infancy are finally saved" (*Theology of Infant Salvation*, 21; italics removed).

and salvation in the Old Testament was understood primarily in this-worldly terms. This leads to the following question: If someone would have asked David, "Where is your child now?" would he have said "heaven"? On the fairly reasonable assumption that David's views reflected the personal eschatology in the Old Testament, David would have likely believed that his son was in Sheol, the place of the dead. Consequently, his statement "I will go to him" was plausibly simply a statement that David, like his son, would someday die.[9]

In addition, the problem with the age of accountability position on infant salvation is that it does not seem to fit well with the affirmation of original sin. The essence of the doctrine of original sin is that even though infants have not yet chosen to sin, they still have a sin nature that separates them from God. They are, in other words, not in the same boat, spiritually speaking, as Adam and Eve prior to their sin. Now there are complexities here and variations of the doctrine of original sin that begin to speak to this problem, but for our purposes it is sufficient to note that the matter of original sin is a potential barrier to the simple affirmation that infants who die prior to the reaching the age of accountability are saved.[10]

Baptismal regeneration. A second common solution to the problem of infant salvation is to affirm that infant baptism removes the stain of original sin and therefore, if an infant who has received the sacrament of baptism dies, they are understood as part of God's covenant people. Jesus' words to Nicodemus in John 3:5, "No one can enter the kingdom of God unless they are born of water and the Spirit," have been taken as supportive of the doctrine of baptismal regeneration, as has Titus 3:5: "He saved us, not because of righteous things we had done, but because of his mercy. He saved us through the washing of rebirth and renewal by the Holy Spirit." Opinions on the salvific efficacy of infant baptism

---

[9]An argument also made by John Sanders, *No Other Name: An Investigation into the Destiny of the Unevangelized* (Grand Rapids, MI: Eerdmans, 1992), 289.

[10]Erickson has a helpful treatment of the issues surrounding this dilemma (*How Shall They Be Saved?*, 249-53). It is interesting to note that he suggests that an infant's postmortem appearance before Christ has the effect of purifying his or her depraved nature (252).

have varied throughout history, but the primary difficulty with the baptismal regeneration view comes not in upholding the importance of infant baptism. Rather, the difficulty lies in making infant baptism *sufficient* by itself for salvation without rendering unnecessary a personal decision of commitment and the explicit faith that accompanies it. It is one thing to say that baptism is salvifically efficacious in the sense of bringing one into the community of God or by removing the taint of original sin; it is another thing altogether to say that infant baptism is sufficient all by itself for salvation. Suffice it to say that there are interesting arguments that suggest that infant baptism is not salvific in any simple sense and, to the degree that those arguments are valid, then even baptized infants might still be seen as unevangelized in an important sense. And, even apart from these debates, the salvific destiny of unbaptized babies remains a pressing question.

Elect infant. The final common solution to the problem of infant salvation is to allow that infants are capable of being elected by God even though they are unable to conceptualize and embrace the gospel of Jesus Christ.[11] This perspective was embraced by the Westminster Confession: "Elect infants dying in infancy are regenerated and saved by Christ through the Spirit who worketh when, and where, and how he pleaseth" (10.3). The logic of this perspective is closely tied to the Calvinist notion of salvation. Since Calvinism views adults as dead in their sin and incapable of doing anything to contribute to their salvation, "there is no more inconsistency in the infant being saved by Christ's atoning death than in the adult being saved."[12] Erickson summarizes this position as follows: "Infants are savable because they are electable and they are electable because election is the work of God, not of human beings."[13] In fact, some go so far as to say that all persons who die in infancy must necessarily be elect, because "providence must delay

[11]See, for example, Terrance L. Tiessen's reference to "infant faith" (*Who Can Be Saved? Reassessing Salvation in Christ and World Religions* [Downers Grove, IL: InterVarsity Press, 2004], 213).
[12]Erickson, *How Shall They Be Saved?*, 246.
[13]Erickson, *How Shall They Be Saved?*, 246.

the death of the reprobate infant until he comes to maturity, and translates his original sin into conscious actual sin, so that there may be a basis, not simply in law and truth, but in consciousness and conscience and experience for penalty."[14] This solution to the problem of infant salvation is, of course, only available to those who embrace a Calvinist soteriology. Those who find Calvinist soteriology to be problematic must look elsewhere for an answer.

Sam. The third category of "unevangelized" are those who, due to various types of disabilities, never develop the cognitive capacity to grasp the gospel.[15] There has been extensive attention paid throughout the centuries to the problem of infant salvation, but the problem of those with cognitive disabilities has only recently been given its due attention. Unfortunately, when the issue of the salvation of the cognitively disabled is discussed, it is often treated as a subset of the problem of infant salvation. This is understandable because there are significant parallels between the Anna and Sam cases. In particular, if there is such a thing as the age of accountability for infants, it is plausible to apply it to at least some of the cognitively disabled as well. Similarly, if infants like Anna can be saved due to infant baptism or election, then undoubtedly, so can the Sams of the world. However, while there are undoubtedly parallel differences between the two cases of Anna and Sam, I treat them as separate because there are significant differences between the two. One of the most important of these differences is the significant variety of cognitive disabilities. There might be some differences within the set of Anna cases, depending on how close the child is to the age of accountability, but the range of differences in Sam cases are much greater. Undoubtedly, some cognitive disabilities are so

---

[14]Webb, *Theology of Infant Salvation*, 291.

[15]I would also include in this category children who were not born with any cognitive disability, but sustained a cognition-impairing injury prior to the age of accountability. I have chosen the name Sam for this case study, but the name Sam does not refer to any actual person. This is because there is such a wide variety of cognitive disabilities that it would be problematic to have the name of this case study be associated with a single type of disability.

severe as to utterly rule out any possibility of grasping the gospel in any way, but there are some who are diagnosed with cognitive disabilities that nonetheless have the ability to cognize at least some of what is necessary for salvation. The second difference between Anna and Sam cases is the fact that, in terms a number of important virtues such as kindness, faith, commitment—virtues usually taken as being crucially important to relationship with God—it is plausible to see at least some with cognitive disabilities as a model toward which those *without* disabilities can aspire.

The questions about salvation that Sam cases force us to engage are profound. The question is not simply whether the individuals represented by Sam cases have or have not received the gospel. Rather the question is how we should understand the concept of salvation when considering people who have been created in God's image and who are loved by God, but who may lack certain intellectual categories often thought to be essential for salvation, like awareness of sin, grace, and conversion. In fact, one might go so far as to ask how the concept of sin applies to individuals who do not reason in power-over categories like the rest of us. This is not, of course, to deny that individuals like Sam are sinful and in need of salvation. Rather it is to point out that our typical ways of describing sin and salvation probably have to be at least complicated and perhaps reimagined to successfully engage the situation of those with cognitive disabilities.[16]

COMPLICATING OUR QUESTION: THE PSEUDOEVANGELIZED

The unevangelized are those who have not *heard* the gospel of Jesus Christ, either due to geographic or temporal isolation from the gospel (George), or due to cognitive limitations due to premature death (Anna), or due to cognitive limitations due to developmental disability (Sam).

---

[16]Some helpful steps toward this reimagining have been taken by Amos Yong, *Theology and Down Syndrome: Reimagining Disability in Late Modernity* (Waco, TX: Baylor University Press, 2007). See also his "Disability and the Love of Wisdom: De-forming, Re-forming, and Per-forming Philosophy of Religion," *Ars Disputandi* 9 (2009): 54-71.

This understanding of the state of being "unevangelized" arises from the belief that "faith comes from hearing" (Romans 10:17). This auditory understanding of "hearing" fits perfectly with the George case, but less well with Anna and Sam. Anna and Sam may have actually "heard" (auditorially) the gospel, but their problem is their capacity to understand what they have heard. However, it is important to note that there are more barriers to truly hearing the gospel than merely failure to hear or failure to understand what has been heard. To make this point concrete, I will offer three more cases, each of which articulates a different kind of barrier to having a genuine opportunity to respond to the gospel.

Kunta Kinte. Kunta Kinte is the main figure from Alex Haley's novel *Roots*.[17] Born in 1750 in Juffure, Gambia, Kunta was taken captive by white slave traders at age seventeen and brought over to America. While in America, Kunta hears about his slave owners' God. This God, Kunta is told, thinks that African slaves are not quite human and that the enslavement, rape, and torture of Africans by white Christians is perfectly acceptable. Kunta Kinte utterly rejects this God, not just because he is a devout Muslim, but because the Christian "gospel" he hears is morally repugnant. Moreover, all Christians should agree with Kunta's assessment of this "gospel" and should regard Kunta Kinte's rejection of this bastardized "gospel" as not only eminently rational, but even morally praiseworthy. Has Kunta heard the name of Jesus and rejected it? Yes, but only in the most superficial sense. He has heard *the name* "Jesus" and he has heard some information *about* Jesus, but the gospel that he has heard is certainly not good news—not for him and I suggest not even for his white slave owners, for a God who blesses their actions is neither good nor worthy of worship.

[17]Alex Haley, *Roots* (New York: Dell, 1976). Recent studies have questioned the historical accuracy of Haley's portrayal of Kunta Kinte. Even if Haley's account of Kunta Kinte's life is fictionalized, that does not affect the point I am making because it is impossible to doubt that many of the over 10 million slaves brought to the United States from Africa were placed in a situation very similar to Kunta Kinte's.

Notice that this category does not just include African slaves like Kunta Kinte. It also includes the many indigenous people who were forced to give up their "heathen" cultural heritage and convert to a Western cultural mindset. Undoubtedly, some of the hearers of this Westernized gospel rejected it because of the dismissal of their culture, not because they were rejecting the genuine good news of Jesus Christ. Have they heard the gospel? Yes and no.

Micha. Micha was born in South Korea to a prostitute who gave her up for adoption to an American couple.[18] Her adoptive parents, however, divorced shortly after her adoption and after years of neglect and abuse, Micha ended up in the foster care system. Sadly, while from the outside Micha's situation with her foster family seemed to be a vast improvement, it was not. Her foster father sexually abused her, and when she told her foster mother, she accused Micha of seducing her husband and told her that she didn't want to talk about it anymore. In high school, Micha started attending church and mustered up the courage to tell her youth pastor, who she had come to trust and respect, of her experience at home. But instead of helping her, her youth pastor took advantage of Micha's vulnerability and began abusing her as well. Moreover, he was spiritually abusive and sought to justify his actions on biblical and theological grounds. Having been rejected and abused by every person that was supposed to love and protect her, Micha considered ending her life, but chose instead to survive. To survive, Micha refuses to trust anybody and she masks her pain with drugs and alcohol.[19]

The details associated with each situation vary widely, but there is no doubt that there are many, many Michas out there. They may have heard the gospel in one sense, but their childhood experiences have rendered them unable to genuinely grasp the idea of an all-powerful,

[18]"Micha" does not refer to any one person, but her experiences are an amalgam of the experiences of various people with whom I have become acquainted over the years.

[19]Marilyn Adams makes a similar point in "The Problem of Hell: A Problem of Evil for Christians," in *Reasoned Faith*, ed. Eleonore Stump (Ithaca, NY: Cornell University Press, 1993), 313.

loving God and unable to drop their protective defenses to allow them to trust anybody. The mindset "Sure, maybe God exists, but he obviously doesn't love me (because I'm intrinsically unlovable or because if he did he would have protected me, etc.)" is tragically common.

Rapunzel. The third example is controversial, because like Kunta Kinte and Micha, Rapunzel has heard the gospel, but unlike Kunta Kinte, the version of the gospel she has heard is not bastardized, and unlike Micha, she has not had experiences that have left her unable to trust. Rapunzel is a young woman who has heard the gospel and who (we have every reason to believe) is on a trajectory toward repentance and relationship with God.[20] Gretel and Rapunzel are identical twins who are very close and who have very similar backgrounds, personalities, and preferences. They have started attending church and have both felt some attraction to both the Christian community and to the gospel message. One day Gretel and Rapunzel were both heading to a church event, but because Rapunzel needed to do some errands, they drove separately. Gretel arrived and, during the event, became aware of her need for salvation and committed her life to Jesus Christ in an authentic and wholehearted way. What she doesn't know is that her sister, Rapunzel was involved in a fatal car crash on her way to church.

While there is no way to be certain, it seems highly plausible that Rapunzel would have followed a path similar to Gretel had she survived the accident or if the accident never happened. This is reasonable to believe not only because Rapunzel is so similar to Gretel, but also because the closeness of Gretel's and Rapunzel's relationship would itself become one of the reasons pulling Rapunzel toward faith. While the Gretel and Rapunzel story is just that, a story, it seems extremely probable that there are many Rapunzels out there, people who are on a

---

[20]I am borrowing Jerry Walls's example here. See Jerry L. Walls, *Purgatory: The Logic of Total Transformation* (New York: Oxford University Press, 2012), 127. I have modified Walls's example slightly (but in a manner that I expect Walls would approve of). In a more recent work, he has made a similar point with a slightly different example, one referring to John and Charles. See his *Heaven, Hell, and Purgatory* (Grand Rapids, MI: Brazos, 2015), 191-92.

trajectory toward faith, a trajectory interrupted by an untimely death. It is not technically true that Rapunzel is *un*evangelized, but it is certainly plausible to think that a God who desires to be in relationship with every person would want to ascertain whether Rapunzel's trajectory toward repentance was going to continue.[21]

Considering cases of pseudoevangelism. Considering these cases is difficult, for a variety of reasons. First, there are what might be called "threshold issues." For example, how bastardized does the gospel have to be before one is considered "pseudoevangelized" instead of evangelized? Or how personally damaged does one have to be before one is deemed to be unable to really hear the gospel? It is undoubtable that the situation of each and every person is unique and that some of those differences are significant. So one must be aware of the very real problem of painting with too broad a brush or assuming that what is true in one case must be true in another subtly different case.

Second, I have agonized a fair amount over how to refer to these sorts of cases. I considered three candidates for the label: *pseudoevangelized*, *quasievangelized*, and *semievangelized*. While in contemporary parlance, each of these prefixes carries the meaning "sort of" or "somewhat," no one prefix captures all of the cases I wish to highlight.[22] Kunta Kinte is pretty clearly pseudoevangelized, Micha is either pseudoevangelized or semievangelized, depending on how you look at her situation, and Rapunzel is pretty clearly quasievangelized. However we label these cases, they force us to reconsider simply placing all people into two categories: "those who have heard the gospel" and "those that have not." At the very least, these cases suggest (at least) that the question of who has and who has not heard the gospel is more complex

[21]In fact, as Walls points out, given a middle knowledge, God might even know that Rapunzel would have repented if she would have not died an untimely death (*Purgatory*, 128; *Heaven, Hell, and Purgatory*, 192.)

[22]The prefix *pseudo-* comes from the Greek for "false" and indicates a lack of genuineness, *quasi-* comes from the Latin for "almost" and indicates something that is almost but not quite something else, and *semi-* comes from the Latin for "half" and indicates something that is half of something else.

than has been acknowledged. I will continue to use the label *pseudo-evangelized* for these difficult cases, acknowledging that the term is not ideal in a number of respects.

THE STRUCTURE OF THE QUESTION OF THE DESTINY OF THE UNEVANGELIZED

The question set before us, therefore, is this: How should Christians think about the soteriological status of the unevangelized and the pseudo-evangelized? But, in order to answer this question, our first task is to seek to better understand the question itself. This is important, because it is unfortunately common to understand the question of the destiny of the unevangelized as an oblique way of asking whether explicit faith in Jesus Christ is necessary for salvation. Those who understand the question in that way will frame the discussion around what is called the threefold typology—that is, they will see the primary answers to this question as being Exclusivism, Inclusivism, and Religious Pluralism. Exclusivists hold that Jesus Christ is ontologically the only savior and epistemologically, one must have explicit faith in him on order to be saved. Inclusivists affirm the ontological necessity of Christ, but deny the epistemological necessity of Christ—they hold that it is possible that some who do not know the name of Christ might still be saved by him. Pluralists deny both the ontological and epistemological necessity of Christ, holding that there are paths to salvation other than the Christian path.

The threefold typology has been the recipient of withering criticism in recent years, for reasons both good and bad. I do not object to using the threefold typology when addressing certain questions, but the question of the destiny of the unevangelized is most decidedly not one of those questions—for two reasons. First, Religious Pluralism is not an answer to the question of the destiny of the unevangelized—in effect, Religious Pluralism denies that there are any who are genuinely and in principle unevangelized, for all can be saved through whatever salvific path preferred by their culture.[23] Second, using the threefold typology would reduce the conversation to an Exclusivism/Inclusivism debate. And doing so is misleading because two of the alternative views I will discuss *and* the view I will end up defending end up in the exclusivist camp. Moreover, my view bears some structural similarities to Inclusivism. In short, while the threefold typology is an effective way of presenting the various options on the exclusivity/finality of Jesus question, it is not an effective way of presenting the options in the question of the destiny of the unevangelized.

So what is the best way to understand the question of the destiny of the unevangelized? The key to answering that question is to recall that while the destiny of the unevangelized is a theological question, it is also an apologetic question. (Or perhaps it is best to say that it is a theological question with unavoidably apologetic overtones.) To put it bluntly, the salvific status of the unevangelized does not merely pose an interesting opportunity to discuss the extent of salvation, it is a straightforward and in-your-face objection to the meaning and even coherence of the Christian claim that God loves all people and that he is providentially in control of his creation. Stated in this way, it is easy to see that the best way to understand the question of the destiny of the unevangelized is to see it as running parallel to and perhaps even a conjunction of two classical apologetic problems: the problem of divine hiddenness and the problem of evil.

The problem of divine hiddenness. Succinctly stated, the problem of divine hiddenness is "If God exists, then why isn't his existence more obvious?" This is a question that believers might ask in a moment of doubt and trial—a "dark night of the soul"—but our topic is more closely related to the version of the question that nonbelievers might ask as an objection to the very idea of God's existence. J. L. Schellenberg falls into the latter camp and phrases the objection this way: "Why would God . . . permit his or her own existence to be hidden even from

[23]More accurately, Pluralism denies that George cases are "unevangelized." Pluralists still have to deal with Anna and Sam cases.

those who are willing to see it? . . . Wouldn't a loving personal God have good reason to prevent such obscurity?"[24] Of course, there are some conceptions of the divine where this isn't as pressing of a problem—pictures of the divine that do not require belief or where relationship with the divine is not the goal—but for Christians who believe in a perfectly loving, personal God who desires to be in relationship with his creation, this is a pressing question indeed.

The problem of divine hiddenness can be interpreted either qualitatively or quantitatively—that is, the question can be either, "Why isn't the evidence of God's existence better, clearer, more obvious?" or "Why isn't it given to everyone?" Thus stated, it is clear that the destiny of the unevangelized is closely related to the quantitative version of the problem of divine hiddenness, although, as we will see, qualitative concerns are relevant as well. Moreover, while the problem of divine hiddenness is epistemic in nature (it presses the question of the lack of evidence of God's existence), the destiny of the unevangelized is soteriological (it inquires why some do not have an opportunity to be saved).[25] Finally, both the destiny of the unevangelized and the problem of divine hiddenness can be understood as arguments against God's existence. They each highlight a feature of reality—either the existence of the unevangelized or pseudoevangelized or the existence of "reasonable nonbelief" due to lack of evidence for God's existence on the part of some persons[26]—that seems out of step with God as we understand him. Schellenberg formalizes the problem of divine hiddenness this way:

1. If there is a God, he is perfectly loving.
2. If a perfectly loving God exists, reasonable nonbelief does not occur.

[24]J. L. Schellenberg, "Why I Am a Nonbeliever?—I Wonder . . . ," in *50 Voices of Disbelief: Why We Are Atheists*, ed. Russell Blackford and Udo Schüklenk (Malden: Blackwell, 2009), 30.

[25]I leave as homework the interesting task of figuring out the various interconnections between the problem of divine hiddenness and the problem of the destiny of the unevangelized.

[26]According to Schellenberg, reasonable nonbelief occurs "if and only if it is not the result of culpable actions or omissions on the part of the subject." See Schellenberg, *Divine Hiddenness and Human Reason* (Ithaca, NY: Cornell University Press, 2006 [1993]), 3n2.

3. Reasonable nonbelief occurs.

4. No perfectly loving God exists.

5. There is no God.[27]

For Christians who cannot embrace the conclusion of this argument, there are two possibilities: deny (2) and argue that reasonable nonbelief is compatible with the existence of a perfectly loving God or deny (3) and argue that reasonable nonbelief does not occur. In other words, the two choices are to acknowledge and explain divine hiddenness or to deny divine hiddenness.

For our purposes, what is interesting here are some of the parallels between the destiny of the unevangelized and the problem of divine hiddenness. First, it is possible to use Schellenberg's argument as a way of expressing the problem of the destiny of the unevangelized by replacing "reasonable nonbelief" in (2) and (3) above with "lack of salvific opportunity." And second, these two answers are also possible with respect to the destiny of the unevangelized—one can argue that lack of salvific opportunity is compatible with the existence of a perfectly loving God and one can argue that lack of salvific opportunity does not occur. But before we pursue these answers, let's consider the relationship between the destiny of the unevangelized and the problem of evil.

The problem of evil. Consider the classic articulation of the problem of evil, a way of stating the problem that goes back to Epicurus.

1. If God is perfectly good, he should want to eliminate evil.

2. If God is all-powerful, he should be able to eliminate evil.

3. Evil exists.[28]

This formulation of the problem of evil is called the trilemma because it presents three statements that all seem to be true but also

[27]Schellenberg, *Divine Hiddenness and Human Reason*, 83.

[28]Some formulations add an additional proposition: (4) if God is all-knowing, he knows that evil exists, if it does.

seem to be logically incompatible. One can affirm any two of these three statements, but (on the surface, at least) not all three. It seems axiomatic that a perfectly good being would want to eliminate evil—in fact, the desire to eliminate evil seems to be a fundamental part of the definition of what it means for a person to be "good." If somebody sees an evil and thinks, "I'm absolutely okay with that," then they are not a good person. Similarly, it seems that an all-powerful being should be able eliminate evil. Moreover, on the orthodox Christian understanding of divine omnipotence (or all-powerfulness), there is nothing outside of God who can thwart his will. Finally, it seems difficult in the extreme to deny that evil exists. Defining what is meant by the term *evil*, of course, is important; it is also very difficult. When I say that evil is difficult to define, what I mean is that providing a list of necessary and sufficient conditions for "evil" is enormously difficult. Even more difficult is doing so in a way that is useful by people who do not share belief systems or worldviews. For instance, I could define evil as "whatever runs contrary God's moral will," but such a definition would be unhelpful or objectionable to my atheistic friends. Of course, none of this suggests that evil is difficult to describe or identify. Perhaps, therefore, we might say of evil what Supreme Court Justice Potter Stewart said of pornography: "Perhaps I cannot define it, but I know it when I see it."[29] The point is this: however evil is defined, everything in our experience suggests it exists.

To respond to this version of the problem of evil, one has two options. One can deny one of the premises or one can demonstrate that there is no incompatibility in accepting all three propositions by offering a fourth proposition which reconciles the set. Many of the answers to the problem of evil take this later approach. Alvin Plantinga's famous "free will defense," for example, is best seen as a fourth proposition that

[29]The above statement is a paraphrase, but it captures the meaning of Stewart's statement. His original statement was made as part of the concurring opinion on Jacobellis v. Ohio, 1964.

demonstrates how it could be that an all-powerful, perfectly good being would allow evil in his creation.[30]

The question of the destiny of the unevangelized is best thought of as a version (or perhaps subquestion) of the problem of evil—in fact, it is sometimes called the *soteriological* problem of evil (or the problem of evil applied to the question of salvation). The problem of evil is the question of why there is evil (and so much of it and such horrible, unexplainable evil) in a perfectly good God's creation. In so doing, the problem of evil calls our attention to an expectation/reality gap—given the fact that God has created everything that exists other than himself and given that God is perfectly good, one would expect there to be no evil. But those expectations do not match reality. In the arena of salvation, the destiny of the unevangelized issue highlights a similar expectation/reality gap. Given that God loves all people and desires to be in relationship with all people, one would expect that God would make sure that his offer of salvation was universally accessible. But, it seems that it is not.

Consequently, the issue of the destiny of the unevangelized can be helpfully stated in a manner that is structurally similar to the problem of evil. Consider the following three statements:

1. God desires that the gospel be universally accessible.
2. Responding to the gospel of Jesus Christ with explicit faith is necessary for salvation.
3. Some die without having heard the gospel.

The incompatibility between these three statements (at least on the surface) is clear. How can we reconcile God's desire that all have an opportunity to be saved with the fact that some die without any opportunity to receive that which is necessary for salvation? We have an expectation/reality gap. Given the reality of (1), we would expect (2) or

[30]Alvin Plantinga, *God, Freedom, and Evil* (Grand Rapids, MI: Eerdmans, 1977).

(3) to be false. Or (to state the incompatibility in a different way) given the reality of (3), we would expect (1) or (2) to be false. I do not mean to claim that there is an *actual* logical incompatibility between these three statements, such that affirming each of them would necessarily result in a logical contradiction. It is probably best to say that there is *apparent theological* incompatibility here.

This is, I submit, the best way to understand the question of the destiny of the unevangelized. It is an inquiry into the theological coherence of God's apparent desire for universal accessibility of salvation, the apparent requirement that one must hear and respond to the gospel of Jesus Christ to be saved, and the apparent fact that some die without hearing the gospel. Answering this question requires showing that the contradiction here is only apparent, not actual. Before offering and defending my preferred answer, it is appropriate and worthwhile to discuss the traditional ways of answering the question of the destiny of the unevangelized.

THE TRADITIONAL ANSWERS

Discussing the various answers to the destiny of the unevangelized is more complicated than it appears at first blush. The number of closely related theological topics and the various ways of nuancing the underlying issues makes for an explosion of possible views. John Sanders discusses five views (many of which have multiple subviews),[31] Tiessen also identifies five,[32] Millard Erickson discusses seven,[33] and Christopher Morgan[34] and Daniel Strange[35] both identify nine views. While each of

---

[31]Sanders, *No Other Name.*

[32]Tiessen, *Who Can Be Saved?*, 31-47.

[33]Erickson, *How Shall They Be Saved?* Actually, Erickson discusses six views, but then also mentions "Postmortem Evangelization" among the "issues" that should be discussed.

[34]Christopher Morgan, "Inclusivisms and Exclusivisms," in *Faith Comes by Hearing: A Response to Inclusivism*, ed. Christopher W. Morgan and Robert A. Peterson (Downers Grove, IL: IVP Academic, 2008), 17-39.

[35]Daniel Strange, *The Possibility of Salvation Among the Unevangelized: An Analysis of Inclusivism in Recent Evangelical Theology*, Paternoster Biblical and Theological Monographs (Waynesboro, GA: Paternoster, 2002), 294-331.

these treatments of the range of possible view have their merits, I think it is possible to simplify matters a bit—not just because simple is better (because it often isn't), but because such simplification can refocus our attention on the primary issues.

There are either two or three broad categories of traditional views, depending on how one asks the question.[36] If the question is phrased, "Is salvation universally accessible?" then there are two traditional views: *Restrictivism* and *Accessibilism*. Restrictivists restrict salvific access to those that hear the gospel of Jesus Christ and Accessibilists hold that salvation is accessible even to those who have not heard the gospel.[37] However, if the question is phrased, "What are the different theories on universally accessibility of salvation?" then we have three traditional views: *Restrictivism*, which denies universal accessibility, *Universal Opportunity*, which claims that, despite appearances to the contrary, all will receive an opportunity in this life to be saved through special revelation, and *Inclusivism*, which claims universal accessibility is granted by the fact that it is possible to be saved through general revelation.

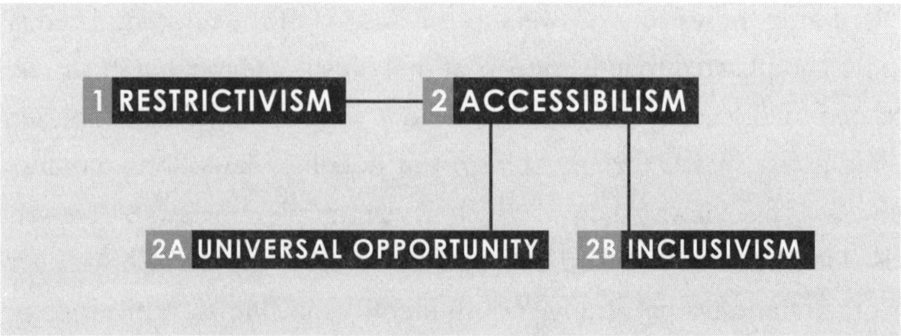

Figure 1

[36]Here I will postpone discussion of agnosticism, the view that says that this is a question that cannot be answered. This is because I think that this view is less of an answer to the destiny of the unevangelized and more of an argument against any and all attempts to answer the question. I will discuss this objection in chapter 7.

[37]The term *accessibilism* was proposed by William Lane Craig, but it has been popularized in the excellent volume by Terrence Tiessen, *Who Can Be Saved?* See William Lane Craig, "Politically Incorrect Salvation," in *Christian Apologetics in the Postmodern World*, ed. Timothy R. Phillips and Dennis Ockholm (Downers Grove, IL: InterVarsity, 1995), 84.

There are, of course, variations within each of these, but my claim is that Restrictivism, Universal Opportunity, and Inclusivism nicely express the primary categories of traditional views on this issue. To see this, recall the trio of statements that together express the objection of the destiny of the unevangelized:

1. God desires that all people have an opportunity to be saved.
2. Responding to the gospel of Jesus Christ with explicit faith is necessary for salvation.
3. Some die without having heard the gospel.

The incompatibility of the three above statements is a product of their conjunction. Any two of the above statements are perfectly compatible, but not all three—or, to say the same thing a different way, to remove the compatibility, one must deny one (or more) of the above statements. Consequently, not only is this a good way of describing the problem of the destiny of the unevangelized, it also nicely highlights the three traditional categories of response: Restrictivism, which affirms both (2) and (3), but denies (1); Universal Opportunity, which affirms (1) and (2), but denies (3); and Inclusivism, which affirms (1) and (3), but denies (2).

Restrictivism. Restrictivists are those that acknowledge that some do not hear the gospel in this life, but nonetheless affirm the necessity of responding with explicit faith to the gospel of Jesus Christ. Some use the term *Exclusivism* to describe this position, but I prefer the term *Restrictivism*, for Exclusivism speaks to a related but subtly different matter—namely, what it is that provides humans with access to salvation. Exclusivists hold that salvation is only possible through Christ's atonement.[38] Restrictivism on the other hand is the idea that access to salvation is restricted to those who hear the gospel and respond affirmatively to it.

Restrictivists support their position by appealing to several lines of biblical and theological evidence. First, Restrictivists appeal to texts

[38]A point made by William Lane Craig in "Politically Incorrect Salvation," 84.

that emphasize the importance of preaching the gospel. For example: "How, then, can they call on the one they have not believed in? And how can they believe in the one of whom they have not heard? And how can they hear without someone preaching to them? . . . Consequently, faith comes from hearing the message, and the message is heard through the word about Christ" (Rom 10:14, 17).

Second, the reason it is important to preach the gospel is because saving faith requires repentance and commitment to Jesus Christ. Romans 10:9-10 is one of the most common texts appealed to by Restrictivists to support this contention. "If you declare with your mouth, 'Jesus is Lord,' and believe in your heart that God raised him from the dead, you will be saved. For it is with your heart that you believe and are justified, and it is with your mouth that you profess your faith and are saved." Restrictivists also find a clear statement of the necessity of personal faith in Jesus in John 3:17-18: "For God did not send his Son into the world to condemn the world, but to save the world through him. Whoever believes in him is not condemned, but whoever does not believe stands condemned already because they have not believed in the name of God's one and only Son." Based on texts such as these, Charles Hodge concludes, "There is no faith, therefore, where the gospel is not heard; and where there is no faith, there is no salvation."[39]

Third, Restrictivists appeal to texts that affirm the particularity and exclusivity of salvation through Jesus Christ. For example:

> Acts 4:12: "Salvation is found in no one else, for there is no other name under heaven given to mankind by which we must be saved."
>
> John 14:6: "[Jesus speaking] I am the way and the truth and the life. No one comes to the Father except through me."
>
> John 3:36: "Whoever believes in the Son has eternal life, but whoever rejects the Son will not see life, for God's wrath remains on them."
>
> 1 John 5:12: "Whoever has the Son has life; whoever does not have the Son of God does not have life."

---

[39]Charles Hodge, *Systematic Theology*, vol. 2 (Grand Rapids, MI: Eerdmans, 1940), 648.

These passages, says the Restrictivist, clearly affirm the necessity of a personal relationship with Jesus for salvation.

Fourth, Restrictivists appeal to texts that talk about the universality of sin and the hopelessness without Christ. Romans 3:23 is the obvious text in this respect: "For all have sinned and fall short of the glory of God." Restrictivists also appeal to Ephesians 4:18, which references Gentiles as examples of those who have not heard the gospel and argues that "they are darkened in their understanding and separated from the life of God because of the ignorance that is in them due to the hardening of their hearts." Carl Henry argues thus: "No man who has never heard of Jesus Christ is condemned for rejecting Christ; all men are condemned for their revolt against the light that they have. . . . In a real sense, a man who has never heard the name of Christ rejects him nonetheless, every time he sins against whatever light he has."[40] Related to the matter of universal human sinfulness, R. C. Sproul points out that the question, "What happens to the poor innocent native in Africa who has never heard of Christ?" is a faulty question. He responds, "The innocent native who never hears of Christ is in excellent shape, and we need not be anxious about his redemption. The *innocent* person doesn't need to hear of Christ. He has no need of redemption. God never punishes innocent people. The innocent person needs no Saviour; he can save himself by his innocence."[41]

Finally, it is important to draw a distinction between the universal accessibility of salvation, which Restrictivists deny, and the universal awareness of God's eternal power and divine nature, as seen in his creation (Rom 1:19-20), which Restrictivists affirm. The awareness of God's character provided by creation is, to use the old saying, sufficient to damn, but insufficient to save. General revelation merely makes humans aware of our need for salvation. Carl Henry claims, "General revelation elicits the anxious interrogation, 'What shall I do to be saved?' It

[40]Carl F. H. Henry, *Giving a Reason for Our Hope* (Boston: W. A. Wilde, 1949), 40, 42.
[41]R. C. Sproul, *Reason to Believe* (Grand Rapids, MI: Lamplighter/Zondervan, 1982), 49.

prompts the question and poses the difficulty, but it cannot provide the solution."[42] In a similar vein, Roger Nicole asks, "Why was it necessary for Christ to come at all if salvation can be attained apart from him?" He continues, "When we reflect on the immensity of his suffering and the paramount significance of the incarnation, it appears incongruous, to say the least, that these great deeds should represent only one of several ways of being reconciled to God."[43]

The above arguments are what unite Restrictivists, but there are also variations on the Restrictivist themes, often correlated with different ways of addressing various challenges. First, there are different opinions within Restrictivism on what is required to hear the gospel.[44] "Gospel Restrictivists" assert only that salvation comes through preaching of the gospel. "Church Restrictivists," on the other hand, hold that one can only hear the gospel through the church—a position typified by Cyprian's "no salvation outside the church" and common in pre–Vatican II Roman Catholicism.[45] And both of these positions can allow that Old Testament patriarchs can be saved despite not hearing the gospel of Jesus Christ in any straightforward way. It is common for Restrictivists to allow that Old Testament patriarchs are saved through a different covenant (or set of covenants) than New Testament Christians and that the old covenant assumed faith in a messiah or Savior to come. Similarly, there are a variety of ways Restrictivists deal with the problem of infant salvation. They might affirm any or all of the following as explaining how infants might be saved: the age of accountability, baptismal regeneration, or election of infants to salvation.

Second, while all Restrictivists affirm that those who do not hear the gospel are lost, some acknowledge that the punishment for those who

---

[42]Bruce Demarest, *General Revelation* (Grand Rapids, MI: Zondervan 1982), 70.

[43]Roger Nicole, "One Door and Only One?" *Wherever* 4 (1979): 3.

[44]Here I utilize the distinctions made by Christopher W. Morgan, although he terms them "Exclusivist" rather than "Restrictivist." See his very nice essay, "Inclusivisms and Exclusivisms," 17-39, especially 27-28.

[45]Morgan also discusses "Special Revelation Exclusivism" ("Inclusivisms and Exclusivisms," 28-30) which would correspond to what I am labeling "Universal Opportunity."

hear the gospel and reject it will be greater than those who did not hear the gospel. Loraine Boettner, for example, appeals to Luke 10:12-14, where Jesus says that the day of judgment will be more severe for those who reject his message than it will be for the people of Sodom.[46] Similarly, in Luke 12:47-48 the punishment is more severe for the servant who knew his master's will but did not do it than it was for the one who was not aware of his master's will.[47]

Third, while Restrictivists are united in their claim that *ultimately* God does not desire the universal accessibility of the gospel, there are very different rationales for this claim. Calvinist Restrictivists connect their denial of God's desire for universal accessibility with their commitment to unconditional election—those whom God has not elected will not be saved and all of those whom God has elected will hear the gospel. Arminian Restrictivists, on the other hand, affirm that *in one sense* God desires the universal accessibility of the gospel, but acknowledge that God has tied the accessibility of the gospel to human efforts to spread the gospel. Hence, because God chooses not to work outside the human proclamation of the gospel, it is true that even for Arminian Restrictivists God does not *ultimately* desire the universal accessibility of the gospel.

Universal Opportunity. Those who accept Universal Opportunity affirm both that God desires all to hear the gospel and that salvation requires explicit faith, but hold that (contrary to appearances) there is no person that has (or will) die without hearing the gospel. This position is not merely an affirmation of universal accessibility of salvation, for anyone who accepts that general revelation is both given to all and is salvific might argue that salvation was universally accessible.[48] Rather, this position is that *the gospel* is universally accessible *in this life* because

---

[46]Loraine Boettner, *The Reformed Doctrine of Predestination*, 8th ed. (Grand Rapids, MI: Eerdmans, 1954), 120.

[47]Boettner, *Reformed Doctrine of Predestination*, 121. See Millard Erickson's helpful discussion in *How Shall They Be Saved?*, 56.

[48]The difficulty for such an argument comes from Anna and Sam cases. Those would have to be handled separately.

God provides special direct access to the gospel via dreams or angelic messengers to all who do not hear it in more traditional ways. Because "universal opportunity to hear the gospel in this life" is a bit of a mouthful, this position has been simply called Universal Opportunity.

There are couple of variations on the Universal Opportunity view.[49] The first of these was fairly popular in the Middle Ages and is called the *Universal Sending* view.[50] Drawing on the stories of the Ethiopian eunuch (Acts 8) and Cornelius (Acts 10), the Universal Sending view asserts that when an unevangelized person genuinely seeks God (as did the Ethiopian eunuch and Cornelius), God will find a way to reveal himself to them. This revelation might come in the form of someone being sent to them (as were Philip or Peter), it might be given by an angelic messenger, or it might come in the form of a supernatural dream or vision. Alexander of Hales (1180–1245) provides a nice summary of this view when, speaking of an unevangelized person, he says, "If he does what is within his power, the Lord will enlighten him with a secret inspiration, by means of an angel or a man."[51] Similarly, Jacobus Arminius asked, "What peril or error can there be in any man in saying, 'God converts great numbers of persons, (that is *very many*), by the internal revelation of the Holy Spirit or by the ministry of angels'; provided it be at the same time stated, that no one is converted except by this very word?"[52] Finally, Norman Geisler claims, "Historically, God has mysteriously conveyed special revelation through dreams and visions. God is more willing that all be saved than we are (cf. 2 Peter 3:9)."[53]

---

[49]In addition to the two I mention here, there is the Universal Opportunity at Death view, which holds that God provides the unevangelized with an opportunity to hear the gospel at the moment of death. For reasons that will become clear later, I will postpone discussion of this view until the next chapter.

[50]This section draws on John Sanders's helpful summary in *No Other Name*, 151-75.

[51]As cited in Ricardo Lombardi, *The Salvation of the Unbeliever*, trans. Dorothy White (Westminster, MD: Newman, 1956), 232.

[52]Jacobus Arminius, *The Writings of James Arminius*, trans. James Nichols, 3 vols. (Grand Rapids, MI: Baker, 1956), 1:331.

[53]Norman Geisler, *Systematic Theology* (Bloomington, MN: Bethany House, 2004), 465; italics removed.

The second variant of the Universal Opportunity view—*Middle Knowledge Universal Opportunity*—is more difficult to explain. It draws on a particular (and somewhat controversial) view of God's foreknowledge called "middle knowledge" or "Molinism."[54] According to middle knowledge, God knows not only what will happen, but also what would have happened. Suppose my wife and I go out to eat at restaurant A and I order a steak. God foreknew what I would order, but he also knows what I *would have* ordered if we would have gone to restaurant B instead. As such, by virtue of his middle knowledge, God knows exactly how each person would respond if presented the gospel, including those who were unevangelized in this life. So imagine all of the people divided into the following categories:

1. Those that hear the gospel in this life and accept it.
2. Those that do not hear the gospel in this life but *would* have accepted it if they would have heard.
3. Those that do not hear the gospel in this life and *would not* have accepted it if they would have heard.
4. Those that hear the gospel in this life but reject it.

The difference between Middle Knowledge Universal Opportunity and other Universal Opportunity theories is that on other theories God makes sure that everybody hears the gospel—they might reject it, but they hear it—and therefore, there is nobody in categories 2 or 3—everybody is in categories 1 or 4.

One could develop this middle knowledge insight in an accessibilist direction and assert that God will save all those who are unevangelized who *would have* responded to the gospel, if it were presented to them.[55]

[54]This view of God's foreknowledge is often called "Molinism" after the Spanish Jesuit Luis de Molina (1535–1600).

[55]For example, Donald M. Lake argues that "God knows who would, under ideal circumstances, believe in the gospel, and on the basis of his foreknowledge, applies the gospel even if the person never hears the gospel during his lifetime." See his "He Died for All: The Universal Dimensions of the Atonement," in *Grace Unlimited*, ed. Clark Pinnock (Minneapolis: Bethany, 1975), 43.

On this view, heaven is populated not only with people who responded to the gospel in this life, but also with the people who would have done so, if they would have been given the opportunity. These people, according to Norman Anderson, "will awaken, as it were, on the other side of the grave, to worship the one in whom, without understanding it, they found forgiveness."[56] But it is also possible to develop this perspective in more restrictive manner. William Lane Craig is the guiding light of this approach.[57] While he avers that "if there were anyone who would have responded to the gospel if he had heard it, then God in His love would have brought the gospel to such a person,"[58] he also argues that those who do not hear the gospel in this world suffer from what might be called "transworld damnation." That is, there is no feasible world in which these people would have accepted the gospel. According to Craig, God has providentially so ordered the world that "anybody who never hears the gospel and is lost would have rejected the gospel and been lost even if he had heard it."[59]

Inclusivism. Inclusivists acknowledge that some do not hear the gospel in this life but maintain that God desires them to have an opportunity to be saved. They reconcile this tension by claiming that it is possible to be saved without hearing the gospel. This position does not in any way deny the value of hearing the gospel, it is simply that it is

---

[56]Norman Anderson, "Christianity and the World's Religions," in *Introductory Articles*, vol. 1 of *The Expositor's Bible Commentary*, ed. Frank E. Gaebelein and J. D. Douglas (Grand Rapids, MI: Zondervan, 1979), 156.

[57]See also Thomas Flint, *Divine Providence: The Molinist Account* (Ithaca, NY: Cornell University Press, 1998), 119; B. A. Little, *A Creation-Order Theodicy: God and Gratuitous Evil* (Lanham, MD: University Press of America, 2005), 154-55; and Paul Copan, *True for You, but Not for Me: Overcoming Objections to Christian Faith*, rev. ed. (Bloomington, MN: Bethany, 2009), 212.

[58]William Lane Craig, "'No Other Name': A Middle Knowledge Perspective on the Exclusivity of Salvation Through Christ," in *Faith and Philosophy* 6, no. 2 (April 1989): 185.

[59]Craig, "Politically Incorrect Salvation," 93. In a recent very impressive article, Kirk R. MacGregor argues that Molina would object to Craig's articulation of transworld depravity. But he also argues that Craig's insights can be incorporated into Molina's scheme. See his "Harmonizing Molina's Rejection of Transworld Damnation with Craig's Solution to the Problem of the Unevangelized," *International Journal for Philosophy of Religion* 84, no. 3 (2018): 345-53.

possible that some who have not heard the gospel can be saved by their response to general revelation.

Inclusivists appeal to a number of strands of biblical and theological evidence. (I will develop these claims more fully in chapter eight; the purpose here is brief summary.) First, Inclusivists reference Romans 1:20: "For since the creation of the world God's invisible qualities—his eternal power and divine nature—have been clearly seen, being understood from what has been made, so that people are without excuse." From this passage they infer that if general revelation is sufficient to damn, it must be sufficient to save. Second, Inclusivists appeal to examples of "holy pagans" in Scripture that were apparently saved apart from special revelation: Melchizedek and Job in the Old Testament and Cornelius in the New. Each of them fell outside the special revelation given to humanity by God, but were nonetheless saved by virtue of their obedience and faith. Finally, Inclusivists argue that the salvation of premessianic believers and Cornelius is perfectly compatible with the definition of faith presented in Hebrews 11:6: "Without faith it is impossible to please God, because anyone who comes to him must believe that he exists and that he rewards those who earnestly seek him." The message of this passage, according to Inclusivists, is that it is not the theological content of faith that saves, it is faith and obedience.

Unlike the other views, the number of varieties of Inclusivism is more manageable.[60] General Revelation Inclusivism is the variety I have described above—salvation is given to those who respond to general revelation. The other variety is World Religions Inclusivism, which involves the claim that the various world religions are means to salvation. This does not amount to the claim that all religions are equally salvific, for a World Religions Inclusivist still affirms the ontological necessity and normativity of Christ's death. Rather, the World Religions are

[60]Here I am also following Morgan, "Inclusivisms and Exclusivisms," 32-34. This pair of terms is preferable, I believe, to the more common pair: Constitutive Inclusivism and Normative Inclusivism.

vehicles of general revelation and perhaps even remnants of special revelation and, therefore, to the degree that they point people to God, they can be salvific.

A DIFFERENT DIRECTION: POSTMORTEM OPPORTUNITY

I believe that there is an answer to the debate over the destiny of the unevangelized that is preferable to each of the views considered so far in this chapter. But I do not claim that there is nothing to be learned from these views. In fact, my purpose in discussing the arguments for each of these views has been to highlight some very important facts. I think that a number of the best insights within the views discussed above should be taken very seriously. From Restrictivism we learn of the universality of sin and that salvation requires conscious and intentional faith in Jesus Christ, from Inclusivism we learn of the universality of God's love and the possibility of salvation of those who have not heard the gospel, and from Universal Opportunity we see unique ways of conceiving of the universal accessibility of the gospel.

These affirmations may seem incompatible, but I will argue they are not. Recall our statement of the issue of the destiny of the unevangelized. There is, I suggested, an apparent logical incompatibility in the following:

1. God desires all to have access to salvation.
2. Hearing the gospel and responding with explicit faith is necessary for salvation.
3. Some die without having heard the gospel.

One way of resolving this incompatibility it to affirm two of the three statements and deny the third. That is the method employed by the answers we have considered thus far. But it is possible to remove the theological incompatibility by adding a statement to the above trio, a statement that renders the previous three consistent. That is the approach

I will take. I affirm each of the three statements and I can do so, without theological inconsistency, because I also believe the following:

4. Those who die without receiving a genuine opportunity to hear and respond to the gospel will receive a Postmortem Opportunity to do so.

The assumption of each of the traditional views discussed earlier in this chapter is that death is the final opportunity to hear and respond to the gospel. It is that assumption that I question. To the Georges, Annas, Sams, Kuntas, Michas, Rapunzels, and millions (or even billions) in similar situations, God provides a Postmortem Opportunity to hear and respond to the gospel. In this Postmortem Opportunity, he makes them aware of his nature, and love, and holiness, and desire for relationship with each person and he gives each one an opportunity to respond.

This answer to the destiny of the unevangelized has been called "Postmortem Evangelization," "Divine Perseverance," and "Future Probation," but I prefer the term "Postmortem Opportunity." There are, of course, many different kinds of objections—scriptural, theological, philosophical—to this view. Those will be dealt with in due time, but first we need to unpack the theory of Postmortem Opportunity itself.

2

POSTMORTEM OPPORTUNITY

My first glimpse of the idea of Postmortem Opportunity was given to me by C. S. Lewis in the final volume of the Narnia Chronicles, *Last Battle*.[1] In Lewis's profoundly evocative account of the day of judgment, Aslan (who represents Jesus in Lewis's Narnia Chronicles) stands in a doorway with all his creatures in a line before him. Lewis writes:

> The creatures came rushing on. . . . But as they came right up to Aslan one or other of two things happened to each of them. They all looked straight in his face; I don't think they had any choice about that. And when some looked, the expression of their faces changed terribly—it was fear and hatred. . . . And all the creatures who looked at Aslan in that way swerved to their right, [Aslan's] left and disappeared into his huge black shadow. . . . The children never saw them again. I don't know what became of them. But the others looked in the face of Aslan and loved him, though some of them were frightened at the same time. And all of these came in at the Door, in on Aslan's right.[2]

Lewis's narrative of the day of judgment is, of course, fictional, but the question of what will happen to those who did not hear in this lifetime is very real. The Postmortem Opportunity theorist suggests an idea that

---

[1]I say this with full awareness that some will pounce on this statement, saying, "See, this Postmortem Opportunity nonsense arises not from careful reading of Scripture, but from nonscriptural sources." In my defense, I will say three things. First, not everything that is theologically important is *explicitly and directly* addressed by Scripture. Second, I am not troubled by the idea of finding theological insights in nonscriptural places: art, literature, story, music, and other places as well. These sources do not overturn Scripture—they don't have that sort of authority—but they can reveal important aspects of theology to us, often in ways that are far, far more powerful than the propositions and arguments that are standard fare in theology textbooks. Third, one must also remember that Lewis's writings are explicitly located within the Christian theological tradition. His writings "go beyond" Scripture in some sense, but he is intentionally seeking to express concepts that are rooted in the Christian theological tradition.

[2]C. S. Lewis, *The Last Battle* (New York: Macmillan, 1956), 144-46.

is as simple as it is controversial: that death is not the end of salvific opportunity and those who have not heard the gospel in this life will have an opportunity to respond to an offer of relationship with God. The task of this chapter is to develop that basic claim. There are many different layers to this claim and there many different kind of objections that must be faced. Discussing these requires a distinction between the core claim of the theory of Postmortem Opportunity and additional claims that add theological depth or detail. The core claim is this: *those who die without receiving a genuine opportunity to hear and respond to the gospel will receive a Postmortem Opportunity to do so.* The task of this chapter is to articulate the rationale for this and then discuss the specific theological claims and assumptions that undergird or flesh out my particular version of Postmortem Opportunity.

THE RATIONALE FOR THE CORE CLAIM OF POSTMORTEM OPPORTUNITY

Offering a rationale for the core claim of Postmortem Opportunity is not the same as offering an argument for any particular version of Postmortem Opportunity. I will offer an argument for my version of Postmortem Opportunity in the next chapter, but here I will articulate the rationale for accepting the core claim itself.

The unevangelized and fairness. I will start by suggesting an unhelpful, misleading, but all too common way to think about the rationale for Postmortem Opportunity. There is some degree of intuitive appeal to the claim that what really drives the problem of the destiny of the unevangelized is an appeal to God's fairness. Undoubtedly, this is partially because fairness is one of our society's most treasured concepts. The sequence of thought in the "fairness" argument goes like this:

1. Some people never receive an opportunity to be saved.
2. The problem with (1) is that it is not fair.

3. God should be fair to all people.
4. Therefore, God will provide a Postmortem Opportunity to the unevangelized.

As common as this argument is, it is spectacularly mistaken. If the theory of Postmortem Opportunity is driven by the concept of fairness, it is on very shaky footing, for two reasons: the concept of "fairness" is much more complex than many people realize and applying it to God is fraught with difficulties. Consider first the question of whether human beings are even in a position to charge God with unfairness. Wouldn't we have to be his moral superior (or at least his moral equal) to do so? This is an important question and one that should not be answered flippantly.

Let's consider the issue of fairness by looking an example. Suppose my kids tell me that I am being unfair because their friends get to travel to Hawaii for spring break and they do not. While my kids' desire for spring break in Hawaii is perfectly understandable, I submit that I am not being unfair in denying them their desire. The simple reason is that my kids do not have a right to vacations in Hawaii (or anywhere, for that matter). And the fact that they passionately desire this vacation does nothing to bolster their claim. There are important qualifications that would have to be made if the subject of fairness and rights was our primary topic, but for the purposes of the present discussion, let's describe unfairness as the withholding (or taking away) of something to which one has a right. If I have a right to be paid a salary by my employer, then it is unfair of them to withhold my pay.

Therefore, the success of the fairness argument hinges on whether humans have a right to salvation. Or, more accurately, since the problem of the destiny of the unevangelized is not that God does not save *everybody*, it is that some do not even have a chance, maybe a better way to think about the "fairness" claim is that human beings have a right to *at least have the chance* to be saved? This claim has a veneer of plausibility, but I think it has the disadvantage of being false (or at least, misleading). To see this, consider what it might be that would give humans this right. Does the fact that God created us require that he give us a chance to be in a saving relationship with him? It is hard to see how it would. Our mere existence does not require our Creator to give us an opportunity for external existence or blissful existence in his presence or anything of the sort. Moreover, even if God created human beings for the purpose of relationship with him, that fact alone would not give any particular person the right to define the terms of that relationship. In fact, there is good reason to think that a relationship with a holy God could be subject to conditions and that one of those conditions would be that humans would not impose their own conditions on the relationship or seek to redefine the terms of the relationship. We are not in a position to demand or even expect anything of God.

If this is true, what explains the persistent intuition that there is something deeply wrong with the state of affairs in which some human beings do not even have a chance to be saved? Perhaps this intuition comes from the fact that the Christian tradition holds that those who are not saved end up in hell and experience terrible punishment. This does seem problematic, but for reasons that are separate from the matter of God's fairness toward the unevangelized. Suppose one adopted a "gentle annihilationist" position on the eternal destiny of the unevangelized. Instead of being punished in hell, the unevangelized are painlessly annihilated; they simply cease to be. Would this be sufficient to remove the sense that there is something wrong with some persons failing to have a chance to be saved? I don't think so. The problem of hell is a very real problem—one that I will attempt to address in the final chapter of this book—but even if the specter of punishment of the unevangelized is removed completely, the intuition that people need the opportunity to be saved is persistent.

This intuition is not driven, I believe, by the claim that fairness demands that God provide an opportunity to be saved, but by something intrinsic to God himself. To see this, let's return to the question of whether humans have a right to an opportunity to be saved. Nicholas Wolterstorff has developed a powerful (and, I think, persuasive) picture of the nature of "rights" and how those rights might be violated.[3] To wrong a person, according to Wolterstorff, is to "treat her in a way that is disrespectful of her worth."[4] But what is it that gives human beings worth? Merely existing or even having been created by God doesn't seem to do it. Wolterstorff argues that the best way to account for human worth is that humans have the "relational property of being loved by God."[5] God's love is given universally and has nothing to do with human abilities or capacities (which are not universally shared or distributed equally). Wolterstorff's point can be illustrated with reference to the children's book *The Velveteen Rabbit.* Just as the worth of a child's stuffed rabbit is not decided by her looks or state of repair, human worth is not decided by our capabilities or achievements.[6] It is a function of the fact that God loves us and created us to be in relationship with him. And it is this fact that explains how humans can acquire rights. "Natural human rights," says Wolterstorff, "inhere in the worth bestowed on human beings by [God's] love" and "are what respect for that worth requires."[7]

To say that God's love grounds human rights does not suggest that human beings automatically have any *particular* right. We do not, by virtue of God's love for us, have the right to be famous, be president of the United States, or be considered moral equals with God. After all, the fact that humans have rights at all is not a product of anything intrinsic to us, they come from the fact that God loves us. Consequently, we need to draw a distinction between an internal requirement and an external

---

[3]Nicholas Wolterstorff, *Justice: Rights and Wrongs* (Princeton, NJ: Princeton University Press, 2008).
[4]Wolterstorff, *Justice*, 296.
[5]Wolterstorff, *Justice*, 352.
[6]An example suggested by Paul Weithman, "God's Velveteen Rabbit," *Journal of Religious Ethics* 37, no. 2 (2009): 243-60.
[7]Wolterstorff, *Justice*, 360.

requirement. It might be the case that God's love is such that, if he creates beings and those beings fall into sin, then he will seek to repair that relationship. But this is a requirement created by an aspect of God's own nature, it is not an external requirement demanded by fairness. My point is that it is difficult to see how there could be any external requirement that requires God to provide salvation for those he has created. As such, what drives the destiny of the unevangelized issue is a particular understanding of God's love.

Therefore, while it is not technically unfair for God to create people who have no opportunity to hear and respond to the gospel, his doing so seems out of touch with his love. When we say this, we are not presenting ourselves as God's moral peers and demanding that he act differently, we are trying to make sense of the fact that Scripture seems to teach that God loves all people and desires that all be saved, but it seems many people never have the opportunity to respond. So in asking the question at the heart of the destiny of the unevangelized issue, we are not really "charging" God with anything, we are trying to make sense of what God has revealed to us about himself.

The love of God for the lost. The hope for those who have not heard the gospel in this life is not grounded on the goodness of the individuals themselves or in any external requirement that God give everybody a "fair chance." The hope that underlies Postmortem Opportunity is rather grounded in the idea that God loves each and every person and genuinely desires to be in relationship with them. Fittingly, Scripture speaks clearly and unequivocally about God's love. But that does not mean that it is not possible to misunderstand this important doctrine. In fact, I submit that *love* is one of the most misused terms in the Western world, and this has had an effect on how we think about God's love. The broader society uses the term *love* to denote everything from sex to infatuation. This misuse, of course, migrates into theology. God is popularly envisioned as a kindly grandpa whose only attribute is love. Or, more commonly in recent years, in a move reminiscent of Marcion's separation of the God of wrath in the Old Testament from the God of love in the New Testament, people bypass God and just speak about Jesus. Or, for those for whom Jesus is still too demanding, perhaps they just focus on a particular expression of Jesus. A recent movie, *Talledega Nights: The Ballad of Ricky Bobby* (2006), nicely caricatures this tendency. Ricky Bobby (a NASCAR driver played by Will Ferrell) is praying before a meal to "Dear Lord Baby Jesus." When asked about his prayer he responds, "Well, look, I like the Christmas Jesus best when I'm sayin' grace. When you say grace, you can say it to Grown-up Jesus, or Teenage Jesus, or Bearded Jesus, or whoever you want." He then continues his prayer: "Dear Eight-Pound, Six-Ounce, Newborn Baby Jesus, don't even know a word yet, just a little infant, so cuddly, but still omnipotent." While Ricky Bobby's prayer is obviously a caricature, this basic mentality is common. Our society is more comfortable with baby Jesus, a God full of love but without holiness, moral expectations, or justice.

Scripture teaches about God's love, but also about God's holiness and justice and wrath at sin. When articulating the doctrine of the love of God, it is crucial that we do not get tunnel vision and ignore other important aspects of God's nature.[8] In fact, there are very good reasons to think that God's nature is such than any abstraction of God's love from God's other attributes is inherently problematic.[9] God's love is not just reflected in his loving actions, rather the concept of love starts within God's own being. 1 John 4:8 teaches that "Whoever does not love does not know God, because God is love." Love is what unites and defines the internal relationships within the Trinity. Love was why God chose to create and when sin entered the world, love was why God provided the possibility of salvation. This idea is powerfully taught in 1 John 4:9-10: "This is how God showed his love among us: He sent his one and only Son into the world that we might live through him. This is love: not that

---

[8]This is one of the main points of D. A. Carson, *The Difficult Doctrine of the Love of God* (Wheaton, IL: Crossway, 2000).

[9]I take this to be true whether or not one accepts a strong formulation of divine simplicity.

we loved God, but that he loved us and sent his Son as an atoning sacrifice for our sins." And then John completes the point by drawing out the responsibility that God's love for us gives: "Dear friends, since God so loved us, we also ought to love one another. No one has ever seen God; but if we love one another, God lives in us and his love is made complete in us" (1 Jn 4:11-12).

The message of Scripture is that the love of God for his creation is not mitigated by the presence of sin. God is wrathful at sin and sin demands justice, but sin does not eliminate or separate us from God's love. In fact, Scripture teaches that God has a unique love for those who are lost. This theme is prevalent in the Old Testament, where God pursues his recalcitrant and unfaithful people, the nation of Israel, and always keeps a remnant. And the love of God for the lost is powerfully evident in the parable of the lost sheep.[10]

> Now the tax collectors and sinners were all gathering around to hear Jesus. But the Pharisees and the teachers of the law muttered, "This man welcomes sinners and eats with them." Then Jesus told them this parable: "Suppose one of you has a hundred sheep and loses one of them. Doesn't he leave the ninety-nine in the open country and go after the lost sheep until he finds it? And when he finds it, he joyfully puts it on his shoulders and goes home. Then he calls his friends and neighbors together and says, 'Rejoice with me; I have found my lost sheep.' I tell you that in the same way there will be more rejoicing in heaven over one sinner who repents than over ninety-nine righteous persons who do not need to repent." (Lk 15:1-7)

This type of parable sets up a hypothetical situation and asks the reader a straightforward question with the purpose of showing that the logic of the answer applies powerfully to another important matter or question.[11] Snodgrass describes the logic of the parable this way: "If, as surely you would agree, a shepherd would go after a lost sheep

---

[10]The other two parables in Luke 15—the parable of the lost coin (Lk 15:8-10) and parable of the prodigal son (Lk 15:11-32)—also convey this message, although in different ways.

[11]Klyne Snodgrass, *Stories with Intent: A Comprehensive Guide to the Parables of Jesus* (Grand Rapids, MI: Eerdmans 2008), 96.

and rejoice when he finds it, how much more will God search for a lost/strayed person and rejoice when he recovers that person."[12] Is Jesus speaking explicitly here of people who do not hear the gospel? No, he is speaking generally about people who are in need to salvation, but the application of what he does say to the arena of the unevangelized is difficult to miss.

Two things are important about this parable with respect to God's love for the lost. First, while the Matthean parallel (Mt 18:12-14) is shorter than the Lukan version, it concludes with a theological reflection on God's will regarding the "lost" not found in the Lukan version: "your Father in heaven is not willing that any of these little ones should perish" (Mt 18:12-14). While Matthew's reference to "these little ones" are set in the context of Jesus' comments earlier in the chapter regarding the importance of having faith like a child, any attempt to restrict the scope of those that God is unwilling should perish is vitiated by the statement "*whoever* takes the lowly position of this child is the greatest in the kingdom of heaven" (Mt 18:4). Second, observe a few features about this lost sheep. This sheep will not be found without effort on the shepherd's part, for, as Snodgrass notes, "a lost sheep usually lies down and gives up and will not find its way back."[13] Moreover, there is no fault ascribed to the lost sheep; this is not an unusually stupid sheep, it's just that sheep sometimes get lost.[14] And finally there is nothing in the parable to indicate that there is anything special about this particular sheep—it is not any better looking, more valuable, or more beloved than the other ninety-nine sheep; the only thing that makes it special is that it is lost.[15]

---

[12]Snodgrass, *Stories with Intent*, 107.

[13]Snodgrass, *Stories with Intent*, 102.

[14]Snodgrass, *Stories with Intent*, 95.

[15]The fact that there is nothing special about the lost sheep in Luke and Matthew stands in sharp contrast to the version of the parable in the Gnostic Gospel of Thomas (107), where the sheep is the largest and loved by the shepherd more than the other sheep. See Snodgrass, *Stories with Intent*, 100.

The other two parables in Luke 15 make a similar point.[16] The lost coin is not blamed for being lost and it has no greater value than the coins that are not lost, and while the prodigal son is not loved more than the older son, his being lost is what makes him special. The father's words to his older son make this point powerfully: "'My son,' the father said, 'you are always with me, and everything I have is yours. But we had to celebrate and be glad, because this brother of yours was dead and is alive again; he was lost and is found'" (Lk 15:31-32). What is most interesting about the parable of the prodigal son is the differences between the son on the one hand and the sheep and coin on the other. While the sheep and the coin are not blamed for their becoming lost, the son bears clear responsibility for his being lost and in fact twice says, "I sinned." And yet, despite the guilt of the son, the father's response is identical to that of the shepherd of the lost sheep and the owner of the lost coin: he does whatever he can to retrieve what was lost. The point of these parables, not just individually, but taken together, is obvious. God seeks those who are lost, even in the cases where the lost are to blame for their being lost.

But we must be careful here. To say that God has a special love for the lost is not to say that he loves his followers any less, or even (technically) that he loves the lost *more*. To illustrate this, consider Nicholas Wolterstorff's powerful words in *Lament for a Son*. His son, Eric, was killed in a climbing accident, and Wolterstorff wrote this book to help process his grief. When speaking of his love for Eric, he writes. "Was he special? Did I love him more—more than his sister and brothers?" He answers his question this way: "Death has picked him out, not love. Death has made him special. He is special in my grieving. When I give thanks, I mention all five; when I lament, I mention only him. Wounded love is special love, special in its wound. Now I think of him every day; before, I did not. Of the five, only he has a grave."[17] So it is not that Nick

---

[16]While there are subtle differences between the three parables, Snodgrass argues, "There can be little doubt that the three parables carry the same essential message" (*Stories with Intent*, 95).

[17]Nicholas Wolterstorff, *Lament for a Son* (Grand Rapids, MI: Eerdmans, 1987), 59.

loved Eric more than his other children, it is that he was lost, separated from him by death. But this illustration only captures part of my point, for Nick has the eminently warranted hope of eventual reunion with Eric. God's love for the lost is fundamentally different than our love for our departed ones, because God is facing the possibility of *eternal* separation from the lost. And that is the "why?" of Christ's incarnation. Nowhere is God's love for the lost more powerfully seen than in the example of Jesus Christ willingly enduring the cross.

Balancing grace and holiness. If the goal in answering the question of the destiny of the unevangelized was to explain how the gospel was universally accessible, then any opportunity would be sufficient. But, if one desires to take seriously the universal salvific will of a loving God, then a mere opportunity is insufficient. Even a "genuine opportunity" seems less than what a perfectly loving God would desire. If God genuinely desires that all people be in relationship with him, then it follows, I submit, that he would give each person the best possible opportunity to be saved. In a similar vein, Jerry Walls has argued that God will not only provide the grace of a Postmortem Opportunity, he will provide "optimal grace."[18] He says, "Optimal grace is not an abstract, impersonal concept. To the contrary, it is a deeply personal notion. It means that God knows each of us as individuals and understands how best to speak to us and reveal himself to us so that we will return his love."[19] This conception of grace stands in stark contrast to that of Terrance Tiessen, who suggests that God will provide "sufficient grace." The appeal to "sufficient grace" raises the question of "sufficient for what?" Tiessen's answer is revealing: the sufficiency of God's grace "lies particularly in its being enough to justify God's condemnation [of sinners]."[20] Not only

[18]Jerry Walls, *Hell: The Logic of Damnation* (Notre Dame: University of Notre Dame Press, 1992), 88-89; Walls, *Purgatory: The Logic of Total Transformation* (New York: Oxford University Press, 2012), 129; Walls, *Heaven, Hell, and Purgatory* (Grand Rapids, MI: Brazos, 2015), 199-203.

[19]Walls, *Heaven, Hell, and Purgatory*, 200.

[20]Terrence Tiessen, *Who Can Be Saved? Reassessing Salvation in Christ and World Religions* (Downers Grove, IL: InterVarsity Press, 2004), 242. Walls also highlights the wide gap between optimal and sufficient grace in his *Heaven, Hell, and Purgatory*, 199-200.

is optimal grace infinitely better suited for a God who loves his lost sheep, I submit that the very idea of sufficient grace as "sufficient to justify condemnation" is self-defeating. Any act done to avoid condemnation is by its very nature insufficient as an act done for its original purpose. If I only teach well enough to sidestep my students' complaints when I fail them, my teaching is insufficient *as teaching*. Similarly, God's provision of grace that is only sufficient to justify his damnation of sinners is insufficient as an account of grace and nonsensical as an account of saving grace.[21]

What would the "best possible opportunity" to be saved look like in any given situation? I am not sure, but I am confident that God does. Since God knows us better than we know ourselves, it seems obvious that he would know what would make the gospel of Jesus Christ most persuasive to each person. One thing is clear: there is no reason to suppose that the best possible opportunity for one person will be the same as another. If Paul can say, "I have become all things to all people so that by all possible means I might save some" (1 Cor 9:22), how much more would God give each person what they need to see him as he is and commit their life to him?

The affirmation that God will give each person the best possible opportunity to be saved must be combined with an accurate picture of what salvation is. Since the essence of salvation is relationship with God, then to be saved we must receive an authentic picture of God. I take it as a truism that salvation is incompatible with what I (following Paul Moser) will call "cognitive idolatry."[22] It is insufficient to commit our lives to the God we hope exists, the God who we want to exist; we

---

[21]The response to this argument might be this: "sufficient grace is insufficient as an account of saving grace, but God does not desire that all people be saved, only that his elect are saved." I find the denial of God's universal salvific will to be problematic on numerous levels, but setting that aside, I would ask the following: If God is truly sovereign over salvation, why would God need to do anything to justify his damnation of the reprobate? So the idea of sufficient grace doesn't even fit that well with Calvinist soteriology.

[22]Paul K. Moser, "Cognitive Idolatry and Divine Hiding," in *Divine Hiddenness: New Essays*, ed. Daniel Howard-Snyder and Paul K. Moser (Cambridge: Cambridge University Press, 2002), 120-48.

must commit ourselves to the God who actually exists. Consequently, in presenting the gospel to us, God will not only give us the best possible chance to be saved, he will also expose any sense in which our trust is placed in a god of our creation. If the goal was merely to get the largest number of people into heaven, then the best way to do that is to give people whatever they want. To the drug addict, heaven should be presented as an unlimited supply of their favorite drug; to the hedonist, heaven is unlimited sensual pleasure; to the arrogant, heaven is a place where they are always right and everybody acknowledges their brilliance; and to the religious fundamentalist, heaven is a place where the only people who are there are those who share their narrow theological interpretations.

Just as there is no reason to think that the best possible opportunity for one person will be the same as another, there is no reason to think that one person's tendency toward cognitive idolatry will be the same as another's. This is because the barriers that hinder each person from fully committing themselves to God are unique to them. Sin and rebellion and the desire for autonomy are universal, but the specific permutations of each of those is person-relative. Consequently, it seems reasonable that God would tailor his presentation of his nature and gospel to expose lingering idolatry.

These two ideas—God giving us the best possible chance to be saved and exposing any and all vestiges of our cognitive idolatry—stand in dialectical relationship with each other and are closely connected, I think, with the biblical themes of Jesus Christ being both our Advocate and our Judge. Because of God's love for the lost, he is our Advocate and desires to give each person the best possible opportunity to be in relationship with him, but because he desires to be in relationship with his creation, he cannot give a false picture of who he is even if doing so would make it more likely for us to accept his offer. Consequently, as Judge, God gives us a true picture of himself and holds us accountable to our response to that picture.

***Salvation and the* Missio Dei.** The final rationale for the core claim of the theory of Postmortem Opportunity is that while God calls us to participate in the task of spreading the gospel, the salvation of the world is ultimately God's work. Salvation *is* the *Missio Dei* (mission of God). Sometimes we fail to appreciate this reality because of the terms we use to describe theological realities. When we hear the term *mission*, we may think of a missionary heading to a faraway destination, or perhaps we think of a Billy Graham crusade, complete with an altar call. In other words, when we think of the *Missio Dei*, our tendency is to think of *our* mission, things that *we* do that fulfill God's mission. Darrell Guder's groundbreaking work *The Missional Church* calls us to think of mission in different ways.[23] Mission is a holistic concept—involving all of what we are as persons—and it is first and foremost God's work. This shift in focus has two important implications. First, we must realize that our collaboration with the *Missio Dei* requires much more than just spreading the gospel. We are called to love our neighbor and fight injustice and evil wherever it may be found and whatever form it is found in. Second, and more importantly for the purposes of this book, while God calls us to participate in the *Missio Dei*—as the Great Commission (Mt 28:19-20) and Acts 1:8 make clear—he gives us the opportunity of participating with him in what he is doing in the world, not because he has no ability to act apart from what we do. While we must take seriously God's call for human beings to spread the gospel, we must not allow ourselves to fall into an evangelistic deism. God uses our efforts to spread the gospel, but it is the height of arrogance, not to mention theological naiveté, to think that our feeble efforts are the sum total of God's plan and work. Donald Bloesch says this well: "The missionary proclamation must go out to the whole world, but we dare not presume on where or how the Spirit of God may work, nor should we deny that

[23]Darrell L. Guder, *The Missional Church: A Vision for the Sending of the Church in North America* (Grand Rapids, MI: Eerdmans, 1998); see especially chapter 1, "Missional Church: From Sending to Being Sent," 1-17.

the hidden Christ may be at work in the most unexpected places in preparing people for the new dispensation of grace."[24]

Therefore, when we think about how people access the gospel, we need to balance two fundamental truths: God's desire to work collaboratively and his desire to accomplish the *Missio Dei*. Our evangelistic work ends at death, but God's "standing at the door and knocking" (Rev 3:20 NET) does not. The theory of Postmortem Opportunity is therefore, most fundamentally, a realization that the task of evangelism is not just our own and God is not a passive observer in his plan to reconcile the world (and each person in it) to himself. God participates with us in the process of bringing the gospel to the world and our work is real and genuinely beneficial—both to those with whom we share the gospel and to us, the sharers of the gospel. But it is still God's mission and God will not allow our failure to fully accomplish the Great Commission to make it such that some of his creatures will never have a chance to be saved.

One final point regarding the *Missio Dei* is crucial. Just as we should not see our efforts at spreading the gospel as the sum total of what God is doing to bring salvation to the world, we should not see Postmortem Opportunity as the sum total of God's action. In addition to the saving work of the Son, God has been working through the Holy Spirit to reconcile the world to himself, and the Holy Spirit does not just work in Christian contexts, in places where the message of Jesus Christ has already gone. This is, of course, not to diminish the role of the Son in salvation, for as Clark Pinnock nicely says, "One does not properly defend the uniqueness of Jesus Christ by denying the Spirit's preparatory work that preceded his coming. Let us try to see continuity, not contradiction, in the relation of creation and redemption."[25] Amos Yong has helpfully extended this insight in a

[24]Donald Bloesch, *The Church: Sacraments, Worship, Ministry, Mission*, Christian Foundations, vol. 6 (Downers Grove, IL: InterVarsity Press, 2002), 41.

[25]Clark Pinnock, *Flame of Love: A Theology of the Holy Spirit* (Downers Grove, IL: InterVarsity Press, 1996), 63. See also 198.

number of his works, arguing that an emphasis on pneumatology can reframe soteriology in helpful ways. I understand Yong's emphasis as operative on a trio of levels. The first is the universality of God's action through the Spirit of God, the second is the specific affirmation of the presence of the Holy Spirit in each person through the *imago Dei* and as the presupposition in all human relationships and communities, and the third is the acknowledgment that the Spirit is not locked out of working within the cultural and religious expressions of particular communities, but rather uses them to draw people to God.[26] The point is that even if there are people who have not heard the gospel, there is no sense in which they are isolated from God's salvific efforts.

Some will undoubtedly worry that a theology of religions focused on the work of the Holy Spirit will cede too much soteriological value to non-Christians religions.[27] While Yong could be interpreted as doing just that, I think such worries are misplaced, primarily because he is not diminishing the importance or necessity of the Son for soteriology. He claims explicitly that "because the Spirit is the Spirit of Jesus, any desire to bracket the soteriological question [to pneumatological rather than christological concerns] can only be momentary."[28] As I understand him, he is worried that a particular kind of focus on Christology will result in collapse of soteriological questions into ecclesiological questions, and the restriction of the work of the Holy Spirit to the footprint of the church.[29]

Pinnock's and Yong's pneumatological theology of religions pairs very nicely with the theory of Postmortem Opportunity. Their emphasis

---

[26]Amos Yong, *Beyond the Impasse: Toward a Pneumatological Theology of Religion* (Grand Rapids, MI: Baker, 2003), 44-46. These points parallel his three axioms. For a more complete picture of Yong's pneumatological emphasis, see also *Discerning the Spirits: A Pentecostal-Charismatic Contribution to Christian Theology of Religions* (Sheffield, UK: Sheffield Academic Press, 2000); and *The Spirit Poured Out on All Flesh: Pentecostalism and the Possibility of Global Theology* (Grand Rapids, MI: Baker, 2005).

[27]I will address the matter of the soteriological relevance of non-Christian religions in chapter 8.

[28]Yong, *Beyond the Impasse*, 22.

[29]Yong, *Beyond the Impasse*, 21.

on the role of the Spirit avoids the evangelistic deism of traditional understandings of the fulfillment of the *Missio Dei*—God, through the Spirit, is truly active in seeking the lost—and the theory of Postmortem Opportunity provides an explicit and unavoidably christological telos for the work of the Spirit—all of those who respond to the Spirit must still stand before the Son of God and embrace his gracious offer of salvation.

SPECIFIC CLAIMS OF (MY VERSION OF) POSTMORTEM OPPORTUNITY

The core claim of the theory of Postmortem Opportunity is this: *those who die without receiving a genuine opportunity to hear and respond to the gospel will receive a Postmortem Opportunity to do so.* All Postmortem Opportunity theorists accept this core claim, but it would be surprising if anyone left the matter there. Most add to the core claim in a variety of ways. These additions are used to answer objections and flesh out theological details. My version of Postmortem Opportunity may be further specified through offering answers to the following questions: Who will receive a Postmortem Opportunity, when will it occur, and how many will be saved by it?

Who will receive a Postmortem Opportunity? This question is vastly more complicated than it seems on the surface. The easy answer is "those who are geographically or temporally isolated from the presentation of the gospel" (i.e., "George" and those in similar situations). I have already tried to complicate this easy answer by arguing that it is best to see babies like Anna and persons with cognitive disability like Sam as also being possible recipients of a Postmortem Opportunity. Further, I argued that there exists a set of people who have heard the gospel in one sense, but still are in need of a Postmortem Opportunity—the "pseudoevangelized." And the fact that there might be some that are pseudoevangelized suggests the deeply uncomfortable conclusion that we might not know who has and has not actually heard the gospel.[30] This is because "hearing" is more than auditory; to hear the gospel is to grasp at some minimum level the import of what is being said. As such, it might be the case that some who *seem to have heard* the gospel in this life (and have either accepted it or rejected it) will still receive a Postmortem Opportunity to hear and respond to the gospel. If so, in a manner reminiscent of C. I. Scofield's comment on those who are in heaven, perhaps we might say of Postmortem Opportunity that we will be surprised by two things: who receives it and who does not.[31]

So, how should we think about the extent of Postmortem Opportunity? This is an interesting and complicated question, but happily, I think it is possible to simplify a good bit and merely say that God will provide a Postmortem Opportunity *to whomever he deems to be in need of it.* All of those who have heard a gospel in this life that is adequate and responded in a way that God deems to be appropriate will hear the blessed words, "Well done, good and faithful servant," and all of those who have heard a gospel that God deems to be adequate and rejected it will hear the words, "I never knew you." But those who God knows have not heard the gospel, whether it be because they know nothing of Christ or because they have heard a gospel that is misleading, will receive a Postmortem Opportunity to hear and repent.

When will the Postmortem Opportunity occur? The Postmortem Opportunity is, by definition, "after death." This answer invites speculation about personal eschatology, or the study of what happens to people after they die. Let's consider four different theories.

[30]To be clear, I am not claiming that there is no one who has actually heard the gospel. I merely assert that the question of who has and has not heard the gospel is an order of magnitude more complicated than typically acknowledged.

[31]Scofield wrote, "When the Lord comes we shall be greatly surprised by two things: First, we shall be surprised to find some people rising with us in the air, whom we had not supposed to be Christians; secondly, we shall be greatly surprised that some very eminent professors will not be there." See his "The Doctrine of the Last Things as Found in the Epistles and Revelation," in *The Coming and Kingdom of Christ* (Chicago: The Bible Institute Colportage Association, 1914), 175. This quote has been commonly attributed to C. S. Lewis. Thanks goes to William O'Flaherty and Jerry Walls for clarifying the actual source for me.

1. Immediate Judgment—Immediately after death, humans are resurrected, judged, and sent to either heaven or hell.
2. Soul Sleep—Humans cease to be (or at least, cease to be aware) until the resurrection.
3. Common Intermediate State—Humans enter an intermediate state to await resurrection.
4. Separate Intermediate States—Humans go to different intermediate states: Hades for unbelievers, paradise for believers.

There are, obviously, complex debates here—debates that are far beyond the scope of this project to consider in depth—but there are three issues that should be mentioned, even if only briefly. The first concerns theological anthropology. Are humans essentially embodied, as materialists claim, or can human persons exist as immaterial souls, separated from their body, as dualists claim? Second, for those views that envision divine judgment occurring immediately after death—Immediate Judgment, but also Separate Intermediate States (for how else are people separated into different intermediate states?)—how can this be reconciled with the biblical witness that the day of judgment is a future reality, following the second coming of Jesus and the resurrection of the dead (Jn 12:48; Acts 17:31; 1 Cor 4:5; Rev 20:11-15)? The third concerns whether the process of sanctification is fully completed at death or not, or whether postmortem purification is possible and necessary.

How do these different understandings of personal eschatology interface with the affirmation of Postmortem Opportunity? Happily, the theory of Postmortem Opportunity is compatible with any of these understandings of personal eschatology. It is possible to affirm Postmortem Opportunity as a materialist or as a dualist—one will just have to change one's understanding of the nature of the resurrection and what the period prior to the end times looks like. One can affirm Postmortem Opportunity and believe in either Immediate Judgment or Soul Sleep. In either case, the Postmortem Opportunity would occur on the day of judgment. And, one can affirm Postmortem Opportunity and accept either Common or Separate Intermediate State(s). On these views, the Postmortem Opportunity could occur either during the intermediate state or on the day of judgment.

So the theory of Postmortem Opportunity can be modified to fit any of these views.[32] But can we say more than that; does it fit especially well with any particular view of personal eschatology? I think so. Jerry Walls has argued extensively and persuasively that persons might undergo a process of purgatorial purification or preparation for their Postmortem Opportunity.[33] The rationale for this view is not one of punishment for unforgiven sins, but preparation for standing before a holy God and, as such, this understanding of postmortem preparation has more in common with the Eastern Orthodox picture of purgatory than with the understanding of medieval Roman Catholics.[34] Perhaps C. S. Lewis had something like a purgatorial view in mind when he said,

> Make no mistake, if you let me, I will make you perfect. The moment you put yourself in My hands, that is what you are in for. Nothing less, or other, than that. . . . Whatever suffering it may cost you in your earthly life, whatever inconceivable purification it may cost you after death, whatever it costs Me, I will never rest, nor let you rest, until you are literally perfect.[35]

---

[32]Are there views of personal eschatology that are incompatible with Postmortem Opportunity? Yes, Postmortem Opportunity is incompatible with the denial of a conscious afterlife. But this is hardly damning, since the question of the destiny of the unevangelized itself is rendered irrelevant by such a view.

[33]See Walls, *Purgatory* and *Heaven, Hell, and Purgatory*.

[34]Lewis (in *Letters to Malcolm*) said that the Protestant reformers had good reasons for rejecting purgatory, because by the sixteenth century it has become degraded by abuses (the selling of indulgences) and by being changed from "a place of cleansing for people already saved (in Dante's *Purgatorio*) to a temporary hell in Thomas More's *Supplication of Souls*" (Will Vaus, *Mere Theology* [Downers Grove, IL: InterVarsity Press, 2004], 206). Jerry Walls argues that the main difference between the Roman Catholic and Eastern Orthodox version of purgatory is that Eastern Orthodoxy always had it as a process of growth and maturation, whereas Roman Catholics had it as a place of punishment for individuals who have not repented sufficiently before death. (Jerry L. Walls, "Purgatory for Everyone," *First Things* 122 [April 2002]: 27). I'm not sure that Jerry is right that the Roman Catholic view has always been about punishment, but his distinction between the Eastern Orthodox view and the Roman Catholic view is helpful.

[35]C. S. Lewis, *Mere Christianity* (New York: Macmillan, 1978), 176.

Those who argue for this view argue that if salvation essentially involves transformation, what becomes of those who plead the atonement of Christ for salvation but die before they have been thoroughly transformed? The common Protestant answer that God transforms them and finalizes their sanctification based on death works much better for those who have had an opportunity to hear the gospel in this life and have responded to it. For those who are unevangelized or pseudo-evangelized, there might be a call for some sort of postmortem preparation for standing before God. But, to be clear, my claim here is only that an understanding of postmortem preparation fits nicely with Postmortem Opportunity; I am not claiming that Postmortem Opportunity requires postmortem preparation.

Two additional perspectives on the timing of Postmortem Opportunity are important to note. First, there is a Universal Opportunity view called Universal Opportunity at Death involving the idea that the unevangelized have an encounter with Jesus Christ *at or just prior to the moment of death*. This has been called the "final option" view and has been common in Roman Catholic circles from the nineteenth century to today. The most famous exponent of this view is Saint John Henry Newman.[36] The final option theory posits that the moment the soul is separated from the body, the unevangelized person has the ability to make a free choice to commit themselves to Christ. Terrence Tiessen articulates a variation of this view, adding the caveat that "the response one makes to Christ at the moment of death will be *consistent* with the response one has been making to God in whatever forms God has been revealing himself *prior* to death."[37] And J. Oliver Buswell applies this approach to Anna cases, arguing that just before death all

[36]See Alan Fairhurt, "Death and Destiny," *The Churchman* 95 (1981): 324n75. A contemporary exponent of final option theory is Jospeh Di Noia, "The Universality of Salvation and the Diversity of Religious Aims," *World Mission* 32 (Winter 1981–1982): 4-15.

[37]Terrence Tiessen, *Who Can Be Saved? Reassessing Salvation in Christ and World Religions* (Downers Grove, IL: InterVarsity Press, 2004), 219. See also his "Salvation and the Religions: An Accessibilist Perspective," *Mission Focus: Annual Review* 15 (2007): 213. I believe that he asserts this requirement, in part, because of his compatibilist stance on human free will.

infants who are about to die are given the full consciousness and cognitive capabilities of an adult, and that allows them to make the decision to accept God's gift of salvation.[38] This opportunity to hear and respond, of course, is not *postmortem*, but neither is it in the normal course of the earthly experience of the person. So perhaps it is best to describe this view as a "postvita" (after life) opportunity.[39] In the coming chapters, I will argue that the assumption that death is the end of salvific opportunity is mistaken, but for those who find that argument difficult to stomach, Universal Opportunity at Death is a perfectly reasonable view. Consequently, while I will argue for the possibility of a salvific opportunity after death, I do not have any vigorous objection to a salvific opportunity at death. I consider the view a close cousin to Postmortem Opportunity.

Second, some believe that God continues to provide opportunities for salvation, even to those in hell. Most of these are Universalists—that is, they believe that eventually every human will be saved. Some make a more chastened claim: some, but maybe not all, will be saved out of hell. I reject both of these claims. While I would love Universalism to be true, I don't believe it squares with the biblical data.[40] While I do not believe that death is the end of salvific opportunity, I do believe that salvific opportunity ends at the day of judgment. After judgment has been passed, it is final. There are no salvific opportunities in hell.

How many will be saved via Postmortem Opportunity? Some who hold to the theory of Postmortem Opportunity are very optimistic about the number of unevangelized that will be saved, while others are more pessimistic. Pessimistic Postmortem Opportunity theorists hold that God's love dictates that he provide the unevangelized and

[38]"The Holy Spirit of God prior to the moment of death, does so enlarge the intelligence of one who dies in infancy . . . that they are capable of accepting Jesus Christ." J. Oliver Buswell, *A Systematic Theology of the Christian Religion*, vol. 2 (Grand Rapids, MI: Zondervan, 1963), 162.

[39]Despite the fact that *Postvita Opportunity* is perhaps a better way of describing my view, I will continue to use the term *Postmortem Opportunity* because that is more recognizable.

[40]I will address the thorny issues surrounding Universalism in the final two chapters of this book.

pseudoevangelized with a genuine opportunity to hear and respond to the gospel, but they also hold that the nature of sin is such that very few if any will be able to respond affirmatively to this Postmortem Opportunity. It is not that God fails to do all he can to secure their salvation, it is that sin blinds the eyes of the sinner.

More optimistic variants of the theory of Postmortem Opportunity hold that many of the unevangelized and pseudoevangelized will respond to God's postmortem presentation of the gospel. Those who make this claim might do so by downplaying the effects of sin on the unevangelized, but that is not necessary. Optimistic Postmortem Opportunity theorists who desire to still hold an orthodox picture of human sin do so by emphasizing the work of the Holy Spirit in the life of those who have not heard the gospel. Even if the unevangelized have not heard the gospel of Jesus Christ, they have still been recipients of the internal testimony of the Holy Spirit and, therefore, when they stand before Jesus Christ on judgment day, they are more likely to respond. The most optimistic Postmortem Opportunity theorists are Universalists, who claim that eventually all will be saved. It might be possible to believe that all who stand before Jesus Christ on judgment day will respond with faith, but it is more common for Universalists to affirm that some people will end up in hell, but that God will continue to pursue those in hell and that eventually all will be saved.

In terms of what I *know* to be the case, I am neither an optimist nor a pessimist on how many people will respond affirmatively to Postmortem Opportunity. This is because I am what might be called a "soteric skeptic." I do not believe that I am in a position to comment on whether *anybody* is or is not saved. A person's salvific status is a function of a complex set of affections, dispositions, commitments, beliefs, and actions and as such a person's soteriological status is opaque to us. This is because a person's public words and deeds may or may not reflect their actual spiritual disposition, and the actual effect of the Holy Spirit's work may not be immediately (or even ever) apparent to others. For example, to use an extreme example, do we *know* that Adolf Hitler was not saved at the time of his death? Do we know that there was no final Damascus Road experience that precipitated a genuine conversion? Now, of course, we have no reason to believe that there was and a good number of reasons to believe that there was not, but the most this gives us is a rational or perhaps a justified belief that he was not saved, not knowledge.[41] Another example: Even if we see a person praying the sinner's prayer, do we thereby know that they are saved? No. This is because the sinner's prayer is not a magical act that performs salvation apart from the intentions of the person praying, and a person's actual intentions are still ultimately unknown to us. Consequently, I am neither an optimistic nor a pessimist because I believe that I am not in a position to claim that there is any human person that is unsaveable by God, and neither am I in a position to claim that there is any particular person that will certainly be saved by God. Both assessments are beyond my ken.

RETURNING TO OUR CASE STUDIES

Let's apply the claims of my version of Postmortem Opportunity to the case studies of unevangelized and pseudoevangelized discussed in chapter one.

George. The most straightforward case is that of George. George, you will recall, is a denizen of Upper Mongolia in the ninth century BCE. He never hears the gospel of Jesus Christ because he never comes in contact with anybody who can give him the good news. Suppose that George, while he never hears the gospel of Jesus Christ, does see God's majesty in creation. One night as he walks under the stars he is led by the Holy Spirit to believe in and worship the Creator of the stars. The defender of Postmortem Opportunity holds that this commitment is

[41]More accurately, those who do not epistemize knowledge (reduce it to justification) or, in other words, those who retain a truth condition for knowledge, must remain skeptical about Hitler's final soteric status.

important (even life shaping), but not sufficient for salvation. What enables George's salvation is his standing before Jesus and seeing him as the Creator of the stars he had worshiped his entire life. Without that postmortem commitment to Jesus, George's religious overtures are insufficient and potentially idolatrous; with a postmortem commitment to Christ, George's religious belief in this life are seen as steps along the way to relationship with Christ.

If George responds positively to the postmortem presentation of the gospel it is because of three things: first, because Jesus is objectively his Savior—he has paid the price for George's sin and the extent of the atonement is universal; second, because God has given prevenient grace to George—in creating him with a *sensus divinitatis* (to use John Calvin's language) or "a God-shaped hole in his heart" (to use Lewis's language), in Christ's drawing him to himself on the cross (Jn 12:32), and in the Holy Spirit's calling of every individual to himself; and third, because in the postmortem encounter God gives George the best possible opportunity to hear and respond. But none of this should give the impression that the salvation of people like George is a foregone conclusion. As indicated above, I am not willing to take a stand on the number of Georges who will respond to the Postmortem Opportunity, or even that any will respond. I claim only that God provides the best possible opportunity to George and that it is possible for George to respond affirmatively.

Why are Anna and Sam cases included? Before we discuss Anna and Sam cases, a few words need to be said about their inclusion in the category of "unevangelized." While some will find this fact disturbing, Terrance Tiessen is exactly right when he says, "The two cannot be so easily separated."[42] There are two objections to placing Anna and Sam cases in the same category as George. The first is that George has the capability to respond in the postmortem context, but (it seems) neither

[42]Tiessen, *Who Can Be Saved?*, 206.

Anna or Sam do, and therefore, it is difficult to claim that they will benefit from a Postmortem Opportunity. The second objection claims that, unlike George, the salvation of Anna and Sam is not in question and therefore they are not in need of a Postmortem Opportunity to be saved.

With respect to Anna, the first objection raises this question: How old are people in heaven? Does she stand (or sit? Or sprawl?) before her Maker as a baby? The answer, of course, is no. Because age is a nonfactor in heaven, it is difficult to imagine that anybody would claim that Anna retains her infancy (and certainly not the cognitive inability of her infancy) in heaven. If her relationship with God in heaven requires a level of understanding that she never developed in this life, then it is reasonable to believe that that resurrection includes an idealization of Anna's cognitive capacities, such that when she stands before Jesus on judgment day, she does so as a fully intellectually capable person. This assumption is unproblematic, for it is commonly assumed that something very like that is the case with older people. My grandfather, who died at the age of ninety-one, was at the time of his death intellectually a shadow of his former self. But no one would assert that, on judgment day, he will stand before Jesus Christ with his intellectual capacities compromised by advanced age. Rather, it is assumed that people like my grandfather will have their intellectual capacities idealized. The same will be true for infants.

This idealization raises some important questions about the nature of personhood. I assume that there is nothing incoherent about the idea of an infant who dies in infancy having their cognitive faculties idealized—say, improved to the state they would have been if they would have lived to the age of forty (the precise age is not important). The person who dies in infancy and the intellectually forty-year-old version of that person are *in terms of personhood* identical, just as the one year old and forty-year-old version of me are the same person.

Can we say the exact same thing about Sam? Does the resurrection idealize Sam's cognitive faculties and allow him to experience a postmortem presentation of the gospel? This is a much thornier issue, not because of any lack of desire on God's part for the salvation of Sam, but due to the way the assumption of an eschatological "healing" of disabilities affects our view of disabled people on this side of the eschaton—they tragically become, in the eyes of many people, less, partial, incomplete.[43] This dismissive attitude toward persons with disabilities needs to end. Amos Yong argues powerfully for a perspective in which "there will be no more tears in the eschaton not because our impairments will be eliminated, but because they will be redeemed."[44] Such a perspective is crucially important if, as Yong argues, "some impairments are so identity-constitutive that their removal will involve the obliteration of the person as well."[45]

What does this all mean? How should we think about the specific experience of the Postmortem Opportunity of people like Sam? In a real sense, I don't know; there are many unanswered questions here, so many that I am suspicious of anyone offering simple or sweeping answers. Moreover, there is a need to have a fine-grained approach to this question, for whatever we would say about the specific experience of Sam would not apply to people with different types of disabilities. But I do think we can say with confidence two things: first, anything that keeps Sam from being able to enter into relationship with God will be removed, and second, anything essential to Sam's identity will be retained, redeemed, and even perfected in heaven. Does this mean that every aspect of Sam's "disability" will cease to be in heaven? Perhaps not. What will be eliminated is our tendency to view people in terms of their abilities and disabilities. In heaven, Sam will not be seen as "cognitively disabled," he will just be Sam.

---

[43]"The problem with such an eschatological expectation is what it generates on this side of eternity." Amos Yong, *The Bible, Disability, and the Church: A New Vision of the People of God* (Grand Rapids, MI: Eerdmans, 2011), 121.
[44]Yong, *Bible, Disability, and the Church*, 135.
[45]Yong, *Bible, Disability, and the Church*, 121.

The second objection to putting Anna and Sam in the same category, soteriologically speaking, as George is that, unlike George, the salvation of Anna and Sam is already secured. The objection is twofold. First, while George has access to information about God's character provided to him through creation and "suppress[ed] the truth" and "exchanged [it] . . . for a lie" (Rom 1:18, 25), Anna and Sam have not rejected God's general revelation.[46] Second, while George is judged to be personally guilty for sins committed while "in the body" (2 Cor 5:10), Anna and Sam "have no personal guilt of that type."[47]

Biblical passages that suggest that infants and cognitively disabled are already saved due to their dying before the age of accountability, through baptismal regeneration, or through their being saved because they are elected, are at best unclear. Millard Erickson, for example, says that many of the texts that people utilize to defend infant salvation (2 Sam 12; Mt 19:14-15; Mk 10:13-16; Lk 18:16-17) "really do not seem to bear sufficiently upon the issue to be of help."[48] In addition, holding that Anna and Sam are not in need of salvation has significant implications for some important theological beliefs, including especially the nature and scope of original sin and the necessity of personal faith. Finally, such a view has an awkward implication, as pointed out by John Sanders: "[This] position means that all those throughout history who died in infancy in unevangelized countries are saved, while those who are unfortunate enough to live into adulthood are damned."[49] And Norm Geisler's horrifying suggestion that this fact explains why there is such a high infant

---

[46]Christopher W. Morgan and Robert A. Peterson, "Answers to Notable Questions," in *Faith Comes by Hearing: A Response to Inclusivism*, ed. Christopher W. Morgan and Robert A. Peterson (Downers Grove, IL: InterVarsity Press, 2008), 243.

[47]Ronald Nash, "Restrictivism," in *What About Those Who Have Never Heard? Three Views on the Destiny of the Unevangelized*, ed. John Sanders (Downers Grove, IL: InterVarsity Press, 1995), 119.

[48]Millard Erickson, *How Shall They Be Saved? The Destiny of Those Who Do Not Hear of Jesus* (Grand Rapids, MI: Baker, 1996), 236. He does go on to mention two passages that he thinks might be of more help, but acknowledges that "even these carry significant problems."

[49]John Sanders, "Response to Nash," in Sanders, *What About Those Who Have Never Heard?*, 146.

mortality rate in unevangelized countries comes close to attempting to justify infanticide.[50]

So there are genuine problems for the views that seek to explain how infants and the cognitively disabled are saved apart from a Postmortem Opportunity. But more fundamentally, I submit that the nature of salvation itself upholds the importance of providing a Postmortem Opportunity to Anna and Sam. Even if there is a disanalogy between George cases and Anna and Sam cases with respect to personal guilt, that does not mean that Anna and Sam are not in need of a postmortem encounter, it just means that their encounter will likely be favorable. They will be standing before their loving Creator and not before the one they have been idolatrously wrestling with in a battle of spiritual wills. Since salvation is more than just freedom from personal guilt and it is in fact a chosen, committed relationship with God the Father, Son, and Spirit, wouldn't God desire to provide Anna and Sam an opportunity to hear and respond to the gospel? And wouldn't Anna and Sam desire an opportunity to commit themselves to God—the spiritual equivalent of the wedding day? I think the answer is yes.

Anna. So Anna, like George, will have an opportunity to stand before her Maker and see him as he is. The difference between George and Anna, however, is that unlike George, Anna is not personally guilty for sin. The doctrine of original sin means that even babies have a sin nature, but there is no biblical justification for taking the additional step and holding that they are *personally* guilty of sin.[51] What the theory of Postmortem Opportunity says is that infants like Anna will have the same opportunity as George to see God as he actually is and when they do so, to respond to his offer of relationship. Ronald

---

[50]Norman Geisler, "All You Wanted to Know About Hell and Were Afraid to Ask" (Pippert Lectures, Alliance Theological Seminary, Nyack, NY, 1982); cited in John D. Ellenberger, "Is Hell a Proper Motivation for Missions?" in *Through No Fault of Their Own? The Fate of Those Who Have Never Heard*, ed. William V. Crockett and James G. Sigountos (Grand Rapids, MI: Baker, 1991), 222.

[51]For an excellent defense of this view see Oliver D. Crisp, "On Original Sin," *International Journal of Systematic Theology* 17, no. 3 (July 2015): 252-66.

Nash finds the fact that Anna will have an opportunity to respond to God's offer of salvation extremely worrisome. As such, he objects to the theory of Postmortem Opportunity on the grounds that "large numbers of children will reject the gospel during the interval after death."[52] Is he right? Does the fact that Anna has a free choice to respond to God in the postmortem state paint so dismal a picture of the likelihood she will embrace relationship with God? On this I will say two things: first, neither Nash nor I *know*—in a philosophically precise sense of that word[53]—what Anna will decide because we are not God, and assessing how people will choose when presented with that choice is substantially beyond our pay grade. But, second, I will also say that I cannot imagine a scenario where Anna (and the millions of others in her shoes) would stand before God, the God who created her to be in relationship with him, the God who wept with her parents when her time on earth was cut short, and have her not recognize God as her Lord and Savior. I cannot say with dogmatism that there are no such scenarios, but I cannot imagine what they might be. As such, because little ones like Anna have not spent their life in sin, running from God, and because Jesus said, "Let the little children come to me, and do not hinder them, for the kingdom of heaven belongs to such as these" (Mt 19:14), I am firmly confident that the Annas of the world—and those who demonstrate Anna's simple love and acceptance—will spend an eternity with their Creator.

Some might object to this response as follows. If it is true that "we cannot imagine" the Annas of the world saying no to an offer of relationship to their Creator, are we not saying that the choice they are making is not free? No. What removes their freedom is if they *must* choose their Creator. I am not claiming that. I am merely claiming that I think that they will embrace relationship with their Creator (or, more

[52]Ronald Nash, *When a Baby Dies: Answers to Comfort Grieving Parents* (Grand Rapids, MI: Zondervan, 1999), 37.

[53]This is because the most plausible definitions of knowledge include a truth condition—one cannot know a proposition that is false.

accurately and minimally, that I cannot envision a scenario where they will not). Being free with respect to a choice does not mean that one of the options must be chosen, only that it is possible to do so. The fact that when offered either a Miller Lite or HammerHeart's Thor's Porter aged in rum barrels, I will *never* freely choose the former does not mean that my choice is not free. It means that I have good taste in beer and that I freely chose accordingly.

Sam. Sam cases are the most complex of the three traditional cases—for two reasons.[54] First, as we engage this question, we must be wary of an overintellectualization of the process of salvation. It is undoubtedly true that salvation includes an intellectual component, for this is what raises the questions about the salvation of person's with cognitive disabilities. But salvation involves a lot more than cognition. For instance, salvation includes an affective component, and it might be said that persons with cognitive disabilities are better suited to embrace the affective component of salvation than nondisabled persons. So even if there are things that people like Sam cannot understand about their Creator, that does not mean that they will not be able to connect emotionally in their postmortem encounter.

Second, Sam cases are complex because, as in Anna cases, it seems that one must posit an idealization of cognitive faculties to enable the requisite level of understanding of the postmortem presentation of the gospel. And this understanding of cognitive disabilities, as something that requires "fixing" in order to make people like Sam "better" or "more fully human," is one that has been rightly subjected to withering criticism in recent years. In fact, contrary to this confused perspective, it is possible to suggest that it is *nondisabled people* who are more in need of "becoming more fully human."

[54]In addition, it should be acknowledged that cognitive disabilities come in degrees. As such it would be folly to presuppose that there is some sort of a clear line on which everybody on one side of that line can understand the gospel and everybody on the other side cannot. We must acknowledge that there are boundary cases where we may simply not know the degree to which soteriologically relevant realities are known.

This second complexity is an extremely important issue, one that begs for a more thorough response than is possible here. Nonetheless, the defender of Postmortem Opportunity has two possible avenues of response to this sort of challenge. The first is to question the assumption that there is something inherently problematic about a postmortem idealization of cognitive faculties. In particular, this line of argument questions whether there is any sense in which the idealization of cognitive faculties entails that a disabled person was of less value or less human. This line of argument involves the claim that people with cognitive disabilities are more than their disability. They are persons with a disability, not disabled persons. God's love for them was no different with or without their disability, and therefore their value is the same with or without their disability. The claim is that, to the degree the disability is a barrier to genuine relationship with God and since relationship with God is a maximally good thing, it is desirable that the disability be mitigated to the degree necessary to enable relationship with God. The person remains the same, it is simply that they have the ability to respond to an offer of relationship from their Creator. The second response is to affirm that people with cognitive disabilities will have a Postmortem Opportunity to enter into relationship with God, but to deny that this requires idealization of their cognitive faculties. While it is both understandable and highly plausible to assume that some level of cognitive ability is necessary for *understanding* God's offer of relationship, it does not follow that the same level of cognitive ability is necessary for *entering into* relationship. Certain persons with disability cannot perhaps understand the concepts of sin and grace and free will and salvation, but this does not suggest that they cannot experience and reciprocate God's love. Now, of course, because every cognitive disability is different, the reciprocation of love and relationship is going to look different in each case. But the point is that there is nothing that says that disabled persons cannot respond in love and relationship to their postmortem encounter with God. Moreover, as with Anna cases, there is no reason to think that persons with cognitive disabilities will not do so.

The pseudoevangelized. The pseudoevangelized are a set of people who have heard the gospel in one sense, but not in another sense. The version of the gospel some hear is bastardized (Kunta Kinte), or some may be so damaged that we cannot trust or put our faith in anything or anybody (Micha), or some may have their opportunity to respond cut short (Rapunzel). The traditional approach to the theory of Postmortem Opportunity is that the postmortem presentation of the gospel should be limited to the unevangelized (like George, Anna, and Sam). Those that hear the gospel in this life in any shape, way, or form are held accountable to their response to that gospel. This seems incorrect. If one was only interested in answering the question, "How can God be considered to be just?" then *maybe* one might be able to justify not providing a Postmortem Opportunity to the pseudoevangelized on grounds that they have already had some sort of opportunity. But operating on the assumption that it is *possible* that some of the pseudoevangelized would respond to the gospel if given the opportunity, is there any doubt that a God who desired all to be saved would not want to give the semievangelized an opportunity to hear and respond?

Reasons why God would want to provide a Postmortem Opportunity to the pseudoevangelized are not difficult to come by. First, it is very difficult to claim that a loving God would take Kunta Kinte's rejection of the gospel he has heard as the final answer. Ironically, the general revelation Kunta Kinte has received—his awareness of God's character seen in creation—is certainly more true and revelatory of God's actual character than the gospel he hears from his white captors. I don't mean to suggest that general revelation in Kunta Kinte's case is *more complete* than the gospel he hears, only that the picture of God presented by general revelation in nature is more accurate (even if lacking many important details) than the gospel presented to him by his white slave owners. Consequently, it is clear to me that a God who loves Kunta Kinte, and genuinely desires to be in relationship with him, would make it possible for him to see a true picture of his nature, one very different from that presented to him in this life.

Second, is it possible to believe that Micha's failure to trust God in this life is wholly her fault? This is not to question the idea that all are sinful, rather this question highlights the truth of the following counterfactual: if Micha's life experiences were different, her response to the gospel might have been different. In fact, it might be possible to see the Micha example as a variation on the Sam case. Due to Sam's developmental disability, he does not have the capacity to understand the gospel. Micha cases highlight the fact that the gospel requires more of us than mere understanding. Faith requires intellectual understanding, but also trust and volitional commitment—and it is the fact that some like Micha have had experiences that, in a very real sense, disable their ability to trust, that drives the Micha case. There is an important disanalogy between the two cases, of course. There is no scenario where Sam has the capacity to cognize the gospel, but there are Micha-like examples where people develop the ability to trust despite crushing circumstances. Why do some "Michas" retain the ability to trust whereas others do not? It is probably impossible to answer this question with anything like finality or clarity, but the inability to provide an answer does not vitiate the fundamental point that Micha's experiences have made it impossible for her to truly hear the gospel in the way that God would desire.

Dealing with this situation requires that we not only blame those who are responsible for Micha's situation, which Scripture surely does: "If anyone causes one of these little ones—those who believe in me—to stumble, it would be better for them to have a large millstone hung around their neck and to be drowned in the depths of the sea" (Mt 18:6). We must also recognize the desire for God to overcome the damage we receive in this life. Consider Jesus' words in the Sermon on the mount:

> Blessed are the poor in spirit,
> for theirs is the kingdom of heaven.
> Blessed are those who mourn,
> for they will be comforted. (Mt 5:3-4)

What if we took these words not as eliminating the need of those who suffer to respond affirmatively to the gospel, but as an affirmation that God will not allow the experience of those who have suffered to define their answer to the gospel? In other words, suppose God could reveal himself to Micha in a way that could transcend the damage to her ability to trust and make it possible for her to respond in faith? Would not a God who desires that all be saved do exactly that?

Third, cases like Rapunzel highlight the incompleteness of many people's trajectories toward God. This is obviously true for babies like Anna, but it is also true of those who live much longer. This is not to suggest that all cases like Rapunzel's end up in a genuine faith commitment; many of those cases are such that a Postmortem Opportunity would not make a difference. But that is not the point. One shouldn't justify a person not receiving a Postmortem Opportunity on the grounds that they might not ultimately commit themselves to Christ, rather one should justify the reception of a Postmortem Opportunity on the grounds that they might do so. Jerry Walls states the issue this way: "So let us assume for the moment that God could find a way to present the gospel to Rapunzel after she has died. The deeper question, perhaps, is whether God *would* do this even if he could. To raise this question is to go to the heart of our conception of the character of God. It is to ask if God truly loves all persons, and is truly willing to save them. How far is he willing to go to save them?"[55] If a postmortem presentation would make the difference, why wouldn't God do it? Or, if

---

[55]Walls, *Purgatory*, 128-29.

God would not, then how can we claim that God truly loves all and truly wants all to be saved?

CONCLUSION

Jerry Walls's question—"If a Postmortem Opportunity could make a difference, why wouldn't God offer it?"—is the crucial question for understanding the rationale of the theory of Postmortem Opportunity. The Postmortem Opportunity theorist surmises that a Postmortem Opportunity could, in fact, make a difference. And, given that fact, the Postmortem Opportunity theorist claims that God would in fact offer a Postmortem Opportunity. Of course, these claims need to be argued for. That is the task of the next chapter.

3

A THEOLOGICAL ARGUMENT FOR POSTMORTEM OPPORTUNITY

In the previous chapter, I discussed the core claim of the theory of Postmortem Opportunity—namely, *those who die without a genuine opportunity to hear and respond to the gospel will receive a Postmortem Opportunity to do so.* I explained the rationale for the core claim and attempted to flesh out what such an opportunity might look like and what the implications of such an opportunity might be. But an explanation is not the same thing as an argument; therefore, it is the task of this chapter to provide a theological argument for the core claim of Postmortem Opportunity.[1] But first, it is important to acknowledge the soteriology that undergirds and, to a significant extent, drives the argument for my version of the theory of Postmortem Opportunity.

SOTERIOLOGICAL ASSUMPTIONS

There are a number of assumptions about soteriology that have a particularly significant impact on how one views the plight of the unevangelized and God's salvific desires with respect to those who have not heard the gospel. Crucially important is one's understanding of the nature of salvation, grace, faith, rewards, and how those concepts are interrelated. One's understanding of these core soteriological concepts will not determine one's answer to the destiny of the unevangelized issue, but it will greatly influence which views are considered plausible.

[1]When referring to the theory of Postmortem Opportunity, Clark Pinnock once said, "Although the scriptural evidence for a postmortem encounter is not abundant, its scantiness is relativized by the strength of the theological argument for it" (*A Wideness in God's Mercy: The Finality of Jesus Christ in a World of Religions* [Grand Rapids, MI: Zondervan, 1992], 169).

In addition, the nature of my theological argument raises the specter of the well-worn debates between Calvinism and Arminianism. As soon as one starts talking about the extent of God's salvific desire and the extent of the atonement, the Calvinist/Arminian debate is the elephant in the room. It would be a mistake to try to plumb the depths of Calvinist/Arminian polemics, but it would also be folly to pretend that these debates are not relevant to my current topic.

The nature of faith and salvation. There is a pernicious sequence of thought about salvation that is disturbingly common in the Western world. It goes like this: God wants people to believe in him, believing in God means you are saved, and those who are saved receive heaven as reward when they die. It is not that everything about this is false, for God does want to be in relationship with the people he has created and those who are in relationship with God will be with him in heaven. But this sequence of thought is deeply mistaken in a couple of important respects.

The nature of faith: heart allegiance, not just beliefs. Salvation involves beliefs, but it is not just or even primarily about what you believe about God. Rather, salvation is about the disposition of a person's heart and particularly whether that disposition involves a commitment or allegiance to God. While it is impossible to have any sort of heart disposition or allegiance without having some beliefs about God (most obviously that he exists), salvation is not granted to those who "believe that God exists" or "believe the right things about God" or even to those who "have some sort of trust in God."[2] Understanding this idea requires confronting the allergic reaction many Protestants have to the notion that there might be some expectations placed on those who would choose salvation. Granted, nothing that we can do is deserving of salvation in the sense that we can claim it as our right, but that does not mean that salvation requires nothing of us other than having some sort of belief or trust that Jesus has punched our ticket into heaven. In a

[2]For instance, if my trust in God is defined by a trust that he will see how spectacularly worthy I am of salvation, it is extremely doubtful that my trust will be even remotely salvific.

splendid recent volume entitled *Salvation by Allegiance Alone*, Matthew Bates has argued for realignment of the language we use to describe faith.[3] The gospel is not just or even primarily about our ability to go to heaven when we die, but "the good news about the enthronement of Jesus as the atoning king."[4] From us, what is required is not belief in Jesus and trust in the "forgiveness-of-sins process," but allegiance: "Paul does not *primarily* call us to 'faith' ('belief' or 'trust') in some sort of atonement system in order to be saved (although affirmation that Christ died for our sin is necessary), but rather to 'faith' ('allegiance') unto Christ as *Lord*."[5] As such, the fundamental nature of the Postmortem Opportunity is an inquiry into whether the unevangelized (or pseudoevangelized) person will declare allegiance to Jesus Christ.

The result of salvation: relationship, not reward. Contrary to the assumption of large segments of the Western church, salvation is not about the attainment of reward ("getting people into heaven") or the avoidance of punishment ("keeping people out of hell"), rather, salvation is about relationship with God, or, if you wish, "getting heaven into people." The painfully common picture of salvation as "fire insurance" has been powerfully deconstructed by C. S. Lewis. In *Reflections on the Psalms*, he argues that one of the reasons why the Old Testament has such an undeveloped account of heaven and hell is that only those who first learned to "to desire and adore God" as an end in itself, could hope to properly understand the idea of heaven as reward and hell as punishment. Those who do not see the concept of the rewards and punishments associated with final destinations "as corollaries of a faith already centred upon God"[6] would inevitably treat relationship with God as a means to an end, and thereby fundamentally misunderstand the Christian concept of salvation. When considering his own motives for faith development, Lewis expressed relief that his conversion was

[3]Matthew W. Bates, *Salvation by Allegiance Alone* (Grand Rapids, MI: Baker, 2017).
[4]Bates, *Salvation by Allegiance Alone*, 30.
[5]Bates, *Salvation by Allegiance Alone*, 39.
[6]C. S. Lewis, *Reflections on the Psalms* (New York: HarperOne, 1986 [1958]), 47.

disconnected from any particular picture of the afterlife. Otherwise he worried that he too would have desired heaven "chiefly as an escape from Hell."[7]

This doesn't imply that there is no sense of reward embedded in salvation, but rather, as Kevin Kinghorn says, "Salvation and the attainment of heaven are not additional awards we earn because we have responded to God's invitation and thereby related to him. Rather the relationship is the reward. Heaven provides a place where this relationship can flourish for eternity."[8] This understanding of salvation is important because it speaks directly to one of the rather obvious objections to Postmortem Opportunity—an objection that I will address more fully in chapter seven: "Who would say no to heaven?" The answer of course is nobody. Nobody who is given the choice between the popular conception of heaven (clouds, golden streets, harps, and halos) and hell (fire and burning) would ever choose the latter. But that is not the question that concerns the Postmortem Opportunity. We are not asked to choose between heaven and hell, but between acknowledging Jesus as Lord or retaining our claim on the lordship of our life. Therefore, the question asked at the Postmortem Opportunity is better represented by Milton's famous words: "Do you want to serve in heaven or reign in hell?"[9] Those who choose to serve in heaven receive the reward of relationship with God. This perspective also explains why those who seek heaven as an end in itself will fail to receive it. Those who understand heaven as a reward distinct from relationship with God—as a means to avoid the punishment of hell—will hear the horrifying words, "I never knew you." In other words, those who want heaven, not relationship with God, will receive neither.

---

[7]Lewis, *Reflections on the Psalms*, 48.

[8]Kevin Kinghorn, "Pursuing Moral Goodness: C. S. Lewis's Understanding of Faith," in *C. S. Lewis as Philosopher: Truth, Goodness, and Beauty*, ed. David J. Baggett, Gary R. Habermas, and Jerry L. Walls (Downers Grove, IL: InterVarsity, 2009), 140.

[9]John Milton, *Paradise Lost*, intro. Philip Pullman (New York: Oxford University Press, 2005), bk.1, line 263; p. 22.

Monergism and Postmortem Opportunity. One of the fundamental questions in soteriology concerns the relationship between God's role and the human's role in salvation. To engage these question is to trespass on the Calvinist/Arminian dispute over election, predestination, and human free will. Does salvation require the contribution of humans, a free choice that might be withheld? Or is salvation wholly the work of God and the result of saving grace that God gives to some persons, a grace that cannot be resisted? Monergism is the notion that God is the sole causal agent in salvation. Those who are saved are those that who have been chosen by God to be saved (the elect) and God's choice of individuals for salvation from eternity past is both necessary and sufficient for those individuals choosing salvation. When God provides saving grace, it is irresistible and effectual. Moreover, God provides effectual saving grace only to a proper subset of humans (the elect) and God's election of individuals for salvation is unconditional. In terms of human freedom, monergists embrace compatibilist freedom, an account of freedom that is compatible with the prior determination of the choice in question. While humans who are free in a compatibilist sense are not free in the sense that their choice is causally sufficient to bring about that aspect of reality, the "freedom" of compatibilist freedom is defined psychologically—humans are free because they undergo a psychological process of selecting among options.

It is certainly possible to combine Postmortem Opportunity and monergism. God may, in his freedom, elect individuals who have not heard the gospel in this life and offer a Postmortem Opportunity at which he provides effectual grace that enables the decision to embrace relationship with him. That being said, while there is no theological or logical reason a monergist could not embrace Postmortem Opportunity, neither is there any strong motivation for a monergist to do so. This is because while God could save some of his elect by means of a postmortem presentation of the gospel, there is no reason (from a monergistic perspective) he could not save those very same people in a premortem context. He could send the gospel to them (for Restrictivists) or miraculously make himself known to them (for Universal Opportunists) or make it such that their response to general revelation was genuinely salvific. Terrence Tiessen, for example, has developed a monergistic version of accessibilism where God presents himself to the unevangelized elect at the moment of death.[10] In short, the monergist has little reason to accept Postmortem Opportunity, because God, as the sole causal agent in determining the salvation of individuals, can accomplish the salvation of the unevangelized even if they have not received a genuine opportunity in this life—a Postmortem Opportunity is unnecessary.

There is another doctrinal reason why monergist Calvinists are much less likely to embrace the theory of Postmortem Opportunity. While Universalistic Calvinists (those who believe that God elects all of humanity to be saved) might hold that some of the elect are saved in a postmortem context, non-Universalist Calvinists have already embraced the idea that some persons have no chance to be saved. In other words, since, on the Calvinist scheme, those who will be saved are those who God has elected to receive salvation, the question of how we can reconcile God's love with the fact that some never have the opportunity to hear the gospel is answered the same way one answers the question, "Why do those who have heard the gospel reject it?" The answer, whether or not the person is evangelized, is the same: they did not receive God's saving grace and therefore they are left in their sin.

Synergism and Postmortem Opportunity. My version of Postmortem Opportunity assumes an explicitly Arminian soteriology. Arminians start from the assumption that salvation is, in a crucially important sense, *synergistic*. As the name implies, synergism assumes that there are two forces that work together to produce salvation. But, contrary to the objections of Calvinists, this does not suggest that humans earn their

[10]Terrence Tiessen, *Who Can Be Saved? Reassessing Salvation in Christ and World Religions* (Downers Grove, IL: InterVarsity Press, 2004), 217-29.

salvation, it merely means that God created a plan of salvation requiring that there is something that humans contribute to the process, something that can be and sadly too often is withheld. Moreover, also contrary to the claims of some Calvinists, a human contribution is necessary not because human freedom itself is inherently valuable or inviolable, but rather because God values the sort of relationship that includes self-determined free choice. This human contribution can be described in various ways, but most plausibly, it is simply a willingness to allow God to save them, a free choice to accept God's offer of salvation, and a commitment to live life in allegiance as a disciple of Christ. Synergists typically embrace a libertarian account of human freedom, holding that choices that are predetermined cannot be free and that at least some choices are not predetermined. At the extreme risk of oversimplifying, libertarian free will places an emphasis on the fact that human choices are the cause of the reality that is chosen. A "free choice" is one that is not predetermined by God or by one's nature or anything else. The version of libertarian freedom that I embrace is called agent causation, which locates the "why" of the choice in the nature of agency itself.[11] Human agents are beings that have the capacity to choose among options, and in doing so, they quite literally shape that aspect of reality.

The connection between Postmortem Opportunity and synergism is intuitive. God has structured salvation such that humans need to choose to be in a saving relationship with him and, therefore, those that do not have a genuine opportunity in this life are given a Postmortem Opportunity. The motivation for synergism comes directly from a positive affirmation about God's character, an affirmation revealed in the following question: If God desires all to be saved, how come Scripture seems to suggest that not all will be? For the Arminian synergist, the answer is clear: some are not saved because there is a contribution we must make in our salvation and those who do not participate with God

---

[11] An excellent defense of this basic perspective can be found in Kevin Timpe, *Free Will: Sourcehood and Its Alternatives* (New York: Continuum, 2008).

in his salvific efforts will not be saved. Moreover, there is nothing in synergism itself that involves a denial or even diminishing of human sinfulness. Calvinists assume that if there is something that humans are contributing to salvation, they must be able to accomplish that on their own, and consequently, there is something about which humans can boast. Their argument proceeds like this:

1. Sin renders human beings spiritually dead.
2. A spiritually dead being can do nothing to contribute to her or his salvation.
3. Therefore, if humans are to be saved, it must come wholly from God's action.

The error here is not in either (1) or (2). In their desire to deny monergism (and all it entails), some Arminians have felt that the best way to do so is to downplay the sinfulness of human beings. I do not concur—because I think that such a diminishing of human sinfulness runs contrary to the pretty clear teaching of Scripture in Romans 3 and 5 (and elsewhere). But the affirmation of the total depravity of human beings does not entail monergism. The faulty assumption by the monergist is that if God does anything, he must do everything. Contrary to monergism, synergism (or at least the synergism that I am interested in defending) holds that God provides grace that makes it possible for humans to respond to his offer of salvation. Arminians label this "prevenient grace," because it is grace that *goes before* our desire to say yes to God's offer of salvation. Prevenient grace is universal, given to all, but it is resistible. Humans can reject God's prevenient grace and in doing so remain unmoved by God's gracious offer of salvation.

Finally, synergism does not entail a denial of predestination or election. Arminians, of course, reject the idea that in eternity God chooses who will and who will not be saved, but that does not mean that Arminians reject the idea of election *en toto*. Rather Arminians argue that the many biblical references to election refer either to God's foreknowledge of who will freely choose to accept his offer of salvation or, more likely, to God's unconditional choice to elect a group that individuals must choose to enter. In the Old Testament, this group is Israel and comprises those who chose to keep covenant with Yahweh, and in the New Testament, the group is the church, those who have chosen to declare allegiance to Christ. God's choice to elect a group is unconditional, but our membership on that group is conditional on our responding with faith to God's prevenient grace.

In summary, the primary impact of the Calvinist/Arminian and monergism/synergism debates on the question of the destiny of the unevangelized is not to define which positions are possible, but what positions one is likely to find persuasive. There is, for example, a strong correlation between the Calvinist idea that God elects a particular group of people who will be saved and the Restrictivist notion that only those people who hear the gospel will be saved. The connecting idea between these two correlates is the notion that God, in his sovereign providence, sends the gospel to all of those he has chosen to save and those who are not elect will not be saved. Similarly, there is a strong correlation between the Arminian view of God's love and "universal accessibility" theories. The idea that "God so loved *the world*" and therefore desires all to be saved strongly suggests that he has plans to save those who do not hear the gospel in this life. In short, I am addressing the Calvinist/Arminian and monergism/synergism debate only to set it aside. Because the version of Postmortem Opportunity I am developing is explicitly Arminian, I will be invoking many ideas (universal salvific will, unlimited atonement, libertarian freedom) that the Calvinist/monergist rejects.

THE ARGUMENT

The theological argument for Postmortem Opportunity can be stated as simply as this: God desires that all people be saved, some people do not have a premortem opportunity to be saved, and therefore, God will provide those people with a Postmortem Opportunity. This way of stating it has the advantage of brevity and (at least surface) clarity, but this comes at the price of leaving a rather large number of questions unanswered. Consequently, I will articulate and seek to defend a more thorough argument. Before I do so, one caveat: while this argument has some of the trappings of a deductive argument, the inferences in this argument should not be understood as deductive. Deductive arguments are arguments where the truth of the conclusion is guaranteed, given the truth of the premises. Deductive arguments can be useful in many different ways, but I submit, establishing the truth of complicated theological positions is just not one of them. A deductively valid argument for Postmortem Opportunity—or, for that matter, social trinitarianism or transubstantiation or the verbal plenary theory of inspiration—even if possible, would require dozens of steps and quite a few premises that would be likely to be rejected by anyone who wasn't already inclined to accept the conclusion. Rather, my argument for Postmortem Opportunity employs abductive reasoning, a form of argument often called "inference to the best explanation" (hereafter, IBE). The fundamental difference between deductive reasoning and abductive reasoning is in the strength of the conclusion. Abductive inferences do not guarantee the truth of the conclusion, given the truth of the premises. Rather, abductive inferences give one a good reason to believe that the conclusion is true, given the truth of the premises.

My argument for Postmortem Opportunity is as follows:

1. God desires that all people be saved. (Premise)
2. Being saved requires having an opportunity to be saved. (Premise)
3. Therefore, God desires that all people receive an opportunity to be saved. (IBE from 1, 2)
4. There are some who do not receive an opportunity to be saved in this life. (Premise)

5. There are no good, all-things-considered reasons to think that death is the end of salvific opportunity. (Premise)
6. Therefore, God desires that those who do not receive a premortem opportunity to be saved will receive a Postmortem Opportunity. (IBE from 3, 4, 5)
7. There are no good, all-things-considered reasons to think that God's desire to provide a Postmortem Opportunity will be thwarted or overridden. (Premise)
8. Therefore, we have good reason to believe that God will provide a Postmortem Opportunity to those who do not receive a premortem opportunity. (IBE from 6, 7)

Some of these premises are less controversial than others, but there is no premise in this argument that is seen as obviously true by all thoughtful Christians.[12] That's no real slight to this argument; there are very few arguments for complex theological positions that can boast having uncontroversial or universally accepted premises. Controversial assertions come with the territory. I do not claim that they are the only reasonable abductive inference from the premises; I do claim that they are the most reasonable inferences.

DOES GOD DESIRE THAT ALL BE SAVED?

The first proposition—"God desires that all people be saved"—asserts a belief that lies at the heart of Arminian/synergistic soteriology, God's universal salvific will. The claim that God desires all to be saved does not, of course, entail that all will be saved, for Arminians believe that God's desires are sometimes frustrated by the decisions of his creation—hence the existence of evil. What God's universal salvific will most clearly entails is a denial of the claim that God only desires to save a proper subset of human beings, his elect. The scriptural rationale for

[12]The exception to this claim might be proposition 1, but there are certainly orthodox Christians who deny this claim.

God's universal salvific will is nicely summed up in John 3:16: "For God so loved *the world* that he gave his one and only Son, that *whoever* believes in him shall not perish but have eternal life." The natural human tendency is to love only one's own people or, at least, "those who deserve it," but that is not the message of Scripture. Scripture makes it clear that God's love is not given only to the righteous, but for sinners with whom he desires relationship (Eph 2:4-5; Rom 5:8). How wide is God's love? And for whom did Christ die? I believe that the clear teaching of Scripture is that God loves all people and especially the lost, those who are in danger of being eternally separated from him. In chapter two, I discussed the expression of this theme in the parable of the lost sheep. But there are many places in which this theme is powerfully expressed.

> John 3:16: "For God so loved the world that he gave his one and only Son, that whoever believes in him shall not perish but have eternal life."
>
> 1 Timothy 2:4: "[God] wants *all people* to be saved and to come to a knowledge of the truth."
>
> 2 Peter 3:9: "The Lord is not slow in keeping his promise, as some understand slowness. Instead he is patient with you, not wanting *anyone* to perish, but *everyone* to come to repentance."
>
> Ezekiel 33:11: "Say to them, 'As surely as I live, declares the Sovereign LORD, *I take no pleasure in the death of the wicked*, but rather that they turn from their ways and live.'"[13]

These verses convey both a positive and a negative message about God's salvific desire. The positive message is that he desires the salvation of all people and the negative message is that God does not desire the eternal destruction of anybody, not even the wicked.[14]

---

[13]Others: Mt 23:37; Jn 12:32, 47; Rom 5:17-21; 11:32; 2 Cor 5:14-19; Heb 2:9; 1 Jn 2:2.

[14]Logicians will correctly point out that these two points are redundant, for "X desires that all have A" entails "X desires that none lack A," but the redundancy serves the purposes of clarity and emphasis. In fact, the entailment is reflexive, for "X desires that none fail to have A" entails "X desires that all have A" as well.

Those who deny God's universal salvific will have a difficult task when faced with these verses. They need to deuniversalize the clearly universal implications of John 3:16 ("the world," τὸν κόσμον), 1 Timothy 2:4 ("all people"), and 2 Peter 3:9 ("anyone") and show how God's desire to save even the most sinful ("the wicked") is *not* thwarted by the failure to "turn from their ways." Further, they need to explain why nobody in the early church until Augustine's shift in 396 saw anything other than universal salvific will in these passages.[15] Calvinists who deny that these verses teach universal salvific will do so, frankly, not because, *taken by themselves*, there is a clear meaning of these passages that teaches that God does not desire all to be saved, but because of their interpretation of other passages they take to teach concepts that are incompatible with universal salvific will. For example, there are passages Calvinists believe teach that God unconditionally chooses to save only some people, most significantly Romans 9:6-24. They then are obliged to interpret the passages listed above in a way that is compatible with their belief that Scripture teaches that God unconditionally elects only some individuals to salvation.

Given their commitment to unconditional election of individuals,[16] Calvinists reinterpret the passages listed above in a variety of ways. For example, they argue that 1 Timothy 2:4 should be understood as saying

[15]On Augustine's 396 shift, see Paul R. Eddy, "Can a Leopard Change Its Spots? Augustine and the Crypto-Manicheaeism Question," *Scottish Journal of Theology* 62, no. 3 (2009): 316-46. See also William S. Babcock, "Augustine's Interpretation of Romans (AD 394–396)," *Augustinian Studies* 10 (1979): 55-74; Babcock, "Augustine and Paul: The Case of Romans IX," in *Studia Patristica* 16, ed. E. A. Livingstone (Berlin: Akademie, 1985), 2:473-79; Gregory E. Ganssle, "The Development of Augustine's View of the Freedom of the Will (386–397)," *Modern Schoolman* 74 (1996): 1-18; J. Patout Burns, *The Development of Augustine's Doctrine of Operative Grace* (Paris: Etudes Augustiniennes, 1980), 30-44. On the pre-Augustinian treatment of human freedom and divine election, see Peter Gorday, *Principles of Patristic Exegesis: Romans 9–11 in Origen, John Chrysostom, and Augustine* (New York: Mellen, 1983); Maurice F. Wiles, *The Divine Apostle: The Interpretation of St. Paul's Epistles in the Early Church* (New York: Cambridge University Press, 1967), 94-110, 135-36; Robert L. Wilken, "Free Choice and the Divine Will in Greek Christian Commentaries on Paul," in *Paul and the Legacies of Paul*, ed. William S. Babcock (Dallas: Southern Methodist University Press, 1990), 123-40.

[16]Also important here are effectual grace and limited atonement. Those will be considered in the next section.

that God desires *all kinds of people* to come to salvation, Gentiles as well as Jews.[17] Similarly, some seek to create the distinction in 2 Peter 3:9 that God died for all people *without distinction*—namely, all kinds of people—but not all people *without exception*. The problem with such interpretations are that they are not interpretations of what the texts actually *say*; they are clever ways of avoiding the implications of what the texts say. More to the point, if the author of these passages wanted to make the claim that God desires all kinds of people to be saved, there is a much clearer way of making that point.[18]

A more plausible Calvinist treatment of these "universal salvific desire" passages is the "two wills of God" answer. John Piper (and others) argues that these sorts of passages genuinely express *an aspect* of God's desire.[19] God does want all people to be saved and he does not want anyone to perish, but because he desires something that conflicts with that desire—that he have an opportunity to demonstrate his justice and wrath at sin—he chooses not to act on his desire that all be saved. Piper's claim can be explained by the following analogy: As a teacher I genuinely want to give all of my students As. But I do not act on that desire and give them all As because I desire something more—namely, that the grades I give mean something, that students earn the grades

[17]See Jonathan Gibson, "For Whom Did Christ Die? Particularism and Universalism in the Pauline Epistles," in *From Heaven He Came and Sought Her: Definite Atonement in Historical, Biblical, Theological, and Pastoral Perspective*, ed. David Gibson and Jonathan Gibson (Wheaton, IL: Crossway, 2013), 313.

[18]This very point is made forcefully by the Calvinist Charles Spurgeon: "[This is how] our older Calvinists friends deal with this text. 'All men,' say they—'that is, some men': as if the Holy Ghost could not have said 'some men' if he had meant some men. 'All men,' say they—'that is, some of all sorts of men': as if the Lord could not have said 'All sorts of men' if he had meant that. The Holy Ghost by the apostle has written 'all men,' and unquestionably he means 'all men.'" See Charles Spurgeon, "A Critical Text—C. H. Spurgeon on 1 Timothy 2:3-4"; cited in Iain Murray, *Spurgeon v. Hyper-Calvinism: The Battle for Gospel Preaching* (Carlisle, PA: Banner of Truth, 1996), 150. Spurgeon offers this explanation for the apparent inconsistency of this comment with his affirmation of Calvinist theology: "I do not know how this squares with [Calvinism]. . . . I would sooner a hundred times over appear to be inconsistent with myself than be inconsistent with the word of God" (154).

[19]John Piper, "Are There Two Wills in God?" in *Still Sovereign: Contemporary Perspectives on Election, Foreknowledge, and Grace*, ed. Thomas Schreiner and Bruce Ware (Grand Rapids, MI: Baker, 2000).

they get. Similarly, Calvinists like Piper assert that passages like 1 Timothy 2:4 genuinely teach an aspect of God's will, an aspect that is overridden by God's desire (and therefore, decision) to save only a particular subset of people.

I will say more about the notion of God's will or desire later, but for now let's merely notice that Piper's "two wills" argument is only plausible if it is clear that Scripture teaches the Calvinistic notions of effectual grace and limited atonement. So as an explanation of how Calvinists should deal with passages like 1 Timothy 2:4, Piper's argument is helpful. But if one does not take it as settled theology that the details of Calvinist soteriology is true, it is pretty clear that 1 Timothy 2:4 (and the other passages) teach universal salvific will. So, adopting the principle of interpreting more controversial passages in light of those that are clear, it is most reasonable to take these passages as teaching that God desires all people to be saved.

DOES BEING SAVED REQUIRE AN OPPORTUNITY TO BE SAVED?

The second proposition—"Being saved requires having an opportunity to be saved"—is the simple notion that humans participate in God's salvific efforts by responding to the gospel and declaring allegiance to Christ. Exploring this idea fully is complicated and worth a book in its own right, but for the purposes of my argument it is sufficient to say that I am not necessarily wedded to any particular account of what is involved in conversion, only that some sort of moment of choice is necessary. Whatever salvation is, it does not take place outside the awareness of the person being saved. It does not "happen to them" in the sense that they are unaware of any spiritual change or ascribe no religious significance to the phenomenon they experience.

From the perspective of synergism, this proposition is trivially true. If salvation necessarily requires human cooperation, there must be a moment (or series of moments) in which a human person has an opportunity to cooperate. It is important to note, however, that I am not assuming that a person requires any particular kind of opportunity; I claim only that there must be an opportunity and can envision a wide range of possibilities for what that opportunity might look like. Ironically, most monergists are inclined to accept that salvation requires an opportunity to be saved. That is because even though monergists aver that the causal impetus behind salvation comes solely from God, they hold that humans play a role in responding with compatibilist freedom.

The notion that salvation requires an opportunity to be saved also has firm biblical support. For instance: "For, 'Everyone who calls on the name of the Lord will be saved.' How, then, can they call on the one they have not believed in? And how can they believe in the one of whom they have not heard? And how can they hear without someone preaching to them? And how can anyone preach unless they are sent? As it is written: 'How beautiful are the feet of those who bring good news!'" (Rom 10:13-15). Passages such as these, of course, raise the question at the heart of the debate over Inclusivism of whether explicit faith in Jesus Christ is required for salvation or whether implicit faith is sufficient. But for the purposes of the discussion of this proposition, it must be said that even if George responds with implicit faith to God's general revelation, that still amounts to an opportunity to be saved.

The understanding of salvific opportunity that does contradict my claim is the belief that salvation is provided by infant baptism or by being born into a covenant community. In those cases, salvation is something that happens to the person and operates outside their intentional awareness. There are deep and complex issues here and I will not pretend to be able to do them justice. But for the purposes of my topic, it is important to note that even if it could be argued that infants are saved through baptism (and, therefore, they are not consciously aware of their salvation), this possibility does little to address the problem of the destiny of the unevangelized. This is because infant baptism (and all such sacramental or covenantal events) occur within the Christian community and therefore are irrelevant to the question of how those who are unevangelized might have an opportunity to be saved.

DOES GOD DESIRE THE UNIVERSAL ACCESSIBILITY OF SALVATION?

The third proposition—"Therefore, God desires that all people receive an opportunity to be saved"—is an inference to the best explanation from the first and second propositions. If God desires that all be saved (he has universal salvific will) and if being saved requires receiving an opportunity to be saved, then that gives one good reason to believe that God desires that each and every person will have an opportunity to be saved. Logically speaking, this argument is stated in something close to the form of *modus ponens*.[20]

1. God desires that all be saved.
2. If all people are saved, then all people have an opportunity to be saved.
3. Therefore, God desires that all people have an opportunity to be saved.

On the surface, this argument might seem pretty solid. Suppose I desire that all my students get a good grade in my class. Doesn't that suggest that I also desire that they have what is necessary to receiving a good grade—clearly defined requirements, achievable assignments, and so on?[21] The objection to this argument, however, is that desire is not necessarily transitive. For example, I might desire a body fat percentage of less than 8 percent, but realize that achieving that goal would require a strict diet in which I chose not to consume things that I like very much (like beer and ice cream), and therefore not desire the diet that is a means to the end I desire. If it is true that desire is not necessarily

[20]Typically *modus ponens* is stated as "If P, then Q; P; therefore, Q." I am reversing the major and minor premises.

[21]Of course, both of these desires are thwartable, but that doesn't call into question my desire for both the end (good grades) and the means to the end (clear assignments).

transitive, God might desire all to be saved, but not desire all to have an opportunity to be saved.[22]

This objection correctly identifies that there are cases when desire is not transitive, but it doesn't establish that, generally speaking, God's desire is not transitive. In fact, there are good reasons to think that desire is transitive for God, even if it often is not for humans. Consider the sort of things that produce an intransitivity of desire in humans: the lack of awareness of causal connections between means and ends, or the unfortunate ability to think about a particular end in a way that is divorced from the means to that end. These are things that we would never predicate of God. For God to desire a particular end necessarily includes an awareness of what would be required to bring that end about. If there was an end that entailed things that God did not desire or could not bring about, then God would not desire that end.[23]

In addition, notice that there are good biblical reasons to believe that God desires all to have an opportunity to be saved, reasons that are independent of an inference from God's universal salvific will. These reasons focus on how Scripture speaks about God's actions with respect to salvation. Not only does Scripture speak about God's desire that all be saved, Scripture speaks about what God has done with respect to salvation. Most relevant, in this respect, is the biblical evidence for Christ's atonement for human sins being unlimited in scope. Scripture teaches, for example, that Jesus "gave himself as a ransom for *all* people" (1 Tim 2:6); Jesus is described as "the Lamb of God, who takes away the sin of *the world*" (Jn 1:29); Jesus said that "when I am lifted up from the earth, [I] will draw *all people* to myself" (Jn 12:32); "For the grace of God has appeared that offers salvation to *all people*" (Titus 2:11); that Jesus "suffered death, so that by the grace of God he might taste death

---

[22]Thanks to Tim Pawl for a helpful conversation surrounding this matter.

[23]Does this entail that God does not desire that all people be saved because he doesn't desire to override the freedom of humans to reject him? No, because his desire that all people be saved is a desire that all people choose relationship with God, not a desire that all people end up saved. If he merely desired that all people be saved, of course, he could bring about that end.

for *everyone*" (Heb 2:9); and that "God did not send his Son into the world to condemn *the world*, but to save *the world* through him" (Jn 3:16-17).[24] Moreover, the texts for universal salvific will discussed above are themselves arguments in favor of unlimited atonement, for given the transitivity of desire for God, if Scripture teaches that God desires that all be saved, it is reasonable to believe that God's atonement was intended for all. And it won't do to appeal to the fact that sometimes God's desires are frustrated by human choices, for the atonement is an act of God. If God intends to make the scope of the atonement universal, then there is no other choice that can frustrate that. It might be case that humans reject his offer of salvation and thereby frustrate his desire that all be saved, but there is nothing to stop his intending the atonement to apply to all.

One final passage should be mentioned: 1 Timothy 4:10 says, "That is why we labor and strive, because we have put our hope in the living God, who is the Savior of all people, and especially [*malista*] of those who believe." Millard Erickson sees this text as the strongest verse in favor of unlimited atonement. Some draw the opposite conclusion from this verse, assuming that the second phrase ("especially those who believe") limits the first ("the Savior of all people"). This argument, however, is flawed because you cannot limit Christ's atoning work to only "those who believe" without explicitly denying that Christ is "the Savior of all people." I. Howard Marshall argues that "the Pastor makes a statement of the character of God as the Savior of all men, and then he makes a necessary qualification: 'I mean, of those [among them] who believe.'"[25] As such, the qualification is not meant to deny Christ being the Savior of all, but to draw attention to the necessity of belief to appropriate Christ's universal saving work. Jesus' atonement is given to all, but only those who believe can take advantage of that gracious gift.

---

[24]Other texts taken to teach unlimited atonement include Is 53:6; Jn 4:42; 12:32, 47; Rom 5:18-19; 2 Cor 5:14-19.

[25]I. Howard Marshall, "Universal Grace and Atonement in the Pastoral Epistles," in *The Grace of God and the Will of Man*, ed. Clark H. Pinnock (Grand Rapids, MI: Zondervan, 1989), 55.

Consequently, this qualification does not undermine unlimited atonement, it undermines the simple inference from Christ's universal atonement to Universalism.[26]

Detractors of unlimited atonement claim that the universal intent of the atonement taught in these passages is merely formal. On this view, the death of Christ could have applied to all if God would have decided to save all. The problem with this claim is twofold. First, there is nothing in these passages themselves that suggests such a distinction. Second, and more significant, there are other texts that clearly and deliberately expand the intent of the atonement beyond the circle of believers. 1 John 2:2 says, "He is the atoning sacrifice for our sins, and *not only for ours* but also for the sins of the whole world" (italics added). And 2 Peter 2:1 extends the atonement not only to "the world" but to false teachers and heretics: "But there were also false prophets among the people, just as there will be false teachers among you. They will secretly introduce destructive heresies, even denying the sovereign Lord *who bought them*—bringing swift destruction on themselves" (italics added).

Those that assert that the intent of the atonement is limited to the elect have three primary ways of responding to these texts. The first is to argue that the offering of salvation to "all people" should be understood not as all individuals, but all *kinds* of people (for example, Jews and Gentiles) or all social classes (slave and free). Second, defenders of limited atonement might argue that the intent of these passages is universal, but still does not teach that Christ died for all. Instead passages like 1 Timothy 4:10 indicate that God bestows common grace on all people. Christ is the Savior in the sense of "patron" of all, even if he only died for the elect.[27] Finally, one might claim that the language of

[26]This point applies whether one translates *malista* as "especially" or as "namely." T. C. Skeat and I. Howard Marshall prefer translating *malista* as "namely." See T. C. Skeat, "'Especially the Parchments': A Note on 2 Timothy 4:13," *Journal of Theological Studies* 30 (1979): 174-75 and Marshall, "Universal Grace and Atonement," 55.

[27]An example of this kind of argument is found in Steven M. Baugh, "'Savior of All People': 1 Timothy 4:10 in Context," *Westminster Theological Journal* 54 (1992): 331-40.

universality is merely phenomenological—it merely *seemed* that the atonement was offered to the whole world. Tom Schreiner applies this reasoning to 2 Peter 2:1; it merely *seemed as though* Christ died even for false teachers.[28] A thoroughgoing treatment of this issue would require a detailed response to these claims. For our purposes, let's note what seems undeniable—these interpretations of these passages are prima facie far less plausible than universal intent interpretations. The reason these passages are being read in this limited way is because the interpretations of other passages are thought to require such a reading.

There are undoubtedly passages that seem to convey limited atonement. For example: John 5:21 says, "The Son gives life to whom he is pleased to give it." Likewise, John 6:37 says, "All those the Father gives me will come to me, and whoever comes to me [of those the Father has given] I will never drive away."[29] And John 17:9 says, "I pray for them. I am not praying for the world, but for those you have given me, for they are yours." These passages teach an important truth, but it is not that the scope of the atonement is limited to the elect. I. Howard Marshall argues that the purpose of the language in John some have taken to limit the scope of the atonement

> is not to express the exclusion of certain men from salvation because they were not chosen by the Father . . . but to emphasize that from start to finish eternal life is the gift of God and does not lie under the control of men. A person who tries to gain eternal life on his own terms will find himself unable to come to Jesus because it has not been granted to him by the Father (John 6:65); he has, in fact, been resisting the leading of the Father.[30]

Similarly, the many passages that speak of God's specific love for the church or the elect or believers and the fact that he has come to

[28]Thomas Schreiner makes this very argument with respect to 2 Peter 2:1. See his "'Problematic Texts' for Definite Atonement in the Pastoral and General Epistles," in Gibson and Gibson, *From Heaven He Came and Sought Her*, 390-92.

[29]The parenthetical phrase is not in the text, but it is the best rendering of the grammar of the passage.

[30]I. Howard Marshall, *Kept by the Power of God* (Minneapolis: Bethany, 1975), 177.

redeem "his people" do nothing to limit the universal intent of the atonement. Matthew 1:21 and Luke 1:68 each speak of the purpose of the birth of Jesus, saying that he has come to save "his people," Ephesians 1:4 says that God "chose us," 1 Corinthians 15:3 says that "Christ died for our sins," and Ephesians 5:25 commands that husbands love their wives "just as Christ loved the church and gave himself up for her."[31] While these passages articulate an undeniable truth, that Christ loves and died for his people, it is an egregious logical error to use these passages to argue that the scope of Christ's atonement is limited to the elect. Simply put, there is no contradiction in saying that Christ loves and died for his people and still affirming that Christ died for all people. Scripture clearly teaches God's special love for the church, but should not be articulated in opposition to his love for the lost, for it is God's desire that the lost become a part of his church.

IS SALVATION UNIVERSALLY ACCESSIBLE IN THIS LIFE?

The fourth proposition asserts that there are some who are people who do not have a genuine opportunity to be saved in this life. Actually, this argument would work just fine with the assertion that "there is at least one person who does not receive an opportunity to be saved in this life," but the claim that "some do not receive an opportunity" is perfectly reasonable. The claim that there are some who do not have a genuine opportunity to be saved in this life is not widely regarded as terribly controversial; nonetheless, there are three theories that seek to establish universal accessibility in this life: Inclusivism, Middle Knowledge Universal Opportunity, and Universal Sending.[32] These views all arrive at the universality of a salvific opportunity in different ways. Inclusivism appeals to the universality of general revelation, Middle Knowledge

---

[31]The parable of the Good Shepherd in Jn 10:11-30 is also commonly used in this context.

[32]There are also some who argue (drawing on Rom 1:18-20) that there are no truly unevangelized persons, but that all are left "without excuse" given that they should be able to see God's existence and divine nature in creation. I will wait to discuss that view in the next chapter.

Universal Opportunity attains universality through God's exhaustive knowledge of what would have happened, and Universal Sending posits a universally accessible special revelation. There are two questions to be faced here: (1) Are these explanations of salvific opportunity actually universal and (2) if they are universal, are they better explanations of universal salvific opportunity than Postmortem Opportunity? In addition, with respect to Inclusivism, there is the pressing question of whether a person's response to general revelation can be salvific. That important question is the primary topic of chapter eight, so I will here focus on the other two Accessibilist theories.

Middle Knowledge Universal Opportunity. Middle Knowledge Universal Opportunity is the most difficult Universal Opportunity theory to evaluate. For starters, there are very real questions regarding whether God even has the sort of knowledge required by this theory, knowledge of what individuals would freely choose to do in various counterfactual (or different than actual) situations. It seems obvious that God would know the truth of things like "If I was offered one million dollars with no strings attached, I would freely accept," but it isn't obvious (at least to me) that this is an example of God knowing what I would freely choose to do in a specific situation. It is more likely that this is an example of God simply knowing my character (and perhaps the diminutive size of my bank account) and applying that knowledge in uncontroversial ways. For God to actually have middle knowledge, he would have to know the results of more difficult choices: "If offered one million dollars to vote for a particular unsavory political candidate, I would freely accept." He would also need to know the results of more (seemingly) meaningless choices: "If presented with an opportunity to write with either a blue pen or a black pen, I would freely choose the blue pen." These issues raise what is called the "grounding objection" to middle knowledge, which (in short) raises the question of what grounds God's knowledge that I would have (or would not have) chosen a particular course of action in a counterfactual situation; what makes it true that I would have chosen to write with the blue pen, but not the black pen? The debate over the grounding objection rages on and shows no signs of abating, and I will not try to resolve it here. For the purposes of this volume it is sufficient to note that the attractiveness of the idea of God's knowing how unevangelized persons would have responded if they would have been given the gospel is mitigated by the complexity of the questions and substance of the objections to the theory of middle knowledge.

To see how God's middle knowledge might be an important part of an answer to the question of the destiny of the unevangelized, let's look at the particularly difficult example of Kunta Kinte. While Kunta Kinte has rejected the "gospel" he has heard, given middle knowledge God might know how Kunta Kinte would have responded to the gospel if he had not been violently mistreated by the people who called themselves Christians and who provided a theological justification for their rape, murder, and torture. And perhaps we could say something similar about Micha and Rapunzel cases. God could use his middle knowledge to determine how they would have responded in more ideal stations—for Micha, without her trust destroying experiences and for Rapunzel, with more time to respond.

If middle knowledge could be employed in this way, then it would go a long way to providing a satisfactory answer to the problem of the destiny of the unevangelized. However, I submit that even with these advantages, it would not be superior to Postmortem Opportunity, for one important reason. If God provides the unevangelized with an ideal Postmortem Opportunity to hear the gospel, then their salvation would not be based on God's knowledge of how those individuals *would have* responded, it would be based on their *actual* response. This is crucially important from the perspective of the unevangelized person, for it is surely a better understanding of salvation for them to find themselves in eternal relationship with God because of their specific choice to embrace that relationship rather than merely having a hypothetical, nonactual situation in which they would have accepted God's offer of salvation. To see this, consider the following example: suppose I am offered the congressional Medal of Honor. When I ask how I achieved this honor (since I have never served in the military), I am told that God knows that if I would have served in the military and been placed in a particular difficult situation, I would have acted in a way to warrant receiving the Medal of Honor. Even if the idea that God has knowledge of counterfactual situations makes perfect sense to me, would I feel like I earned the medal? Would I wear it proudly? I think the answer is no. For similar reasons, it is far better that a person's final destination be decided by a decision that they consciously and explicitly make, not by decisions that they would have made.

Therefore, despite its name, Middle Knowledge Universal Opportunity does not affirm actual universal accessibility of the gospel. It affirms a closely related point with an apologetic motive. It affirms (positively), "All of those who would respond, will receive an opportunity" and (negatively), "Those who never hear the gospel, never would have responded under any circumstances." The goal is to defend God's goodness in *not giving some the opportunity to be saved*, not to explain how all persons will have an opportunity to be saved. This is not irrelevant, but it is also not sufficient.

Universal Sending. The Universal Sending theory involves the claim that God reveals himself supernaturally to each of the unevangelized at some time prior to death. As such, unlike Middle Knowledge Universal Opportunity, Universal Sending theorists affirm the actual universal accessibility of the gospel, and because of this affirmation, Universal Sending bears some similarities to Postmortem Opportunity. There are, however, a number of objections to Universal Sending. First, suppose we believe that God has sent the gospel to some people by dream or vision, as seems to be the case from the example of Cornelius and the Ethiopian eunuch. But there doesn't seem to be a good reason to believe that all of the unevangelized, or even all of the George cases receive a similar revelation. So even if Universal Sending sketches a possible scenario in which George might hear the gospel, there is no good reason to think that he actually does. The only argument that he does is an indirect one and it goes roughly like this:

1. God desires all people to have an opportunity to be saved.
2. Death is the end of salvific opportunity.
3. Therefore, God will provide all people an opportunity in this life through a dream or vision.

For starters, I don't think that it is true that death is the end of salvific opportunity, and I will make an argument to that end in the coming chapters. But even if we set aside that argument, Universal Sending has prima facie implausibility. Is it reasonable to believe that all of the people who lived before the time of Christ and outside the influence of the nation of Israel received special revelation from God via vision or angelic messenger? If so, would there not be some evidence of such a pervasive divine interaction or at least powerful indications of such supernatural divine evangelism in the respective cultures? The lack of such evidence places a significant burden of proof on Universal Opportunists who would suggest that all receive special revelation.

Moreover, Universal Sending relies on a fairly straightforward definition of what it means to be "unevangelized." The unevangelized are those like George. Even if the Universal Sending theory can deal with George cases, it is pretty clear that persons like Anna and Sam will not benefit from dreams and visions, so Universal Sending theories are not helpful in those cases. But the most pressing cases for universal sending are not Anna and Sam—they could be handled by positing an age of accountability. The most pressing cases for universal sending are the pseudoevangelized. Kunta, Micha, and Rapunzel are, for different reasons and in different ways, not quite fully evangelized and not quite unevangelized. The challenge they raise for Universal Opportunity theories is substantial. Even if the various Universal

Opportunity theories can explain how George might be given an opportunity to hear the gospel via dream or angelic messenger in this life, the same cannot be said of the pseudoevangelized. Would a dream or angelic visitation be sufficient to open Kunta Kinte's mind to Jesus Christ, given the picture of Jesus painted for him by his slave owners? Would Micha's inability to trust be magically cured? And would Rapunzel be given more time? It is difficult to answer any of these questions definitively, of course, nonetheless, these cases highlight a very real difficulty for the Universal Sending theory.

IS DEATH THE END OF SALVIFIC OPPORTUNITY?

The fifth proposition is the most controversial in my argument. It proposes that, contrary to traditional belief, we lack good reasons to believe that death is the end of salvific opportunity.[33] As we saw in the previous section, the best argument for Universal Opportunity theories flows from the commitment that God desires all to be saved and assumes that death is the end of salvific opportunity. From those beliefs, the belief in the universal accessibility of the gospel in this life follows naturally. There are a variety of justifications for the belief that death is the end of salvific opportunity. First, some argue that Scripture either explicitly rules out Postmortem Opportunity or teaches things that entail the impossibility of postmortem repentance. Second, others simply claim that even if Scripture does not rule out Postmortem Opportunity, it does not teach it, and therefore Christians should not see it as a viable option. Third, some appeal to the fact that the majority of the Christian tradition has held that death is the end of salvific opportunity—which is true, as long as you ignore the witness of numerous key figures in the early church. Finally, some appeal to various theological objections to the idea of Postmortem Opportunity.

---

[33]Defending this claim is a large task and will be the primary focus of chapters four and five and a secondary focus in chapters six and seven.

Addressing these arguments is obviously a larger task than can be shouldered in this chapter. Since I do not complete my argument for this claim in this chapter, it might be fruitful to think of my argument for Postmortem Opportunity as contingent on a successful defense of this claim.

DOES GOD DESIRE TO PROVIDE A POSTMORTEM OPPORTUNITY?

The sixth proposition is an inference to the best explanation from (3), (4), and (5). If one believes that God desires that all people have an opportunity to be saved, that there are some that do not have an opportunity in this life, and that it is possible to be saved after death, then it is most reasonable to believe that God desires those who did not receive an opportunity to be saved in this life to receive a Postmortem Opportunity. Why a Postmortem Opportunity? Simply because a person's existence can be divided into two mutually exclusive and jointly exhaustive categories: premortem and postmortem. And if a person does not hear in their premortem existence, then hearing in their postmortem existence is the only other option. Now one who wishes to deny the premortem/postmortem binary could claim that there is a third category, the moment of death, between a person's premortem and postmortem existence. This is true, but as I detailed in chapter two, I am using the term *postmortem* to encompass all experiences after the experiences within this life, including the moment of death.[34] As such, I consider those who argue for a Universal Opportunity at the moment of death to be allies to Postmortem Opportunity theorists—they see the need for universal opportunity and they acknowledge that there are some who do not have an opportunity to be saved in this life. The primary difference is that they are laboring under the (I think) mistaken notion that postmortem repentance is impossible.

---

[34]I grant that the term *postvita opportunity* would, therefore, be better to describe this position, but I am using the more traditional term: *Postmortem Opportunity*.

To be clear, I am not yet claiming that God will follow through on his desire and provide a Postmortem Opportunity. That claim is saved for the next proposition. My claim is merely that God desires to provide a Postmortem Opportunity because his doing so is the only way for some people to receive an opportunity. And if God does not desire to provide a Postmortem Opportunity to these people, it is difficult to claim that he desires that all people receive a salvific opportunity.

Now, of course, as we discussed with respect to proposition 3, desire is not *necessarily* transitive—it certainly often fails to be transitive with humans—but nonetheless, there are good reasons to think that desire is transitive for God. Moreover, this very issue is a good illustration of this claim. Suppose that propositions 3, 4, and 5 are all true—namely, God desires all people to have an opportunity to be saved, there are some that do not receive an opportunity in this life, and there are no good reasons that death is the end of salvific opportunity. One who would accept these propositions as true, but argue that God still did not have a desire to provide a Postmortem Opportunity to those who did not receive a premortem opportunity would have to explain why God's desire was not transitive in this case. Moreover, they could not appeal to any lack of knowledge on God's part or any ambivalence about the implications of offering a Postmortem Opportunity, for God would know the implications of all of his actions. Ultimately, if one insisted that God did not desire to provide a Postmortem Opportunity, when doing so was both possible and the only salvific avenue for some people, the most reasonable conclusion would not be that the desire was not transitive for God, but that proposition 3 was false: ultimately, God did not desire all to have an opportunity to be saved. Either way, desire seems to be transitive for God.

But there is another reason to think that it is true that "God desires that those who do not receive a premortem salvific opportunity will receive a Postmortem Opportunity"—namely, God's offering of a Postmortem Opportunity is the best (and maybe only) way for a synergist to eliminate soteriological vagueness. To explain this claim, I will employ (and adapt) an argument made by Theodore Sider that I will call the "Vagueness Problem."[35] He notes that orthodox Christians believe each of the following:

1. There are only two ultimate postmortem states, heaven and hell.
2. Heaven is very, very good and hell is very, very bad—or, more minimally, hell is much worse than heaven.
3. Not everybody ends up in heaven, some are sent to hell and stay there for an eternity.
4. God is the arbiter of who is sent to heaven and who is sent to hell; a person's final destiny is based on his decision.[36]

The Vagueness Problem is that while there are only two ultimate postmortem states, God must judge humans according to a standard that comes in degrees and admits of borderline cases. One could develop the idea of soteriological vagueness along the lines of C. S. Lewis's suggestive comment: "The world does not consist of 100 per cent Christians and 100 per cent non-Christians. There are people (a great many of them) who are slowly ceasing to be Christians but still call themselves by that name: some are clergymen. There are other people that are slowly becoming Christians though they do not call themselves so."[37]

I think Lewis's more general claim is correct, but given the purposes of this volume, I am interested in the soteriological vagueness that results from being unevangelized or pseudoevangelized. The soteriological vagueness for George, Anna, Sam, and Kunta Kinte cases should be obvious—none have rejected the gospel in any meaningful sense, George and Kunta may have responded in some way to the grace God provides through general revelation, and Anna and Sam have never personally chosen to sin or rebel against God in any way. The essence

[35]Theodore Sider, "Hell and Vagueness," *Faith and Philosophy* 19, no. 1 (January 2002): 58-68.
[36]Sider, "Hell and Vagueness," 58.
[37]C. S. Lewis, *Mere Christianity* (New York: Macmillan, 1978), 176.

of the Vagueness Problem is that God must draw the line somewhere and, because the person just on the heaven side of the line is not that different than the person just on the hell side of the line, it seems that there will be injustice (or at least a lack of clarity) wherever God draws the line. The idea of an unevangelized or pseudoevangelized person "not being very different" than a person who heard the gospel is a function of the difficult-to-deny fact that if the unevangelized person would have heard the gospel, they might have responded and if the evangelized person would have failed to hear the gospel, they would have lacked saving faith—the differences between the two people concern their geographical and temporal location, not differences in virtue, disposition toward faith, or any other morally significant property. And yet, the person who has heard the gospel has an opportunity to experience a massively dissimilar ultimate postmortem state. And this seems to conflict with God's love, goodness, and justice, for it is highly plausible to say that God's goodness would prohibit very unequal ultimate postmortem destinations of persons who are very similar in terms of faith.[38]

There are three ways of addressing soteriological vagueness. The first is to be a monergist. If one is a monergist than any genuine step toward relationship with God is a result of effectual grace given to that person by God, and no one who has not received effectual saving grace from God can genuinely desire relationship with God. People may seem to desire relationship with God, but this is illusory; without effectual grace, what we desire is an idol of our choosing or power and control over our destiny. There is, therefore, no vagueness. The causal human element in salvation is completely eliminated. Those that will be saved are those whom God has given effectual grace. A second response to soteriological vagueness comes from those who embrace middle knowledge. On this view, soteriological vagueness is eliminated by God's exhaustive

[38]Sider, "Hell and Vagueness," 59.

knowledge of what people would do in counterfactual situations. Assuming middle knowledge is a viable concept, this would eliminate vagueness, but the problem is that salvation would be based on what people would have done rather than on what they actually choose. And that problem is, I believe, damning.

Suppose one rejects both monergism and Middle Knowledge Universal Opportunity. From a synergistic point of view, it seems impossible to eliminate vagueness *in this life*. If the human element is causally important in salvation, then whether a person has or has not heard the gospel or whether the gospel they have heard is genuine or misleading is of crucial importance. The only way for a synergist to avoid soteriological vagueness is to acknowledge that God will provide a Postmortem Opportunity to all of those he knows did not receive a genuine a premortem opportunity.[39] If a person's salvific status is decided by their response to a genuine presentation of the gospel in this life or a Postmortem Opportunity, there is no soteriological vagueness. And because the elimination of soteriological vagueness is a good thing, this is yet another reason why God would desire that those who do not receive a premortem opportunity to be saved will receive a Postmortem Opportunity.

WILL GOD PROVIDE A POSTMORTEM OPPORTUNITY?

Let's recapitulate the argument thus far. God desires that all be saved, and being saved requires an opportunity to be saved; therefore, it is most reasonable to believe that God desires that all have an opportunity to be saved. But it seems most reasonable to believe that some do not have an

[39]In their response to Sider's argument, Trent Dougherty and Ted Poston argue that Sider's argument only works when additional premises are employed, the most problematic of which (from their perspective) is the "existence thesis," the claim that there are some persons who are very similar, yet who end up in radically different eternal destinations. I don't contest their claims, but one could see my argument for Postmortem Opportunity as not only an argument that the existence thesis is unsupported, but that in offering a Postmortem Opportunity to those whose salvific status is vague, God makes sure that the existence thesis is false. See their "Hell, Vagueness, and Justice: A Reply to Sider," *Faith and Philosophy* 25, no. 3 (July 2008): 322-28.

opportunity to be saved in this life. So, assuming a successful defense of the claim that death is not the end of salvific opportunity, it is most reasonable to believe that God desires that persons who fail to have a genuine premortem opportunity receive a Postmortem Opportunity to be saved. The final question to be faced is whether God will act on this desire and offer a Postmortem Opportunity to those he deems to be in need of it. As such, the seventh proposition proposes that there are no persuasive reasons to think that God's desire to provide a Postmortem Opportunity to those who need it will be thwarted or overridden.

Two initial clarifications. First, the difference between this question and the question faced in the previous section is that the previous section considered the transitivity of desire—if God desires X, sees that X requires Y, does he desire Y?—whereas this section is about the translation of desire into action—given that he desires Y, do we have reasons to believe that he will act on his desires and bring about Y? Second, my claim here is epistemic, not metaphysical. I am not claiming that there *are no reasons* why God might not provide a Postmortem Opportunity—for I believe that such a determination is beyond my ken. Rather, I am claiming that *we have no good reasons* to believe that he will not provide a Postmortem Opportunity.

Clark Pinnock argues that the universal accessibility of the gospel is a straightforward inference from God's universal salvific will. He says, "If God really loves the whole world and desires everyone to be saved, it follows logically that everyone must have access to salvation. There would have to be an opportunity for all people to participate in the salvation of God. . . . God's universal salvific will implies the equally universal accessibility of salvation for all people."[40] As such, for Pinnock, if there are people who have not heard the gospel in this life, it follows that God will provide a Postmortem Opportunity. While it is tempting to agree with Pinnock's argument, this issue is more complicated than

[40]Pinnock, *Wideness in God's Mercy*, 157.

it appears on the surface. The problem arises because, as an Arminian, Pinnock believes that human beings can frustrate God's will with their choices.[41] The fact that humans have self-determining freedom means that not all of God's desires are actualized. This is why God's universal salvific will does not necessarily entail Universalism; God's desire that all be saved can be thwarted by humans who freely choose to reject his gracious offer of salvation. But, given self-determining freedom, isn't it possible that the same thing might be said for universal accessibility of salvation? Daniel Strange presses this very point: "God may desire everyone to hear the gospel, but this desire for everyone to hear can be frustrated. . . . God may desire the salvation of all but getting the gospel to those people is our task, and this task can succeed or fail."[42]

To see the import of Strange's argument, consider the following two arguments:

	ARGUMENT A		ARGUMENT B
1	God desires that all be saved.	1	God desires that salvation be universally accessible.
2	Human choices can thwart God's desires.	2	Human choices can thwart God's desires.
3	Therefore, it is possible that not all will be saved.	3	Therefore, it is possible that salvation will not be universally accessible.

Figure 2

The point of Strange's argument seems to be that one who accepts Argument A should also accept Argument B. I don't think this follows.

[41]Pinnock is also an open theist, but on the matter of human freedom there is not much daylight between the classical Arminian and the open theist.

[42]Daniel Strange, "Salvation, Atonement and Accessibility: Towards a Solution of the 'Soteriological Problem of Evil,'" *Foundations* 44 (Spring 2000): 12.

The problem with Strange's argument is that he assumes that the provision of the salvific opportunity is something that humans must *necessarily* participate in. From a synergistic point of view, this is false because God cannot guarantee that all will be saved without being willing to override human freedom, but he can make salvation universally accessible without overriding human freedom. As such, there is an asymmetry between God's desire that all be saved and God's desire that all have an opportunity to be saved simply because the former requires human participation where the latter does not necessarily do so. That is precisely the point of the theory of Postmortem Opportunity. God has chosen to allow humans to participate in spreading the gospel, but he does not leave the task of bringing opportunities for salvation to those who need it completely up to humans. He does not do so because he knows that there are some people who will live in a time and place that will rob them of a salvific opportunity. And he knows that some person's situation will be such that the "gospel" they hear will be compromised and not even remotely "good news" (as in the case of Kunta Kinte). As such, because God desires the universal accessibility of salvation, he retains the right to provide postmortem salvific opportunities to those who do not receive a premortem opportunity.[43]

So there is nothing external to God that can thwart his provision of a Postmortem Opportunity to those he deems to be in need of it. But might there be something internal to God that would override his desire for the universal accessibility of the gospel? This is an important question because, for Arminian non-Universalists, something like this happens with respect to universal salvific will. God desires that all be saved, but because he desires that salvation be something that is chosen

[43]In a more recent essay, Strange has extended this argument, claiming that the fact that the unevangelized do not hear the gospel in this life means that the scope of the atonement is not unlimited as Arminians claim, but definite or limited. See his "Slain for the World? The 'Uncomfortability' of the 'Unevangelized' for a Universal Atonement," in *From Heaven He Came and Sought Her: Definite Atonement in Historical, Biblical, Theological, and Pastoral Perspective*, ed. David Gibson and Jonathan Gibson (Wheaton, IL: Crossway, 2013), 585-605, especially 591-92.

by human persons, he allows the possibility that there will be some who will choose to reject his offer of salvation. Or, in other words, he does not act on his desire for universal salvation, because his desire that humans choose to be in relationship with him overrides that desire. Are there any candidates for overriding desires that might prevent God from acting on his desire to provide a Postmortem Opportunity?

There are a number of possibilities, but each would involve denying one of the earlier propositions in the argument. For instance, anyone who rejected the idea that God desires all people to be saved might also believe that God would have an overriding desire that would prevent him offering a Postmortem Opportunity. Even more clearly, anybody that believed that there were good objections to the very idea of a Postmortem Opportunity—perhaps if they believed that the nature of the relationship resulting from a Postmortem Opportunity was substandard or idolatrous—would also certainly believe that God might have good reasons not to act on his desire to provide a Postmortem Opportunity. But these are ideas already addressed earlier in the argument, in Propositions 1 and 5, respectively, so they aren't really reasonable objections to Proposition 7, for one who rejected either Proposition 1 or 5 wouldn't even be considering whether or not there are persuasive reasons to think that God's desire to provide a Postmortem Opportunity to those who need it will be thwarted or overridden. As such, for one who has accepted Propositions 1 to 6, it is exceedingly difficult to see why God would desire to provide a Postmortem Opportunity, but choose not to act on that desire. The rationale for this claim comes not only from the assertions in the first six propositions—that God desires all to be saved, to have an opportunity to be saved, and so on—but also from the fact that salvation and the resulting relationship with God is not just one good among others, but the greatest good imaginable. This is true not only from a human perspective, but arguably from God's perspective. Given that God is love and that he has created humans to be in a loving relationship with him, it is obviously true that he would desire the humans he has created to be able to see him as he is and to enter into relationship with him.

This brings us to the final proposition of the argument for Postmortem Opportunity. Proposition 8 is an inference to the best explanation from (6) and (7). If God desires that those who do not receive a premortem opportunity receive a Postmortem Opportunity and if there are no all-things-considered reasons to think that his desire is thwarted or overridden, then it is perfectly reasonable to conclude that God will, in fact, provide a Postmortem Opportunity to those who need it.

CONCLUSION

But is it true? Do we have sufficient reason to believe that God will provide a Postmortem Opportunity to those he deems to need it? Answering this question is the burden of the next four chapters. We must address the biblical evidence for and against the belief that postmortem repentance is possible, we should consider historical arguments that this is a matter that the church has already settled, and we need to consider the theological objections that might be raised against the theory of Postmortem Opportunity.

4

SCRIPTURAL OBJECTIONS TO POSTMORTEM OPPORTUNITY

The previous chapters introduced the problem of the destiny of the unevangelized, laid out the basic concepts of the theory of Postmortem Opportunity, and presented a theological argument for it. One of the premises of that argument was as follows: "There are no good all-things-considered reasons to think that death is the end of salvific opportunity." While segments of the early church acknowledged the possibility of postmortem repentance, the theory of Postmortem Opportunity is currently *not* the dominant answer to the question of the destiny of the unevangelized. In fact, it has largely fallen off the church's radar for much of the last 1500 years. And the primary factor keeping Postmortem Opportunity off the radar screen for most contemporary Christians is the belief that there are decisive reasons to believe that a Postmortem Opportunity is impossible—namely, that it runs contrary to Scripture. This is, I believe, mistaken, and in the next two chapters I will seek to demonstrate that fact.

There are three kinds of scriptural objections to the theory of Postmortem Opportunity. The first is the most aggressive—that the theory of Postmortem Opportunity is unreasonable because Scripture explicitly rules it out by teaching that salvific status is fixed at death. The second is slightly less aggressive. It is the assertion that, even if Scripture does not directly rule out Postmortem Opportunity, it says things that imply it is false. The third objection is that, even if Scripture does not explicitly rule Postmortem Opportunity out, it still should not be held because Scripture does not directly or explicitly teach it. In this chapter

I will consider the first two of these objections and will take up the third in the next.

IS SALVIFIC STATUS FIXED AT DEATH?

There are a number of passages that have been marshaled to support the notion that one's salvific status is fixed at death. These include Hebrews 9:27, the parable of Lazarus and the rich man in Luke 16:19-31, Luke 13:25, 2 Corinthians 5:10, 2 Corinthians 6:2, Psalm 49, and the noncanonical text 2 Clement 8:3. Let us consider each of these in turn.

Hebrews 9:27. The text most commonly cited in opposition to Postmortem Opportunity is Hebrews 9:27: "Just as people are destined to die once, and after that to face judgment." Of this verse, Millard Erickson says that it "seems to assume an *invariable* transition from one to the other, with no mention of any additional opportunities for acceptance."[1] And Ronald Nash claims that this verse teaches that "the judgment of each human reflects that person's standing with God *at the moment of death*."[2] These interpretations are surprising, for there is nothing *in the text* whatsoever to justify these specific claims.[3] Hebrews 9:27 is set in the context of a discussion of the death of Jesus Christ as the atonement for the sins of humanity.

> [25] Nor did he enter heaven to offer himself again and again, the way the high priest enters the Most Holy Place every year with blood that is not his own. [26] Otherwise Christ would have had to suffer many times since the creation of the world. But he has appeared once for all at the culmination of the ages to do away with sin by the sacrifice of himself. [27] Just as people are destined to die once, and after that to face judgment, [28] so Christ was sacrificed once to take away the sins of many; and he will appear a second time, not to bear sin, but to bring salvation to those who are waiting for him. (Heb 9:25-28)

---

[1]Millard Erickson, *How Shall They Be Saved? The Destiny of Those Who Do Not Hear of Jesus* (Grand Rapids, MI: Baker, 1996), 173.

[2]Ronald Nash, *When a Baby Dies: Answers to Comfort Grieving Parents* (Grand Rapids, MI: Zondervan, 1999), 43; italics mine.

[3]If one starts from the assumption that salvation after death is impossible, then these passages could be interpreted in a way that could be supportive of that commitment, but that's about it.

The broader context of this passage is the difference between the old system of atonement and Jesus Christ's atoning sacrifice. Hebrews 9:25 and 26 asserts that Jesus did not atone for sins the way the high priest did, for that would require ongoing sacrifice on his part. Rather, just as human beings only die once, and after that face judgment (Heb 9:27), so Christ will only die once to pay the price for human sin, and after that "appear a second time" to bring salvation to those who are being judged (Heb 9:28). The parallelism between Hebrews 9:27 and 28 as well as the context draws attention to the fact that humans only die once. That is the point of the passage. The point of saying "death then judgment" is to reinforce the idea that death only occurs once. Consequently, if this text is an argument against any particular position or belief, it is reincarnation, not Postmortem Opportunity. There is nothing in the claim that judgment follows death that is problematic for the Postmortem Opportunity theorist. In fact, even if this passage could be interpreted to teach that the day of judgment followed *immediately* after death, that would do nothing to impugn Postmortem Opportunity,[4] for it is possible to believe that the judgment that an unevangelized person experiences includes an opportunity to hear the gospel and that they are judged by their response to that offer. This is not the place to discuss the labyrinthine issues surrounding personal eschatology, but suffice it to say that there are numerous possibilities here, and even if Hebrews 9:27 teaches an immediate transition from death to judgment, that does nothing to undermine the theory of Postmortem Opportunity.[5]

Luke 16:19-31. The second most common passage used to demonstrate that salvific status is fixed at death is the parable of Lazarus and the rich man.[6]

---

[4]And the parallelism between Heb 9:27, 28 works against such an inference. The assumption that death is followed *immediately* by judgment is problematized by the fact that Christ's second coming does not follow immediately after Christ's death.

[5]A similar point can be made about Rev 20:11-13.

[6]See Erickson, *How Shall They Be Saved?*, 172; Nash, *When a Baby Dies*, 43.

> There was a rich man who was dressed in purple and fine linen and lived in luxury every day. At his gate was laid a beggar named Lazarus, covered with sores and longing to eat what fell from the rich man's table. Even the dogs came and licked his sores. The time came when the beggar died and the angels carried him to Abraham's side. The rich man also died and was buried. In Hades, where he was in torment, he looked up and saw Abraham far away, with Lazarus by his side. So he called to him, "Father Abraham, have pity on me and send Lazarus to dip the tip of his finger in water and cool my tongue, because I am in agony in this fire." But Abraham replied, "Son, remember that in your lifetime you received your good things, while Lazarus received bad things, but now he is comforted here and you are in agony. And besides all this, between us and you a great chasm has been set in place, so that those who want to go from here to you cannot, nor can anyone cross over from there to us." He answered, "Then I beg you, father, send Lazarus to my family, for I have five brothers. Let him warn them, so that they will not also come to this place of torment." Abraham replied, "They have Moses and the Prophets; let them listen to them." "No, father Abraham," he said, "but if someone from the dead goes to them, they will repent." He said to him, "If they do not listen to Moses and the Prophets, they will not be convinced even if someone rises from the dead."

On the surface, this text presents a sequence of events after death that are difficult (though not impossible) to square with the theory of Postmortem Opportunity. Not only is there no mention of postmortem opportunities to hear the gospel, the "great chasm" that "has been fixed" is often taken to suggest that one's salvific fate is set at death. Most problematic for the idea of Postmortem Opportunity (or so claim the theory's detractors) is the fact that the rich man is never offered a Postmortem Opportunity to be saved despite seeming to be repentant (at least on some level). In fact, his desire that a message of warning be brought to his still living brothers assumes that he has no salvific hope for himself.

What may be said about this passage? Does it support the contention that death is the end of salvific opportunity? I don't think so. The first thing to say regarding the Lazarus parable is that it is just that: a parable.[7] As a parable, we need to be careful not to make theology out of the details of the parable, for there are many details in Jesus' parables that we accept as window dressing and not part of what the parable is teaching. Granted, it is a unique parable—it is not explicitly labeled a parable and it is the only parable where names are given.[8] Richard Bauckham suggests that the uniqueness of this parable is explained (at least in part) by the fact that it draws on a preexisting story, originating in Egypt, with various Jewish versions of the story all utilizing a common story motif. It is likely that these stories would have been around in the first century and that Jesus would have known of them.[9] Why is Lazarus named? Perhaps just for the simplicity of telling the story or perhaps because "return from the dead" stories like this commonly gave the dead person a name.[10]

If parables are stories designed to make a particular point, what then is the point of this parable? It is instructive to note that there are three parables in Luke 16, each of them addresses the issue of wealth and how it is used, and that these three parables bracket Jesus' words to the Pharisees who "loved money" (Lk 16:14). It is difficult to avoid the point that the Luke 16 parables concern money, not eschatology.[11] Bauckham argues, "The parable's unity hinges on Abraham's unexpected refusal of the rich man's request, directing attention away from an apocalyptic revelation of the afterlife back to the inexcusable injustice of the coexistence of rich and poor."[12] The point of the rich man and Lazarus parable fits perfectly with this context: God does not judge as humans

---

[7]Hence Snodgrass: "Certainly Luke viewed this as a parable." See his *Stories with Intent* (Grand Rapids, MI: Eerdmans, 2008), 426.

[8]Not only is the poor man named Lazarus, there are textual variants where the rich man is named as well.

[9]Bauckham, *The Fate of the Dead: Studies on the Jewish and Christian Apocalypses*, Supplements to Novum Testamentum, vol. 93 (Leiden: Brill, 1998), 101. See also J. Jeremias, *The Parables of Jesus*, trans. S. H. Hooke, 2nd ed. (London: SCM, 1972), 178-79, 183.

[10]Bauckham, *Fate of the Dead*, 115-16.

[11]Bauckham, *Fate of the Dead*, 118. See also Bauckham, "The Rich Man and Lazarus: The Parable and the Parallels," *New Testament Studies* 37 (1991): 225-46.

[12]Bauckham, *Fate of the Dead*, 118.

judge—the rich man was spiritually poor and the poor man was spiritually rich. The inclusion of eschatology in this parable is arguably to drive home the point that the rich man "winds up where children of Abraham are not supposed to go, Hades."[13] Finally, the case for a topical grouping of the parables in Luke 16 is strengthened when one notices that Luke 15 also has three parables that each address the same general topic—defending Jesus' mission to the outcasts of Israelite society.[14]

Millard Erickson, however, rightly points out that it is fallacious to assume that the only point that can be drawn from a passage is the primary point.[15] It is possible that Luke 16 assumes a particular stance on eschatology even if it does not argue for it. As such, the "this is a parable" response only goes so far. What other reasons are there for thinking that the eschatological details of Luke 16 are either not a threat to Postmortem Opportunity or not part of the intended teaching of Scripture? Two things. First, the location described by Luke 16 is either the final resting places of the rich man and Lazarus or an intermediate state. If the rich man and Lazarus are in hell and heaven, what this parable rules out is that the denizens of hell can enter heaven, which does not contradict Postmortem Opportunity at all. True, the passage does not describe either the rich man or Lazarus receiving a Postmortem Opportunity, but that is, at best, an argument from silence, and their failure to receive a Postmortem Opportunity can be rather easily explained by the fact that they were neither unevangelized nor pseudo-evangelized. If this passage places Lazarus and the rich man in the intermediate state, then this would also not rule out a Postmortem Opportunity, for the statement "you cannot cross from there to here" most plausibly only applies to the intermediate state and the inability of persons to move from Hades to paradise. Second, some of the

---

[13]Kline Snodgrass, "Jesus and Money—No Place to Hide and No Easy Answers," *Word & World* 30, no. 2 (Spring 2010): 141.

[14]William Manson, *The Gospel of Luke*, Moffatt New Testament Commentary (London: Hodder and Stoughton, 1930), 182.

[15]Erickson, *How Shall They Be Saved?*, 172.

eschatological details in Luke 16 are likely to be questioned by most orthodox Christians. The parable describes a scenario where those in heaven (or paradise) can peer down into hell (or Hades) and observe the suffering of the unregenerate. These beliefs were common in the Middle Ages and resurface here and there in the writings of other theologians—most notably in Jonathan Edwards's "Sinners in the Hands of an Angry God"—but there is very little to justify these beliefs and quite a few reasons to question them. In particular, it is difficult to reconcile the eternal bliss of believers with the idea that the torture of unbelievers is experientially present to them. For these reasons, the attempt to use this passage to prove death is the end of salvific opportunity is to try to get this parable to speak to theological matters it does not address. For these reasons it seems best to say with N. T. Wright, "The parable is not, as often supposed, a description of the afterlife."[16] Robert Yarbrough goes even further: "It is widely accepted that this story is parabolic and not intended to furnish a detailed geography of hell."[17] This is, of course, not to deny that there is nothing in this parable about the importance of one's choices in this life. My point is that there is nothing in the parable of Lazarus and the rich man that teaches that one's salvific status is fixed at death.

Luke 13:25. One of the people following Jesus asks the question: "Lord, are only a few people going to be saved?" (Lk 13:23). As was his wont, Jesus does not answer the speculative question but instead calls attention to practical considerations, saying, "Make every effort to enter through the narrow door, because many, I tell you, will try to enter and will not be able to" (Lk 13:24). In the next verse, Jesus extends this thought by explaining why many will be unable to enter, saying, "Once the owner of the house gets up and closes the door, you will stand outside knocking and pleading, 'Sir, open the door for us.'

---

[16]N. T. Wright, *Jesus and the Victory of God*, vol. 2 of *Christian Origins and the Question of God* (London: SPCK, 1996), 255.

[17]Robert Yarbrough, "Jesus on Hell," in *Hell Under Fire*, ed. Christopher W. Morgan and Robert A. Peterson (Grand Rapids, MI: Zondervan, 2004), 74.

"But he will answer, 'I don't know you or where you come from'" (Lk 13:25). When those who are locked out protest, "We ate and drank with you, and you taught in our streets" (Lk 13:26), the owner responds, "I don't know you or where you come from. Away from me, all you evildoers!" (Lk 13:27).

The objection to the theory of Postmortem Opportunity comes in the fact that once the owner closes the door, there are no further opportunities for salvation. The careful reader will notice that there is nothing about this argument—call it the "once shut, always shut" argument—that impugns the theory of Postmortem Opportunity. To suggest the impossibility of a Postmortem Opportunity, one must assume that death is when the owner of the house closes the door. But that is nowhere stated or even implied in the text and consequently, this argument begs the question against the Postmortem Opportunity theorist by assuming what is to be proved.

What then is this passage teaching? Two things. First, this text (and Lk 13:25 in particular) does constitute an argument against any view that would claim that there are infinite opportunities to be saved, even while in hell. Consequently, this text calls into question Universalism, but it says nothing against the theory of Postmortem Opportunity. Second, this text is a sharp rebuke against those who believe that superficial acquaintance with Jesus or his teachings is sufficient for salvation. What is required is committed relationship. But, again, there is nothing in this claim that suggests that death is the end of salvific opportunity.

2 Corinthians 5:10. This text reads: "For we must all appear before the judgment seat of Christ, so that each of us may receive what is due us for the things done while in the body, whether good or bad." The claim is that judgment is solely for things done "in the body" or in this life—or, as Ronald Nash terms it, "postmortem judgment is for premortem conditions." There are, in fact, a set of passages that teach this theme, and regarding them Nash claims, "In these passages and others, I contend, one simple point stands out: physical death marks the boundary of human opportunity."[18]

Deciding whether 2 Corinthians 5:10 teaches that salvific opportunity ends at death depends on who Paul is speaking to in this passage, believers only or all people, believers as well as unbelievers. Some say that Paul is speaking to all people in this passage, believers and unbelievers, and on the basis of that claim they assert that people are judged solely by premortem decisions and actions. There are two problems with this assertion. First, there is no explicit justification using this passage to claim that people are judged *solely* based on premortem factors. This passage implies only that judgment includes premortem factors and to claim that there could be no postmortem factors is an argument from silence. Second, there are good reasons to see Paul as speaking to believers only in this passage. It fits the context more naturally than seeing Paul as talking about both believers and unbelievers. Moreover, Murray Harris argues, "there is one consideration . . . that favors the restriction of the expression to all Christians. Where Paul applies the principle of recompense according to works to all people (Rom 2:6), there is found a description of two mutually exclusive categories of people (Rom 2:7-10), not a delineation of two types of action . . . which may be predicated of all people."[19] In other words, if Paul is speaking to both believer and unbelievers, he is making a point that runs strongly counter to his ubiquitous claim that salvation is not by works. But, if Paul is speaking only to Christians, then the claim that "each of us may receive what is due us" is not about salvation, it is about rewards.

Understanding the "we" of this passage as believers fits nicely with the explanation that this passage is likely an explicit refutation of the idea in segments of the Corinthian church that it didn't matter what one

---

[18]Ronald Nash, "Is There Salvation After Death? The Answer to Postmortem Evangelism," *Christian Research Journal* 27, no. 4 (2004): 5.

[19]Murray J. Harris, *The Second Epistle to the Corinthians*, New International Greek Testament Commentary (Grand Rapids, MI: Eerdmans, 2005), 406.

does in this life—a problem documented in 1 Corinthians 6:12-20. The sequence of logic is (2 Cor 5:9) believers are to be committed fully to God and (2 Cor 5:10) this means that nothing we do in the body is irrelevant.[20] But this understanding means that there is nothing in this passage that calls into question the theory of Postmortem Opportunity. This passage is speaking to those who have heard and responded to the gospel in this life. Nothing whatsoever is said about those who haven't heard the gospel.

But some will see this as sidestepping the real issue and in so doing, setting up 2 Corinthians 5:10 as a strawman argument. Isn't the real dilemma for the defender of Postmortem Opportunity the pervasive scriptural evidence for there being two paths, one that leads toward God and the other that leads toward destruction? God will separate the sheep from the goats (Mt 25:31-46) and there are two types of resurrection, one to life and one to judgment (Jn 5:29). Consequently, even if 2 Corinthians 5:10 isn't the best verse to express this concept, isn't there still copious scriptural evidence for the fact that the decisions one makes in this life either reflect a movement toward God or away from God? I think this is correct. The problem, however, comes in seeing those "choosing God" as those who have heard the gospel and "became a Christian," and those who are "choosing destruction" as those who have not heard the gospel and haven't "become a Christian." The problem with this way of seeing things is not in seeing that our decisions in this life have eternal implications, but in the simplistic way of expressing those decisions—either you become a Christian or you don't. It is this simplistic assumption that I question. In *Mere Christianity*, C. S. Lewis makes the following provocative statement: "The world does not consist of 100 per cent Christians and 100 per cent non-Christians. There are people (a great many of them) who are slowly ceasing to be Christians but still call themselves by that name: some are clergymen.

[20]Victor Paul Furnish, *II Corinthians*, Anchor Bible Commentary (Garden City, NY: Doubleday, 1984), 305.

There are other people that are slowly becoming Christians though they do not call themselves so."[21] Some Christians hear the gospel and appear to respond affirmatively. Does that mean that they will be saved? Not necessarily. In a disconcerting passage for those with the aforementioned simplistic view, Matthew 7:21-23 reads, "Not everyone who says to me, 'Lord, Lord,' will enter the kingdom of heaven, but only the one who does the will of my Father who is in heaven. Many will say to me on that day, 'Lord, Lord, did we not prophesy in your name and in your name drive out demons and in your name perform many miracles?' Then I will tell them plainly, 'I never knew you. Away from me, you evildoers!'"

On the other hand, some people never have the opportunity to hear the gospel, but does that mean that they are in opposition to the gospel of Jesus Christ? Not necessarily. I suggest that we cannot speak to the spiritual disposition of those who have not heard the gospel. What I do believe is that the God who loves all people will want to supply those people with an opportunity to demonstrate whether part of their house was built on solid rock. Undoubtedly, the decisions made in this life matter, but we must avoid assuming that we can be the judge of the heart of people whose situations are wildly different than our own. What they need is the refining fire of God's wisdom and judgment that will reveal whether anything they have done was a response to God's grace or whether it will all disappear in flames.

2 Corinthians 6:2. Some who argue that postmortem repentance is ruled out by Scripture appeal to 2 Corinthians 6:2.[22] The context for this passage begins in 2 Corinthians 5:18. Paul says,

> All this is from God, who reconciled us to himself through Christ and gave us the ministry of reconciliation: that God was reconciling the world to himself in Christ, not counting people's sins against them. And he has

---

[21]C. S. Lewis, *Mere Christianity* (New York: Macmillan, 1978), 176.

[22]See Robert H. Gundry, "The Hopelessness of the Unevangelized," *Themelios* 36, no. 1 (2011): 53, and C. D. Morris, *Is There Salvation After Death? A Treatise on the Gospel in the Intermediate State*, 2nd ed. (London: Forgotton Books, 2015 [1887]), 48.

> committed to us the message of reconciliation. We are therefore Christ's ambassadors, as though God were making his appeal through us. We implore you on Christ's behalf: Be reconciled to God. God made him who had no sin to be sin for us, so that in him we might become the righteousness of God. As God's co-workers we urge you not to receive God's grace in vain. (2 Cor 5:18–6:1)

In 2 Corinthians 6:2, Paul continues, citing Isaiah 49:8:

> For he says,
> "In the time of my favor I heard you,
> and in the day of salvation I helped you."
>
> I tell you, now is the time of God's favor, now is the day of salvation.

The argument here against Postmortem Opportunity comes from the sense of urgency conveyed in this text. Now is the time for salvation, not later in this life, not after death, now.

The error in this objection is not in seeing a sense of urgency regarding salvation in this passage, but in seeing this passage as ruling out a Postmortem Opportunity for the unevangelized and pseudoevangelized. This is because the message of urgency is delivered to those who have already heard the "message of reconciliation," not to those who have not heard the gospel. As such, to try to get this passage to speak to those who have never heard the gospel and who have not had an opportunity to be saved is to expand the meaning of this passage beyond what is plausibly a part of Paul's intention. The defender of Postmortem Opportunity heartily concurs with Paul's admonition: when one hears the gospel, one should respond. The idea of putting off committing one's life to Christ until later in life is practically and theologically problematic. But one can assert this and still claim that there are some people who have not heard the gospel and therefore have not be given the opportunity to respond.

Psalm 49. I will mention one final canonical text used to support the idea that death is the end of opportunity to be saved. Millard Erickson says, "The thrust of much of Psalm 49 is that the sinner will go to the grave and perish there, with no indication of any possible release from that place."[23] While the text does have this theme, the point made in developing this is about the spiritual uselessness of accumulating wealth in this world. In this respect, Psalm 49 is similar to the parable of Lazarus and the rich man. But let's not stop there. Let's suppose that, in addition to teaching about wealth, this text teaches that the sinner goes to the grave and stays there, as Erickson claims. How might the defender of Postmortem Opportunity respond to such a claim?

Two points. First, it is difficult to deny that the Old Testament notion of the afterlife was profoundly undeveloped. Not only are many of the questions of personal eschatology simply not addressed in any way, the entire concept of heaven and hell is inchoate at best and plausibly simply absent. Consequently, to use Psalm 49 in this way, a text that raises more theological questions than it answers, seems problematic. Moreover, to use this text and ignore the New Testament material on death and the afterlife—material that at least fleshes out the picture of the afterlife presented in Psalm 49 and, undoubtedly, contradicts many misreadings of the text—is a mistake. Second, setting aside the first point, Erickson's claim really amounts to a pair of claims: "the grave is the same as hell" and "sinners who are sent there have no possible release." These claims, however, do nothing to suggest that Postmortem Opportunity is false. This is because the set of people being referred to in Psalm 49—the "sinners who will go to the grave and perish there"—could easily be understood as those who do not embrace a Postmortem Opportunity for relationship with God. To rule this possibility out, one would have to claim that there is an intervening moment of judgment for those who die and this is far from obvious on strictly biblical grounds.

2 Clement 8:3. In the absence of clear canonical refutations of the possibility of a Postmortem Opportunity to hear and respond to the gospel, some (such as Ronald Nash) cite the noncanonical text 2 Clement 8:3.[24] Their argument is that even if 2 Clement is not Scripture,

[23]Millard Erickson, *How Shall They Be Saved?*, 173.
[24]Nash, "Is There Salvation After Death?," 5.

it is relatively early (best guess: midsecond century[25]) and it reflects a mindset common in the first 150 years of the church. The text of 2 Clement 8:3 reads, "For after we leave this world, we will no longer there be able to confess or repent."[26]

Unlike the passages discussed above, the meaning of this passage is clearly contrary to the theory of Postmortem Opportunity. So does this passage constitute a damaging objection to Postmortem Opportunity? Not even remotely. To make their argument, the detractors of Postmortem Opportunity would have to demonstrate that 2 Clement was either inspired Scripture that somehow missed being canonized or indicative of a common theological mindset in the early church. The first of these is clearly false and the second is nigh impossible to defend. First, 2 Clement itself was not a significant text in the patristic world. Christopher Tuckett avers, "The text of 2 Clement was not widely known (or at least mentioned) in the early centuries of the Christian church."[27] Certainly this passage reflects the theological perspective of at least one person, the author of 2 Clement, but we have no idea who he was[28] and there is no evidence of this text influencing any wider contemporary audience, circle, or group, and no evidence of the influence of this document on any subsequent writer.[29] Moreover, while Karl Paul Donfried takes a slightly more optimistic view of the influence of 2 Clement, he argues persuasively that 8:3 is written to a "congregation in which certain libertinistic tendencies had become manifest."[30] The purpose of this verse, therefore, is not to

[25]Christopher Tuckett, *2 Clement: Introduction, Text, and Commentary*, Oxford Apostolic Fathers Series (Oxford: Oxford University Press, 2012), 64. Karl Paul Donfried dates 2 Clement extremely early (98–100) since he argues for a close connection with 1 Clement (*The Setting of Second Clement in Early Christianity*, Supplements to Novum Testamentum, vol. 38 [Leiden: E. J. Brill, 1974], 1), but the majority of scholars agree with Tuckett, placing 2 Clement somewhere between 120 and 170.

[26]Tuckett, *2 Clement*, 99.

[27]Tuckett, *2 Clement*, 12. "In general, the relatively low level of (explicit) interest shown in the text by patristic writers matches the relatively low amount of extant manuscript evidence for the text" (13).

[28]Tuckett, *2 Clement*, 17.

[29]I have benefited from personal correspondence on this topic with my former colleague, Michael Holmes.

[30]Donfried, *Setting of Second Clement*, 130.

speak to the impossibility of Postmortem Opportunity for the unevangelized, but to the necessity of Christians to strive to live a holy life now. In other words, the text doesn't address the matter of becoming a Christian, but what is expected for those who want to live as a Christian.

Nash's use of 2 Clement to argue for death being the end of salvific opportunity also creates an interesting dilemma for him. The strength and clarity of 2 Clement's critique of postmortem hope relative to the canonical text might cause one to wonder why Scripture was relatively less clear on this supposedly important issue. Nash responds to this question as follows: "I also suggest that comments as clear as 2 Clement 8:3 do not appear in the New Testament because they simply were not needed among the members of a community whose every action recognized that physical death marked the boundary of human opportunity to be saved."[31] Setting aside the fact that this is at best an appeal to silence, Nash's claim is curious. He claims that there was ubiquitous affirmation of death being the end of salvific opportunity in the apostolic era, but that (evidently) that commitment had waned by the time of 2 Clement, enough for the writer of 2 Clement to issue such a clear refutation. But if that was the case, if this universally assumed doctrine had begun to be rejected, one wonders why there are not more patristic sources saying roughly the same thing as 2 Clement. In fact, the patristic evidence runs in quite a different direction, for as I will argue in chapter six, there are numerous voices in the first three centuries who did not believe that death marked the boundary of salvific opportunity.

DOES SCRIPTURE IMPLY THE FALSITY OF POSTMORTEM OPPORTUNITY?

Even in the absence of demonstrating that the Bible teaches that salvific status is fixed at death, the detractors of Postmortem Opportunity might fall back on a more chastened claim: that Scripture implies or

[31]Nash, "Is There Salvation After Death?," 5.

assumes things that are incompatible with Postmortem Opportunity. There are a number of these sorts of objections, and the three most sensible are the claim that there are none that can justifiably claim ignorance of God (drawing on Rom 1:18-20), the "only a few will be saved" passages, and the description of the day of judgment in Revelation 20.

"People are without excuse" (Rom 1:18-20). When becoming aware of the problem of the destiny of the unevangelized, the initial response of many is to claim that the question has already been answered by Romans 1. This passage, they aver, teaches that there is no one who is truly unevangelized. All know about God and therefore are left "without excuse."

> The wrath of God is being revealed from heaven against all the godlessness and wickedness of people, who suppress the truth by their wickedness, since what may be known about God is plain to them, because God has made it plain to them. For since the creation of the world God's invisible qualities—his eternal power and divine nature—have been clearly seen, being understood from what has been made, so that people are without excuse. (Rom 1:18-20)

While some have used Romans 1 to justify natural theology and argue that it is possible to arrive at knowledge of God based on logic and observation alone, there is nothing in this text to justify that contention. While it is obvious that this text teaches that people "clearly see" something about God, that which people see is clearly not the result of sophisticated logical argumentation, and Paul does not here refer to or seek to justify "a long process of reasoning by which people come to a knowledge of God's existence and power."[32] Moreover, the claim that this text teaches that humans have "knowledge" of God is liable to be misunderstood. It is better to see this text as teaching than humans have a "vague, unformulated knowledge or experience of God."[33] From this

[32]Thomas R. Schreiner, *Romans* (Grand Rapids, MI: Baker, 1998), 86.

[33]Joseph A. Fitzmyer, *Romans*, Anchor Bible Commentary (New York: Doubleday, 1993), 281. Richard Alan Young argues persuasively that the best way to see the understanding of God described in Romans 1 is a "vague unthematic awareness." See his "The Knowledge of God in

perspective on this passage, Karl Barth says, "We know that God is He whom we do not know, and that our ignorance is precisely the problem and the source of our knowledge."[34] And, in a similar vein, but from the perspective of one more open to the concept of natural theology, Wolfhart Pannenberg argues that "to understand the complex issue, we need to separate the natural human knowledge of God, no matter how it be described in detail, very sharply from the phenomenon of natural theology, which may be related to it in some way but which must not be equated with it. The lack of clear differentiation in this matter is partly responsible for the hopeless confusion in the modern discussion of natural theology."[35]

But doesn't the fact that all people are aware of God, even if that awareness is vague and unthematic, suggest that there are no people who are truly unevangelized and, therefore, that attempts to argue that some will be given a Postmortem Opportunity to hear the gospel are both unnecessary and presumptuous? No, for two reasons. First, it doesn't seem at all plausible that "all are aware of God's external power and divine nature" and have seen that "through what has been created." For instance, how could Anna and Sam come to an awareness of God's nature through observing creation? Now it might be possible to say that this unthematic awareness of God is only possessed by those who suppress the truth by their wickedness, but such an avenue of argument both raises questions about the nature and extent of original sin and fails to show that all people have an awareness of God. A second reason why Romans 1 does not function as an objection to Postmortem Opportunity is that even if this text teaches that all are aware of God in some sense, people are not aware in the requisite sense that renders the question of the destiny of the unevangelized moot or undercuts the Postmortem Opportunity answer to that question. To see this, consider

---

Romans 1:18–23: Exegetical and Theological Reflections," *Journal of the Evangelical Theological Society* 43, no. 4 (December 2000): 695-707.

[34]Karl Barth, *The Epistle to the Romans* (London: Oxford University Press, 1968), 45.

[35]Wolfhart Pannenberg, *Systematic Theology*, 3 vols. (Grand Rapids, MI: Eerdmans, 1988), 1:76.

the question, What does it mean to say that "people are without excuse"? Does this mean that "people do not need to hear the gospel"? Surely not, for such a claim would invalidate the Great Commission. Does it mean that God does not desire the salvation of those who do not hear the gospel? Again, no. Human sinfulness and our unworthiness to stand before God and demand anything does not change the fact that "God so loved the world that he gave his one and only Son" (Jn 3:16). The lesson here is that our need for a salvific opportunity is unchanged by the fact there is a very important sense in which people are aware of God and therefore lack an excuse.

It would be one thing if people who pressed this sort of objection to answers to the problem of the destiny of the unevangelized also asserted that it was possible to be saved via awareness of God's invisible qualities on display in creation. Unfortunately, many who press the "no excuse" argument claim that God's general revelation is sufficient to damn, but insufficient to save. For instance, Restrictivists like J. I. Packer argue, "The Bible says that God's general revelation, even when correctly grasped, yields knowledge of creation, providence, and judgment only, not of grace that restores sinners to fellowship with God."[36] This is problematic, as I argued in chapter two, not because God owes humanity an opportunity to be saved, but because this articulation of God's love and salvific will is incompatible with what Scripture itself actually teaches. And perhaps that is the heart of what the "no excuse" objection is all about. What they are objecting to is a sense that the problem of the destiny of the unevangelized is being driven by a demand for "equal opportunity" or "soteriological opportunity justice." The problem of the destiny of the unevangelized is driven by the sense that there are some that do not have an opportunity to be saved combined with the belief that this state of affairs is deemed to be undesirous by God himself.

[36]J. I. Packer, "The Way of Salvation, Part IV: Are Non-Christian Faiths Ways of Salvation?," *Bibliotheca Sacra* 130, no. 518 (April 1973): 115.

"Only a few will be saved." There are a couple of passages in Scripture that are taken to indicate that the number of people who will receive salvation will be few. These are the following:

> Matthew 7:13-14: "Enter through the narrow gate. For wide is the gate and broad is the road that leads to destruction, and many enter through it. But small is the gate and narrow the road that leads to life, and only a few find it."
>
> Matthew 22:14: "For many are invited, but few are chosen."[37]
>
> Luke 13:23-24: "Someone asked him, 'Lord, are only a few people going to be saved?' He said to them, 'Make every effort to enter through the narrow door, because many, I tell you, will try to enter and will not be able to.'"

The assumption behind this argument is that if people are given a Postmortem Opportunity to hear and respond to the gospel, many, most, or even all of those people will be saved—which contradicts these passages.

The first problem is with the assumption that underlies this argument against Postmortem Opportunity. The assumption that "if people are given a Postmortem Opportunity to hear and respond to the gospel, then many of those people will be saved" is faulty. I will address this issue more fully in the final chapter of this book when I take up the issue of the relationship between Postmortem Opportunity and Universalism, but for now it is sufficient to note that it is not the case that those who hear the gospel after death will necessarily respond affirmatively. What the theory of Postmortem Opportunity asserts is merely that there will be a Postmortem *Opportunity* to hear and respond; it is no part of the theory (or at least the version I am interested in defending) that all, most, or even *any* who receive a Postmortem Opportunity *must* respond with genuine faith.

The second problem, however, is with the interpretation of these passages.[38] While the theory of Postmortem Opportunity does not

---

[37]These words close the parable of the wedding banquet (Mt 22:1-14).

[38]This section draws on John Sanders's excellent discussion in *What About Those Who Have Never Heard? Three Views on the Destiny of the Unevangelized*, ed. John Sanders (Downers Grove, IL: InterVarsity Press, 1995), 30-35.

entail that most of humanity will respond to the gospel, I genuinely hope that many or even most people will embrace relationship with Jesus. Do these passages undercut that hope by teaching that percentage-wise only a few will be saved? I don't think so. First, there have been many Christians who rejected that interpretation of these passages, including conservative stalwarts Charles Hodge and B. B. Warfield.[39] Second, there are other passages that might be taken to suggest that many will be saved. For example, in Matthew 13:24-30 the kingdom of heaven is compared to a wheat field in which the enemy comes and sows some weeds. And Revelation 7:9 speaks of "multitudes" in heaven: "After this I looked, and there before me was a great multitude that no one could count, from every nation, tribe, people and language, standing before the throne and before the Lamb. They were wearing white robes and were holding palm branches in their hands." Psalm 22:27:

> All the ends of the earth
> will remember and turn to the LORD,
> and all the families of the nations
> will bow down before him.

Revelation 5:9 refers to the "persons from every tribe and language and people and nation" who have been "purchased" by Christ's atonement. But it must be admitted that these passages do not entail that a high percentage of people will be saved. The parable in Matthew does not provide the percentage of wheat to weeds, and while Revelation 7:9 speaks of "multitudes," it might still be the case that only a small percentage of humanity is saved, and the Psalm text and Revelation 5:9 speaks only of the breadth of those who will be saved—"from every

[39]Granted, as Sanders points out it is possible that they did so because they were appealing to a postmillennial theology that assumed that a period of human history was coming in which the vast majority of people on the planet would be Christians (*No Other Name: An Investigation into the Destiny of the Unevangelized* [Grand Rapids, MI: Eerdmans, 1992], 41n4). But the point is that these giants of conservative theology had no problem reconciling the Matthew passage with their theology that a great many will be saved.

nation"—not the actual percentage of people saved. As such, the danger of overreading these texts is very real.

Ironically, I think that the strongest argument against the contention that "few will be saved" comes from the very passages that many claim teach that idea—the aforementioned "narrow road" passages. It is arguable that the very passages that seem to restrict salvation to only a few are teaching quite the opposite. John Sanders makes a compelling argument that one of the "narrow path" passages—the parable of the king's son (Mt 22:1-14)—does not teach that few are saved.[40] Instead, Sanders claims that the passage is about reversal, because before anybody is excluded, all are invited. On this parable, Robert Farrar Capon argues,

> Nobody in the parable is outside the king's favor; everybody starts out by being, as far as the king himself is concerned, *irrevocably in. . . . Nobody is kicked out who wasn't already in.* Hell may be an option; but if it is it is one that is given us only after we have already received the entirely non-optional gift of sitting together in the heavenly places in Christ Jesus.[41]

This is a principle that Sanders sees as reflected throughout Scripture: God "includes all in his grace, and excludes in judgment only those who spurn that grace."[42] Consequently, the "narrow road" passages are not statements about the relatively small percentage of people who will be saved, they are indictments of the religious leaders of Jesus' day who were confident that their lineage assured their salvation. In this, as in other places, Jesus' words are meant to comfort the afflicted and afflict the comfortable. The statement that many are called and few are chosen is designed to call into question the religious leaders' soteriological comfort and provide hope to those who had little.

In the Matthew 7 passage, Jesus concludes his statement about the narrow road with a direct statement calling into question the soteric confidence of even those who have spoken words of prophecy, driven

---

[40]John Sanders, *What About Those Who Have Never Heard?*, 32.
[41]Robert Farrar Capon, *The Parables of Judgment* (Grand Rapids, MI: Eerdmans, 1989), 125.
[42]John Sanders, *What About Those Who Have Never Heard?*, 33.

out demons, and performed many miracles in God's name (Mt 7:22). Of Jesus' words in Matthew 7:23, Capon says, "The dreadful sentence: 'I never knew you,' is simply the truth of their condition. He does not say, 'I never called you.' He does not say, 'I never loved you.' He does not say, 'I never drew you to myself.' He only says, 'I never knew you—because you never bothered to know me.'"[43]

My assessment is that there is both a "narrow way" theme and a "broad way" theme in Scripture, but that properly understood, there is no conflict between them. The narrow way theme indicates the high bar set for salvation and, in particular, the difficulty of the path to salvation for those who seek to assert religious control over it and define it for themselves. And the broad way theme indicates not God's desire that all be saved but his efforts and provision to save as many as possible. All are graciously invited, but there are conditions on accepting God's invitation of salvation. Moreover, there is nothing in either of these themes that calls into question the theory of Postmortem Opportunity. It is perfectly possible to affirm both of these themes and believe that the unevangelized will receive a Postmortem Opportunity to hear and respond to the gospel.

The day of judgment and the book of life. This objection to Postmortem Opportunity is based on the account of the day of judgment in Revelation 20:11-15, which reads as follows:

> Then I saw a great white throne and him who was seated on it. The earth and the heavens fled from his presence, and there was no place for them. And I saw the dead, great and small, standing before the throne, and books were opened. Another book was opened, which is the book of life. The dead were judged according to what they had done as recorded in the books. The sea gave up the dead that were in it, and death and Hades gave up the dead that were in them, and each person was judged according to what they had done. Then death and Hades were thrown into the lake of fire. The lake of fire is the second death. Anyone whose name was not found written in the book of life was thrown into the lake of fire.

---

[43]Capon, *Parables of Judgment*, 165.

Millard Erickson articulates the objection this way: "Revelation 20:11-15 contains the scene of the Great White Judgment Throne at which each person who wanted to be judged on the basis of his or her works is judged, and all are accounted guilty. There is no offer of any sort of salvation."[44]

Initially, it is difficult not to get distracted by Erickson's restriction of judgment to those "who wanted to be judged on the basis of his or her works."[45] The context doesn't seem to allow for any sort of restriction—all are judged. Ignoring that difficulty, Erickson's claim is that there is no mention of a Postmortem Opportunity for salvation in this, the biblical description of the day of judgment. The initial response to this objection to Postmortem Opportunity would be to point out that this is, at best, an argument from silence. Scripture says that humans will be judged, but gives us very few details about what exactly (or even approximately) that will look like. But there is a more direct response available to the defender of Postmortem Opportunity—namely, that the day of judgment is *itself* a presentation of the gospel and an opportunity for response.

Does this understanding of judgment fit with these passages? It depends on how one understands the nature of the judgment described in this passage and in particular how should the "books" referred to in this passage be understood. There are two kinds of books. The first—"and books were opened" (Rev 20:12)—is an allusion to Daniel 7:10, in which books were opened before the heavenly council. These books in Jewish thought were a record of "the deeds of both the righteous and unrighteous."[46] The second—"Another book was opened, which is the book of life," and "Anyone whose name was not found written in the book of life" (Rev 20:12, 15)—is built on the idea of "a roll of citizens in a city or nation; thus, those written in it are citizens of heaven and God's special people."[47]

---

[44]Erickson, *How Shall They Be Saved?*, 173.

[45]Erickson, *How Shall They Be Saved?*, 173.

[46]Grant R. Osborne, *Revelation*, Baker Exegetical Commentary on the New Testament (Grand Rapids, MI: Baker, 2002), 722.

[47]Osborne, *Revelation*, 722. The same idea is found in Psalm 69:28 and Daniel 12:1, which refer to a heavenly book in which the names of the righteous were kept (Osborne, 503).

The first kind of book is no problem for the defender of Postmortem Opportunity—judgment undoubtedly includes a judgment of our actions, dispositions, and character and none of that is incompatible with judgment also being an opportunity to bow a knee to God. But the second kind of book might be understood in a way that would be problematic for the Postmortem Opportunity theorist. The first way of expressing this objection is to claim that the book of life is finalized prior to death and therefore a Postmortem Opportunity to salvation is impossible. The response here is simple. There is nothing in the text that says that; this interpretation reads the impossibility of a Postmortem Opportunity into the text—or, in other words, given the assumption that death is the end of salvific opportunity, it makes sense to read the text this way, but absent that assumption, there is nothing in this text that requires one to see the book of life being finalized before the day of judgment. The second way of expressing the objection is that, according to Revelation 13:8, the names written in the book of life have been written "from before the foundation of the world."[48] This is a more interesting objection. It is also a complex matter, for it raises the issue of how election and predestination should be understood. Not only is this matter complex theologically, it is complex exegetically; the major translations do not agree.[49] There are genuine difficulties here. Happily, it is unnecessary to delve into such labyrinthine matters to see whether this passage refutes the theory of Postmortem Opportunity. That is because it is irrelevant *when* one's name was placed in the book of life, it

---

[48]There is a similar passage in Rev 17:8.

[49]The ESV translates 13:8 as follows: "and all who dwell on earth will worship it [the Beast], everyone whose name has not been written *before* the foundation of the world in the book of life of the Lamb who was slain" (italics added). The debate is whether the preposition ἀπό should be translated as "before" or "from/since" and whether the temporal modifier applied to the "names not written in the book of life" or "the Lamb." The NASB changes the preposition to "since," rendering the passage: "All who live on the earth will worship him, everyone whose name has not been written since the foundation of the world in the book of life of the Lamb who has been slaughtered." And the NIV agrees with the NASB on the preposition, but sees the phrase "from the creation of the world" as modifying "the Lamb" not "the names": "All inhabitants of the earth will worship the beast—all whose names have not been written in the Lamb's book of life, the Lamb who was slain from the creation of the world."

only matters *why* it was so placed. If God ordains that a person who has not heard the gospel be saved (as a Calvinist could claim) then there is nothing that will stop that person from being saved, even if it takes a Postmortem Opportunity to do so. If God does not foreordain who is and who is not saved (as the Arminian claims), then the fact that the person's name is written in the book of life from before the foundation of the world is based on God's foreknowledge of who will respond to his offer of salvation. The only group that this passages creates problems for are open theists, who deny that God possesses exhaustive definitive foreknowledge, and again, that problem is only present given the assumption that the book of life includes a definitive list of those who will be saved and that its contents were foreknown before the foundation of the world. And neither of these assumptions are obviously true.

CONCLUSION

I do not claim that this chapter has provided an exhaustive list of scriptural objections to Postmortem Opportunity, for there are others.[50] But these are the objections that are the most commonly raised against Postmortem Opportunity. What is left to be discussed is the biblical evidence for the theory of Postmortem Opportunity. Is there any sound scriptural reason to accept the notion that the unevangelized and pseudo-evangelized will be given a Postmortem Opportunity to repent and embrace relationship with Christ? This is the task of the next chapter.

[50]Nash mentions a similar point made in each of Mt 7:15-20, 21-23, 24-27. He also points to Mk 13:24-30, 36-43; and Lk 12:16-21. See his *When a Baby Dies* and "Is There Salvation After Death?"

5

SCRIPTURAL EVIDENCE FOR POSTMORTEM OPPORTUNITY

Having discussed scriptural objections to the theory of Postmortem Opportunity in the previous chapter, in this chapter I consider the scriptural support for the theory of Postmortem Opportunity and how we should think about postmortem salvific hope in light of that evidence. As we undertake this task, it is crucial to acknowledge that exegesis does not occur in a vacuum. If our interpretation of individual verses and chapters are the data beliefs, there are also undoubtedly control beliefs that affect how we view, interpret, and apply the data beliefs. For the Postmortem Opportunity theorist, some of the most important control beliefs are those that do not directly or even indirectly address the issue of Postmortem Opportunity, but profoundly affect our assessment of texts that might directly or indirectly speak to it. There are many of these; I will mention only two sets of texts. The first are texts that clearly teach God's love for all—1 Timothy 2:4, 2 Peter 3:9, and John 3:16 are of course commonly mentioned, but there are many others. These texts not only teach the theological concept of God's love, they constitute a powerful answer to one of the most interesting and theology-shaping questions one can ask: Why did God create? This set of texts highlights a broad stream of scriptural data that ground the belief that God created with the purpose of spreading the perfect divine love that exists eternally in the Trinity throughout his creation. The second set of texts are those that speak of God's special love for the lost. The parable of the lost sheep and the parable of the prodigal son are powerful illustrations of this theme. As I argued in chapter two, this theme does not suggest in any way that God loves those who are saved any less or that he loves the lost *more*. Rather, God's special love for the lost is a function of the fact that they are lost and in danger of eternal separation from him. It is love that sends the Good Shepherd out to search for the lost sheep, not any lack of love for the ninety-nine that are already safely home.

INDIRECT SCRIPTURAL EVIDENCE

The first category of scriptural evidence are texts that indirectly support the theory of Postmortem Opportunity. By "indirect support" I mean that these texts do not directly teach the idea that the unevangelized will have a Postmortem Opportunity to hear and respond to the gospel on judgment day, but rather they teach things that render the theory of Postmortem Opportunity more plausible. I will mention four such sets of texts.

Salvific opportunity and the day of judgment. Contrary to the claim that death is the end of salvific opportunity, there is a persistent strand of Scripture that points to judgment day as the culmination of salvific expectations. In his commentary on 1 Peter, John Peter Lange says, "[Scripture teaches] in many passages that forgiveness may be possible beyond the grave, and refers the final decision not to death, but to the day of Christ."[1] Some of the passages Lange alludes to are the following:

> Acts 17:31: "For he has set a day when he will judge the world with justice by the man he has appointed. He has given proof of this to everyone by raising him from the dead."
>
> 2 Timothy 1:12: "That is why I am suffering as I am. Yet this is no cause for shame, because I know whom I have believed, and am convinced that he is able to guard what I have entrusted to him until that day."
>
> 2 Timothy 4:8: "Now there is in store for me the crown of righteousness, which the Lord, the righteous Judge, will award to me on that day—and not only to me, but also to all who have longed for his appearing."

---

[1]John Peter Lange, *The First Epistle General of Peter* (New York: Scribner, 1868), 75.

These texts do not *teach* that there will be a Postmortem Opportunity to be saved. That conclusion would involve reading my desired conclusion into these texts. Rather, in the absence of passages that *teach* that death is the end of salvific opportunity, in speaking of the day of judgment as the moment in which our faith is revealed, judged, and rewarded, these passages open up the *possibility* of that God will offer a Postmortem Opportunity. As such, these passages lend indirect support to the theory of Postmortem Opportunity.

Condemnation only for explicit rejection of Christ. The second kind of indirect scriptural support for the theory of Postmortem Opportunity consists of the passages that seem to teach that people are condemned to hell only for explicit rejection of Jesus Christ. Postmortem Opportunity theorists support this contention by appealing to passages like the following:

> Matthew 10:32-33: "Whoever acknowledges me before others, I will also acknowledge before my Father in heaven. But whoever disowns me before others, I will disown before my Father in heaven."
>
> John 3:18: "Whoever believes in him is not condemned, but whoever does not believe stands condemned already because they have not believed in the name of God's one and only Son."
>
> John 3:36: "Whoever believes in the Son has eternal life, but whoever rejects the Son will not see life, for God's wrath remains on them."
>
> John 15:22: "If I had not come and spoken to them, they would not be guilty of sin; but now they have no excuse for their sin."

The immediate and obvious response to this claim draws on Romans 1:18-20—a passage that was addressed, albeit briefly, in the last chapter. This passage teaches that ignorance is culpable, in at least one sense. All should know important aspects of God's character just by looking at what he has created. But this sort of knowledge is—to use the common phrase—sufficient to damn, but insufficient to save. When raising the issue of salvation, I question whether the affirmation of the love of God for the lost is compatible with affirming that the only knowledge that some receive is only sufficient to damn, but is insufficient to save. Yes, all should know about God's existence and nature based on what they see in creation, but when it comes to salvation, people are condemned to hell only for explicitly rejecting Jesus Christ.

Death and salvific opportunity. There are a couple of suggestive echoes of Postmortem Opportunity in the Old Testament, passages that might be thought to support the idea that God will extend his grace past the grave. In Hosea 13:14 there is a prophecy some have interpreted as justifying the salvation of those who are dead:

> Shall I ransom them from the power of Sheol?
> Shall I redeem them from death?
> Death, where are your thorns?
> Sheol, where is your sting? (NASB)

And Isaiah 24:21-22 refers to a "visitation" of those who are dead:

> And it shall come to pass in that day, that the LORD shall punish the host of the high ones that are on high, and the kings of the earth upon the earth. And they shall be gathered together, as prisoners are gathered in the pit, and shall be shut up in the prison, and after many days shall they be visited. (KJV)

From an evidential point of view, the difficulty of these passages comes from the underdeveloped nature of personal eschatology in the Old Testament.

In addition, there are New Testament echoes of the notion that Christ will be proclaimed to those who are dead, though contemporary ears miss them. Colossians 1:23, for example, says, "This is the gospel that you heard and that has been proclaimed *to every creature under heaven*." Contemporary ears do not hear this as it was intended, for we have a different cosmology, but in the first century, those under heaven included those currently living on the earth and those living under the earth (those who have died and reside in Sheol/Hades). Philippians 2:10 is even more explicit: "that at the name of Jesus every knee should bow, in heaven and on earth *and under the earth*," as is Revelation 5:13:

> Then I heard every creature in heaven and on earth and *under the earth* and on the sea, and all that is in them, saying:
>
> "To him who sits on the throne and to the Lamb
> be praise and honor and glory and power,
> for ever and ever!"

Finally, some such as Gabriel Fackre point to John 5:25 as supporting the claim that God provides a Postmortem Opportunity to the lost: "Very truly I tell you, a time is coming and has now come when the dead will hear the voice of the Son of God and those who hear will live."[2] This conclusion is rendered more difficult by the phrase "and now has come," which has caused the significant majority of commentators to understand "the dead" not as those who will hear the gospel on judgment day, but as those who are now "spiritually dead." This interpretation is possible, but we must remember that, from the temporal perspective of John, Jesus has *already* descended into Hades and "preached to the dead." So it is very possible that John is referring to the same reality referred to by Peter in 1 Peter 4:6: "For this is the reason the gospel was preached even to those who are now dead, so that they might be judged according to human standards in regard to the body, but live according to God in regard to the spirit."[3]

Prayers for the dead. While the idea of praying for the dead is foreign to many contemporary ears, it was present in Second Temple Judaism and in the New Testament, and it was a relatively common practice in

---

[2]Gabriel Fackre, "Divine Perseverance," in *What About Those Who Have Never Heard? Three Views on the Destiny of the Unevangelized*, ed. John Sanders (Downers Grove, IL: InterVarsity Press, 1995), 85.

[3]Another possible way for the Postmortem Opportunity theorist to deal with this passage is to treat the phrase "and now has come" as a textual mistake. It is omitted in one Greek manuscript (Sinaiticus) and a few Latin witnesses (two manuscripts and Tertullian). But it is also quite possible to understand the omission in Sinaiticus and the Latin manuscripts as scribal mistakes and the omission in Tertullian as a theologically motivated redaction. So it would be difficult to place a great deal of evidentiary weight on this claim.

the patristic era.[4] From the Jewish context, the primary example is recorded in 2 Maccabees 12:38-45. During the Maccabean revolt against the Seleucid Empire, after a battle with Gorgias, the governor of Idumaea, the victorious Judas Maccabaeus was horrified to learn that the fallen Jewish soldiers were wearing idolatrous amulets—"sacred tokens of the idols of Jam'nia, which the law forbids the Jews to wear"—designed to provide protection in battle. He responded by entreating the entire army to pray for the fallen soldiers that their sin "might be wholly blotted out" (12:42) and by collecting an offering to make atonement for the sins of the dead soldiers. The narrator[5] then offers the following interpretive comment:

> In doing this he [Judas] acted very well and honorably, taking account of the resurrection. For if he were not expecting that those who had fallen would rise again, it would have been superfluous and foolish to pray for the dead. But if he was looking to the splendid reward that is laid up for those who fall asleep in godliness, it was a holy and pious thought. Therefore he made atonement for the dead, that they might be delivered from their sin. (12:43b-45 RSVCE)

There are a number of other obvious examples of prayers for the dead in Scripture: Elijah prays for a child (1 Kings 17:17-24), Jesus prays for Lazarus (John 11:41-42), and Peter prays for Tabitha (Acts 9:36-44). However, each of these are prayers that the person in question be brought back to life, they are not prayers for an already-dead person's spiritual status. Are there biblical examples of praying for the spiritual status of a dead person? Yes. Consider 2 Timothy 1:16-18. In this passage Paul prays as follows:

> May the Lord show mercy to the household of Onesiphorus, because he often refreshed me and was not ashamed of my chains. On the contrary, when he

---

[4]Even Augustine prayed for his dead mother. See *Confessions* 9.13.36, in vol. 1 of *Nicene and Post Nicene Fathers*, series 1, ed. Philip Schaff (Buffalo, NY: Christian Literature Publishing Co., 1887).

[5]Trumbower identifies the narrator as either Jason of Cyrene or an author who epitomized his five-volume work. See Jeffrey A. Trumbower, *Rescue for the Dead: The Posthumous Salvation of Non-Christians in Early Christianity* (New York: Oxford University Press, 2001), 27. The date would be either the late second or early first century BCE.

> was in Rome, he searched hard for me until he found me. May the Lord grant that he will find mercy from the Lord on that day! You know very well in how many ways he helped me in Ephesus.

The reasons for believing that Onesiphorus was already dead when Paul prayed this prayer are immediately apparent in the text. Paul speaks of "the household of Onesiphorus" in the present tense, but of Onesiphorus himself only in the past tense. Moreover, in the final verses of 2 Timothy, Paul sends greetings to Priscilla, Aquila, and "the household of Onesiphorus," not Onesiphorus himself (2 Tim 4:19-21).[6] This language is perfectly intelligible if Onesiphorus was dead but still had a wife, children, or family living in Ephesus, but is extremely difficult to understand if Onesiphorus was still living. Finally, the content of Paul's prayer is strongly suggestive that Onesiphorus is already dead. He prays that Onesiphorus "will find mercy from the Lord" on the day of judgment, but mentions nothing about his health or happiness in this life. In summary, in the words of Alfred Plummer, "it seems, therefore, to be scarcely too much to say that there is no serious reason for questioning the now widely accepted view that at the time when St. Paul wrote these words Onesiphorus was among the departed."[7] Not only does Paul's prayer for Onesiphorus give biblical sanction for prayers for the dead, J. N. D. Kelly argues that the practice was common in the early church: "There is nothing surprising in Paul's use of such a prayer, for intercession for the dead had been sanctioned in Pharisaic circles at any rate since the date of 2 Macc 12:43-45 (middle of first century B.C.?). Inscriptions in the Roman catacombs and elsewhere prove that the practice established itself among Christians from very early times."[8] What does all of this suggest? Should we begin praying for the sins of

---

[6]Paul also sends greeting from Eubulus, Pudens, Linus, and Claudia, and there is no reference to their households.

[7]A. Plummer, *Pastoral Epistles*, 3rd ed., Expositor's Bible (London: Hodder and Stoughton, 1891), 325.

[8]J. N. D. Kelly, *A Commentary on the Pastoral Epistles* (London: A&C Black, 1963), 171. For a detailed historical survey on this matter, see R. J. Edmund Boggis, *Praying for the Dead: An Historical Review of the Practice* (London: Longmans, Green, and Co., 1913).

the dead? Not necessarily, but these passages do suggest that the idea that one's spiritual status is not fixed at death was certainly present in New Testament and patristic times.[9]

A similar point may be made with respect to the early church practice of baptism for the dead. In 1 Corinthians 15:29, there is an oft-ignored reference to "baptism for the dead." Paul says: "Now if there is no resurrection, what will those do who are baptized for the dead? If the dead are not raised at all, why are people baptized for them?" Interpretive difficulties abound in this text, as evidenced by the more than forty different interpretations cataloged by B. M. Forschini.[10] Of course, even if it is assumed that this text is in fact referring to the practice of vicarious baptism for the dead—which I think is very plausible—it is not obvious that this text should be understood as Paul *teaching* or *defending* the practice. And it also isn't obvious that the practice was designed to affect the dead person's salvific destiny, for it may have just been thought of as posthumous sanctification. Nonetheless, if Paul is referring to a common practice of vicarious baptism for the dead for the purpose of defending the concept of resurrection, this provides additional evidence that some in the first century believed that one's spiritual trajectory was not fixed at death and gives support to belief in the possibility of postmortem repentance.

DIRECT SCRIPTURAL EVIDENCE: THE DESCENT PASSAGES

The most significant set of texts for Postmortem Opportunity are the "descent of Jesus" texts. These texts are also notoriously difficult. On the surface, these texts seem to indicate that while Jesus was dead he "took captives," "made proclamation," and "preached the gospel." Before

[9]An additional piece of evidence for the scriptural invocation of praying for the dead comes from the early church. It is difficult to deny that the earliest Christians believed in the appropriateness and efficacy of prayers for the dead, for such prayers appear on the graves in Jewish cemeteries as far back as the second century. See E. H. Plumptre, *The Spirits in Prison and Other Studies on the Life After Death* (New York: Thomas Whitaker, 1894), 128.

[10]B. M. Foschini, "Those Who Are Baptized for the Dead," *Catholic Biblical Quarterly* 12 (1950): 260-76, 379-99, and *Catholic Biblical Quarterly* 13 (1951): 46-78, 172-98, 276-83.

looking at these individual texts, however, we need to clarify what is meant by Christ's "descent." In particular, to *where* did Christ descend? The quick answer is that Jesus descended into the "realm of the dead" (Greek: Hades; Hebrew: Sheol).[11] In his sermon in the streets of Jerusalem on the Day of Pentecost (Acts 2:14-41), Peter refers to Psalm 16:8-11, and said, "Seeing what was to come, he [the writer of Psalms] spoke of the resurrection of the Messiah, that he was not abandoned *to the realm of the dead*, nor did his body see decay" (Acts 2:31, italics added). The teaching here is straightforward: Jesus died (and therefore descended into the "realm of the dead" or, to Luke's Greek-speaking audience, Hades), but because of the resurrection, he did not stay there. Even apart from the descent texts, there is ample support for the presence of Christ in Hades, both scriptural (Peter's reference in Acts 2:31 and the "firstborn from among the dead" references in Col 1:18 and Rev 1:5) and in early church tradition—so much so that the affirmation became part of the Apostles' Creed: "I believe that Jesus . . . descended into Hades."

Of course, there are plenty of vexed questions surrounding the concept of Hades: Is it a place of punishment? If Jesus descended into Hades, why does he say to the criminal on the cross (in Lk 23:43), "Today you will be with me in paradise"? And why do many churches say that Jesus descended into hell? We will take a closer look at some of these issues in chapter six, but for now suffice it to say that if "hell" is understood as the final resting place for sinners, Jesus *did not* descend into hell. The Greek word for hell is *gehenna*, not Hades. Hades is the place of the dead and therefore it is best to say that Jesus descended into Hades. For our purposes, the most salient question is this: What was the *purpose* for the descent? Is this merely a statement that Jesus did in fact die, or do the descent passages indicate that Jesus offered salvation to those in Hades and thereby provided Christians

[11]For a recent defense of this claim, see Matthew Y. Emerson, *He Descended to the Dead: An Evangelical Theology of Holy Saturday* (Downers Grove, IL: InterVarsity Press, 2019).

with a precedent for Postmortem Opportunity? Let's look at each of the descent passages in turn.

Ephesians 4:8-10.

> This is why it says:
>
> "When he ascended on high,
> he took many captives
> and gave gifts to his people."
>
> (What does "he ascended" mean except that he also descended to the lower, earthly regions? He who descended is the very one who ascended higher than all the heavens, in order to fill the whole universe).

The passage has its share of interpretive issues, notably the fact that the quotation (ostensibly of Ps 68:18) varies from both the MT and LXX in crucial respects,[12] but I will focus on the aspects of this text that are most relevant to the theory of Postmortem Opportunity. The crucial issue is how to understand "ascended" and "descended." To where is Christ ascending and descending?

Let's assume that "ascended" in Ephesians 4:8 refers to Christ's ascension into heaven after his resurrection. The reference to "took many captives and gave gifts to his people" is a reference to a triumph, a practice common in ancient Rome where the conquering emperor would celebrate a major victory over his enemies with a parade in which his captives were led in chains after him, and at which the emperor would distribute presents to his soldiers and military leaders. In other words, this is a metaphor claiming Christ's defeat of evil and sin. This much is relatively clear. The debate concerns the parenthetical remark. Following Calvin, many contemporary exegetes understand the "descended" in Ephesians 4:9 as indicative of the incarnation. The logic here is that Christ's ascension back to heaven first required the incarnation and his descent from heaven to earth. The problem

---

[12]For a helpful discussion, see Frank Thielman, *Ephesians*, Baker Exegetical Commentary on the New Testament (Grand Rapids, MI: Baker Academic, 2010), 265-68.

with this line of thinking is that the Ephesians, like the majority of the first century Mediterranean world, had a three-tiered cosmology: the heavens (the home of God and the angels), the earth (the abode of living humans), the underworld (the realm of the dead). And the phrase "lower, earthly regions" was commonly used to refer to the underworld or Hades. Thielman argues, "It is extremely unlikely that Paul would use the phrase [descended to the lower, earthly regions] in such a cultural environment and expect his readers to understand by it anything over than a descent to the realm of the dead."[13] Not surprisingly, a significant number of patristic figures interpret Paul in just that way, including Tertullian, Irenaeus, Ambrosiaster, and Chrysostom.[14] Among contemporary interpreters, the primary barrier to this interpretation is that it is common to understand the phrase "lower, earthly regions" as an epexegetical or appositional genitive and thus signifies that Christ descended into "the lower parts, namely the earth."[15] Those who understand the phrase this way have a good reason to deny that the "descent' in Ephesians 4:9 is an actual descent of Christ into Hades.

A more serious problem to the attempt to utilize Ephesians 4:8-9 as an argument for Postmortem Opportunity comes from the overall purpose of this passage. Given the context, it just isn't obvious that Paul intended Ephesians 4:8-9 to speak to soteriological concerns. The point being made in Ephesians 4 is not soteriological, but christological. Even if Paul is teaching that Christ descended into Hades, this is in service of Paul's assertion of the lordship of Christ over the "whole creation": the heavens, the earth, and the realm of the dead. In this respect, the

---

[13]Thielman, *Ephesians*, 271. See also C. E. Arnold, *Ephesians, Power, and Magic: The Concept of Power in Ephesians in Light of its Historical Setting*, Society for the Study of the New Testament Monograph Series 63 (Cambridge: Cambridge University Press, 1989), 57.

[14]See W. Hall Harris, *The Descent of Christ: Ephesians 4:7-11 and Traditional Hebrew Imagery* (Grand Rapids, MI: Baker, 1998), 4-5.

[15]For example, see Harold W. Hoehner, *Ephesians: An Exegetical Commentary* (Grand Rapids, MI: Baker Academic, 2002), 535. Hoehner provides an extensive list of scholars who support this interpretation (535n3).

point of Ephesians 4:8-9 should be seen as parallel to the point in Colossians 1:18—"And he is the head of the body, the church; he is the beginning and the firstborn from among the dead, *so that in everything he might have the supremacy*" (italics added). There are also echoes of Philippians 2:10 here: "that at the name of Jesus every knee should bow, in heaven and on earth *and under the earth*." So even if this text does suggest a descent into Hades (I believe it does, but acknowledge that this is contentious), it isn't obvious that it teaches a presentation of the gospel, for the reference to "captives" is most plausibly a reference to Christ's victory over spiritual powers and over death.[16] As such, what on the surface looks like a promising text for Postmortem Opportunity seems somewhat less promising after close analysis.

1 Peter 3:18-20.

> For Christ also suffered for sins once for all, the just for the unjust, so that He might bring us to God, having been put to death in the flesh, but made alive in the spirit; in which He also went and made proclamation to the spirits in prison, who once were disobedient when the patience of God kept waiting in the days of Noah, during the construction of the ark, in which a few, that is, eight persons, were brought safely through the water. (NASB)

Let's be frank, this is an odd text. Martin Luther justifiably said of this text, "A wonderful text is this, and a more obscure passage perhaps than any other in the New Testament, so that I do not know for a certainty just what Peter means."[17] And Robert Mounce goes so far as to say that 1 Peter 3:18-22 is "widely recognized as perhaps the most difficult to understand in the whole New Testament."[18] Interpreters of this passage must confront a cascade of questions, each with a range of possible answers, and each of which affects how one looks at the other questions,

---

[16]The exultation of Christ over the powers who are placed under Christ's feet is a point of emphasis earlier in this letter (Eph 1:20-22).

[17]Luther, *Commentary on Peter & Jude*, 166; cited in Thomas Schreiner, *1, 2 Peter, Jude*, New American Commentary (Nashville: B&H Publishing, 2003), 184.

[18]Robert Mounce, *A Living Hope: A Commentary on 1 and 2 Peter* (Grand Rapids, MI: Eerdmans, 1982), 54.

answers, and reasons for those answers. Some of the most pressing questions are the following: Who are the "spirits in prison"? What was preached? When did this preaching occur? And where did this preaching occur?

It is beyond the scope of this book to analyze all the exegetical intricacies of this passage—others have done that job well.[19] I will instead consider the most pressing objections to seeing this passage as a precedent for Postmortem Opportunity for salvation. And in doing so I will simplify the possible ways of understanding this text down to the four most plausible theories.[20]

1. Enoch, not Christ, delivering a message of condemnation to sinful angels.
2. Noah (animated by Christ's Spirit) preaching to his contemporaries as he built the ark.
3. Jesus providing a message of condemnation to sinful angels after his resurrection.
4. Jesus preaching of the gospel in Hades to those who were killed in the flood.

I will consider each of these in turn.

1. Enoch. First, some argue that this passage does not even teach Christ's descent into Hades, arguing that this passage refers not to the preaching of Jesus in Hades, but the preaching of Enoch.[21] This argument appeals to the Jewish legend, recorded in 1 Enoch, that Enoch

[19]William J. Dalton, *Christ's Proclamation to the Spirits*, Analecta Biblica, vol. 23, 2nd rev. ed. (Rome: Pontifical Biblical Institute, 1989 [1965]); Bo Reicke, *The Disobedient Spirits and Christian Baptism: A Study of 1 Peter III. 19 and Its Context*, ASNU 13 (Copenhagen: Ejnar Munksgaard, 1946); Millard Erickson, *How Shall They Be Saved? The Destiny of Those Who Do Not Hear of Jesus* (Grand Rapids, MI: Baker, 1996), 167-73; Wayne Grudem, "Christ Preaching Through Noah: 1 Peter 3:19-20 in the Light of Dominant Themes in Jewish Literature," *Trinity Journal* 7 (1986): 3-31; John S. Feinberg, "1 Peter 3:18-20, Ancient Mythology, and the Intermediate State," *Westminster Theological Journal* 48 (1986): 303-36.

[20]Erickson lists six different theories (*How Shall They Be Saved?*, 168). I am limiting my list to four because I believe that the other two views on Erickson's list lack prima facie plausibility.

[21]Moffatt's translation goes so far as to insert Enoch's name into the biblical text.

was sent from heaven down to Hades as God's envoy to announce God's judgment and the impossibility of forgiveness (1 En 12:1) to the angels who sinned by coming to earth and seducing human women (Gen 6:1-4).[22] This interpretation has been powerfully advanced by Karen Jobes in her commentary on 1 Peter.[23] Jobes points to a number of grammatical advantages of this view and argues that 1 Enoch "no doubt provides the background to 1 Peter 3:19-20."[24] The difficulty for this view is the lack of any reference to Enoch in the text. We are, therefore left with a couple of explanations for this absence. First, perhaps 1 Peter 3:19 did originally include Enoch in the text, but that it was dropped out by a scribe. There is, however, no textual evidence for such a scribal omission. The second explanation is that Enoch was so well-known in the early church that Peter could allude to a section of it without mentioning it by name.[25] This is a bit of a leap, even if one assumes that the audience of 1 Peter was wholly made up of Jewish Christians, and quite implausible if one assumes an audience of Gentiles.[26]

2. Noah. The second interpretation of 1 Peter 3:19-20 is that this text does not refer at all to the descent of Christ into Hades, but to the fact that, through the spirit of Jesus Christ, Noah preached a message of repentance to his neighbors, those that were eventually killed in the flood.[27] Those that argue for this interpretation appeal to the parallels between Noah's situation and those of Peter's readers (such as both Noah and Peter's audience being surrounded by hostile unbelievers)[28]

---

[22]William Barclay, *The Letters of James and Peter*, rev. ed. (Philadelphia: Westminster, 1976), 239.

[23]Karen H. Jobes, *1 Peter*, Baker Exegetical Commentary on the New Testament (Grand Rapids, MI: Baker Academic, 2005), 242-47. Thanks to Amy Peeler for helping me see the strengths of Jobes's argument.

[24]Jobes, *1 Peter*, 243.

[25]Wayne Grudem, *1 Peter*, Tyndale New Testament Commentary (Grand Rapids, MI: Eerdmans, 1988), 220.

[26]See Jobes's discussion on the audience of 1 Peter (*1 Peter*, 23-27). She makes an interesting case for the audience being Jewish Christians, but she acknowledges that "most modern commentators" disagree (23).

[27]This view has been argued by Grudem, *1 Peter*, 157-65, 203-39; Grudem, "Christ Preaching Through Noah," 3-31; Feinberg, "1 Peter 3:18-20, Ancient Mythology," 303-36.

[28]Grudem, *1 Peter*, 160-61.

and that Noah is referred to as "preacher of righteousness" (2 Pet 2:5). This was Augustine's interpretation and a good number of contemporary commentators follow his lead on this passage.[29] While this view is more plausible than the Enoch view, there are a number of exegetical reasons why this interpretation is problematic. The first is that it is awkward to say that Christ "*went* and made proclamation" when Christ does not go anywhere if he is preaching *through* Noah.[30] Grudem's suggestion that Jesus "did not stay in heaven but 'went' to where the people were disobeying, and there preached to them through the lips of Noah"[31] is utterly implausible given the fact that the preincarnate Christ did not need to be spatially present in order to see a situation and speak through a person.[32]

The second objection to the preaching in 1 Peter 3:19 being done by Noah, not Christ, comes from the structure of the passage itself. It follows the well-known doctrinal formula of crucifixion, death, descent, resurrection, and ascension.

> Crucifixion (1 Pet 3:18): "For Christ also died for sins once for all, the just for the unjust, so that He might bring us to God"
>
> Death (1 Pet 3:18): "having been put to death in the flesh"
>
> Descent (1 Pet 3:18-21): "but made alive in the spirit; in which also He went and made proclamation to the spirits now in prison"
>
> Resurrection (1 Pet 3:21): "through the resurrection of Jesus Christ"
>
> Ascension (1 Pet 3:22): "who is at the right hand of God, having gone into heaven"[33] (all NASB)

Understanding 1 Peter 3:18-22 as expressing a doctrinal formula makes it very difficult to see the descent as anything other than the descent of

[29]Augustine, Letter 164 (To Evodius), 15-17; vol. 2 in *The Works of St. Augustine: A Translation for the 21st Century: Letters (156-210)*, trans. Roland J. Teske (New York: New City Press, 2004), 69-71.
[30]Schreiner, *1, 2 Peter, Jude*, 186.
[31]Grudem, *1 Peter*, 160.
[32]It would be far more plausible for Grudem to claim that the "went" is purely anthropomorphic.
[33]J. A. MacCulloch, *The Harrowing of Hell: A Comparative Study of an Early Christian Doctrine* (Edinburgh: T&T Clark, 1930), 61.

Christ into Hades. MacCulloch goes so far to say, "No other interpretation than that of the work of the discarnate Spirit of Christ in Hades seems natural and self-evident here. Indeed all other interpretations merely evade this evident meaning."[34]

3. *Jesus preaching to sinful angels.* The third interpretation acknowledges that it was Jesus doing the preaching but avers that his message was given to the sinful angels who, according to Genesis 6:1-4, had sex with human women and were imprisoned in the "gloomy dungeons" of Tartarus (2 Pet 2:4). Those who interpret the text this way affirm three things: First, they argue that the word for "spirits" (πνεύμασιν) was commonly used of angelic beings. Second, because Scripture offers no hope for the salvation of rebellious angelic beings, the message that was "proclaimed" cannot be a message offering salvation, it can only be a message of doom, a pronouncement of judgment. And third, the phrase "[Jesus] went" in 1 Peter 3:19 is understood to refer to the same "going" as "has gone" in 1 Peter 3:22 and therefore that the preaching took place after Christ's resurrection and exultation.[35]

This interpretation is probably the most common among contemporary exegetes and interpreters, but it suffers from a number of substantial deficiencies. First, while the word for "spirits" is commonly used of angelic beings, it is not always so used. Hebrews 12:23 uses the term to refer to humans and Grudem identifies ten other similar usages.[36] Moreover, since the beings being referred to in Hades are, in fact, dead, it makes sense that Peter would speak of them as spirits. Second, this view forces an awkward interpretation of the word for "preached" (Greek: ἐκήρυξεν, from the verb κηρύσσω). Schreiner argues that this fact is "the greatest difficulty" for those who claim that Christ preached only to angelic beings.[37] In the New Testament and Septuagint this

---

[34]MacCulloch, *Harrowing of Hell*, 61.
[35]Schreiner, *1, 2 Peter, Jude*, 189.
[36]Grudem, "Christ Preaching Through Noah," 6.
[37]Schreiner, *1, 2 Peter, Jude*, 189.

word is consistently used to refer to evangelistic preaching.[38] These considerations suggest that "on the whole it seems more satisfactory to take κηρύσσω in its normal New Testament sense,"[39] namely as a preaching of the good news of salvation, not as a message of condemnation. Third, it is odd that the proclamation is made only to some of the angels, especially since their sin is long past and they have already received judgment and been imprisoned.[40] Instead of announcing the condemnation of angels already imprisoned, it would seem far more relevant to make a proclamation to Satan, who was not imprisoned and about whom Peter admonishes his readers, just two chapters later, to "Be alert and of sober mind. Your enemy the devil prowls around like a roaring lion looking for someone to devour" (1 Pet 5:8).[41] The fourth objection to the preaching being given to sinful angels is this understanding assumes without reason that the preaching took place after Christ's ascension. It is difficult to see the "went" in 1 Peter 3:19 as the same as the "has gone" in 1 Peter 3:22. Finally, such an understanding ignores the fairly clear presence of the christological formula of crucifixion, death, descent, resurrection, and ascension present in 1 Peter 3:18-22.

4. Jesus preaching to the dead in Hades. The fourth interpretation of 1 Peter 3:19-20 is Jesus preached to dead persons in Hades who had been disobedient in the time of Noah and received God's judgment in the form of the flood.[42] While keeping in mind the difficulty of this

---

[38]Grudem, "Christ Preaching Through Noah," 18. See also Sanders, who lists seventeen examples of ἐκήρυξεν being used as a presentation of the gospel (*No Other Name: An Investigation into the Destiny of the Unevangelized* [Grand Rapids, MI: Eerdmans, 1992], 187). It might also be said that when these two can agree on a highly contentious issue, one should take notice.

[39]C. E. B. Cranfield, *The First Epistle of Peter* (London: SCM, 1950), 85.

[40]Feinberg asks, "What would be the point of announcing such a condemnation? Would they not already know that?" ("1 Peter 3:18-20, Ancient Mythology," 327).

[41]In response to the question, "Why only proclaim to some of the angels?," Schreiner says, "This question is an excellent one" and (very fairly) admits that "we cannot answer every question raised in difficult texts" (*1, 2 Peter, Jude*, 189-90).

[42]Interestingly, this seems to have been Martin Luther's view. In his commentary on Hosea 6:1, he quotes 1 Peter 3:19 and says, "Here Peter clearly teaches not only that Christ appeared to the departed fathers and patriarchs, some of whom, without doubt, Christ, when He rose, raised

passage (and therefore the need for chastened conclusions about its interpretation), I believe that this interpretation is preferable.[43] It has a number of advantages. First, it allows us to see Jesus as the one preaching, not Enoch or Noah, which better fits the immediate context of the passage. Second, it allows the term for "proclamation" (ἐκήρυξεν) to be understood in its most natural sense. Third, the descent of Christ into Hades fits the christological formula perfectly. Fourth and finally, this understanding fits Peter's own words in his Pentecost sermon in Acts 2:24: "But God raised him from the dead, freeing him from the agony of death, because it was impossible for *death* to keep its hold on him" (italics added). Of this usage of "death," MacCulloch says, "'Death' is here, as elsewhere, equivalent to 'Hades' and some MSS. read 'Hades.'"[44] In fact, the earliest manuscript of the New Testament, the Peshito Syriac, renders 1 Peter 3:19 as, "He preached to those souls which were detained in Hades."[45] Further, this understanding of Peter's Pentecost sermon is required by his citation of David's words in Psalm 16:9-10:

> Therefore my heart is glad and my tongue rejoices;
> my body also will rest in hope,
> because you will not abandon me to the *realm of the dead*. (Acts 2:26-27)

There are, of course, genuine objections to this interpretation of 1 Peter 3:19-20. The simplest of these is, "Why are the people from Noah's time singled out for Christ's preaching?" C. E. B. Cranfield

---

with Him to eternal life, but also preached to some who in the time of Noah had not believed, and who waited for the long-suffering of God, that is, who hoped that God would not enter into so strict a judgment with all flesh, to the intent that they might acknowledge that their sins were forgiven through the sacrifice of Christ" (cited in Plumptre, *Spirits in Prison*, 116).

[43]Even as conservative a scholar as J. I. Packer seems to accept this view. He simply seeks to mute the salvific implications of this reading, arguing that the preaching was severely limited in scope and that there is no reason to think that this preaching would be successful. See his "The Way of Salvation—Part III: The Problems of Universalism," *Bibliotheca Sacra* 130, no. 517 (January-March 1973): 8.

[44]MacCulloch, *Harrowing of Hell*, 68.

[45]Frederic Huidekoper, *The Belief in the First Three Centuries Concerning Christ's Mission to the Underworld*, 4th ed. (New York: James Miller, 1882 [1854]), 48n1. I will discuss the early church treatment of the descent texts in the next chapter.

argues that Peter is making a very specific point in speaking of Christ's preaching to these particular people for these were "generally regarded as the most notorious and abandoned of sinners."[46] Cranfield then explains a powerful implication of this point: "If there was hope for them, then none could be beyond the reach of Christ's saving power."[47] Similarly, William Barclay says of this text, "The doctrine of the descent into Hades conserves the previous truth that no man who ever lived is left without a sight of Christ and without the offer of the salvation of God."[48] Oscar S. Brooks extends these ideas further, arguing that the structure of 1 Peter is such that Jesus' actions in Hades were an example to Christian converts: "If Christ, in the time of his abode in Sheol, proclaimed the good news to these notorious evil people, from whom can a faithful convert withhold his witness?"[49]

A second objection to this "Postmortem Opportunity–friendly" reading is that Peter does not use the word typically used to convey evangelism (εὐαγγελίζω), a word that he uses elsewhere (1 Pet 1:12, 25; 4:6). While εὐαγγελίζω is commonly used to convey a proclamation of the gospel, κηρύσσω is used more broadly, as a formal and official proclamation of information. This point is granted, but it is important to note that there is nothing in it that undercuts the notion that Jesus preached the gospel to the dead in Hades. Even if εὐαγγελίζω is more commonly used to convey a proclamation of the gospel than κηρύσσω, there is nothing in the meaning of it or of κηρύσσω that rules out it being used to convey a proclamation of the gospel. In fact, κηρύσσω is used to convey a proclamation of the gospel dozens of times in the New Testament—thirty-two times in the Synoptics alone.[50] Κηρύσσω is also the word used in one of the most obvious "gospel proclamation"

---

[46]Cranfield, *The First Epistle of Peter*, 85.

[47]Cranfield, *The First Epistle of Peter*, 85.

[48]Barclay, *Letters of James and Peter*, 242.

[49]Oscar S. Brooks, "1 Peter 3:21: The Clue to the Literary Structure of the Epistle," *Novum Testamentum* 16, no. 4 (October 1974): 303.

[50]*The New International Dictionary of New Testament Theology*, ed. Colin Brown (Grand Rapids, MI: Zondervan, 1978), 3:52.

passages in the New Testament, Romans 10:14-15: "How, then, can they call on the one they have not believed in? And how can they believe in the one of whom they have not heard? And how can they hear without someone *preaching* to them? And how can anyone *preach* unless they are sent? As it is written: 'How beautiful are the feet of those who bring good news!'"[51] So why κηρύσσω instead of εὐαγγελίζω? It is impossible to say for sure, but perhaps the descent of Christ into Hades was of such significance that Peter chose the word that conveyed a more formal pronouncement—perhaps a pronouncement befitting the entrance of a Conqueror to his conquered realm.

The third objection to this interpretation is that such a reading allows that sinners are given a "second chance" that renders the decisions made in this life irrelevant. While I believe this objection to ultimately be mistaken, it would be a mistake to downplay its significance. This objection is, I believe, the reason why people struggle to see the descent passages as indicative of postmortem hope.[52] For example, in his commentary on 1 Peter, Thomas Schreiner refers to the following "fatal problem": "It makes no sense contextually for Peter to be teaching that the wicked have a second chance in a letter in which he exhorted the righteous to persevere and to endure suffering."[53] Likewise, John Elliott argues, "Any notion of a possibility of conversion or salvation after death would seriously undermine the letter's consistent stress on the necessity of righteous behavior here and now."[54] These objections have an inner logic that is difficult to deny; however, they are based on a misunderstanding of what the Postmortem Opportunity theorist claims. I will address the "second chance" and "irrelevance of decisions in this life" objections in detail in chapter seven, but for now it is enough

[51]Italics added. Κηρύσσω is also used in Rom 10:8.

[52]Examples of dismissing the postmortem hope in 1 Pet 3:19-20; 4:6 due to the impossibility of a second chance: Feinberg, "1 Peter 3:18-20, Ancient Mythology," 326; Grudem, *1 Peter*, 172; John H. Elliott, *1 Peter: A New Translation with Introduction and Commentary*, vol. 37B, Anchor Yale Bible Commentaries (New York: Doubleday, 2000), 662.

[53]Schreiner, *1, 2 Peter, Jude*, 188.

[54]Elliott, *1 Peter*, 662.

to say that Postmortem Opportunity is in no way a second chance. Moreover, the Postmortem Opportunity theorist must not say anything that implies that one's behavior in this life is irrelevant because they can simply choose salvation posthumously. If the Postmortem Opportunity theorist was defending such silly things, Schreiner's and Elliott's objections would be devastating, but they claim nothing of the sort.[55]

1 Peter 4:6.

> For this is why the gospel was preached even to those who are dead, that though judged in the flesh the way people are, they might live in the spirit the way God does. (ESV)

This passage is, on the surface at least, the most straightforward of the descent passages, but that does not mean that there is anything like widespread agreement on how it should be interpreted. While it is clear that the gospel is being preached, there is vigorous debate over the recipients of the preaching of the gospel. There are three primary interpretations of who the "dead" are. The first of these sees the dead as those who are "spiritually dead." This view has had numerous defenders throughout church history, including Augustine, but it is difficult to square with the fact that the text says that "the gospel was preached *even* to those who are dead." If the dead are understood as "spiritually dead," the inclusion of the word "even" (καί) makes no sense, for it would seem that the spiritually dead would be exactly the people who would need to receive the gospel. Moreover, the preceding phrase "the living and the dead" (1 Pet 4:5 ESV) strongly supports that the dead are physically dead.[56] And finally, Peter never used the term "dead" (νεκροῖς) to refer to spiritual death.[57]

[55]More accurately, I am not claiming anything of the sort. There are some defenders of Postmortem Opportunity that make such claims. William Barclay, for example, says that 1 Peter 4:6 "gives a breath-taking glimpse of a gospel of a second chance." See his *Letters of James and Peter*, 249.

[56]David G. Horrell, "Who Are 'the Dead' and When Was the Gospel Preached to Them? The Interpretation of 1 Peter 4:6," *New Testament Studies* 48 (2003): 71.

[57]Schreiner, *1, 2 Peter, Jude*, 206; See also Reike, *The Disobedient Spirits*, 205.

The second interpretation of "the dead" is that the phrase refers to those who heard the gospel when they were alive, but are *now* dead. This view doesn't have the ancient lineage of the "spiritually dead" view, but has garnered increasing support in recent decades, owing largely to the work of W. J. Dalton[58] and E. G. Selwyn.[59] On this view, Peter is assuring his readers that believers who have died have not ceased to be and are enjoying a blessed existence in the eternal realm.[60] The NIV attempts to bolster this reading by inserting the word "now" into the text of this verse—"the gospel was preached even to those who are *now* dead"—while admitting in a study note in the *NIV Study Bible* that the word "now" is not in the original Greek. Their proffered rationale for the addition is that they believe that the Bible teaches elsewhere that there are no opportunities for salvation after death. This is problematic because, as I have argued in the previous chapter, it is *not* obvious that Scripture does rule out salvation after death. Moreover, even given dynamic equivalence ("thought for thought") translation, this is an egregious example of overstepping the task of translation, for there is *nothing* in the text to suggest that the word "now" should be included. As such, the inclusion of "now" in the text of 1 Peter 4:6 constitutes an obvious example of the imposition of the translator's theology onto the text. If they wanted to suggest a particular reading of the text, they should have done so in a footnote.[61]

As popular as the "now dead" interpretation of 1 Peter 4:6 has become, it has a number of serious problems. One problem with this interpretation is that it seems highly unlikely that the author of 1 Peter would need to assure his readers about the salvation of those who had recently died because "there is no indication that the readers of 1 Peter doubted

---

[58]William Joseph Dalton, *Christ's Proclamation to the Spirits*; Dalton, "The Interpretation of 1 Peter 3,19 and 4,6: Light from 2 Peter," *Biblica* 60 (1979): 547-55.

[59]E. G. Selwyn, *The First Epistle of St. Peter* (London: Macmillan, 1952).

[60]Grudem, *1 Peter*, 171.

[61]Keith DeRose makes a similar observation in his "Universalism and the Bible: The *Really* Good News," http://campuspress.yale.edu/keithderose/1129-2/, sec. 8.

this."[62] David Horrell has argued (persuasively I think) that projecting a worry similar to that addressed in 1 Thessalonians 4:13-18 onto the readers of 1 Peter is implausible.[63] Moreover, understanding the preaching of the gospel to those that were alive and are now dead doesn't fit the immediate context of the passage very well. Peter is reminding his readers that those who engage in riotous living, and who "heap abuse" of Christians for refusing to join them "will have to give account to him who is ready to judge the living and the dead" (1 Pet 4:5). As Horrell notes, "Since the phrase 'the living and the dead' has a general reference, we should expect the same to be true of 'dead' in vs. 6."[64] The immediate context provides no justification for limiting the "dead" in 1 Peter 4:6 to only the Christian dead.

The final interpretation is to understand "the dead" simply as those who are physically dead. Joel Green claims that "the dead" in this verse are "dead members of the human family given Postmortem Opportunity to hear the good news."[65] And F. W. Beare asserts that "the dead" are "all the dead from the beginning of time, all that are to stand before the judgement seat of Christ."[66] On this interpretation, 1 Peter 4:6 offers a justification for God's judgment of the living and the dead: "God can justly judge all people, both the living and the dead, since the gospel has been announced to all, to the dead as well as the living."[67] This interpretation doesn't require, as some have surmised, that the events surrounding 1 Peter 3:18-22 and 4:6 are exactly the same, only that "the author of 1 Peter conceives of a proclamation made by the crucified and risen Christ in a realm other than that of the world of living humanity."[68]

---

[62]Horrell, "Who Are 'the Dead,'" 78.

[63]Horrell, "Who Are 'the Dead,'" 74-77.

[64]Horrell, "Who Are 'the Dead,'" 80-81.

[65]Joel B. Green, *1 Peter*, Two Horizons New Testament Commentary (Grand Rapids, MI: Eerdmans, 2007), 122. Green goes on to aver that "the idea of postmortem proclamation and even conversion is not as rare in early Christianity as is often postulated" (127).

[66]F. W. Beare, *The First Epistle of Peter* (Blackwell: Oxford, 1958), 156.

[67]Horrell, "Who Are 'the Dead,'" 78.

[68]Horrell, "Who Are 'the Dead,'" 79.

Objections to this interpretation often mirror objections to a Postmortem Opportunity reading of 1 Peter 3:19-20. It is common to object that offering a "second chance" to sinners runs counter to the call for Christians to persevere through suffering, and Paul Achtemeier adds the objection that offering salvation on the day of the final judgment is incompatible with the New Testament notion that "the final judgment is a time of separation of good from evil."[69] However, as mentioned above, these objections are based on serious misunderstandings of the theory of Postmortem Opportunity—it is not a "second chance," and the notion of Postmortem Opportunity does not entail that none will reject Christ and that there will be no need to separate good from evil.

A more pressing objection to a Postmortem Opportunity reading of 1 Peter 4:6 has been articulated by Thomas Schreiner. He claims that the use of the passive verb in the phrase "the gospel was preached" indicates that it was not Jesus who did the preaching, but the preaching of Christ by human beings.[70] This raises an interesting point. It is true that the passive verb might indicate that it was not Jesus preaching, but it seems to be a reach to claim that the passive voice would *require* such a reading. Moreover, the passive verb might suggest a connection between the "dead" in 1 Peter 4:6 and the "spirits in prison" in 1 Peter 3:19, for "if Christ can announce his own victory to the imprisoned spirits in 3:18-19 then the idea of Christ announcing the good news about himself to the human dead is no less plausible."[71] Moreover, there are interesting parallels between 1 Peter 3:19 and 4:6 that could suggest the relevant connection. In 1 Peter 3:18, Christ is put to death in the body, but made alive in the Spirit, and in 1 Peter 4:6, the dead are judged after the manner of persons in the flesh (1 Pet 3:19) but live after the manner of God in the spirit (1 Pet 4:6).[72]

---

[69]P. J. Achtemeier, *1 Peter*, Hermeneia (Minneapolis: Fortress, 1996), 289.

[70]Schreiner, *1, 2 Peter, Jude*, 207.

[71]Horrell, "Who Are 'the Dead,'" 81.

[72]MacCulloch, *Harrowing of Hell*, 61-62.

The third objection to this reading of 1 Peter 4:6 is a recapitulation of one of the objections to 1 Peter 3:19-20. Dalton states the objection as follows: "The normal meaning of the term, 'preach the gospel,' would imply the possible conversion of these souls" and "such an idea is alien to the rest of the New Testament, which insists on this life as the arena where eternal life is decided."[73] Again, I think that the biblical case against death being the end of salvific opportunity is wildly overstated, but let's step back and take a good look at this claim. It is interesting that the most common objection to these passages teaching a Postmortem Opportunity is external in nature—namely, the (purported) fact that Scripture rules out such a possibility—not internal. Suppose, however, the internal evidence was allowed to speak for itself and these passages were interpreted to teach that there is a postmortem salvific opportunity. If that was the case, then it would be very difficult to claim that Scripture rules out such a view. As such, a great deal depends on one's prior assessment of the scriptural case against postmortem salvific opportunity. One might argue that my approach violates the exegetical principle that we interpret difficult texts in light of clear ones, not vice versa. That is, of course, a fine principle, but it isn't obvious how it should be applied in this situation given the fact that the primary reason many interpreters have deemed 1 Peter 3:18-22 and 4:6 to be so difficult is that these passages seem to teach a view—postmortem salvific opportunity—that is (mistakenly, I believe) deemed to be ruled out by Scripture. If postmortem salvific opportunity is not ruled out, are these texts anywhere near as difficult?

ASSESSING THE SCRIPTURAL EVIDENCE

What should be made of the scriptural evidence for Postmortem Opportunity? The indirect evidence, by its nature, cannot be taken to straightforwardly teach Postmortem Opportunity, but it can open up

---

[73]Dalton, *Christ's Proclamation to the Spirits*, 235.

the possibility that death is not the end of salvific opportunity. Or, more precisely, one who becomes aware of the indirect evidence has a reason to question the common assumption that one's salvific status is fixed at death. And, once one approaches the question of when one's salvific status is fixed with an open mind, the direct scriptural evidence for Postmortem Opportunity becomes much more persuasive.

I believe that Ephesians 4:8-9 does indicate that Jesus descended into Hades, but the christological rather than soteriological focus of the passage means that this text does not indicate that the descent involved preaching of the gospel. As such, while this text is compatible with this the idea of Postmortem Opportunity, it is a stretch to say that it "teaches" it. And while 1 Peter 3:19-20 and 4:6 can be interpreted as indicating that Jesus descended into Hades and preached the gospel to those who had died, the complexity of these passages make it difficult to be too dogmatic about this conclusion. Perhaps the only thing that is clear about the descent texts is that there is no clarity and no widespread agreement on what they mean and what theological positions they sanction or rule out. There are undoubtedly a range of possible interpretations, each of which is supported by respected exegetes.[74] In such a situation, one's appraisal of what a text says (or doesn't say), or what positions it defends (or cannot be taken as defending) are determined less by a reading of the text itself and more by beliefs about Scripture's broader stance on relevant matters (the *metanarrative* of Scripture) or by prior theological or methodological commitments. Crucial among these is the belief of whether death ends salvific opportunity. For those who are open to the possibility of postmortem conversion, 1 Peter 3:19-20 and 1 Peter 4:6 are very plausibly read as teaching that are least some people have experienced a Postmortem Opportunity. But, taken by themselves, it is unlikely that the descent passages will cause one who believes that death is the end of salvific

[74]John Sanders, *No Other Name: An Investigation into the Destiny of the Unevangelized* (Grand Rapids, MI: Eerdmans, 1992), 186; Feinberg, "1 Peter 3:18-20, Ancient Mythology," 312.

opportunity to question that belief. Here, as elsewhere, the role of control beliefs and presuppositions is powerful.

In addition, it must be remembered that there is a logical gap between the most Postmortem Opportunity–favorable interpretation of the descent passages and the theory of Postmortem Opportunity. Millard Erickson states this point this way:

> It should be noted that the argument for postmortem evangelism is not necessarily successful even if we accept the interpretation that Christ descended into Hades and offered salvation to the imprisoned sinners there. For even if that is achieved, that only takes care of those few people. It says nothing about others who have lived since that time or will live in the future. To be sure, the principle of no salvation beyond the grave, or death being the end of all opportunity, has been breached, but that gives no guarantee that others will be saved. That might have been a unique situation. It is necessary to establish an additional link in the argument, namely, that because Christ proclaimed and provided salvation for those imprisoned sinners, there will also be an opportunity for others to come.[75]

Even if it could be claimed that the descent passages straightforwardly *teach* that Jesus presented the gospel during the *tridentum mortis* in Hades, that would not entail that the theory of Postmortem Opportunity was true and that all of those who God deems to need a Postmortem opportunity will receive it. The most they could do is provide a precedent for the postmortem salvific opportunity. Consequently, while there is some scriptural evidence for Postmortem Opportunity, it is not decisive. It is perhaps best to say that, given the background evidence about God's love (which some do not emphasize as much as others) and given the indirect evidence (which some see differently), it is plausible to see the descent passages as providing some support to the theory of Postmortem Opportunity.

In summary, consider three different claims regarding the scriptural evidence for Postmortem Opportunity.

---

[75]Erickson, *How Shall They Be Saved?*, 173.

1. Scripture directly and explicitly teaches that the unevangelized will have a Postmortem Opportunity to be saved.
2. Scripture provides positive evidence for the theory of Postmortem Opportunity.
3. Scripture provides a counterexample to the claim that death is the end of opportunity to hear and respond to the gospel.

The first of these is clearly false. Even if it is granted that the descent passages demonstrated that after his death Jesus descended into Hades and preached the gospel to those there, giving them an opportunity to respond, it would not follow that all of the unevangelized (let alone the pseudoevangelized) will be given the same opportunity. Assessing the second claim is more complicated, for it depends on what is allowed to count as "positive evidence." If what is required for positive evidence is evidence that Scripture teaches that all the unevangelized and semi-evangelized will receive a Postmortem Opportunity, then (2) is also false. Unfortunately, many commentators take this as the end of the story with respect to Scripture and the theory of Postmortem Opportunity, and this is also a serious error. While it is unlikely that Scripture provides positive evidence for the theory of Postmortem Opportunity as a whole, that doesn't mean that it doesn't provide some sort of positive evidence for claims that are relevant to the theory of Postmortem Opportunity. And one of the important pieces of evidence is (3) itself. Even if the descent passages do not teach or evidentially support the notion that the unevangelized will have a Postmortem Opportunity, they might still provide a challenging counterexample to the claim that there can be no Postmortem Opportunities to hear the gospel. And once the claim "death is the end of salvific opportunity" is called into question, the substantial theological evidence for the theory of Postmortem Opportunity can be seen more clearly.

DOING THEOLOGY WHERE SCRIPTURE DOES NOT GO

I have just claimed that Scripture provides positive evidence for the theory of Postmortem Opportunity, even if it does not *directly and explicitly* teach it. It is not that Scripture says nothing that is at all relevant to the idea of Postmortem Opportunity, but it does not directly address the issue of the destiny of the unevangelized, and when it speaks about the salvation of the lost, it does not explicitly say that all people who do not get an opportunity to hear and respond to the gospel in this life will be given an opportunity in the postmortem state. For many, this is a decisive objection to the theory of Postmortem Opportunity. Ronald Nash phrases his objection this way:

> Suppose we concede that God may, if he chooses, continue to pursue believers after their death. That is hardly the issue, I think; rather, the issue is whether that is what God teaches us in His Word. If postmortem salvation is not endorsed by Scripture, we should not be tempted to treat human death as an artificial, human-made boundary that limits God's power.[76]

And even if it is acknowledged that the descent passages (especially 1 Pet 3:19-20 and 4:6) provide some support to the theory of Postmortem Opportunity, Millard Erickson expresses the opinion of many when he says, "It would be strange to rest a doctrine about the eternal destiny of humans on such an obscure passage."[77] Nash concurs: "Wise Christians do not base any important doctrine—especially a controversial teaching that might also contain heretical implications—on one single, highly debatable passage of Scripture."[78] Stephen Wellum extends this objection, arguing, "In the end, we must remember that logical possibilities are not necessarily *biblical* possibilities. And theologizing must be carefully tied to the biblical text. Unless Scripture explicitly

---

[76]Ronald Nash, "Is There Salvation After Death? The Answer to Postmortem Evangelism," *Christian Research Journal* 27, no. 4 (2004).

[77]Erickson, *How Shall They Be Saved?*, 175.

[78]Ronald Nash, *When a Baby Dies: Answers to Comfort Grieving Parents* (Grand Rapids, MI: Zondervan, 1999), 39.

sanctions and warrants it, we must be careful in drawing hypotheses that rise to the level of settled conclusions."[79]

At the heart of this matter is the crucially important question of what it means to say that a particular piece of theology is "based on" Scripture. There are actually a pair of objections here. There is an objection to basing theology on controversial or obscure passages of Scripture and an objection to it not being carefully tied to the biblical text. Let's assume that these are different ways of expressing the same idea (or at least, logically parallel ideas). The desire underlying both is that theology be based on Scripture and flow from what Scripture teaches. From these claims, Nash and Erickson seem to be embracing something like the following argument:

1. Theology must be explicitly and directly based on Scripture.
2. Postmortem Opportunity is not explicitly and directly based on Scripture.
3. Therefore, Postmortem Opportunity is not a viable answer to the problem of the destiny of the unevangelized.

There are two ways for the Postmortem Opportunity theorist to respond to this objection: they can deny the major premise (1) or the minor premise (2). I have already admitted the minor premise, that Postmortem Opportunity is not explicitly and directly taught by Scripture, so that leaves me the task of denying (or at least complicating) the major premise—the requirement that theology, if it is to be acceptable, must be explicitly and directly based on Scripture.

Before critiquing this principle, let's first try to understand it better. Suppose one was to say, "I don't care if my theology is based on

[79]Stephen Wellum, "Saving Faith," in *Faith Comes by Hearing: A Response to Inclusivism*, ed. Christopher W. Morgan and Robert A. Peterson (Downers Grove, IL: IVP Academic, 2008), 183. Wellum is making this argument with respect to the answer to the destiny of the unevangelized problem given by Inclusivists, but it is clear from his statements that he would apply these very same objections to Postmortem Opportunity theorists. In fact, he might find Postmortem Opportunity to be even more objectionable along these lines. But that is just a guess.

Scripture"; what would be wrong with such a stance? The odd thing about this question is that the sense that something is wrong is overwhelming, but it is much less clear exactly why such a stance is problematic. Some might simply say that if one's theology is not based on Scripture, then it isn't biblical. This is, of course, true, but since it is tautologous (true by definition), it doesn't really help us much. Others might claim that if theology isn't based on Scripture then it won't be "Christian"—because Christian theology must be based on the Christian Scriptures. That claim seems more plausible, but it isn't quite right either. Consider a theological teaching of Yahweh before the writing of the Old Testament or a teaching of Jesus before the writing of the New Testament.[80] Can those theological teachings be considered "Christian?" Of course. So it isn't that theology must come from Scripture in order to be Christian. Still others will suggest that theology must be based on Scripture for alethic reasons—Scripture is what makes it such that theology is true. This is also an improvement, but is still confused, for (technically speaking) Scripture itself isn't true or false, it is interpretations of Scripture that are true or false, and it is not the case that just any interpretation of Scripture is true. The proposition "God exists" is not true because it is taught by Scripture, it is true because reality is such that God does, in fact, exist.

The reason for desiring that our theology be based on Scripture is epistemological. The reason it is problematic to ignore Scripture when doing theology is because there is no good reason to believe that the stuff human beings just make up off the top of their heads is true. Scripture is God's Word, it contains God's teaching for humanity, and the church has acknowledged God's inspiration in the biblical text. Of course, fleshing out exactly what is meant by saying that Scripture is God's Word and is inspired is no mean task, and different strands of

---

[80]To make this example work, let's assume that this particular teaching of Jesus is not found anywhere in the Old Testament.

Christianity might explain this basic idea differently.[81] Happily for our task, it can be stipulated that the reason we want our theology to be based on Scripture is because Scripture is God's Word and, however that is understood, there is epistemological warrant granted to the doctrines taught in Scripture that are not granted to the beliefs that are not based on Scripture.[82]

So let's assume that theology must be *based on* Scripture. But because there is enormous complexity in the question of how Scripture and theology are related, it is far from clear what it means that theology must be based on Scripture. Moreover, there is an unfortunate tendency to oversimplify this question—either Scripture teaches something or it does not. For example, James Orr says, "A strong distinction ought to be drawn between things which Scripture expressly teaches and those things on which it gives no light."[83] This seems wrong. It's pretty clear that there are theological issues or questions that Scripture speaks to, but doesn't expressly teach. As such, we need a more fine-grained approach to understanding what it means to say that theology is based on Scripture. Here are a range of possibilities:

1. Specific theological beliefs cannot contradict what Scripture clearly teaches.
2. Specific theological beliefs cannot contradict what Scripture clearly teaches and should be based on reasonable inferences from what Scripture does teach.

---

[81]Theological liberals are more likely to explain the epistemic value of Scripture in ecclesiological terms—these are the books that the church has traditionally seen as being life-guiding and important. Theological conservatives are more likely to explain the epistemic value of Scripture in terms of the divine authority conveyed to these writings in the process of inspiration, a process that preserves what God desires to teach and grounds belief in the inerrancy of Scripture. And there are also a myriad of positions mediating these two.

[82]There is much more that could (and maybe should) be said about the underlying epistemological issues here. Suffice it to say that I think that this general point holds, however "epistemological warrant" is understood.

[83]James Orr, *Christian View of God and the World* (New York: Charles Scribner's Sons, 1907), 338.

3. Specific theological beliefs must have explicit and direct Scripture support.
4. Specific theological beliefs must have explicit and direct Scripture support and cannot be based on anything other than Scripture.[84]

The first of these statements is obviously true, but is clearly not strong enough, for it would suggest that even beliefs like "God wants the Minnesota Vikings to finally win a Super Bowl"—which, contrary to the opinion of some Green Bay Packer fans, is not contradicted by anything in Scripture—could be considered to be "based on Scripture."

On the other end of the continuum, (4) is clearly far too strong. The belief that there is a simple one-to-one correspondence between Scripture and theology must be discarded. Similarly, it must be understood that the Reformation ideal of *sola scriptura* does not mean that nothing outside of Scripture is relevant to the production of our theology. *Sola scriptura* means that Scripture is unique in terms of authority, but there are other "sources" of theology, in the sense that we use our mind to read Scripture and understand its teachings. Moreover, we are never theologically *tabula rasa*; we always read Scripture with certain theological stances and concepts in mind. And our hermeneutical and philosophical assumptions, our culture, our context, our questions, and even our personality plays a role in shaping our theology. All of these things form the plausibility structures which cause us to read Scripture as we do.

So it comes down to (2) and (3). I believe that the best way to think about basing theology on Scripture is (2). This is because the requirement that theological beliefs must have direct and explicit support is incompatible with how theology has actually been done. Consider, for example, the Chalcedonian Creed on Christ's divine and human natures. While this crucially important doctrine is certainly *based on*

[84]Thomas McCall has done something similar in *An Invitation to Analytic Christian Theology* (Downers Grove, IL: InterVarsity Press, 2015). His list is more comprehensive (he offers eight options), but the general point and purpose is basically the same.

Scripture, it is difficult if not impossible to say that it is *directly and explicitly taught* by Scripture. The creed speaks of the relationship between the human and divine nature of Christ using four terms: the two natures are "inconfusedly, unchangeably, indivisibly, inseparably" related. Now there are certainly Scriptures behind each of these points, but the formulation of the creed requires not just an accumulation of the relevant Scriptures, but a delicate balancing act. If one overemphasizes the inconfusability of Christ's natures, the result is Nestorianism, which separated the natures into different persons. And if one overemphasizes the inseparability of the two natures, the result would be Monophysitism, which collapses the two natures into synthesis of the two. Similar points can be made with respect to the doctrine of trinity, creation *ex nihilo*, and the compatibility of divine providence and human freedom. None of these core beliefs of the Christian faith can lay claim to being explicitly and directly taught by Scripture.

In addition, (2) is preferable to (3) because Scripture underdetermines most of our theological doctrines. As Stephan Davis says, we must be careful not to "confuse the claim that the Bible is authoritative on matters of faith and practice with the claim that the Bible authoritatively tells us everything we might want to know about Christian faith and practice."[85] So at issue here is nothing less than our view of what Scripture is and what it sets out to do. Some treat Scripture as a theology text and therefore accept all and only the theology explicitly taught therein. The problems with this view of Scripture are extensive and I will not belabor them here. Suffice it to say that Scripture simply does not directly and explicitly address all of the important questions and issues we have about theological and spiritual matters.

Consider, for example, the theological beliefs on either side of the Calvinist/Arminian debate. While no one would claim that Scripture does not provide the data points that both Calvinists and Arminians

---

[85]Stephen T. Davis, "Universalism, Hell, and the Fate of the Ignorant," *Modern Theology* 6, no. 2 (January 1990): 180-81.

appeal to, there is much in this intractable debate that Scripture does not explicitly and directly teach. For example, the debate between Calvinism and Arminianism depends on differing intuitions about the nature of human freedom, and while it might be the case that Scripture indirectly supports either a libertarian or compatibilist conception of human freedom, it must be admitted that Scripture says *nothing* directly about these labyrinthine debates. Similarly, Calvinist and Arminian debates often hinge on the nature of God's relationship to time, and despite what far too many Christians have claimed in the past, "a day is like a thousand years, and a thousand years are like a day" (2 Pet 3:8) and "A thousand years in your sight are like a day that has just gone by" (Ps 90:4), tell us very little about God's relationship to time. The simple fact is that Scripture simply does not speak to these important elements of our theological beliefs.

The fact that Scripture underdetermines many specific theological doctrines might cause some to suggest the following principle: "Of what Scripture does directly and explicitly not speak, we should remain silent." There are, of course, many places where this principle should be applied. If we have nothing in Scripture that gives us any meaningful information about the question we desire to answer—such as God's will on the Vikings' Super Bowl victories or, dare I say, the precise date of Jesus' second coming—then agnosticism and silence on that matter is in order. But there are many important theological issues that can be fruitfully addressed, even though they are underdetermined by Scripture. The theological task is one of connecting the data points of Scripture and in so doing seeking to provide biblically faithful answers to important theological questions. And, I submit, the question of the destiny of the unevangelized is one that we must at least try to answer.[86]

[86]Those who would say that we do not need to bother with answering this question because we may simply assume that "God will do what is right in judgment," should take seriously Clark Pinnock's rather frontal comments to Lesslie Newbigin, who makes just such a claim: "There is truth in what he says, but such an attitude can also be a cop-out to avoid answering a fair and urgent question in a responsible way. What kind of theologian refuses to speak about the

CONCLUSION

After careful consideration of the various streams of scriptural evidence, I have concluded that Scripture might be seen as offering positive evidential support for the theory of Postmortem Opportunity, even if it cannot be claimed to directly and explicitly teach it. This state of affairs is not a problem, I believe, because the best way to think about the necessity of theology being based on Scripture is that specific theological beliefs cannot contradict what Scripture clearly teaches and should be based on reasonable inferences from what Scripture does teach. Thus understood, there is no problem in affirming both that Scripture does not directly and explicitly teach the doctrine of Postmortem Opportunity and that the doctrine of Postmortem Opportunity can be based on Scripture. But not all objections to the theory of Postmortem Opportunity are scriptural. In the next two chapters I will discuss the historical and theological objections to Postmortem Opportunity.

possibility of salvation of the majority of the human race? Is such a person reticent on other controversial matters? Maybe he or she should find easier work" (*A Wideness in God's Mercy: The Finality of Jesus Christ in a World of Religions* [Grand Rapids, MI: Zondervan, 1992], 152).

6

A HISTORICAL OBJECTION TO POSTMORTEM OPPORTUNITY

The purpose of considering the perspective of the early church is twofold. First, considering the exegesis and theology of the early church can shed some light on the exegetical debates addressed in the previous chapter. This isn't to say that writings of the patristic age possess the same authority as Scripture; it is merely to recognize the fact that the early church stands much closer than contemporary believers to the cultural assumptions and historical context of the human authors and first readers of Scripture. The second purpose is related to the purpose of the next chapter, to respond to the various theological objections to Postmortem Opportunity. There is a fairly common, although rarely explicitly developed, historical objection to Postmortem Opportunity that assumes that this matter has been settled by the church. For the purposes of concreteness, I will state this objection as follows:

> Historical Objection: *Postmortem Opportunity has been almost universally rejected by the church and therefore anyone seeking to defend it has an especially high evidentiary burden to meet.*

While I acknowledge that Postmortem Opportunity has been largely absent from the church since the time of Augustine, the early church was not universal in its rejection of postmortem repentance, and the objections the early church did develop against postmortem repentance need not be seen as decisive against my version of the theory of Postmortem Opportunity. I will argue this response through advancing three claims or theses with respect to the early church—which

I will define, for the purposes of this chapter, as up to the time of Augustine (354–430).[1]

> Thesis 1: The early church fathers believed Christ preached the gospel to people who were dead.
>
> Thesis 2: Postmortem repentance was deemed to be possible by significant segments of the early church.
>
> Thesis 3: The reasons the church rejected the possibility of postmortem conversion can be explained and, for the most part, do not constitute objections to my version of Postmortem Opportunity.

To be clear, I am not claiming that each of these three theses provide direct evidential support for Postmortem Opportunity, but only that they cumulatively offer a sound response to the historical objection and provide contemporary Christians with a reason to reconsider Postmortem Opportunity. After arguing for these three theses, I will briefly highlight the voices calling for a renewed consideration of Postmortem Opportunity.

CHRIST'S DESCENT AND PREACHING IN HADES

> Thesis 1: *The early church fathers believed Christ preached the gospel to people who were dead.*

The primary line of evidence for the first thesis is the claim by many early Christian writers that Christ descended to the underworld during the *triduum mortis* and preached the gospel. The idea of Christ's descent to Hades was significant for early Christians "because it represented that definitive defeat of death from which Christian believers benefit."[2] The descent also fueled the rise of the *Christus Victor* model of the atonement. Of the descent, Archbishop Hilarion Alfeyev says,

---

[1]I do not intend to imply that Augustine should not be considered an early church figure. Drawing such bright lines in history is rarely helpful. Rather I am acknowledging that on this issue as on others, Augustine is a watershed figure who fundamentally changes the shape of the conversation on Postmortem Opportunity.

[2]Richard Bauckham, *The Fate of the Dead: Studies on the Jewish and Christian Apocalypses*, Supplements to Novum Testamentum, vol. 93 (Leiden: Brill, 1998), 44. Bauckham even suggests

> The teaching on Christ's descent is an inseparable part of the dogmatic tradition of the church. It was shared by all members of the ancient church as reflected in the New Testament, the works of the early Christian apologists, fathers and teachers of the church, ancient and later writers of both the East and West, as well as in the baptismal creeds, eucharistic services, and liturgical texts.[3]

Early Christians appealed to a number of scriptural texts as evidence of the descent of Christ to Hades, most significantly, Acts 2:24-32, where Peter quotes from Psalm 16:8-11: "because you will not abandon me to the realm of the dead, you will not let your holy one see decay" (Acts 2:27; Ps 16:10). The descent is used as the explanation as to why "at the name of Jesus every knee should bow, in heaven and on earth and *under the earth*" (Phil 2:10) and how Christ might "enter a strong man's house and carry off his possessions" (Mt 12:29; Mk 3:27). Other texts cited as evidence are Hosea 13:14, "I will deliver this people from the power of the grave; I will redeem them from death"; Zechariah 9:11, "As for you, because of the blood of my covenant with you, I will free your prisoners from the waterless pit"; Matthew 12:40, "the Son of Man will be three days and three nights in the heart of the earth"; and Romans 10:7, "'Who will descend into the deep?' (that is, to bring Christ up from the dead)." In addition to these passages, a good number of early Christian thinkers found a reference to the descent in Ephesians 4:9; 1 Peter 3:19; and 1 Peter 4:6.[4]

The early church on the intermediate state. One of the difficulties of considering the perspective of the early church on the descent, however, is that there was not a single clear understanding of the intermediate state in the early church. The early church's view of the intermediate state was unclear and evolving. The early church was firmly convinced of the idea that there is a realm of the dead, located in the underworld,

---

that, in this respect, the descent played a more prominent role in early Christian thought than the resurrection of Christ because "it showed Christ delivering others from death."

[3]Hilarion Alfeyev, *Christ the Conqueror of Hell: The Descent into Hades from an Orthodox Perspective* (Crestwood, NY: St. Vladimir's Seminary Press, 2009), 203.

[4]Although not as early as might be expected. The first reference to these passages in connection with the descent is from Clement of Alexandria.

labeled Hades (Greek) or Sheol (Hebrew). Regarding the belief in the realm of the dead, John Feinberg says, "As one peruses the extrabiblical literature from the centuries immediately preceding and after the time of Christ, he finds the notion of an underworld very firmly intrenched. This is the case whether one is reading Greco-Roman mythology, inter-testamental Jewish literature, or apocryphal works written shortly after the time of Christ."[5] The debates over the realm of the dead concerned its nature, not its existence. Most significant in this respect were questions of whether Hades was different than hell and whether there were divisions in the "realm of the dead"—Hades for the unrepentant and a separate place for Old Testament patriarchs and New Testament believers, sometimes labeled "paradise" or *limbus patrum* (limbo of the fathers). Moreover, during the early centuries of the Christian era, there was a gradual shift "from the old view that the wicked are not immediately punished after death, but held in detention awaiting punishment at the last judgment, to the latter view that the eternal punishment of the wicked begins already after death."[6] In the earliest literature to address the matter, those in the underworld are merely waiting for the day of judgment, when the wicked will be punished and the righteous rewarded. But starting in the second century CE, it became more popular to see the dead as already experiencing either reward or judgment.[7] On the early view, hell is empty until the day of judgment and all people reside in Hades; on the latter, Hades is where unbelievers experience hell (or at least some of the torments of hell).[8] As such, on the early view, Christ descended to a place of the dead, a place that included those who had embraced relationship with Christ in this life, those who have rejected it, and those who had not received

---

[5]John Feinberg, "1 Peter 3:18-20, Ancient Mythology, and the Intermediate State," *Westminster Theological Journal* 48 (1986): 303.

[6]Bauckham, *Fate of the Dead*, 34.

[7]Bauckham, *Fate of the Dead*, 34, 86.

[8]An additional difficulty is that "the transition from one view to the other apparently took a long time." The latter view is around as early as the first century CE and the former is still common in 200 CE (Bauckham, *Fate of the Dead*, 86).

an opportunity to hear the gospel. This shift is significant with respect to Postmortem Opportunity, since the latter view is correlated with the belief that one's eternal destiny has been sealed at death in a way that the former view is not.

The crucial question at the heart of this dispute concerns the timing of the day of judgment. The difficulty with seeing some in Hades already experiencing the punishments of hell is that it seems to imply that God's judgment has already been rendered. But the consistent witness of Scripture is that the resurrection of the dead will occur during the end times and, after the resurrection, the dead will experience the day of judgment.[9] It is best, therefore, to see the descent of Christ as a preaching not to those who have already experienced the day of judgment, but to those who were awaiting it. As such, it is theologically important to draw a distinction between hell, the final resting place of those who reject relationship with God (Greek: *gehenna*), and the intermediate realm that serves as the "place of the dead."[10] More importantly, it is no part of my version of the theory of Postmortem Opportunity to claim that people can be saved out of hell, if "hell" is understood as the final destination of those who have rejected relationship with God and have experienced the day of judgment. If a Postmortem Opportunity is possible it is only possible at the moment of death, in the context of the intermediate state, or at judgment day itself, not after the day of judgment.

Grudem's objection to the descent. Wayne Grudem has argued that not only did Christ not preach the gospel to those who are dead, he didn't even descend into the realm of the dead at all. His primary piece of evidence for this claim is that while the phrase "He [Christ] descended into Hell [Hades]" (*descendit ad infernos*) is in the Apostles'

---

[9]On this, see the excellent work of N. T. Wright, *For All the Saints: Remembering the Christian Departed* (Harrisburg: Morehouse, 2003), 20-46.

[10]It is undoubtedly true that this distinction was neither clear, nor universally accepted in the early church. This is a substantial complicating factor in considering the early church perspective on postmortem repentance.

Creed, it was not present in the Old Roman Creed, which constitutes the earliest version of the creed. The creed was used as the profession of faith made by those being baptized, and while each church shaped their own baptismal confession, as the significance of the Church of Rome increased, other Christian churches were drawn to the basic structure of Rome's baptismal creed.[11] The phrase is not found in any of the early versions of the Apostles' Creed until Tyrannius Rufinus (345–410) includes it in 390 when speaking of the baptismal confession on his church in Aquileia. Wayne Grudem makes a big deal of the late appearance of *descendit ad infernos* in the Apostles' Creed, claiming that the phrase "never belonged there in the first place and that, on biblical and historical grounds, deserves to be removed [from the Creed]."[12] In addition, he argues that after Rufinus it is not found in any version of the Apostles' Creed until 650, and that Rufinus understood the phrase *descendit ad infernos* not as an affirmation of Christ's descent into Hades, but rather as merely a statement that Christ was "buried."[13] He concludes his argument as follows: "But this means that until A.D. 650 no version of the Creed included this phrase with the intention of saying that 'Christ descended into hell.'"[14]

Grudem's argument is surprisingly weak. First, Grudem's argument that, other than Rufinus, there is no mention of the descent in the creed ignores the avalanche of affirmations of Christ's descent into Hades in the early church. Even Augustine, who agrees with Grudem on the rejection of Postmortem Opportunity, accepted the reality of the *descensus*. He says, "It is established beyond question that the Lord, after he had been put to death in the flesh, 'descended into hell.'"[15] Augustine

[11]Jeffery L. Hamm, "*Descendit*: Delete or Declare? A Defense Against the Neo-deletionists," *Westminster Theological Journal* 78 (2016): 94n6.

[12]Wayne Grudem, "He Did Not Descend into Hell: A Plea for Following Scripture Instead of the Apostles' Creed," *Journal of the Evangelical Theological Society* 34, no. 1 (March 1991): 103.

[13]Grudem, "He Did Not Descend," 103-5.

[14]Grudem, "He Did Not Descend," 105.

[15]Augustine, Letter 164 (To Evodius) 2.3 (*NPNF* 1, 1:515).

supports this contention by quoting Psalm 16:10 and Acts 2:24.[16] Second, Grudem ignores the fact that Rufinus views the statement "Christ was buried" as implying Christ's descent. In the very passage Grudem cites, Rufinus writes, "But it should be known that the clause, 'He descended into Hell,' is not added in the Creed of the Roman Church, neither is it in that of the Oriental Churches. *It* [the descent] *seems to be implied, however, when it is said that He was buried*."[17] Third, and most inexplicably, Grudem fails to mention that Rufinus offers an unambiguous defense of the descent in his commentary on the Apostles' Creed. He quotes Philippians 2:10 and claims that Christ brought "into subjection to Himself the kingdoms of the nether world,"[18] and he closes his commentary with the claim that the purpose of the descent of Christ into Hades was "the delivery of souls from their captivity in the infernal regions."[19] Moreover, Rufinus responds to an imaginary interlocutor challenging him to provide scriptural evidence for the descent,[20] by providing exactly that: evidence for the descent of Christ into Hades from Psalm 16:10; 22:15, 30:3, 9; 69:2; Luke 7:20; and 1 Peter 3:19-20.[21] While it is undoubtedly true that Grudem would find Rufinus's scriptural argument wanting, it is equally true that these passages make it extremely

---

[16]For a helpful treatment of Augustine's views on the descensus, see Paul J. J. Van Geest, "Augustine's Certainty in Speaking About Hell and His Reserve in Explaining Christ's Descent into Hell," in *The Apostles' Creed: "He Descended into Hell,"* ed. Marcel Sarot and Archibald L. H. M. van Wieringen, Studies in Theology and Religion, vol. 24 (Leiden: Brill, 2018), 33-53.

[17]Rufinus, *Commentary on the Apostles'* Creed 18, in *Nicene and Post Nicene Fathers*, series 2, ed. Philip Schaff (Buffalo, NY: Christian Literature Publishing, 1887), 3:550. italics added. See also Hamm, "*Descendit*: Delete or Declare?," 95.

[18]Rufinus, *Commentary on the Apostles' Creed* 14 (*NPNF* 3:549). Hamm makes a similar point in "*Descendit*: Delete or Declare?," 96.

[19]Rufinus, *Commentary on the Apostles' Creed* 48 (*NPNF* 3:562).

[20]Rufinus says, "But in the love and zeal for the Divine Scriptures which possess you, you say to me, I doubt not, these things ought to be proved by more evident testimonies from the Divine Scriptures. For the more important the things are which are to be believed, so much the more do they need apt and undoubted witness. True. But we, as speaking to those who know the law, have left unnoticed, for the sake of brevity, a whole forest of testimonies. But if this also be required, let us cite a few out of many, knowing, as we do, that to those who are acquainted with the Scriptures, a very ample sea of testimonies lies open" (*Commentary on the Apostle's Creed* 18; *NPNF* 3:550).

[21]Rufinus, *Commentary on the Apostles' Creed* 28 (*NPNF* 3:553-54).

difficult (nigh impossible, really) to doubt that Rufinus accepted the doctrine of the descent into Hades. He was unequivocally *not* just using the phrase *descendit ad infernos* as shorthand for "Jesus was buried."

But what shall we make of the lack of inclusion of the phrase *descendit ad infernos* in the early versions of the Apostles' Creed? Even if Grudem's arguments are not successful, isn't there something to the fact that the early Christians did not include it as one of the essential beliefs in the baptismal creed? I don't think so. The absence of the *descensus* in early creeds does not necessarily mean it was not an important part of early Christian belief, for there are important beliefs (and even dogmas) of the church that are not present in the earliest creeds—creation *ex nihilo*, any theory of atonement or justification, and the doctrine of election are obvious examples, but there are many others. Moreover, with respect to the idea of Christ's preaching to and liberation of the departed, Frederic Huidekoper claims,

> The evidence of its general reception is far stronger than if it were a mere doctrine of the creed, for articles of the creed have in nearly every instance been opinions which were *not* generally received, and to which the stronger party therefore gave a place in their confessions of faith as a means of defining their position. On the essential features of the present doctrine the Catholics and the heretics were of one mind. It was a point too well settled to admit dispute."[22]

So why was it added to the Apostles' Creed when it was? The most reasonable explanation is that something shifted in the theological context that justified or rendered necessary its inclusion. Some might argue that, in the years leading up to Augustine, the tides had shifted against belief in the descent and its inclusion was an attempt to reinforce support for this beleaguered doctrine. There isn't much if any evidence for this claim, however, for even Augustine happily accepted the descent. Much more plausible is Huidekoper's suggestion that the

[22]Frederic Huidekoper, *The Belief in the First Three Centuries Concerning Christ's Mission to the Underworld*, 4th ed. (New York: James Miller, 1882 [1854]), 131; note omitted, emphasis original.

inclusion of "Christ descended into Hades" in the fourth century was precipitated by christological debates. He says, "The reason which, in the fourth century, caused the insertion into some of the public and individual confessions of faith of the clause 'He descended into the Underworld' appears to have been, that it was regarded as *implying* a tenet openly denied by the Apollonarians, namely, that Christ had a human soul."[23]

The preaching of Christ in Hades. While there were a host of questions about the nature of the underworld, that the early church believed that Christ descended to Hades is difficult to deny. As such, within the early church, the primary debate over the descent concerned the significance of the descent of Christ into Hades. At the very least, it was believed that "Christ's soul had to descend to Hades in order for him to fully share the human lot in death."[24] But very few patristic sources leave it at that. There are three additional motifs that were articulated to express the significance of the descent of Christ to Hades: (1) he defeated the spiritual powers that kept the dead captive in Hades, (2) he preached to the dead, and (3) some of those to which he preached in Hades were released from the underworld.[25] The defeat of the powers of death and the preaching to the departed are typically presented as the necessary precondition for the release of those held captive in the realm of the dead. Belief in the preaching of Christ to the dead in Hades was not merely sprinkled throughout the church, it was common. Huidekoper argues that "in the second and third centuries, every branch and division of Christians, so far as their records enable us to judge, believe that Christ preached to the departed; and this belief dates back to our earliest reliable sources of information in the former of these two centuries."[26] Moreover, this belief was not merely held in

[23]Huidekoper, *Belief in the First Three Centuries*, 131n9. E. H. Plumptre makes a similar point (*The Spirits in Prison and Other Studies on the Life After Death* [New York: Thomas Whitaker, 1894], 86).
[24]Bauckham, *Fate of the Dead*, 40.
[25]These three motifs are from Bauckham, *Fate of the Dead*, 40.
[26]Huidekoper, *Belief in the First Three Centuries*, 49.

conjunction with belief in the descent; for many the preaching was seen as the purpose of the descent.

It is neither possible nor desirable to discuss all of the early church texts that discuss the preaching of Christ in Hades. A representative list of texts from the first three centuries will have to suffice.[27]

Odes of Solomon 42:11-20. One of the earliest texts describing the preaching of Christ in Hades/Sheol is the Odes of Solomon. The Odes were compiled by a Jewish Christian (perhaps influenced by the Essenes), sometime around 100 CE, likely before the Bar Kokhba Rebellion (132–135 CE). The text describes the descent and the subsequent shattering of Sheol. Verse 14 says, "And I made a congregation of living among his dead; and I spoke with them by living lips; in order that my word may not be unprofitable." In response, "those who had died ran towards me; and they cried out and said, Son of God, have pity on us. . . . May we also be saved with You, because You are our Savior" (vv. 15, 18). Christ responds, "Then I heard their voice, and placed their faith in my heart. And I placed my name upon their head, because they are free and they are mine" (vv. 19-20).

Gospel of Peter 41–42. The Gospel of Peter is an apocryphal gospel[28] with gnostic or docetic undertones, dated by some in the first century, but more likely from the middle of the second century.[29] Unlike other gospels, the Gospel of Peter provides only an account of Christ's death and resurrection. When describing the resurrection, the text describes the following question being asked of Christ as he exited the tomb: "And

[27]A more complete list of sources can be found in Jared Wicks, SJ, "Christ's Saving Descent to the Dead: Early Witnesses from Ignatius of Antioch to Origen," *Pro Ecclesia* 17, no. 3 (2008): 281-309.

[28]On the authorship and purpose of the Gospel of Peter, see Joel Marcus, "The Gospel of Peter as a Jewish Christian Document," *New Testament Studies* 64 (2018): 473-94.

[29]The Gospel of Peter is dated "not much earlier than 150," according to M. R. James, *The Apocryphal New Testament* (Oxford: Clarendon, 1924), 90. More recently, J. K. Elliott claims, "Most scholars date its composition to the second half of the second century" (*The Apocryphal New Testament* [Oxford: Clarendon, 1993], 150). Whenever it is dated, it is clear that the Gospel of Peter is dependent on the canonical Gospels (see R. E. Brown, "The Gospel of Peter and Canonical Gospel Priority," *New Testament Studies* 33 [1987]: 321-43).

they heard a voice out of the heavens crying: 'Have you preached to those who sleep?,' and from the cross there was heard the answer, 'Yes.'"[30]

Epistle of the Apostles 27. The second-century work Epistle of the Apostles is misnamed. Although it begins as an epistle, the form quickly changes to that of an apocalypse.[31] It was written around 160, preserved by a Coptic translation, and was intended to refute the heretical teachings of the Gnostics Cerinthus and Simon Magus.[32] The relevant section of the text reads as follows:

> And on that account I have descended and have spoken with Abraham and Isaac and Jacob, to your fathers the prophets, and have brought them news that they might come from the rest which is below into heaven, and have given them the right hand of the baptism or life and forgiveness and pardon for all wickedness as to you, so from now on also to those who believe in me.[33]

Irenaeus (ca. 130–ca. 200), Against Heresies *4.27.2.* Irenaeus was undoubtedly one of the most significant second-century theologians. His best-known work, *Against Heresies,* was written around 180 and constitutes an influential refutation of the various Gnostic heresies that were common in the latter half of the second century. In the course of his discussion of the sin and repentance of Old Testament figures, Irenaeus says, "It was for this reason, too, that the Lord descended into the regions beneath the earth, preaching his advent there also, and [declaring] the remission of sins received by those who believe in him. Now all those believed in him who had hope towards Him, that is, those who proclaimed his advent, and submitted to his dispensations, the righteous men, the prophets, and the patriarchs, to whom he remitted sins in the same way as he has for us."[34]

---

[30]Elliott, *Apocryphal New Testament*, 156-57.
[31]Elliott, *Apocryphal New Testament*, 555.
[32]Elliott, *Apocryphal New Testament.* See also James, *Apocryphal New Testament*, 485.
[33]Elliott, *Apocryphal New Testament*, 573.
[34]*Irenaeus, Against Heresies* 4.27.2, in *Ante Nicene Fathers: Translations of the Writings of the Fathers Down to A.D. 325*, ed. Alexander Roberts and James Donaldson (1885-1887; repr., Grand Rapids, MI: Eerdmans, 1973), 1:499; hereafter *ANF*.

Hippolytus of Rome (170–235), Treatise on Christ and Anti-Christ *26.* Hippolytus was a presbyter in the church of Rome and the disciple of Irenaeus. He is widely regarded as one of the most important theologians in the pre-Constantinian era. His work *Treatise on Christ and Anti-Christ* was written around 202 and is a discussion of biblical prophecies. Commenting on Daniel 7:13-14, Hippolytus says,

> He [Christ] showed all power given by the Father to the Son, who is ordained Lord of things in heaven, and things on earth, and things under the earth, and Judge of all: of things in heaven, because He was born, the Word of God, before all (ages); and of things on earth, because He became man in the midst of men, to re-create our Adam through Himself; and of things under the earth, because He was also reckoned among the dead, preaching the Gospel to the souls of the saints, (and) by death overcoming death.[35]

Tertullian (160–220), A Treatise on the Soul *55.* Another giant in the early third century was Tertullian. Writing from Carthage, he waged an unremitting war on paganism and heresy in all its forms. *A Treatise on the Soul,* written around 210, stands among his dogmatic works. In the course of his discussion on death, Tertullian states, "With the same law of His being He fully complied, by remaining in Hades in the form and condition of a dead man; nor did He ascend into the heights of heaven before descending into the lower parts of the earth, that He might there make the patriarchs and prophets partakers of Himself."[36]

These texts are representative of the early church literature affirming the descent of Christ and his preaching to the souls on Hades. But this is not to imply that there are no differences of opinion on the preaching in Hades in the first two centuries. It raised a number of questions, on which there were a variety of answers given in the early church.[37] For

[35]Hippolytus of Rome, *Treatise on Christ and Anti-Christ* 26 (*ANF* 5:209).
[36]Tertullian, *A Treatise on the Soul* 55 (*ANF* 3:231).
[37]Loofs points out a number of additional questions raised by the descent and preaching, the two most pressing of which are the following: (1) How can we reconcile the descent of Christ into Hades with the witness of Lk 23:43 that Christ was in paradise after his death, and (2) if Christ did not ascend to heaven for forty days after his resurrection, where did the souls of those he liberated dwell during that period? It should be noted that these are not only difficulties for the

instance, who did the preaching in Hades? Was it Christ, as claimed by most, or only the disciples, as claimed by the Shepherd of Hermas?[38] Did John the Baptist descend to Hades prior to Christ, serving as the forerunner in death as he had in life, as Hippolytus and many others claim?[39] And was Christ followed by the disciples, as suggested by Clement of Alexandria?[40]

What scriptural evidence did early Christians point to with respect to Christ's descent and preaching in Hades? Many early Christians believed that Matthew 27:52-53 ("The bodies of many holy people who had died were raised to life. They came out of the tombs after Jesus' resurrection and went into the holy city and appeared to many people") *presupposes* a nation called the "harrowing of Hades"—the belief that Christ's descent involved the defeat of the powers of death. Origen, in fact, interprets Matthew 27:52 as a fulfillment of Psalm 68:18: "When you ascended on high, you took many captives," which is cited by Paul in Ephesians 4:6. Another text cited by early Christians is Hosea 13:14:

> Shall I ransom them from the power of Sheol?
> Shall I redeem them from death?
> Death, where are your thorns?
> Sheol, where is your sting? (NASB)

Moreover, early Christians saw a reference to the descent and preaching in Hades in the passages that speak of Christ's lordship over all three

---

defender of Postmortem Opportunity. One possible answer to these questions was suggested by the Gospel of Nicodemus—namely, that Christ brought those to whom he preached to paradise. See Friedrich Loofs, "Descent into Hades (Christ's)," in *Encyclopedia of Religion and Ethics*, ed. James Hastings, vol. 4 (New York: Charles Scribner's Sons, 1911), 655.

[38]The Shepherd of Hermas, Similitude 9.16 (93.5): "When these apostles and teachers who preached the name of the Son of God fell asleep in the power and faith of the Son of God, they preached also to those who had previously fallen asleep, and they themselves gave them the seal of the preaching" (Michael W. Holmes, *The Apostolic Fathers*, 3rd ed. [Grand Rapids, MI: Baker, 2007], 653).

[39]"He [John the Baptist] also first preached to those in Hades, becoming a forerunner there when he was put to death by Herod, that there too he might intimate that the Saviour would descend to ransom the souls of the saints from the hand of death" (Hippolytus, *Treatise on Christ and Anti-Christ* 45 [*ANF* 5:213]).

[40]*Stromata* 6.6 (*ANF* 2:491).

layers of ancient cosmology: Colossians 1:23: "This is the gospel that you heard and that has been proclaimed *to every creature under heaven*," and Philippians 2:10: "that at the name of Jesus every knee should bow, in heaven and on earth *and under the earth*." And, finally, Matthew 13:17 was referred to in this context—"many prophets and righteous people longed to see what you see but did not see it, and to hear what you hear but did not hear it."

Another possible, albeit substantially more contentious scriptural justification for the descent and preaching of Christ lies in the complex textual history of the prophets. In *Dialogue with Trypho*, Justin Martyr accused the Jews of mutilating a prophecy of Jeremiah,[41] which according to him, says, "The Lord God remembered his dead people of Israel who lay in the graves; and he descended to preach to them his own salvation."[42] In *Against Heresies*, Irenaeus quotes the very same passage five times,[43] but it is unclear whether he is drawing on Justin's citation or if he has his own manuscript source. Referred to as the "Jeremiah-logion" by scholars, the exact source of this passage is unknown, but the text of the prophets possessed by Justin Martyr was not identical to either the LXX or Masoretic text. It can be speculated that Justin's citation draws on a non-LXX testimony source in a time before the text of Jeremiah had been stabilized.[44] Moreover, a fascinating feature of this text is its similarity to 1 Peter 4:6.[45]

---

[41]This was a common complaint by Justin. See Eric Francis Osborn, *Justin Martyr* (Tübingen: Mohr Siebeck, 1973), 110-12.

[42]Justin Martyr, *Dialogue with Trypho* 72 (*ANF* 1:235). See also E. H. Plumptre, *The Spirits in Prison and Other Studies on the Life After Death* (New York: Thomas Whitaker, 1894), 83.

[43]Irenaeus attributes the citation once to Isaiah (3.20.4), once to Jeremiah (4.22.1), once to "others" (4.33.12), and once to "the prophet" (5.31.1). One other time he leaves it unattributed (4.33.1).

[44]Oscar Skarsaune suggests this possibility. See his *The Proof from Prophecy: A Study in Justin Martyr's Proof-Text Tradition*, Supplements to Novum Testamentum, vol. 56 (Leiden: E. J. Brill, 1987), 42. In addition, Osborn suggests that Justin's quotations bear a striking affinity to a first century scroll found in 1952, which is a Palestinian revision of the LXX from a Hebrew text. See his *Justin Martyr*, 112.

[45]Hence Dalton: "It must be admitted that there is a considerable similarity between 4:6a and the Jeremiah logion" (William J. Dalton, *Christ's Proclamation to the Spirits*, Analecta Biblica, vol. 23, 2nd rev. ed. [Rome: Pontifical Biblical Institute, 1989 {1965}], 51).

One might also expect that early Christians would invoke the putative scriptural references to Christ's descent into Hades in Ephesians 4:8-9, 1 Peter 3:19-20, and 1 Peter 4:6 as justification for their belief in Christ's work in Hades. Surprisingly, references to these texts in connection with the descent are absent in the first two centuries of the early church, and references to Ephesians 4 and 1 Peter 4 in connection with the descent are relatively rare.[46] But the connection between 1 Peter 3:19 and the descent and preaching of Christ in Hades was fairly common in the Alexandrian school by the late second and early third century. Chad Pierce says, "It appears that a majority of the Alexandrian view of 1 Pet was that Christ, during the *triduum mortis*, proclaimed a message of salvation of human souls imprisoned in the underworld."[47] Clement of Alexandria,[48] Origen,[49] Tyrannius Rufinus,[50] and Cyril of Alexandria[51] all refer to 1 Peter 3:19 in connection with the descent and preaching to those in Hades. In addition, Athanasius claims that while Jesus' body was in the grave, the Word proclaimed the gospel to the spirits in prison.[52] Therefore, "while the early church leaders might not have linked these verses [1 Pet 3:19-20] with the *descensus*, this view of Christ's proclamation to the spirits was widely held from the time of Clement to Augustine."[53]

The soteriological significance of the descent and preaching. The objection to the foregoing evidence is that it does not describe anything of soteriological significance; all that Christ's descent provided to the Old Testament patriarchs was a change in postmortem location, a

[46]Cyprian quotes 1 Peter 4:6 in reference to the idea that all who are saved must be saved through Jesus Christ (*Testimony Against the Jews* 2.27 [*ANF* 5:526]).

[47]Chad Pierce, "Spirits and the Proclamation of Christ: 1 Peter 3:18-22 in Its Tradition-Historical and Literary Context" (PhD diss., Durham University, 2009), 4.

[48]*Stromata* 6.6 (*ANF* 2:490).

[49]*De Principiis* 2.5 (*ANF* 4:279); *Against Celsus* 2:43 (*ANF* 4:448).

[50]*Commentary on the Apostle's Creed* 28 (*NPNF* 3:554).

[51]*Commentary on John* 11.2, in *Ancient Christian Texts: Commentary on John: Cyril of Alexandria*, vol. 2, trans., David R. Maxwell, ed., Joel C. Elowsky (Downers Grove, IL: IVP Academic, 2015), 260-61.

[52]Athanasius, *Letter 59: Ad Epictetum* 5 (*NPNF* 4:572).

[53]Pierce, "Spirits and the Proclamation of Christ," 4.

transfer from Hades to paradise. However, there are some good reasons to think that this is false and that Christ's descent and preaching was soteriologically significant. To be clear, I am not defining "soteriological significance" in terms of a full-fledged theory of Postmortem Opportunity. Rather, when I say that the early church saw the descent and preaching as soteriologically significant I am claiming that it provided *something* that was necessary to the salvation of the recipients of the preaching, even if there is a wide range of opinion on what that something was. They did not just receive an upgrade in eschatological abode.[54]

The "no soteriological significance" view of the descent and preaching doesn't fit very well with how the early church described the *descensus*. The fact is that, as Bauckham says, "Christians from a very early date saw in the descent an event of soteriological significance for the righteous dead of the period before Christ, whose souls were in Hades."[55] The pattern of preaching in Hades parallels the preaching on earth: John the Baptist is a forerunner (Hippolytus) and the apostles follow after (Clement of Alexandria). Christ is consistently described as "preaching" to the souls in the underworld, and Hippolytus (and others) say that Christ preached "the gospel." Moreover, the result of Christ's preaching is "salvation," "the remission of sins," "salvation from all evil," and so on. Those who would resist the soteriological implications of the descent and preaching should explain why those words were used. While Irenaeus was firm on seeing Christ's preaching in Hades as being given only to the Old Testament fathers, he clearly saw the descent and preaching as soteriologically relevant since he repeatedly quotes the Jeremiah-logion, which affirms that Christ "descended to them to make known to them His salvation, that they might be saved."[56] Finally, Shepherd of Hermas offers a variation on the descent and preaching by claiming that it was the "apostles and teachers" who descended and

---

[54]One of the difficulties to be faced here is the lack of clarity in the early church.

[55]Bauckham, *Fate of the Dead*, 40.

[56]Irenaeus, *Against Heresies* 4.22.1 (*ANF* 1:493-94).

preached the gospel, but the text is very clear that there was a postmortem event of soteriological significance for even the righteous dead, namely baptism: "They [the apostles and teachers] preached also to those who had previously fallen asleep, and they themselves gave them the seal of the preaching. . . . So they [Old Testament fathers] were made alive through them [the apostles and teachers] and came to full knowledge of the name of the Son of God. . . . They [the Old Testament fathers] fell asleep in righteousness and in great purity, only they did not have this seal."[57]

Ultimately, from an orthodox Christian perspective, one is hard-pressed to say that the preaching of the gospel of Jesus Christ is irrelevant to the salvation of anyone who ever lived. There are some who want to see the salvation of Old Testament figures as completely separate from the salvation of people through the death and resurrection, but those arguments are difficult to make. It is best to see the Old Testament saints as people who had responded to the grace they had already been given and were given a proclamation of the full revelation of God's grace in Christ Jesus. And that proclamation is certainly soteriologically significant, even if it is preached to those who are dead.

EARLY CHURCH BELIEF IN POSTMORTEM REPENTANCE

> Thesis 2: *Postmortem repentance was deemed to be possible by important segments of the early church.*

The previous thesis made a more minimal point—that early Christians saw soteriological relevance in the descent—with reference to a broad range of early Christian sources. The second thesis makes a more aggressive point—that postmortem repentance was deemed to be possible—with respect to a narrower, but still important range of early Christian sources. In calling these sources "important," I am claiming that these texts should not and cannot be dismissed as fringe, heterodox,

[57]Shepherd of Hermas, Similitude 9.16 (93.5, 7); Holmes, *Apostolic Fathers*, 653.

or otherwise irrelevant. To defend this thesis, I will point to two lines of evidence: the practice of offering prayers for the dead and the belief that during his descent to Hades, Christ preached not only to the Old Testament saints, but also to those who had no prior response to God's grace.[58]

Prayers for the dead in the early church. In the previous chapter, I mentioned a pair of examples of praying for the dead, one from Second Temple Judaism and the other from the New Testament—Judas Maccabeus's prayer for fallen soldiers in 2 Maccabees 12:38-45 and Paul's prayer for Onesiphorus in 2 Timothy 1:16-18. While the practice of praying for the dead is largely absent among Protestants, it is much more common in other strands of the Christian faith. Moreover, it is a theme that is found in numerous sources in the early church. The following are some representative examples.[59]

Testament of Abraham. Admittedly, the 2 Maccabees text is an outlier among Second Temple Judaism; the majority of texts from this period do not countenance postmortem repentance. The other outlier is a recension of the Testament of Abraham, dated to approximately 100 CE.[60]

---

[58]A third line of evidence has also received attention from some: the practice of baptism for the dead, alluded to opaquely by Paul in 1 Cor. 15:29. It is probable that there was some sort of practice of vicarious baptism for the dead, perhaps paralleling the Roman custom of "providing for dead and praying for the them during the Parentales festival" (Jeffrey A. Trumbower, *Rescue for the Dead: The Posthumous Salvation of Non-Christians in Early Christianity* [New York: Oxford University Press, 2001], 38; see also 16-17), but it is likely that the persons being baptized for were already believers but had died before being baptized. The practice of baptism for the dead was only to "set a posthumous seal onto a faith that was already present in this life" (36). This is not irrelevant to the theory of Postmortem Opportunity, for it still suggests the belief that a person's spiritual direction can be altered after death, but it doesn't speak to the question of the early church's stance on postmortem repentance, which is the primary focus of this chapter. There are a number of Mormon theologians who advance the early church practice of baptism for the dead as evidence for Postmortem Opportunity, which makes sense given that the Church of Latter Day Saints still practices vicarious baptism. See David L. Paulsen and Brock M. Mason, "Baptism for the Dead in Early Christianity," *Journal for the Book of Mormon and Other Restoration Scripture* 19, no. 2 (2010): 22-49.

[59]There are other patristic passages that contain the theme of God having mercy on sinners at the request of the righteous, most notably, Sibylline Oracles 2:330-338, Coptic Apocalypse of Elijah 5:27-29, and Epistle of the Apostles 40. Bauckham argues that these passages are dependent on Apocalypse of Peter, which I discuss below. See his *Fate of the Dead*, 147-48, 156.

[60]Trumbower, *Rescue for the Dead*, 29.

In 14:1-5 and 10-15, Abraham is depicted as asking God to show mercy on a pair of dead individuals, one whose sins are exactly balanced by Abraham's righteous deeds and another whom Abraham had mistakenly cursed in this life.[61] Of this text, E. P. Sanders says, "This may be the earliest instance in Jewish sources in which intercessory prayer is considered effective after the death of the person on whose behalf it is offered."[62]

Thecla's prayer for Falconilla. The Acts of Paul and Thecla is a mid-second century work by an unknown author[63] that describes the ordeal of one of Paul's converts, a virgin named Thecla. Thecla was unjustly condemned to the lions for rejecting the advances of a powerful man in Antioch, but was befriended by a rich woman named Tryphaena whose daughter had recently died. Tryphaena's dead daughter, Falconilla, had told Tryphaena in a dream that Thecla would come into her house and, because of her prayers that she would be "transferred to the place of the righteous."[64] When Tryphaena asked Thecla to pray for Falconilla, Thecla did so. The relevant portion of the text of Acts of Paul and Thecla reads as follows: "So Thecla, without delay, raised her voice and said, 'O my God, the Son of the Most High, who is in heaven, grant her according to her wish, that her daughter Falconilla might live for ever.'"[65] After Thecla was miraculously preserved from the beasts, Tryphaena and all her female slaves become converts and Tryphaena exclaims: "Now I know that my daughter [Falconilla] lives."[66]

---

[61]Trumbower, *Rescue for the Dead*, 29.

[62]Sanders's comment assumes a distinction between the sacrificial atonement offered by Judas Maccabeus and the prayer offered by Abraham. See E. P. Sanders, "The Testament of Abraham," in *Old Testament Pseudepigrapha*, ed. J. H. Charlesworth, vol. 1 (New York: Doubleday, 1983), 891n14b.

[63]Although Tertullian describes the author as a presbyter from Asia (*On Baptism* 17.5; *ANF* 3:677).

[64]Acts of Paul and Thecla 28; Elliott, *Apocryphal New Testament*, 369; Trumbower, *Rescue for the Dead*, 61.

[65]Acts of Paul and Thecla 29; Elliott, *Apocryphal New Testament*, 370; Trumbower, *Rescue for the Dead*, 61.

[66]Acts of Paul and Thecla 39; Elliott, *Apocryphal New Testament*, 371; Trumbower, *Rescue for the Dead*, 61.

Perpetua's prayer for Dinocrates. The well-known Martyrdom of Perpetua and Felicitas relates the story of the martyrdom of a young woman from North Africa named Perpetua, probably at the games held in the Emperor Geta's honor in Carthage on March 7, 203 CE.[67] Narrated in the first person, Perpetua records a number of visions, including two of her younger brother, Dinocrates, who died some years earlier. In her first vision, her brother was in agony, dirty, thirsty, and still possessed the wounds he had on his deathbed. After her vision, Perpetua is moved to pray for Dinocrates, saying, "I was confident I could help him in his trouble. . . . And I prayed for my brother day and night with tears and sighs that this favor might be granted me."[68] Before her martyrdom, Perpetua had another vision of Dinocrates in which his wounds were healed and he was clean, well-dressed, refreshed, drinking water, and playing happily. As Perpetua awoke from her vision, she realized that Dinocrates "had been delivered from his penalty."[69]

Apocalypse of Zephaniah. The Apocalypse of Zephaniah is a pseudepigraphon of Jewish origin (but possibly reworked or redacted by Christian scribes) that exists in two fragments (and one probable citation by Clement of Alexandria).[70] Plausibly dated between 100 BCE and 70 CE,[71] the narrative consists of Zephaniah being taken to see the fate of souls after death. Upon seeing the torments of unbelievers, Zephaniah prays for mercy for them (2:8-9) and is joined by "multitudes," including Abraham, Isaac, and Jacob, who daily offer prayers of intercession "on behalf of these who are in all these torments" (11:1-6).[72]

Apocalypse of Peter. The final, and most important, witness to the patristic idea of prayers for the dead comes from the second-century Apocalypse of Peter. Richard Bauckham argues that the Apocalypse

---

67 Trumbower, *Rescue for the Dead*, 78.

68 Passion of Perpetua and Felicitas 7; in Trumbower, *Rescue for the Dead*, 81.

69 Passion of Perpetua and Felicitas 8; trans. Trumbower, *Rescue for the Dead*, 81.

70 Bauckham, *Fate of the Dead*, 36; O. S. Wintermute, "The Apocalypse of Zephaniah," in Charlesworth, *Old Testament Pseudepigrapha*, 1:500-501.

71 Wintermute, "Apocalypse of Zephaniah," 501.

72 Wintermute, "Apocalypse of Zephaniah," 515.

derives from "Palestinian Jewish Christianity during the Bar Kokhba war of 132-135 CE."[73] Moreover, not only was it "a very popular work in the church as a whole, from the second to the fourth centuries" and "widely read in east and west,"[74] it was treated in some circles as Scripture, and "along with *Shepherd of Hermas*, it was probably the work which came the closest to being included in the canon of the New Testament while being eventually excluded."[75] The text of the Apocalypse of Peter includes a vision in which Peter is shown the judgment of sinners on the last day (ch. 3). After a lengthy description of the punishments due to each of twenty-one different types of sinners (chs. 7–12), the sinners cry for mercy (13:1-2), are informed by Tartarouchos, the angel in charge of hell, that it is too late for repentance (13:3), and the damned acknowledge that their punishment is just (13:4). Two versions of chapter 14 survive, the Ethiopic and the Greek (from the Rainer Fragment, dated from the third or fourth century[76]). Both Buchholz[77] and James[78] argue that the Greek text is earlier and that the Ethiopic text reflects a deliberate attempt to erase any suggestion of postmortem salvation.[79] In the Greek (Rainer fragment) the elect intercede for the damned and Christ grants their prayers, and those for

[73]Richard Bauckham, *Fate of the Dead*, 160. On authorship and date, see also Jan N. Bremmer, "Christian Hell: From the Apocalypse of Peter to the Apocalypse of Paul," *Numen* 56, nos. 2–3 (2009): 300-301.

[74]Bauckham, *Fate of the Dead*, 160-161. See also D. D. Buchholz, *Your Eyes Will Be Opened: A Study of the Greek (Ethiopic) Apocalypse of Peter*, SBLDS 97 (Atlanta: Scholar's Press, 1988), 20-80.

[75]Bauckham, *Fate of the Dead*, 161.

[76]Trumbower, *Rescue for the Dead*, 50.

[77]Buchholz, *Your Eyes Will Be Opened*, 344-51.

[78]M. R. James, "Rainer Fragment of the *Apocalypse of Peter*," *Journal of Theological Studies* 32 (1931): 270-79.

[79]Trumbower, *Rescue for the Dead*, 50. An additional argument for the reliability of the message in the Rainer fragment comes from Augustine. In *City of God*, he considers seven different positions on the scope of salvation, ranging from Origen's extremely optimistic Universalism to the view that only those Christians who perform acts of mercy can be saved. The third view to which he responds refers to a position virtually identical to that found in the Apocalypse of Peter 14:1, and the way in which he speaks of these Christians—"our own compassionate ones"—makes it clear that he is not referring to a merely possible position, but a theological stance argued by people in the early church (*City of God* 21.18, trans. Henry Bettenson [New York: Penguin, 1972], 996-98). Bauckham makes this argument in *Fate of the Dead*, 155.

whom the elect pray are baptized in the Acherusian lake and share the destiny of the elect (14:1).[80]

Among the many interesting questions raised by this text is the fact that the angel Tartarouchos rebukes the sinners who plead for mercy in a manner reminiscent of 2 Clement 8:3, saying, "Now you repent, when there is no time for repentance, and life is past" (13:5). But this statement of the impossibility of postmortem repentance is followed just a few verses later with Christ offering salvation to those for whom the elect have interceded. The juxtaposition of these two, seemingly opposite messages—the disapproval of postmortem repentance and the actuality of postmortem grace—is crucially important. Contrary to appearances, these messages are not contradictory. The warning about the impossibility of postmortem repentance is designed to prevent any sort of a wait-and-see approach on the part of sinners, and the ultimate offering of grace is a powerful statement of the freedom of God to offer grace. Bauckham articulates this idea as follows: only after it is acknowledged that "hell is required by God's justice," can "can mercy be allowed a voice which does not detract from justice."[81]

THE PREACHING TO THE UNCONVERTED IN HADES

When discussing the theory of Postmortem Opportunity, the most obvious piece of evidence is the claim that in his descent to Hades, Christ preached the gospel not only to the righteous dead, but to all the dead. The relevance of this claim to Postmortem Opportunity should be obvious. If this is true, there exists a clear example of the claim that the gospel is preached to those who are dead and in need of salvation. Even more importantly, since the vast majority of denizens of Hades were people who had no interaction with God's revelation through the nation of Israel, the

[80]Bauckham, *Fate of the Dead*, 66-167. The text reads as follows: "Then I will grant to my called and elect ones whomsoever they request from me, out of the punishment. And I will give them [i.e. those for whom the elect pray] a fine baptism in salvation from the Acherusian lake (which is, they say, in the Elysian field), a portion of righteousness with my holy ones," 145.

[81]Bauckham, *Fate of the Dead*, 233. See also 147n50.

descent to Hades to preach to all the dead constitutes an example of the provision of a Postmortem Opportunity to the unevangelized.

Clement of Alexandria (150–ca 215), Stromata *6.6.* The earliest and strongest voice making this claim is Clement of Alexandria. Clement was born in Athens of pagan parentage and traveled to Athens in search of the best Christian teaching available. He became the head of the catechetical school at Alexandria. St. Jerome pronounced him the most learned of all the ancients and Eusebius testified to his theological attainments, and applauded him as an "incomparable master of Christian philosophy."[82] In the early years of the third century, Clement authored the *Stromata*, a collection of reflections "in opposition to Gnosticism, to furnish the materials for the construction of a true gnosis, a Christian philosophy, on the basis of faith, and to lead on to this higher knowledge."[83] Starting in 6.6, Clement considers the knowledge of God by the Greeks, and in chapter 6 he discusses the preaching of the gospel in Hades to the Jews and the Gentiles.

> If, then, the Lord descended to Hades for no other end but to preach the Gospel, as He did descend; it was either to preach the Gospel to all or to the Hebrews only. If, accordingly, to all, then all who believe shall be saved, although they may be of the Gentiles, on making their profession there. . . . If, then, He preached only to the Jews, who wanted the knowledge and faith of the Saviour, it is plain that, since God is no respecter of persons, the apostles also, as here, so there preached the Gospel to those of the heathen who were ready for conversion. . . . What then? Did not the same dispensation obtain in Hades, so that even there, all the souls, on hearing the proclamation, might either exhibit repentance, or confess that their punishment was just, because they believed not?[84]

Clement's argument here is clear: since God obviously desired the salvation of the Gentiles in this life, then Christ either preached the gospel to them as well as the Jews in Hades or, as in this life, he left that task to

---

[82]A. Cleveland Coxe, "Introductory Note to Clement of Alexandria," *ANF* 2:166.
[83]A. Cleveland Coxe, "Introductory Note to Clement of Alexandria," *ANF* 2:168.
[84]Clement, *Stromateis* 6.6 (*ANF* 2:491).

his apostles to do so. Even more striking is the rationale he offers for this claim.

> And it were the exercise of no ordinary arbitrariness, for those who had departed before the advent of the Lord (not having the Gospel preached to them, and having afforded no ground from themselves, in consequence of believing or not) to obtain either salvation or punishment. For it is not right that these should be condemned without trial, and that those alone who lived after the advent should have the advantage of the divine righteousness. . . . If, then, He preached the Gospel to those in the flesh that they might not be condemned unjustly, how is it conceivable that He did not for the same cause preach the Gospel to those who had departed this life before His advent?[85]

Here, more than any other early Christian figure, Clement is pressing the question that lies at the heart of the question of the destiny of the unevangelized. And he is clearly advancing the possibility of Christ's provision of a Postmortem Opportunity to answer that challenge.

Origen (185–255), Against Celsus *2:43.* Origen was Clement's most famous disciple and is well-known for his far-reaching version of Universalism, in which he envisioned the salvation of even Satan. He is also undoubtedly early Christianity's most prolific author. *Against Celsus* is Origen's best-known apologetic work and is a response to a polemic against Christianity by a learned Platonist. In 2.43, in response to Celsus's sarcastic objection, "You will not, I suppose, say of him, that, after failing to gain over those who were in this world, he went to Hades to gain over those who were there," Origen responds that Christ not only converted many in this life, but that "when He became a soul, without the covering of the body, He dwelt among those souls which were without bodily covering, converting such of them as were willing to Himself, or those whom He saw, for reasons known to Him alone, to be better adapted to such a course." The preaching in Hades envisioned by Origen is clearly given to all, but interestingly Origen's Universalism is

[85]Clement, *Stromateis* 6.6 (*ANF* 2:491, 492).

muted in this passage as salvation is given only to those who were "willing" and those that Christ saw "to be better adapted to such a course."

Hippolytus, Easter Homily. An extremely interesting text comes from Hippolytus. As indicated above, Hippolytus clearly accepted the preaching of Christ in Hades to the Old Testament saints. However, in his Easter Homily (from a preserved Syriac fragment[86]) he extends the scope of that preaching to the unconverted. After describing the "holy souls" awaiting a visit from Christ in Hades, Hippolytus claims, "For it behooved him to go and preach *also* to those who were in Hell [Sheol], namely those who have once been disobedient."[87] The allusion to 1 Peter 3:19-20 ("he went and made proclamation to the imprisoned spirits—to those who were disobedient long ago") here should be impossible to miss. This text provides an example of a broader preaching in Hades outside the school of Alexandria and it is the first Western text to refer to 1 Peter 3:19-20 in connection with the descent.[88]

Cyril of Alexandria, Commentary on John *11.2.* Cyril became bishop of Alexandria in 412 and was undoubtedly the worst of enemies to those he deemed to be heretics, especially Nestorius. His *Commentary on John* is impressive and addresses many of the theological issues of the day. As a part of a discussion of Jesus' words to his disciples just prior to his ascension, Cyril includes this comment on the descent of Christ to Hades: "For on the third day He revived, having preached unto the spirits in prison. The proof of His love towards mankind was hereby rendered most complete by His giving salvation, I say, not merely to the quick, but also by His preaching remission of sins to those who were already dead, and who sat in darkness in the depths of the abyss

[86]For an extended discussion of Hippolytus's Easter Homily, see Bo Reicke, *The Disobedient Spirits and Christian Baptism: A Study of 1 Peter III. 19 and Its Context*, ASNU 13 (Copenhagen: Ejnar Munksgaard, 1946), 23-27.

[87]Italics mine. Riecke's translation (*Disobedient Spirits*, 25). Even Dalton, who is no fan of the idea of postmortem repentance, argues (pace Riecke) that Hippolytus has in mind the preaching to the unconverted in Hades. See *Christ's Proclamation to the Spirits*, 37.

[88]Trumbower also lists Hilary of Poitiers and Ambrosiaster as western figures who believed in a general offer of salvation to the dead during Christ's descent (*Rescue for the Dead*, 128).

according to the Scripture."[89] Not only does this text include a clear reference to 1 Peter 3:19-20, Cyril makes explicit reference to God's love as driving his universal salvific will.

Assessing the evidence for postmortem repentance. How should we assess the fact that some members of the early church offered prayers to affect the salvific status of the dead? Some will want to argue that while members of the early church prayed for those who had died, they did not think that their prayers affected the dead person's salvific status; the best that could be hoped for was an improvement in one's postmortem setting. But this argument just doesn't fit with the evidence. That claim might be made of Dinocrates, but not of Falconilla and certainly not of those being prayed for in the Apocalypse of Peter. At this point, the Postmortem Opportunity skeptic may argue that we have no good reason to believe that the texts that have been alluded to in this section have any theological authority whatsoever and, moreover, that we don't have reason to believe that these texts are correct in teaching that prayers can affect the salvific status of the dead. Those points are granted. But the point of offering these stories is not to argue that Christians *actually have* the intrinsic power to affect the salvific status of the dead through their prayers, for my version of Postmortem Opportunity makes no such claim. Rather, I argue that these accounts of prayers for the dead reflect a mindset among some in the early church that salvific destiny was not sealed at death and that God's mercy could extend beyond the grave. And perhaps one who objects to the theory of Postmortem Opportunity would grant that point but simply claim that these figures in the early church were confused. However, this admission is more evidentially significant than it may seem on the surface, for many of the biblical arguments against Postmortem Opportunity hinge on the assumption that it was universally assumed that death was the end of salvific opportunity. Once it is admitted that

[89]Cyril of Alexandria, *Commentary on John* 11.2.

postmortem repentance was considered possible by some in the apostolic age, the hand-waving dismissal of the postmortem import of 1 Peter 3:18-20 and 1 Peter 4:6 on the grounds that "everybody believed that death was the end of salvific opportunity" no longer seems persuasive. Something similar may be said of the fact that some figures in the early church believed in the preaching to the unconverted in Hades. While their testimony is not decisive evidence that the gospel was actually preached to all the souls in Hades, the witness of those like Clement, Origen, and Hippolytus provides good reason to believe that significant segments of the early church did not believe that death was the end of salvific opportunity.

But even if it was true that the whole of the early church accepted the possibility of postmortem repentance (which, of course, I have not claimed), would that suggest that the theory of Postmortem Opportunity is true? Not necessarily; even if one accepted that Jesus Christ descended into Hades and preached the gospel to all of the dead, that does not mean that the same opportunity will be given to the unevangelized on judgment day. Recall Millard Erickson's argument to this effect in the previous chapter. He argued that even if Christ preaches to the dead in Hades "that only takes care of those few people. It says nothing about others who have lived since or will live in the future."[90] As a point of logic, Erickson's claim is correct. Nonetheless, I believe that this objection misses the theological force of the argument for Postmortem Opportunity. The argument is not simply that Jesus happened to descend into Hades to preach to those held in bondage there, it is that his love compelled him to do so. If the possibility of postmortem repentance is granted, then it is exceedingly difficult to see why a God who desires the salvation of all people would not provide a Postmortem Opportunity to those who did not receive a genuine opportunity in this life. As Clark Pinnock says, from the

[90]Millard Erickson, *How Shall They Be Saved? The Destiny of Those Who Do Not Hear of Jesus* (Grand Rapids, MI: Baker, 1996), 173.

standpoint of salvific opportunity, "a person who is informationally pre-messianic, whether living in ancient or modern times, is in exactly the same spiritual situation."[91] Moreover, Erickson does not seem to fully appreciate the evidential implications for the theory of Postmortem Opportunity of granting the preaching of the gospel in Hades. As he himself acknowledges, if one grants that some were given a Postmortem Opportunity, the claim that Scripture teaches that death is the end of salvific opportunity is, itself, dead. And once one grants that death is not the end of salvific opportunity, the question of the destiny of the unevangelized starts to look very different. It is no longer possible to dismiss the descent passages on the grounds that Scripture envisions no postmortem possibilities for salvation. And those who believe both that God desires the salvation of all people and that some people never have an opportunity to hear the gospel in this life are now given textual evidence for a new and powerful way of answering this perennial question.

FACTORS INFLUENCING THE LOSS OF POSTMORTEM HOPE

> Thesis 3: *The reasons the church rejected the possibility of postmortem conversion can be explained and, for the most part, do not constitute objections to my version of Postmortem Opportunity.*

If segments of the early church believed in postmortem repentance, why has the doctrine been reduced to its current state? Before we consider this question, it is crucial to note that this question is one that can only be asked by those in standing the shadow of the Western church, for it is arguable that the Eastern Orthodox church *never did* lose sight of postmortem hope. Speaking of the doctrine of the Eastern Orthodox church, Archbishop Alfeyev says, "The belief in Christ's descent into Hades and his preaching to the dead is not a

[91]Clark Pinnock, *A Wideness in God's Mercy: The Finality of Jesus Christ in a World of Religions* (Grand Rapids, MI: Zondervan, 1992), 161.

theologoumenon [personal opinion], but belongs to general church doctrine. The belief is based on the New Testament, works of the church fathers, and liturgical texts. It is, therefore, as significant for today's Orthodox Church as it was for the Christian church of early centuries."[92] So then our question, more properly stated is, Why was postmortem hope lost in the Western Church?

The direct influence of Augustine. Augustine represents a watershed on this question in church history, as he does on a number of other matters. His opposition to Postmortem Opportunity has cast a long shadow on the Christian church. Augustine's influence on medieval theology and exegesis is illustrated by the common medieval saying: "If one had Augustine on his side, it was sufficient" (*Si Augustinus adest, sufficit ipse tibi*).[93] But even within his own writings, there is evidence of evolution and a lack of certainty.[94] The early Augustine does not have much to say about Postmortem Opportunity, but in *Commentary on the Sermon on the Mount* (393) he tentatively allows the possibility that one might secure a postmortem release from punishment.[95] However, as the Pelagian controversy escalates, his previous tentativeness wanes.[96] This perspective is reflected in his well-known letter to Evodius in which he argues that the two Petrine passages (1 Pet 3:19-20 and 4:6) have nothing to do whatsoever with the descent of Christ into Hades.[97] He dismisses 1 Peter 3:19-20 as the preaching of the preincarnate Christ to those in Noah's time and 1 Peter 4:6 as a preaching of the gospel to those who were spiritually dead.[98] Not only did many medieval theologians (including Thomas Aquinas) and most of the reformers follow Augustine's interpretation

---

[92]Alfeyev, *Christ the Conqueror of Hell*, 208; italics original. See also his comments on 213-18.

[93]David Schley, "Introductory Essay: St. Augustin as an Exegete," *NPNF* 1, 6:vii.

[94]Trumbower has a very helpful discussion of the development of Augustine's thought on postmortem repentance, *Rescue for the Dead*, 128-33.

[95]Augustine, *Commentary on the Sermon on the Mount* 1.11.30 (*NPNF* 6:40-41).

[96]Trumbower, *Rescue for the Dead*, 129-130.

[97]Augustine, Letter 164 (To Evodius) (*NPNF* 1, 1:515-21).

[98]Loofs, "Descent into Hades (Christ's)," 655.

of these passages,[99] Augustine's interpretation of the descent passage continues to be influential to this day.

In addition, Augustine provides a powerful statement of two arguments that have become central to the rejection of Postmortem Opportunity. First, he argues that Postmortem Opportunity is an insuperable barrier to the motivation to preach the gospel in this life. If one accepts Postmortem Opportunity, he says, "forasmuch as all men shall certainly die, and ought to come to hell wholly free from the guilt of having despised the gospel, since otherwise it can be of no use to them to believe it when they come there, the gospel ought not to be preached on earth—a sentiment not less foolish than profane."[100] Second, Augustine argued that if one had the sort of free will that allowed one to say yes to Christ in a postmortem state, what would prevent that same free will from resulting in sin in heaven?[101] As Trumbower notes, "The mere mention of such a possibility is anathema to Augustine, since for him any beatitude that is not eternal is no beatitude at all."[102] While these objections are widely regarded as devastating to the theory of Postmortem Opportunity, I will argue in the next chapter that they are not.

Objection to the notion of a second chance. Many of the objections to postmortem repentance by early church figures are not really objections to Postmortem Opportunity, but to the notion of a second chance at salvation after death. The very reasonable worry was that the offer of a second chance at salvation could create a lackadaisical approach to

[99]But not all. Pierce lists the following figures who continued to espouse the idea that 1 Peter 3:19; 4:6 referred to the descent of Christ to Hades ("Spirits and the Proclamation of Christ," 5n13, 9n28): Maximus Confessor (580–662; *Quaestiones ad Thalassium* 7 [PG 90:284C]), Joannes Zonaras (12th century; *Epistolarum* 10 [PG 76:1124A-C]), Theophylact (ca. 1055–ca. 1108; *Expositio in Epistolas catholicas: Jacobi* [PG 125:1232]), and Nicephorus Callistus (ca. 1256–ca. 1335; *Historia Ecclesiastica* 1.31 [PG 145: 724ff]).

[100]Augustine, Letter 164 (To Evodius) 4.13 (*NPNF* 1, 1:519).

[101]Referring to Origen, Augustine says, "For in fact he lost even the appearance of compassion in that he assigned to the saints, genuine misery, by which they paid their penalties, and false bliss, in which they could not experience the joy of everlasting good in genuine security—I mean that they could not be certain of it without any apprehension" (*City of God* 21.17, p. 995).

[102]Trumbower, *Rescue for the Dead*, 131.

sin and discipleship based on a "just repent later" mindset. For example, in the aftermath of the Decian persecution (250–251), Cyprian argued that those who had lapsed should be restored before they die, because "there is no confession among the dead."[103] It is crucial to see that Cyprian's objection is not to the unevangelized having a salvific opportunity, but to the offering of a second chance to those who had a chance in this life and squandered it by recanting their faith in the face of persecution. This, of course, is not to claim that Cyprian was a defender of Postmortem Opportunity, only that his objections to postmortem repentance do not speak directly to the question of the unevangelized. A similar example can be found in Augustine's *Enchiridon* (421). He cites 2 Corinthians 5:10, " For we must all appear before the judgment seat of Christ, so that each of us may receive what is due us for the things done while in the body, whether good or bad," and argues, "It is here, then, that is won all merit or demerit whereby a man's state after this life can either be improved or worsened. But let no one hope to obtain, when he is dead, merit with God which he earlier neglected to acquire."[104] This passage articulates an important truth, but it is one that is wildly irrelevant to the question of the destiny of the unevangelized. At issue here is the decision to ignore or put off the decision to follow Christ and live a godly life, not the lack of salvific opportunity in this life.

This is not to suggest that all early church objections to postmortem repentance are really objections to a second chance. It is quite plausible that many, like 2 Clement 8:3 (which reads, "For after we leave this world, we will no longer there be able there to confess or repent") are straightforward objections to any sort of postmortem repentance. The difficulty of assessing this lies in the lack of clarity in the early church on personal eschatology (alluded to earlier in this chapter). There was

[103]Cyprian, *Epistle* 55.17.3, in *St. Cyprian: Letters*, trans. Rose Bernard Donna, CSJ, Fathers of the Church, vol. 51 (Washington, DC: Catholic University of America Press, 1964), 144.

[104]Augustine, *Faith, Hope and Charity*, trans. Bernard M. Peebles, Fathers of the Church vol. 2 (Washington DC: Catholic University of American Press, 1950), 462.

a shift in opinion on the nature of Hades in the second and third century from a place of waiting for judgment to a place where punishments are already experienced and, therefore, plausibly, divine judgment had already been dispensed. For those who ascribe to this "judgment immediately after death" view, any postmortem salvific offer becomes a second chance view.

The fear of Universalism. It is difficult to overstate the importance of the fear of Universalism had on the waning of postmortem hope. On one level, this is understandable, for there is a definite correlation between postmortem repentance and Universalism. Those who believe that all will be given an opportunity to be saved, in this life or the next, must grant that it is *possible* that all will be saved. Consequently, postmortem hope fuels the hope for Universalism. Moreover, the only plausible version of Universalism is one in which some will be saved in the postmortem context. The doctrine of postmortem hope has been used by a number of Christian theologians—Origen and Gregory of Nyssa are prominent examples in the early church—as an explanation of *how* all will be saved. As such, for those who believe that Scripture clearly teaches that not all will be saved, the concept of Postmortem Opportunity resides squarely on a slippery slope to heresy. As evidence of this fact, notice that in the Western church in particular, the anathemas directed toward those who proclaimed the release of souls from Hades were reserved for those who claimed that *all* were released from Hades. While the teaching that Christ descended to Hades remained a part of the teaching of the Roman Catholic Church, there were attempts to mitigate its soteriological significance,[105] culminating in the edict by the Council of Florence (1442) in which Augustine's skepticism toward Postmortem Opportunity was fully embraced. The edict made use of the statement by Augustine's disciple, Fulgentius of Ruspe (468–533):

[105]For example, Bauckham identifies a refutation inserted in a manuscript of Sibylline Oracle 2:331 that explicitly links the notion that Christ will listen to the postmortem entreaties of the righteous and grant mercy to some sinners with "babbling Origen" (*Fate of the Dead*, 148).

> The Holy Roman Church firmly believes, professes and proclaims that none of those who are outside the Catholic Church—not only pagans, but Jews also, heretics and schismatics—can have part in eternal life, but will go with eternal fire, which was prepared for the devil and his angels, *unless they are gathered into the Church before the end of life.*[106]

The most plausible justification for linking the belief in postmortem salvific opportunity and Universalism comes from the belief in that those who experience a Postmortem Opportunity will, of necessity, be saved. This objection is powerfully stated by John Chrysosytom. Chrysostom is desperately disinterested in any affirmation that the unrepentant might benefit from Christ's postmortem preaching. He says, "If unbelievers are after death to be saved on their believing, no man shall ever perish" and he cites Philippians 2:10-11 and 1 Corinthians 15:26, saying, "But there is no advantage in that submission, for it comes not of a rightly disposed choice, but of the necessity of things, as one may say, thenceforth taking place."[107] I will seek to refute the claim that those who receive a Postmortem Opportunity do not have the free choice to reject it in the final chapter of this book. For now, it is instructive to see how Chrysostom completes his thought. Chrysostom allows that there might be some who could benefit from Christ's postmortem preaching:

> But in proof that they who, not having known Christ before His coming in the flesh, yet refrained from idolatry and worshipped God only, and showed forth an excellent life, shall enjoy all the blessings; hear what is said: But glory, and honor, and peace to every one that works good, to the Jew first, and also to the Gentile. Do you see that for their good deeds there are many rewards, and chastisements again, and penalties for such as have done the contrary?

What Chrysostom's claims really amount to is the claim that Postmortem Opportunity cannot be a means to save those who have no desire to submit to Christ's Lordship. And on that all Christians should agree.

---

[106]Cited in Alan M. Fairhurst, "Death and Destiny," *Churchman* 95 (1981): 314; italics mine.
[107]John Chrysostom, *Homily on Matthew* 36.3 (*NPNF* 1, 10:241).

Extra ecclesiam nulla salus. In addition to the fear of Universalism, belief in Postmortem Opportunity was suppressed by the increasingly pervasive and influential belief that there was "no salvation outside the church." The expression *extra ecclesiam nulla salus* comes from Cyprian (200–258) and is often used as shorthand for the doctrine that communion with the church is necessary for salvation. This doctrine gained increasing significance and visibility under Augustine (354–430) and Gregory the Great (540–604). In his Letter 72, Cyprian addressed the question of whether it was necessary to baptize church applicants who had previously been baptized by heretics. Cyprian argues that baptism performed by heretics was not valid. In the writings of Augustine, the barrier to salvation of the unevangelized was strengthened. He affirmed that unbaptized children who die before committing actual sin would receive a lesser punishment in *limbus infantum*, but their lot was still one of damnation and exclusion from the blessedness of the redeemed. Moreover, Augustine firmly excluded any person who was not blessed with the message of salvation taught by the church, saying,

> No man can find salvation except in the Catholic Church. Outside the Catholic Church he can have everything except salvation. He can have honor, he can have the sacraments, he can sing alleluia, he can respond with Amen, he can have the gospel, he can hold and preach the faith in the name of the Father and of the Son and of the Holy Spirit: but nowhere else than in the Catholic Church can he find salvation.[108]

It is likely that Augustine understood the statement "No salvation outside the church" as a statement that the church is the *source* of salvation—saying, "If someone is saved, it is because they are saved by the church." After all, in certain moods, Augustine acknowledged that there might be some outside the church that are saved: "How many sheep there are without, how many wolves within!"[109] But over time the

[108]Augustine, *A Sermon to the People of the Church of Caesariensis* 6 (CSEL 53:174-75); cited in Francis A. Sullivan, *Salvation Outside the Church: Tracing the History of the Catholic Response* (Eugene, OR: Wipf & Stock, 1992), 32.

[109]Augustine, *Homilies on John* 45.12 (*NPNF* 1, 7:254).

statement "No salvation outside the church" increasingly functioned to define a *barrier*—saying, "If one is not inside the church, they cannot be saved." Hence by the time of Thomas Aquinas the metaphor of the church as Noah's ark was common: "There is no entering into salvation outside the Church, just as in the time of the deluge there was none outside the Ark, which denotes the Church."[110] Those who do not receive the gospel message from the church, therefore, are hopelessly lost in the flood waters of sin.

In this context, postmortem hope of a sort was maintained, but attenuated severely. The effect of Christ's preaching in Hades was restricted to only the Old Testament patriarchs and postmortem spiritual progress was given only to those who had been baptized in the church. In short, the notion of postmortem hope was morphed into the doctrine of purgatory, which is a sort of postmortem hope, offered only to those who were within the church and whose sins were venial. It is fair to wonder how Postmortem Opportunity would have been received in the early church if the sensibilities about salvation outside the church expressed in Vatican II would have been present in Augustine's time. The post–Vatican II *Catechism of the Catholic Church* explains the phrase "outside the Church there is no salvation," as follows: "All salvation comes from Christ the Head through the Church which is his Body," and "is not aimed at those who, through no fault of their own, do not know Christ and his Church."[111]

The indirect influence of Augustine. Augustine's pernicious influence on Postmortem Opportunity can be seen in another, less direct manner, namely in his influence on the doctrine of election.[112] Prior to Augustine, the early church was largely marked by a synergistic understanding of salvation: salvation was God's work, but required human participation. God's grace was absolutely necessary for salvation, but human beings

[110]Thomas Aquinas, *Summa Theologica*, part 3, Q. 73, a. 3 (New York: Benzinger Brothers, 1947), 2435. That being said, the use of the ark analogy dates all the way back to Cyprian.

[111]*Catechism of the Catholic Church* (New York: Doubleday, 1995), 846-47.

[112]A point made by Bauckham, *Fate of the Dead*, 158-59.

could freely resist God's call to salvation. Augustine's earliest writings mirror this perspective, but in 396, Augustine's view of election and human freedom undergoes a dramatic and enormously influential shift.[113] God's election of human beings could not, he claimed, be based on his foreknowledge of who would freely respond to the gift of grace, rather election must precede the choice of the individual and be the cause of that person's choice to accept God's grace. Thus salvation was not synergistic, it was monergistic. The grace that God gives to the elect is irresistible and no one who is not elected can be saved.

The primary impact of Augustine's shift is on belief in God's universal salvific will. Instead of seeing God as desirous of the salvation of all, instead Augustine held that there are some who, due to God's unconditional election, have no chance of being saved. Augustine's theological argument against prayers of mercy for the unrepentant is found in the *City of God* 21:24:

> In fact the reason which now prevents the church from praying for the evil angels, whom she knows to be her enemies, is the same reason which will prevent her at that time of judgement from praying, however perfect her holiness, for the human beings that are to be tormented in eternal fire. . . . If the church had such certain information about people as to know who were already predestined, although still under the conditions of this life, to go into the eternal fire with the devil, then the church would pray as little for them as it does for him.[114]

The impact of the loss of universal salvific will on the theory of Postmortem Opportunity is significant, but complicated. In chapter three, I argued that there is no necessary relationship between monergism and the denial of Postmortem Opportunity, but nonetheless if salvation is monergistic there is no strict *need* to posit a Postmortem Opportunity

[113]Augustine, "To Simplician: On Various Questions," in *Augustine: Earlier Writings*, ed. J. H. S. Burleigh (Philadelphia: Westminster, 1953), 376-406. On Augustine's shift, see the helpful article by William S. Babcock, "Augustine's Interpretation of Romans (A.D 394–396)," *Augustinian Studies* 10 (1979): 55-74. I am not claiming that the entirety of Augustine's shift is seen in 396, for there are undoubtedly additional shifts made during the Pelagian Controversy.

[114]Augustine, *City of God* 21.24, pp. 1002-3.

for the unevangelized to hear the gospel, for all of those that God has elected can be saved in this life. As such, it is not that Augustine's monergism is technically incompatible with Postmortem Opportunity, it is rather than the motivational core of Postmortem Opportunity is eviscerated by monergism. While the Western church never fully adopted Augustine's view of predestination, adopting a semi-Augustinian stance against the Pelagians and semi-Pelagians at the Synod of Orange (529), it is undeniable that Augustine's influence was profound. Even if his soteriology was not adopted *en toto*, his way of framing the question about the destiny of the unevangelized and particularly his way of understanding the extent of the opportunity for salvation was assumed.

The role of experience (or the lack thereof). The final cause of the loss of Postmortem Opportunity is the most difficult to state precisely, but is nonetheless crucially important. Consider the case studies of the unevangelized detailed in chapter one: George, Anna, and Sam. Anna and Sam cases are typically taken to be easily answered by the saving power of infant baptism or with reference to an age of accountability principle. The first of these still does not speak to the fate of unbaptized infants, but there has been a movement in many segments of the church to subsume them under the second answer: the age of accountability. And the fact that the age of accountability principle sits rather poorly with the belief that explicit allegiance to Christ is necessary for salvation is usually ignored. The net effect of this is that, for the most part, the contemporary church has been relieved of soteriological worry with respect to Anna and Sam cases. Moreover, since Christians, by definition, do not meet anybody who falls in the category of George, and since the probability you would meet a person whose father or grandfather was unevangelized is vanishingly small, contemporary Christians are in a situation where they have been experientially isolated from the question of the destiny of the unevangelized. This reality is combined with the fact that the soteriological problem of cases of pseudoevangelism has been almost wholly ignored by Christian theologians.

Raising this issue is not to offer an experiential argument for the truth of Postmortem Opportunity—"if we only knew some truly unevangelized people, we would feel bad for them and accept the truth of Postmortem Opportunity." Experience does not, in my opinion, have that sort of argumentative power. If we desired Postmortem Opportunity to be true, that wouldn't make it true. But the fact that contemporary Christians—and indeed, most Christians for the last 1500 years—do not have any relational experience of unevangelized persons does, I believe, explain why postmortem hope has dwindled. Making this case would require more words than I have space for here, because it is very likely that there are culturally specific factors involved in the acceptance of postmortem hope, but let me offer a single example: Japan. A number of sources have alluded to the interest the theory of Postmortem Opportunity has for Japanese Christians.[115] Undoubtedly, the cultural importance ascribed to ancestors in Japanese culture is a partial explanation for this fact. More important, however, might be the fact that Japanese converts to Christianity, especially converts in the nineteenth century, likely had parents who never had an opportunity to hear the gospel. As such, the possibility of postmortem repentance was a pressing issue for them in a way that it is not for the vast majority of Western Christians.

CONTEMPORARY RECONSIDERATIONS OF POSTMORTEM OPPORTUNITY

The dismissal of postmortem hope in the West inaugurated by Augustine began to lift in the nineteenth century, when the consensus surrounding Restrictivism was under increasing pressure. Some will

[115]Gavin James Campbell, "To Make the World One in Christ Jesus: Transpacific Protestantism in the Age of Empire," *Pacific Historical Review* 87, no. 4 (Fall 2018): 575–92; Hirokatsu Yoshihara, "A Study of 1 Peter 3:18b-20a and 4:6: A Response to the Notion of Christ's Postmortem Evangelism to the Un-evangelized, a View Recently Advocated in Japan," *Asian Journal of Pentecostal Studies* 20, no. 2 (2017): 183-97. Campbell speaks to the situation in the late nineteenth century in Japan, Yoshihara speaks to the current situation.

dismiss this as paralleling the rise of liberal theology. Perhaps there is something to that claim, but if so, it is not simply that the alternatives to Restrictivism were motivated by a liberal approach to Scripture or theology. More plausibly, as people's awareness of the world expanded throughout the nineteenth century, the seriousness of the problem of the destiny of the unevangelized became more difficult to ignore. Moreover, while it is undoubtedly true that liberal theologians felt comfortable raising questions that exposed tensions inherent in conservative theological method, particularly in misreadings of the implications of *sola scriptura*, Postmortem Opportunity was motivated more as a reaction to liberalism, not an acquiescence to liberalism. As wider hope views proliferated, many of them began questioning fundamental Christian beliefs. Inclusivists set aside the commitment that explicit faith in Jesus Christ was necessary for salvation and Universalists discarded the belief that there will be some who reject relationship with Jesus Christ and spend an eternity separate from him in hell. Consequently, the rise of Postmortem Opportunity was due to Christians who were anxious to find an *orthodox* and *christocentric* way of answering the question of the destiny of the unevangelized that resisted the narrowness of Restrictivism and the quiescence of agnosticism.

It was in Germany that postmortem hope saw its first resurgence, perhaps because Martin Luther himself planted the seeds of its return. While Luther did not assert that the unevangelized will receive a Postmortem Opportunity, he was more open to the idea than the vast majority of early Protestants. While upholding the absolute necessity of faith for salvation, Luther acknowledged, "It would be quite a different question whether God can impart faith to some in the hour of death or after death so that these people could be saved through faith. Who would doubt God's ability to do that?"[116] But he was also clear that this

[116]Martin Luther, "Letter to Hans von Rechenberg, 1522," in *Luther's Works* 43, trans. Martin H. Bertram (St. Louis: Concordia, 1968), 54; cited in Sharon Taylor, "Future Probation: A Study in

could not be a teaching of the church, saying, "That God could do so could not be denied; that God does so cannot be proved."[117] In addition, late in his life, Luther seemed to find scriptural ground for Postmortem Opportunity. In a commentary on Hosea 6:1, Luther cites 1 Peter 3:19 and says,

> Here Peter clearly teaches that Christ not only appeared to the departed fathers and patriarchs, some of whom, without doubt, Christ, when he rose, raised with him to eternal life, but also preached to some who in the time of Noah had not believed, and who waited for the long-suffering of God, that is, who hoped that God would not enter into so strict a judgment with all flesh, to the intent that they might acknowledge that their sins were forgiven through the sacrifice of Christ.[118]

These seeds of openness to postmortem salvation planted by Luther flowered in the nineteenth century with the work of John Peter Lange (1802–1884)[119] and Isaak A. Dorner (1809–1884),[120] among others.[121] From Germany, the theory of Postmortem Opportunity spread to England and found expression in the writings of Joseph Butler (1692–1752),[122] Herbert Luckock (1833–1909),[123] Edward H. Plumptre (1821–1891),[124] Frederic

---

Heresy, Heterodoxy, and Orthodoxy," *American Theological Library Association Summary of Proceedings* (January 1, 2004): 156.

[117]Martin Luther, *Dr. Martin Luthers Briefe, Sendschreiben und Bedenken*, ed. W. M. L. de Wette, vol. 2 (Berlin: G. Reimer, 1826), 455; cited in Taylor, "Future Probation," 156.

[118]Luther, *Commentary on Hosea*; cited in Plumptre, *Spirits in Prison*, 116.

[119]John Peter Lange, *Commentary on the Holy Scriptures: Critical, Doctrinal, and Homiletical: Peter* (Grand Rapids, MI: Zondervan, 1960 [1872]), 62-65, 67-71, 74-75.

[120]Isaak A. Dorner, *A System of Christian Doctrine*, trans. Alfred Cave and J. S. Banks, vol. 4 (Edinburgh: T & T Clark, 1896), 127-32.

[121]Friedrich Loofs also names J. L. König, E. Güder, and C. Clemen as German defenders of Postmortem Opportunity. See his "Descent into Hades (Christ's)," 658. Taylor claims that Philip Schaff fell into the Future Probation camp as well ("Future Probation," 157).

[122]Joseph Butler, *Analogy of Religion: Natural and Revealed, to the Constitution and Course of Nature* (New York: Harper and Brothers, 1889), pt. 1, ch. 3, 119, 131; pt. 2, ch. 6, 259. Jerry L. Walls highlights the fact that Butler argued for a Postmortem Opportunity "to make up for the inequalities of this life" (*Purgatory: The Logic of Total Transformation* [New York: Oxford University Press, 2012], 196n61).

[123]Herbert M. Luckock, *The Intermediate State Between Death and Judgment* (New York: Thomas Whitaker, 1890), 137-216, especially 187-96.

[124]Plumptre, *Spirits in Prison*. John Sanders rightly notes that Plumptre argues for an inclusivist understanding of salvation for those who have lived since the incarnation (*No Other Name: An Investigation into the Destiny of the Unevangelized* [Grand Rapids, MI: Eerdmans, 1992], 212-13);

W. Farrar (1831–1903),[125] P. T. Forsyth (1848–1921),[126] Joseph H. Leckie (1865–1938);[127] and J. A. MacCulloch (1868–1950).[128]

In the United States, in the late nineteenth century, these voices catalyzed what came to be called the "Andover Theory," centered at Andover Seminary in Massachusetts. Many of the faculty at Andover—most notably the president of the faculty, Egbert C. Smyth (1829–1904)[129]—embraced the theory of Postmortem Opportunity, calling it the theory of "Future Probation." The popularity of Future Probation at Andover, however, caused a backlash within the Congregational church (with which Andover was affiliated). The result was a theological trial of sorts in which Smyth and four other Andover professors were charged with holding beliefs contrary to the stated doctrinal convictions of Andover Seminary, one of which was the theory of Future Probation. While the lengthy and convoluted trial eventually made it to the Massachusetts Supreme Court, the matter of the acceptability of future probation was never decided. What the trial did accomplish, however, was to cause Andover Seminary to close until it combined with Newton Theological Institution and reopened as Andover-Newton Theological Seminary in 1931.[130]

The other effect of the Andover Trial—and more important for the specific point being made here—was to drag Future Probation into the theological wars between liberals and conservatives in America in the late nineteenth and early twentieth centuries. In short, Postmortem

---

however, as I will argue in chapter eight, it is not necessary to see Inclusivism and Postmortem Opportunity as contradictory, and Plumptre certainly believes that death is not the end of salvific opportunity.

[125]Frederic W. Farrar, *The Early Days of Christianity* (New York: Cassell & Company, 1889), 93-95.

[126]P. T. Forsyth, *This Life and the Next* (Boston: Pilgrim, 1948), 36-37. As Jerry Walls notes, there is some ambiguity in when Forsyth thinks conversion occurs (see *Purgatory*, 139-40; *Heaven, Hell, and Purgatory* [Grand Rapids, MI: Brazos, 2015], 206).

[127]Joseph H. Leckie, *The World to Come and Final Destiny*, 2nd ed. (Edinburgh: T&T Clark, 1922), 90-101.

[128]J. A. MacCulloch, *The Harrowing of Hell: A Comparative Study of an Early Christian Doctrine* (Edinburgh: T&T Clark, 1930).

[129]Egbert C. Smyth, "Probation After Death," *The Homiletic Review* 11, no. 4 (April 1886): 281-91.

[130]Taylor, "Future Probation," 163-65.

Opportunity found itself caught between the pincers of the modernist/fundamentalist controversy, with the result that the moderate, non-Universalistic version of Postmortem Opportunity was rejected by both. Liberals rejected non-Universalist Postmortem Opportunity because it was not Universalistic and because the burgeoning growth of the social gospel caused theological liberals to define salvation more in worldly, economic terms. Conservatives likewise rejected Postmortem Opportunity, for three reasons. First, Postmortem Opportunity was irreparably tainted by the fact that a number of pseudo-Christian sects embraced the doctrine: the Swedenborgians, Mormons, and the Russellites (who later took the name Jehovah's Witnesses).[131] Second, the theory of Postmortem Opportunity was unfairly and incorrectly lumped together with the Catholic doctrine of purgatory, a simplistic and erroneous connection made due to the fact that some of the defenders of Future Probation in the nineteenth century saw the intermediate state as the context for Postmortem Opportunity. Finally, the theory of Future Probation was co-opted by some Unitarians who used it to explain how all souls will eventually be saved. In this context, the doctrine of Future Probation was inextricably linked with Universalism and became something of a litmus test for orthodoxy.

In recent years, however, the theory of Postmortem Opportunity has resurfaced in a wide variety of theological currents and is ripe for renewed consideration. Recent proponents of Postmortem Opportunity include the following: C. E. B. Cranfield (1915–2015),[132] one of the leading British New Testament scholars in the second half of the twentieth century; George Beasley-Murray (1916–2000),[133] former New Testament professor at Southern Baptist Theological Seminary; George Lindbeck (b. 1923), influential founder of the "Yale School" of

[131]Taylor, "Future Probation," 157.

[132]C. E. B. Cranfield, *The First Epistle of Peter* (London: SCM, 1950), 84-86, 90-91.

[133]George Beasley-Murray, *Baptism in the New Testament* (Grand Rapids, MI: Eerdmans, 1962), 258-59.

postliberalism;[134] Gabriel Fackre (b. 1926), professor emeritus from Andover Newton Seminary;[135] Donald Bloesch (1928–2010), longtime professor at University of Dubuque Theological Seminary who describes himself as either a "progressive evangelical" or as "Ecumenical orthodox";[136] Carl Braaten (b. 1929),[137] professor emertius from Lutheran School of Theology at Chicago and widely known Lutheran theologian; and Clark Pinnock (1937–2010),[138] noted evangelical theologian and former professor at McMaster Divinity College. Recently, there have also been a number of philosophical theologians who have argued for Postmortem Opportunity, including Richard Swinburne,[139] Stephen T. Davis,[140] Kevin Timpe,[141] and especially Jerry Walls.[142] And finally, mention should be made of Stephen Jonathan's book *Grace Beyond the Grave*.[143] It is the most complete recent defense of Postmortem Opportunity.

I do not tally these voices as evidence of the truth of Postmortem Opportunity. That would be folly, for there are far more dissenting voices than defenders. But these "defending voices" demonstrate that the theory of Postmortem Opportunity is not a radical or fringe position and neither is it located only in a particular strand of Christian

---

[134]George A. Lindbeck, *The Nature of Doctrine: Religion and Theology in a Postliberal Age* (Philadelphia: Westminster, 1984), 55-63; "Unbelievers and the *Sola Christi*," *Dialog* 12 (1973): 182-89.

[135]Gabriel Fackre, *The Christian Story: A Narrative Interpretation of Basic Christian Doctrine*, rev. ed. (Grand Rapids, MI: Eerdmans, 1984), 232-35; "Divine Perseverance," in *What About Those Who Have Never Heard?*, ed. John Sanders (Downers Grove, IL: InterVarsity Press, 1995), 71-106.

[136]Donald Bloesch, "Descent into Hell," in *Evangelical Dictionary of Theology*, ed. Walter Elwell (Grand Rapids, MI: Baker, 1984), 313-14; *The Last Things: Resurrection, Judgment, Glory* (Downers Grove, IL: InterVarsity Press, 2004), 240.

[137]Carl Braaten, "Lutheran Theology and Religious Pluralism," *Lutheran World Federation* 23–24 (January 1988): 122; *The Flaming Center: A Theology of the Christian Mission* (Philadelphia: Fortress, 1977), 117.

[138]Pinnock, *Wideness in God's Mercy*, 168-72. I would like to add that Clark was one of the most kind and personally warm people I have ever met.

[139]Richard Swinburne, *Faith and Reason* (New York: Oxford University Press, 1981), 169.

[140]Stephen T. Davis, "Universalism, Hell, and the Fate of the Ignorant," *Modern Theology* 6 (1990): 173-86.

[141]Kevin Timpe, "An Argument for Limbo," *Journal of Ethics* 19 (2015): 277-92.

[142]Jerry Walls, *Hell: The Logic of Damnation* (Notre Dame: University of Notre Dame Press, 1992) and *Purgatory*.

[143]Stephen Jonathan, *Grace Beyond the Grave* (Eugene, OR: Wipf & Stock, 2014).

belief, in a particular field of expertise, or in a particular culture. The common theme in each of the scholars named above seems to be a desire to clearly affirm God's universal salvific will while maintaining a clear commitment to the necessity of explicit faith in Jesus Christ for salvation. And that goal is, I think, a very good one.

7

THEOLOGICAL OBJECTIONS TO POSTMORTEM OPPORTUNITY

In previous chapters, I developed an argument for Postmortem Opportunity, discussed the scriptural evidence for and against that account, and responded to the historical objection to Postmortem Opportunity. Along the way, I have acknowledged various theological objections to my proposed theory and promised to address them eventually. It is now time (and probably past time) to make good on that promissory note. The majority of this chapter will address a variety of objections that fall under two broad categories. The first includes objections to the implications the theory of Postmortem Opportunity has for this life. This sort of objection focuses on the following theme: "If humans have a Postmortem Opportunity to be saved then that trivializes important aspects of this life." The second category of objections addresses the eschatological details of the theory of Postmortem Opportunity and suggests that they are theologically problematic in a number of respects. In addition to objections that fall into those categories, I will open this chapter with a consideration of an objection not to my theory in particular, but to any and all attempts to answer the question of the destiny of the unevangelized, and I will close with an objection to my use of the category of the pseudoevangelized.

SHOULD AN ANSWER BE GIVEN?

There are some who think that the question of the destiny of the unevangelized is a perfectly coherent question, and even at some level, a pressing question, but who nonetheless believe that it cannot and should not be answered. These people are in a similar boat to those who believe that it is perfectly reasonable to wonder if there is life elsewhere in the universe, but who hold that it is impossible to answer the question one way or another and that any yes or no would be problematic. This stance has been aptly titled Agnosticism. The most common rationale offered for the Agnostic position is that Scripture speaks only to what the gospel is and what the gospel requires of sinners, it does not speak to the fate of those who do not hear the gospel. And because Scripture does not speak to this issue, any answer that we might give to the status of those who do not hear the gospel would be speculative at best, and presumptuous at worst.[1]

Some who advocate Agnosticism strike an optimistic tone. For example, John Stott says,

> I believe the most Christian stance is to remain agnostic on this question. . . . The fact is that God, alongside the most solemn warnings about our responsibility to respond to the gospel, has not revealed how he will deal with those who have never heard it. We have to leave them in the hands of the God of infinite mercy and justice, who manifested these qualities most fully in the cross. Abraham's question, "will not the Judge of all the earth do what is right?" (Genesis 18:25) is our confidence too.[2]

Others strike a more pessimistic tone, acknowledging that for all we know, God may save some of the unevangelized, but we do not know how he will do so and we have no biblical reasons to affirm that he will do so. For example, J. I. Packer says, "We have no warrant to affirm categorically that this is true in the sense of having actually happened to people to whom God's promises never came; nor are we entitled to

[1]There are a number of examples of the Agnostic position in William V. Crockett and James G. Sigountos, eds., *Through No Fault of Their Own? The Fate of Those Who Have Never Heard* (Grand Rapids, MI: Baker, 1991): Timothy R. Phillips, "Hell: A Christological Reflection," 47-60; Aida Besançon Spencer, "Romans 1: Finding God in Creation," 125-36; and Tite Tiénou, "Eternity in Their Hearts," 209-16. They all "prefer to leave the matter in the hands of God" (259n3).

[2]David L. Edwards and John Stott, *Evangelical Essentials: A Liberal-Evangelical Dialogue* (Downers Grove, IL: InterVarsity Press, 1988), 327.

expect that God will act thus in any single case where the Gospel is not known or understood."[3]

I am sympathetic with some of what drives the Agnostic position. I think that Christians often ask questions that Scripture does not answer and, too often when we do so, we try to shoehorn the biblical evidence into our own preferences. And I agree that Christians should be very aware of when they are going beyond what Scripture explicitly teaches. But, contrary to those who take the Agnostic position, I think that the question of the destiny of the unevangelized is not a question that should be ignored. To make this case, let's consider the more general question: When should we be reticent to answer a theological question? It is important to note that our question is *not*, "When do we think we will be unable to answer a theological question fully?" For it is unlikely that any theological questions are ever answered fully. Instead, the relevant question is, "When is it not worth it to even try to give an answer?" It seems reasonable to avoid answering a theological question when any of the following three conditions are met.

1. We have reason to believe that we will be unable to make any meaningful headway on answering the question. The issue in question is beyond our ken and/or there are no data points in Scripture that speak to the issue or even to the penumbral issues or questions.
2. When the question is theologically irrelevant and/or when the answer provides nothing more substantial that theological trivia.
3. When even the attempt to engage a question would involve heresy.[4]

Stated from the opposite perspective, we should attempt to answer a theological question when we think we have something to say, when the answer is theologically important, and when doing so does not

---

[3]J. I. Packer, "What Happens to People Who Die Without Hearing the Gospel?" *Decision* (January 2002): 11.

[4]Of course, there may be disagreements about what constitutes meaningful headway, irrelevance, and heresy.

cross the bounds of orthodoxy. And by these lights, I think we can confidently say that engaging the destiny of the unevangelized is appropriate. I think it is possible to make meaningful headway on this question. Perhaps we cannot offer theories that are uncontroversial or obviously true, but that is not a meaningful objection to such theories—or if it is, it is simultaneously an objection to almost all theological theories. Moreover, despite the difficulty of seeking to answer the question of the destiny of the unevangelized, I suggest that we must do so because the questions at the heart of this matter cut to the very heart of the Christian theological system of belief. In seeking an answer to the question of the destiny of the unevangelized we are asking, "Can we really affirm God's universal love?" and "How should we understand the idea that God desires all to be saved?" To merely affirm the universality of God's love and salvific will but ignore these questions is to remove the mind from the Christian faith. So, given the assumption that the life of the mind matters to the Christian faith, both for individual persons and for the church as a whole, ignoring questions like the destiny of the unevangelized is something we do at our extreme peril. It is crucial to note, however, that one's theological stance makes a difference here. The affirmation of universal salvific will is most comfortable in an Arminian soteriological framework. So perhaps it is more accurate to say that it is severely problematic for an Arminian to avoid the problem of the destiny of the unevangelized and, for parallel reasons, it is more plausible for a Calvinist to embrace Agnosticism.

I would add that the Agnostic stance on the question of the destiny of the unevangelized is rendered more problematic by the fact that the way it is defined makes it such that one never encounters a person for whom this is an issue. Once we make an "age of accountability" exception for the Annas and Sams of the world, then we have guaranteed that we will never meet an unevangelized person and that therefore we can feel quite comfortable about ignoring the difficult question about their soteriological plight. This is not only theological cowardice, this is a failure to do what theologians must do—namely, engage the difficult theological issues that arise at the intersection of our fundamental theological commitments and our reasonable questions and experiences. Of course, the question of the destiny of the unevangelized is a particularly thorny question, but Clark Pinnock is exactly right when he asks, "Isn't theology supposed to face tough questions as well as easy ones?"[5] But one might respond to this argument this way: "Fine, but that implies only that we should *want* to answer the question of the destiny of the unevangelized, but that is not the same as actually being able to give an adequate, biblically reasonable answer." True. There are two questions here: First, does the question of the destiny of the unevangelized address a matter of genuine importance? And, second: Is it possible to give a reasonable answer? As I have argued, the answer to the first question is unequivocally yes—the question of the destiny of the unevangelized is a genuine and important question, a question that cuts right to the heart of the understanding of God's love and plans for his creation. The answer to the second question depends on what is meant by a "reasonable answer." If by a reasonable answer you mean "an answer that is clearly and uncontroversially taught in Scripture" then, of course, the question of the destiny of the unevangelized cannot be reasonably answered *in that sense*. Then again, if that is what is required to provide a reasonable answer, we must cease to ask most of our pressing questions about God's attributes, Trinity, the incarnation, and election. But if by "answered" we mean, "Can we offer internally coherent and scripturally valid ways of thinking about this question that result in greater understanding of the issues that are raised?" then, I believe, it is clear that we can answer the question of the destiny of the unevangelized in that way. We should not allow the quest for the perfect theological answer to become the enemy of a fruitful, edifying, reasonable answer.

[5]Clark Pinnock, *A Wideness in God's Mercy: The Finality of Jesus Christ in a World of Religions* (Grand Rapids, MI: Zondervan, 1992), 151.

"IRRELEVANCE OF THIS LIFE" OBJECTIONS

One of the most substantial objections to Postmortem Opportunity is to ask, If salvation is possible in the postmortem state, then what is this life for? In essence, this objection states that the affirmation of Postmortem Opportunity undercuts the rationale or motivation to do a variety of important things, things that Scripture clearly requires of Christians. There are a number of permutations of this objection. First, one might argue that the motivation to respond to God's offer of salvation is undercut by the fact that a Postmortem Opportunity to do so amounts to a second chance to be saved. And that raises the question, Why should we (or anybody) see any urgency in responding to a first chance to be saved, if we are given another chance? Second, and closely related to the first, If one will have a Postmortem Opportunity to respond to the gospel, why undergo the difficulty of living as a Christian in this life? Why seek to live holy lives and, certainly, why experience hardship, persecution, or martyrdom? Finally, if those who do not hear the gospel will have a Postmortem Opportunity to do so, why expend the effort to do missions now?

Is Postmortem Opportunity a "second chance" to be saved? As we saw in chapter five, one of the most pervasive and serious objections to seeing 1 Peter 3:18-20 and 1 Peter 4:6 as teaching (or, more minimally, providing precedent for) the theory of Postmortem Opportunity is that such a reading would imply that there was a "second chance" for salvation. Similarly, the "second chance" objection was one of the reasons for the waning of postmortem hope in the years following Augustine. It would be difficult to overstate how significant this objection is for those who find the idea of a postmortem repentance to be problematic. This objection is not only seen as a direct attack on the theory of Postmortem Opportunity, it undermines the theory in another way. Since (it is argued) that Postmortem Opportunity is equivalent to a second chance to be saved, then the belief that there will be no second chance is used as decisive evidence against biblical arguments for Postmortem

Opportunity. Any passage that might have been thought of as teaching Postmortem Opportunity cannot be teaching that view, because that would be a "second chance." With the possible biblical evidence for Postmortem Opportunity effectively set aside, it is then argued that one should not believe in the theory of Postmortem Opportunity, because the biblical evidence is insufficient.

There is also a logical problem with the idea of a second chance. As Jonathan Kvanvig says, "If a second chance is deserved, then it is hard to see why the same considerations would not justify a third chance if the second chance were passed on, thereby launching an infinite sequence of delays of consignment to hell."[6] As Kvanvig's quote suggests, the only way the concept of a second chance makes sense is if one already believes on biblical or theological grounds that no one will be sent to hell for an eternity and that all will eventually be saved. For Universalists, God's provision of a second chance is merely an expression of God's infinite love and salvific patience. But for those who reluctantly believe that some will reject God and end up in hell, the allowance of a salvific opportunity that is truly a "second chance"—it is provided even to those who had a perfectly good first chance—is difficult to justify.

Let me say unequivocally that if the theory of Postmortem Opportunity amounts to offering a second chance to those that have had a viable first chance, then it should end up on the scrap heap of theological theories. There is no second chance. For Postmortem Opportunity to be a "second chance," people would have to hear the gospel in a way that was truthful and viable, have a genuine opportunity to respond, refuse to do so, but then also be given a second chance to respond in heaven. That claim would indeed be problematic, but that is not what the Postmortem Opportunity theorist claims. What they argue is not that the unevangelized should be given a second chance, but that it seems that they have not received a genuine first chance. As such, affirming

[6]Jonathan Kvanvig, "Hell," in *Oxford Handbook of Eschatology*, ed. Jerry L. Walls (New York: Oxford University Press, 2008), 418.

Postmortem Opportunity is not affirming a second chance, it is affirming (in the words of Donald Bloesch) "the universality of a first chance, an opportunity for salvation for those who have never heard the gospel *in its fullness*."[7]

One of the problematic rationales for the "second chance" objection to Postmortem Opportunity goes as follows. Romans 1 teaches that there are no people who have not had a viable first chance, for God has clearly revealed his "eternal power and divine nature" in creation. As such, if a Postmortem Opportunity is offered, it would have to be a second chance. This assumption is problematic for a number of reasons. First, it is extremely implausible to suggest that Anna and Sam have had any sort of viable salvific opportunity, and certainly not one based on their observation of God's creation.[8] Second, the Romans 1 response conflates "having an awareness of God as Creator" with "having a genuine salvific opportunity." This conflation is especially unjustified for Restrictivists who claim that the knowledge that all people receive through general revelation is sufficient to damn but insufficient to save. As such, they can hardly claim that Romans 1 supports the notion that all people have a genuine opportunity to be saved. Knowing that God exists and, by virtue of that knowledge, not being able to say to God, "I didn't know you existed" is very different than having a genuine opportunity to be saved, hearing the gospel, and embracing a relationship with Jesus Christ through his plan of salvation. Those who try to collapse the latter into the former must deal with James 2:19: "You believe that there is one God. Good! Even the demons believe that—and shudder!" Satan clearly knows that God exists and knows all about his greatness and essential nature. Salvation is not a function of the

---

[7]Donald Bloesch, "Descent into Hell," in *Evangelical Dictionary of Theology*, ed. Walter Elwell (Grand Rapids, MI: Baker, 1984), 314; italics added. Daniel Strange makes this same point. The theory of Postmortem Opportunity, he says, is "not to be confused as a 'second chance' theory, but rather the universality of a first chance" ("Salvation, Atonement and Accessibility: Towards a Solution of the 'Soteriological Problem of Evil,'" *Foundations* 44 [Spring 2000]: 14).

[8]It is far more reasonable—although still not unproblematic—to claim that Anna and Sam fall in classes of people who do not need any sort of salvific opportunity to be saved.

correctness of our knowledge, but the disposition of our heart toward God's offer of salvation in Jesus Christ.

Suppose it is granted that the unevangelized have not had a salvific opportunity and, by virtue of that fact, their Postmortem Opportunity is not a second chance. But some might press the "second chance" point with respect to the pseudoevangelized. Does my inclusion of the pseudoevangelized as possible recipients of a Postmortem Opportunity involve the offering of a second chance to these classes of people? One's perspective on this matter depends crucially on what is meant by "hearing the gospel." If "hearing" is solely auditory, then Kunta, Micha, and Rapunzel have "heard" the message of Jesus. (In fact, if hearing is merely auditory, Anna and Sam have probably heard the message of Jesus as well). But they haven't heard the gospel. If the gospel is God's good news of salvation through Jesus Christ, then what is required is not some bare minimum auditory "hearing," but a hearing that leads to understanding of the good news represented by the gospel. Can anyone claim with seriousness that Kunta Kinte had an opportunity to respond to the good news of the gospel *in this life*? Obviously, he heard about Jesus, but he did not hear *the* gospel. Similarly, Micha's experiences are such that even if she heard the gospel (auditorially), her life experiences were such that she was still unable to respond and, therefore, it is difficult to see her first chance as genuine. The Rapunzel case is perhaps the most difficult in this respect, for it might be argued that she could have responded to the gospel immediately, before her untimely death. Sure, she might have responded immediately, but there is a serious problem with disallowing Rapunzel as a possible recipient of a Postmortem Opportunity on the grounds that such an opportunity would out of necessity be a second chance. One who claims that the provision of a Postmortem Opportunity to Rapunzel would be a second chance pretends to know a lot more than they actually know about what is and what is not an adequate opportunity. Ultimately, the crucial determinant is not our opinion about what is or is not adequate, but whether God himself considers Rapunzel's opportunity to be sufficient.

As a final point on this matter, it is important to reiterate that I claim absolutely no knowledge of who has and has not actually heard the gospel in this life. Similarly, I don't know who will and who will not receive a Postmortem Opportunity. What I claim is that (1) God knows who has and who has not received an adequate opportunity and (2) we have good reason to believe that he will provide a Postmortem Opportunity to those who did not receive an adequate premortem opportunity.

Why does this life matter? Perhaps the worry at the heart of the "second chance" objection is not "the unevangelized themselves get a second chance," but if Christian soteriology allows for the possibility of postmortem conversion, then that undercuts the motivation to respond to the gospel and live a holy life now. Speaking about 1 Peter, J. H. Elliott argues, "Any notion of a possibility of conversion or salvation after death would seriously undermine the letter's consistent stress on the necessity of righteous behavior here and now."[9] Likewise, this seems to be what Tom Schreiner refers to as a "fatal problem" for reading 1 Peter 3:18-20 as suggesting a postmortem salvific opportunity. He argues, "It makes no sense contextually for Peter to be teaching that the wicked have a second chance in a letter in which he exhorted the righteous to persevere and to endure suffering."[10] This objection has more teeth—at the very least, it is not based on a simple misunderstanding of what the Postmortem Opportunity theorist claims—but it is still misguided in a number of respects. I will offer four responses to this challenge.

1. The initial problem with this objection is that it is less than clear how, according to the objector, the theory of Postmortem Opportunity

---

[9]John Hall Elliott, *1 Peter: A New Translation with Introduction and Commentary*, Anchor Yale Bible Commentaries, vol. 37 (New York: Doubleday, 2000), 662.

[10]Thomas Schreiner, *1, 2 Peter, Jude*, New American Commentary (Nashville: B&H Publishing, 2003), 188. Many others have made a similar argument, including John S. Feinberg, "1 Peter 3:18-20, Ancient Mythology, and the Intermediate State," *Westminster Theological Journal* 48 (1986): 326, and Wayne Grudem, *1 Peter*, Tyndale New Testament Commentary (Grand Rapids, MI: Eerdmans, 1988), 172.

undermines the clear biblical requirement to live a righteous and holy life. It cannot be the mere fact that God will offer a Postmortem Opportunity to those who are in need of it. Because, if nobody who was living was aware of God's provision of a Postmortem Opportunity, it would not affect anybody's decision of how to live. In fact, even if humans were aware of the fact that God will provide a Postmortem Opportunity to people who have not heard the gospel, it should not cause anyone to change how they live. One who is aware of the possibility of a Postmortem Opportunity to hear and respond to the gospel would also have to be aware of the gospel and, by virtue of that fact, not be a candidate for a Postmortem Opportunity. Therefore, one who justifies their decision to delay repentance until the afterlife on the basis of God's provision of a Postmortem Opportunity to the unevangelized has severely misunderstood the theory. They have illicitly assumed that if the unevangelized are given a Postmortem Opportunity, then all must be given one. And while it is perhaps true that the theory of Postmortem Opportunity is open to being misunderstood in this way, a theory should be judged by how it should be understood, not by how it could be misunderstood.

2. The "Why does this life matter?" objection assumes that it could be reasonable for one who hears of the existence of a Postmortem Opportunity to delay the decision to follow Christ in this life. Consequently, the affirmation of the possibility of a Postmortem Opportunity trivializes decisions made in this life. Setting aside the fact that this objection is based on a misunderstanding of Postmortem Opportunity, the problem with this objection is that, even if it is successful, it probably proves too much. As Jerry Walls perspicuously points out, "If allowing postmortem repentance would trivialize this life, the same might be said for deathbed repentance."[11] Unless one is willing to claim that we should not allow for the possibility of a deathbed conversion,

[11]Jerry Walls, *Heaven, Hell, and Purgatory* (Grand Rapids, MI: Brazos, 2015), 194.

it seems inconsistent to argue that a postmortem conversion should be disallowed.

3. Even if we set aside the first two responses, there is a debilitating problem with the assumption that one who becomes aware of the existence of postmortem repentance might make the strategic decision to postpone commitment to Christ until after death. The logic behind such a move is clear. Avoid what is difficult, distasteful and, on this line of thinking, unnecessary—namely, all the messy and difficult requirements of actually living as a Christian—while still gaining the ultimate goal: eternal life in heaven and avoidance of eternal punishment in hell. While this logic is all too common in segments of American Christianity, it is utter gibberish from a biblical, orthodox Christian perspective. The choice to postpone commitment in this life reveals that what is desired is not relationship with God, but the eternal benefits that come with being a Christian. And that is simply not the Christian message of salvation. As N. T Wright reminds us, the Christian understanding of salvation is not about getting people into heaven, but getting heaven into people.[12] Salvation is not about having the correct belief, it is not about saying the right magic words to receive an eternal prize, and it is certainly not about jumping through whatever hoops are necessary to avoid eternal punishment. It is a life-transforming love and commitment that should result in loving God and neighbor. The fundamental truth of Christian soteriology is that one who merely seeks heaven is likely not to find it, but one who seeks first the kingdom of God in this life, not as a means to an end, but as an end in itself, will receive the reward of heaven (Mt 6:33). The claim that God loves all people and desires to be in relationship with them does not mean that God is willing to lower his standards for relationship or to allow humans to negotiate the terms of eternal relationship in heaven. One who says,

[12]Wright's exact wording is, "Jesus's resurrection is the beginning of God's new project not to snatch people away from earth to heaven but to colonize earth with the life of heaven. That, after all, is what the Lord's Prayer is about." See his *Surprised by Hope: Rethinking Heaven, the Resurrection, and the Mission of the Church* (New York: HarperOne, 2008), 293.

"Okay God, I will agree to commit myself to you, but only on the condition of . . ." is deeply confused about who they are and who God is. Such a mindset is clearly idolatrous, and idolatry is incompatible with relationship with God. Consequently, the "why live a holy life now" objection assumes that one can choose to postpone relationship with God now but choose to embrace it later. And that is far from obvious. Moreover, even if one could postpone their commitment, it is likely that what they would be choosing would not be God, but eternal life or avoidance of hell, or something else, and there is nothing even remotely salvific about the desire to avoid death or eternal punishment.

4. There is a final sense in which how one lives in this life matters, even if a Postmortem Opportunity for repentance exists for some people. It matters in terms of our experience in heaven. The concept of rewards *in* heaven is common in Scripture, but it must be distinguished from the concept of the rewards *of* heaven. All who stand before Jesus on judgment day and choose to serve him in heaven receive the rewards of heaven: the presence of God, freedom from pain and suffering, eternal bliss.[13] Rewards in heaven, on the other hand, are something meted out to those who have lived lives of faith and commitment. Matthew 16:27: "For the Son of Man is going to come in his Father's glory with his angels, and then he will reward each person according to what they have done" is representative of the numerous references to one's reward being based on what one has done (Rom 2:5-7; Prov 24:12; Mt 25:14-30[14]).

When I was a kid and I heard about the idea of rewards in heaven, I combined the idea with Jesus' words "I go and prepare a place for you"

---

[13]Some have seen the parable in Mt 20:1-15 as indicative of the rewards of heaven. All who commit their life to Christ will receive the rewards of heaven, whether they spent their life following Christ or, like George, only received and responded to the gospel message on judgment day.

[14]There is fairly substantial debate over whether the parable of the talents should be understood as referring to stewardship in this life or rewards in the eschatological state. With Klyne Snodgrass, I think that the former is probably better, but that does not rule out an eschatological application. See his *Stories with Intent: A Comprehensive Guide to the Parables of Jesus* (Grand Rapids, MI: Eerdmans 2008), 540, 542.

(Jn 14:1-3) and assumed that if I was a good Christian, I would get to live in a mansion in heaven, but if I was not (something I judged to be the more likely scenario), I would live in a box in somebody's backyard. Even if we set aside some of the childishness of my imagery, some object that the state of affairs in which there are some who receive a greater reward than others in heaven is problematic. Would not those with less reward eventually come to resent those with the greater reward? And, even if we assume that existence in heaven is incompatible with that sort of resentment, it might still be asked whether the concept of maximal bliss in heaven is compatible with the variable bliss associated with the idea of rewards in heaven.

Here is a way of explaining how the rewards in heaven are dependent on one's earthly deeds and how this idea is consistent with our intuitions about the nature of heaven. Let's draw a distinction between the *degree of joy* and the *quantity of joy* a person experiences. Let me illustrate this with an example. Imagine a person who has never golfed and never really followed the sport watching Bubba Watson hit his shot on the second playoff hole in the 2012 Masters. He had hit his drive way right and was in a thick stand of trees, 163 yards from the pin, with no shot at the green. Instead of punching out, he chose to aim to the left, almost 60 degrees offline from a straight path to the green. His shot from his 52 degree wedge hooked 45 yards and ended up on the green, only 15 feet from the pin.[15] Even a golf novice would have to be impressed with such a shot. If you asked them to rate the impressiveness of the shot on a scale of 1 to 100, they would undoubtedly rate it a 100. In other words, their degree of appreciation for the shot would be maximal. Now compare that person's experience with my own experience watching the same shot. I have golfed for much of my life and have spent hours at the driving range trying to control shots like that. Because of my experience playing the game, I know that Watson's shot

[15]For more on the absurd numbers associated with this shot, see the relevant episode on ESPN's Sports Science program: www.espn.com/video/clip?id=19076712.

was not only amazing, it was borderline miraculous. My degree of appreciation for Bubba's shot, like that of the golf novice, is maximal—I rate it a 100. But I submit that my *quantity* of appreciation for Bubba's shot exceeds the golf novice's by many orders of magnitude. (If golf examples don't work for you, imagine the appreciation of a hearing a Stradivarius by a world-class concert violinist compared to one who have never heard a violin, or a Jimi Hendrix guitar solo by an accomplished guitarist compared to one who had never picked up a guitar.)

Similarly, while every person's *degree* of joy in heaven will be the same, the quantity of joy will be much, much greater for those who have spent their life following Christ. Further, this difference will be a purely subjective, internal one and therefore, even if resentment was possible in heaven, there would be nothing to resent, for the differences in experiences would not be discernible. Consequently, one of the reasons why this life matters is because our experiences in heaven will be a function of and an extension of our decisions and behaviors in this life. N. T. Wright powerfully articulates the point of this life.

> The point of the resurrection . . . is that the present bodily life is not valueless just because it will die. . . . What you do with your body in the present matters because God has a great future in store for it. . . . What you do in the present—by painting, preaching, singing, sewing, praying, teaching, building hospitals, digging wells, campaigning for justice, writing poems, caring for the needy, loving your neighbor as yourself—will last into God's future. These activities are not simply ways of making the present life a little less beastly, a little more bearable, until the day when we leave it behind altogether (as the hymn so mistakenly puts it . . .). They are part of what we may call building for God's kingdom.[16]

And the crucial point is that this is true whether or not anybody is given a Postmortem Opportunity to repent. This life matters.

Why do missions? One of the perennial objections to Postmortem Opportunity is that it undercuts the Great Commission. This objection

[16]Wright, *Surprised by Hope*, 193.

asks what reason there is to "go into all the world" if those in all the world will receive an opportunity to hear and respond to the gospel even if one does not go. In fact, as Augustine argues, it might even be worse for those who heard the gospel in this life. If one accepts Postmortem Opportunity, he says, "forasmuch as all men shall certainly die, and ought to come to hell wholly free from the guilt of having despised the gospel, since otherwise it can be of no use to them to believe it when they come there, the gospel ought not to be preached on earth."[17] As powerful as Augustine imagined this objection to be, I think it might be put even more strongly than that. In chapter two, when describing my version of Postmortem Opportunity, I argued that it was insufficient to merely claim that everybody will receive some kind of chance to hear the gospel. Instead, I argued that God's love for the entire world and his desire that none should perish required that people be given *the best possible opportunity* to respond to the gospel. Given that claim, it might be objected that the motivation for missions is doubly undercut. Not only will everybody receive an opportunity to hear even if we shirk the call to go into all the world, everybody will receive a far better presentation of the gospel than we can manage in our feeble missionary efforts. So, it might be claimed, if Postmortem Opportunity is true, wouldn't it be better to just stay at home and let God present himself to the unevangelized on judgment day?

On its face, this objection has a certain plausibility, but there are two responses available to the Postmortem Opportunity theorist. The first questions whether it is justifiable to tie our obedience to the Great Commission to our assessment of the success of our missionary efforts, and the second argues there is nothing in the theory of Postmortem Opportunity that implies that conversion in this life does not matter or that postmortem conversion would be more likely.

Obedience. The first response to the "Why do missions?" objection is to simply point out that we do missions because God has commanded

---

[17]Augustine, Letter 164 (To Evodius) 4.13 (*NPNF* 1, 1:519).

us to do so. Our assessment of the improbability of our success or the probability of God's success on judgment day does not change the fact that God has asked us to "Go into all the world and preach the gospel." To see this more clearly, consider the following analogy. Suppose I ask my son to cut the grass in our yard. (Perhaps I might say, "Go ye therefore, into all the lawn, cutting the grass to a height of three inches.") Would I (or any father) accept the following response: "Well, dad, I know that you care how your lawn looks and if I don't do it, I know that you will mow it yourself before the grass gets too long." And suppose he continues, "What's more, dad, there's not much point in me mowing the lawn because you are the mower-than-which-none-greater-can-be-conceived-of and so when you mow the lawn you will do a better job than I would have done." Even if he is perfectly justified in his belief that I will not let the lawn get too long and will eventually do it myself and that I would probably do a better job than he, his response is a spectacular exercise in missing the point. The question is not whether the lawn is going to get mowed eventually, but whether I have a right to (1) make such a request of my son and (2) expect to be obeyed. Extricating ourselves from the lawn care metaphor, it should be clear that our ignoring (or treating lightly) the Great Commission due to our awareness of God's eventual offer of a Postmortem Opportunity to the unevangelized is even less justified than my son's protestations, because I am not God and sharing the gospel is infinitely more important than cutting the lawn. Therefore, our first and primary reason to fulfill the Great Commission is that we have been commanded to do so by God. And this command holds whether our efforts are going to be fruitful or not and whether there will be opportunities to be saved other than those provided by our efforts.

Moreover, there is no theological justification for seeing the task of fulfilling the Great Commission as drudgery. Yes, we fulfill the Great Commission because God has required us to do so. But it is also true that in doing so we will find joy. Lesslie Newbigin makes this point in a characteristically poignant fashion, saying, "The deepest motive for mission is simply the desire to be with Jesus where he is, on the frontier between the reign of God and the usurped dominion of the devil."[18] So obeying Christ's call to go into all the world should not be thought of as analogous to a sixteen-year-old being asked to push mow the lawn on a hot summer day, but as a four-year-old being asked to open their presents on Christmas morning.

Premortem conversion matters. The second response to the "Why do missions?" objection is that it matters if people have accepted Christ in this life. The theory of Postmortem Opportunity entails that those who did not have a genuine chance to hear and respond to the gospel in this life will have a Postmortem Opportunity. Moreover, I have argued that God's love entails that the opportunity will be the best possible opportunity for that person to hear and respond. But none of that entails that it is certain or even likely that any given person will respond to the gospel. In fact, it is *possible* that none of the people who receive a Postmortem Opportunity to repent will do so.

This idea is likely to strike some as absurd. How could persons who are standing before God on judgment day deny God's existence? The answer is that, of course, they could not, but salvation is not simply a matter of acknowledging God's existence. If it was, then Romans 1:18-20, which teaches that all are aware of God's existence and divine nature, would straightforwardly entail Universalism. And, one who claims that salvation only requires acknowledging God's existence would be unable to explain Lucifer's fall, who was in heaven with God and rebelled against him. Salvation is not merely an intellectual matter, it is also a matter of the heart and will.

Therefore, there is reason to question the assumption that underlies the "Why do missions?" objection. The underlying assumption is that if an unevangelized person will receive a Postmortem Opportunity to

[18]Lesslie Newbigin, *A Word in Season: Perspectives on Christian World Missions* (Grand Rapids, MI: Eerdmans, 1994), 129.

hear the gospel then there is no value in having a premortem opportunity to do so. And this is simply false. One who has wholeheartedly embraced the gospel in this life and has allowed the Holy Spirit to rewrite their spiritual DNA through the process of regeneration will be one who hears the blessed words "Well done good and faithful servant" on judgment day. Those who have not heard the gospel in this life will have an opportunity to hear and respond to the gospel, but there is no guarantee that their answer will be in the affirmative. We may well hope that all such people will embrace relationship with Christ, but it is certainly not a given that George (for example) will say yes to a Postmortem Opportunity, because the morally significant choices humans make in this life matter. Choices create dispositions to choose in similar ways in the future, repetitively acting on dispositions creates habits, and habits create our character. This is a phenomenon called "solidification of character" and should be a crucial aspect in any full-fledged account of soteriology.

This is why not all unevangelized and pseudoevangelized cases are created equal. Anna and Sam cases are unique because even if there is no intentional decision in this life to enter into relationship with Christ, neither is there a history of "self-choosing" choices that become dispositions, habits, and character. There is also justification for being hopeful for the Rapunzels of the world—although for different reasons than for Anna and Sam. Because she died on the brink of committing her life to God, there is reason to think that the dispositions and character that grounded the decisions that brought her to that place will encourage and ground a decision for Christ in judgment day. But the Georges, Kuntas, and Michas are more difficult and it is well beyond our pay grade to say anything definitive about how they will respond to a Postmortem Opportunity. On the one hand, I believe that there is no human person who, by their nature, is beyond God's grace, but on the other hand, we cannot simply assume that those who receive a Postmortem Opportunity will repent. Grace is a reality, but so is sin and free will.

A probability argument. But perhaps my response doesn't quite get to the heart of the "Why do missions?" objection. Perhaps the core issue concerns our assessment of what might be called the relative probability of conversion. I have argued that even if some will be offered a Postmortem Opportunity, there is no reason to believe that premortem evangelism is irrelevant. But one might grant this argument but press the point that the probability of conversion through premortem evangelism is less than (and maybe much less than) the probability of conversion through a Postmortem Opportunity. Stated more formally (where C stands for Conversion, EV stands for Premortem Evangelism, and PMO stands for Postmortem Opportunity), this claim is as follows:

$$P(C/EV) < P(C/PMO)$$

The pretty obvious rationale for this claim is that God's postmortem presentation of the gospel is not infected with any of the maladies that inhibit our evangelism—sinfulness, pride, false pictures of God, imperfect understanding of the person being talked to, cultural barriers, and so forth—and, as such, God's evangelism is infinitely better than ours. In fact, this objection might be pressed further. Given the fact that our evangelistic attempts are often imperfect (to say the least), it might be the case that premortem evangelism, if it was misleading or problematic enough, could decrease the probability of conversion through a Postmortem Opportunity. This objection, therefore, is as follows:

$$P(C/EV \;\&\; PMO) < P(C/PMO)$$

The rationale for this argument is that it is not difficult to imagine a situation where our evangelistic attempts are so problematic that we leave our interlocutor pseudoevangelized (and therefore in need of a Postmortem Opportunity) and less likely to accept that Postmortem Opportunity by virtue of their anger at Christians.

I take these statements, and perhaps especially the latter, to express the intuition at the heart of the "Why do missions?" objection. The response to the first of these objections hearkens back to some themes developed in the previous section. Suppose our premortem evangelistic efforts were less effective than God's provision of a Postmortem Opportunity. Would that suggest that our motivation for missions was undercut? Not at all. Just as I have a right to expect my son to mow the lawn when I ask him, even if I would do a better job than he, God has a right to expect to be obeyed when he gives his followers the Great Commission. And I think that this expectation would stand even if the probability we would find success in our missionary efforts were zero, because God is interested in the process, not just the end. Our missionary work may or may not provide salvific benefit to others, but it can (if we allow it to) provide real benefit to us as we seek to partner with what God is doing in the world.[19]

But what about the second objection, that our evangelistic efforts might make postmortem conversion less likely? First of all, it is absurd to say that we have anything like a reasonable guess on what the relevant probabilities would be here. I doubt that our vague guesses would or should do much of anything to shape our current decisions about how and when to do evangelism. Second, and more importantly, we should never assume that evangelistic success hinges on our words and actions. It is the Holy Spirit that changes hearts, not us. Of course, this doesn't mean that we can evangelize recklessly, with no thought to the future impact of our actions. Above all, our actions should be Christlike and

[19]It might be possible to push the response to this objection even further. Thus far, the assumption that our premortem evangelistic efforts are less effective than God's postmortem efforts has not been challenged. But there are reasons to think that this assumption is false in at least some cases. Consider the difference between my premortem evangelistic encounter with a fourteen-year-old and God's postmortem encounter with that same person after a long life. Yes, the quality of my evangelism cannot be compared to God's, but we should also consider the solidification of character and belief that takes place over a long life. The religious beliefs of those open to God tend to increase in intensity over time, but those who are not believers also tend to become less open over time. In fact, it is possible that there are some people who over time completely close their heart to God. Now this response might suggest to some that killing people before they are solidified against God would be the best evangelistic strategy. However, it should go without saying that such an approach flies in the face of God's direct commands. It also reflects a presumption that we can accurately divine which people will and will not become solidified against God, a presumption that is beyond absurd.

our communication of the gospel must be audience focused and context sensitive.[20] As such, if we properly understand our role in evangelism, there is no reason to think that accepting Postmortem Opportunity should give us any reticence toward sharing the gospel now. So, in short, the "Why do missions?" objections fails on two fronts. It doesn't adequately explain why we do missions even if we are given no guarantee of success and it doesn't acknowledge that there is a good reason to believe that our evangelistic efforts in this life do in fact matter, even if there will be a Postmortem Opportunity for the unevangelized to repent.

"ESCHATOLOGICAL" OBJECTIONS

A second umbrella category of theological objections to Postmortem Opportunity take issue with the eschatological details of the theory. There are, of course, many questions about the eschatological details of the theory of Postmortem Opportunity, but the vast majority of them do not constitute objections to Postmortem Opportunity. For instance, just to pick two examples, one might wonder if a human person can exist as a disembodied soul after death—that is one might wonder how the dualism versus materialism debate might impact the details of postmortem repentance. And one might wonder whether the unevangelized (or pseudoevangelized) would require a postmortem period of purification before receiving their Postmortem Opportunity to repent—a purgatorial (or better, preparatory) experience designed to clarify and solidify their dispositions toward God.[21] These are very good questions, and it would be interesting to work out answers to them. But these questions are not really objections to the theory of Postmortem Opportunity per se. That is, there are plausible

---

[20] I have argued for just such an approach to apologetics in my *Thinking About Christian Apologetics: What It Is and Why We Do It* (Downers Grove, IL: IVP Academic, 2011).

[21] Another reason not to try to unpack the implications of a purgatorial experience for Postmortem Opportunity is that very much I doubt I could improve on the work Jerry Walls has already done. See his *Purgatory: The Logic of Total Transformation* (New York: Oxford University Press, 2012) and *Heaven, Hell, and Purgatory*.

ways of explaining the details of postmortem repentance from the assumption of either materialism or dualism and with or without a purgatorial/preparatory experience. As such, I will focus on what I take to be actual objections to the theory of Postmortem Opportunity, acknowledging that I will have to leave some of the details undeveloped. I will consider two objections: that postmortem repentance is intrinsically impossible and that allowing a Postmortem Opportunity opens up the door to sin in heaven. Another pair of eschatological objections—that a postmortem choice could not be a free choice and that allowing for the possibility of postmortem repentance requires one to accept the ongoing repentance of persons in hell—will be dealt with in the final chapter, because these objections are directly relevant to the matter of the relationship between Postmortem Opportunity and Universalism.

Repentance after death is impossible. One of the significant causes behind the rejection of Postmortem Opportunity has been the belief that repentance after death is impossible. There are a variety of justifications offered for this claim. The first appeals to Scripture and involves the claim that the Bible teaches that postmortem repentance is impossible. The problem with this claim is that, as I argued in chapter four, the biblical warrant for this claim is surprisingly weak. If we assume that postmortem repentance is impossible, it is possible to see evidence for that claim in Scripture, but if we approach Scripture with an open mind on the subject, it is exceedingly difficult to see how Scripture makes that argument. A second justification comes from church tradition. For instance, the Roman Catholic catechism says, "Death puts an end to human life as the time open to either accepting or rejecting the divine grace manifested in Christ."[22] Of course, this justification will be persuasive only to those within the Roman Catholic Church, and even faithful Roman Catholics might want to know why the Church

[22]*Catechism of the Catholic Church* (New York: Doubleday, 1995), 1021.

teaches that repentance after death is impossible. Further, as I argued in chapter six, the historical objection to Postmortem Opportunity is not as strong as it is commonly thought to be. The third possible reason to believe that postmortem repentance is impossible is on the basis of a persuasive theological or philosophical argument. It is this third avenue that is in view in this chapter.

One way to think about death being the end of opportunity for salvation is to say that after death God no longer grants the grace that is necessary to respond with faith.[23] The problem is that, given the assumption that there are those who die without having received a genuine opportunity for salvation, this is incongruous with the clear teaching of Scripture that God desires all people to be saved. A Calvinist will, of course, demur; but that fact is of little relevance here, since Calvinists also believe that God does not provide the grace that is necessary for repentance *in this life* to the nonelect. As such, there is nothing in Calvinism *simpliciter* that implies that postmortem repentance is impossible.

For those who believe that God desires that all people have an opportunity to respond to the gospel, it remains difficult to see why death itself would make repentance impossible. Jerry Walls finds an attempted explanation in Thomas Aquinas's *Summa Contra Gentilies*:

> The soul is, of course, in a mutable state so long as it is united to the body, but it will not be after it has been separated from the body. A disposition of the soul is changed incidentally with some change in the body, for, since it is at the service of the soul for its very own operations, the body was given to the soul by nature with this in view: that the soul existing within the body be perfected, be, as it were, moved toward its perfection. When it shall, then, be separated from the body it will not be in a state of motion toward the end, but in a state of rest in the end acquired. The soul's will, therefore, will be immovable regarding a desire for the ultimate end.[24]

---

[23]Kevin Timpe, *Freewill in Philosophical Theology* (New York: Bloomsbury, 2014), 76.

[24]Thomas Aquinas, *Summa Contra Gentiles*, 4.95.5; trans. Charles J. O'Neil (New York: Doubleday, 1957), 344.

The idea here is that, in Walls's words, "repentance after death is impossible because a soul cannot change its fundamental preferences without the body."[25] Aquinas assumes a hylomorphic view of human persons, or the idea that a human person is a union of soul and body. Souls can exist without bodies, but they cannot change without them. This is certainly one way of looking at human nature, but it is not the only one. Walls argues that "[Aquinas's] argument will carry very little weight with dualists who believe that the soul is the essential self . . . [and] retains its basic powers even without the body."[26] Similarly, materialists will not be persuaded by Aquinas's argument, since they believe that the person standing before God on judgment day has been physically resurrected, and necessarily so, since they hold that persons cannot exist without bodies. Finally, even apart from the dualist/materialist debates over the composition of humanity, the teaching of Scripture is that in the end times, all will be resurrected to face judgment. As such, the defender of Postmortem Opportunity has many options for thinking about the nature of human constitution.

Suppose, however, that one is insistent that there is something about death that ends all possibility of repentance. Perhaps they are persuaded by Aquinas's hylomorphism or, even if they are not, perhaps they believe that the weight of church tradition requires that postmortem repentance is impossible. The latter rationale seems to be the crucial one for Kevin Timpe. He says, "Whatever reasons one thinks there might be for why it is that death secures the psychological impossibility in question, *that* it does so is secured by the church tradition."[27] Leaving aside the question of *which* church tradition one should take as definitive on this matter—for it is pretty clear that the Eastern Orthodox church demurs—if one takes this stance, is Postmortem Opportunity done for? It depends what freight is loaded on the "post-" in "postmortem." If "postmortem"

---

[25]Walls, *Heaven, Hell, and Purgatory*, 195.
[26]Walls, *Heaven, Hell, and Purgatory*, 195.
[27]Timpe, *Free Will in Philosophical Theology*, 77.

requires repentance in the afterlife, then those who are persuaded by the tradition argument will be unable to embrace Postmortem Opportunity. But if "postmortem" merely means "after conscious existence in this life" ("postvita"), then maybe not. As I mentioned in chapter two, it is possible that the Postmortem Opportunity occurs in the moment of death. Life has ended, but they are not yet in the afterlife. This is a position that is common in the Roman Catholic Church and it is possible to modify Postmortem Opportunity accordingly.

What might this look like? Here is a one highly speculative suggestion. Suppose there is such a thing as hypertime. Hypertime is a complex and controversial notion that suggests that it is possible that multiple moments can be contained within a single moment—or, more precisely, there are multiple hypermoments contained in a single temporal slice of time.[28] If hypertime is real, it is possible to think of the moment of death as encompassing, from the perspective of the person, years of opportunities to repent.[29] The opportunities to repent, while lasting as long as necessary in hypertime, are all contained in the moment of death. Hence, repentance after life ends (or maybe *as* life ends) is possible, even if repentance in the afterlife is not.

Postmortem Opportunity and the possibility of sin in heaven. The previous objection was psychological in nature. It involved the claim that, given human nature, repentance after death was impossible. The "possibility of sin in heaven" objection is different. It argues that postmortem repentance is problematic because of its implications—namely, accepting the theory of Postmortem Opportunity entails the possibility of sin in heaven. If one had the sort of free will that allowed one to say yes to Christ in a postmortem state, what would prevent that same free

[28]For a very nice discussion of the idea of hypertime (and a fascinating application of it to the problem of reconciling evolution and the biblical notion of the Garden of Eden), see Hud Hudson, "An Essay on Eden," *Faith and Philosophy* 27, no. 3 (July 2010): 273-86. See also his book *The Fall and Hypertime* (New York: Oxford University Press, 2014). Thanks to Hud for correspondence and advice on this matter.

[29]I am indebted to Tom McCall for suggesting this possibility.

will from resulting in sin in heaven? This is perhaps the objection to Postmortem Opportunity with the oldest pedigree. In *City of God*, Augustine objects to Origen's articulation of postmortem hope as follows: "For in this theory he lost even the credit of being merciful, by allotting to the saints real miseries for the expiation of their sins, and false happiness, which brought them no true and secure joy, that is, no fearless assurance of eternal blessedness."[30] The question of the possibility of sin in heaven is a question for all theologies that affirm libertarian freewill, but it is especially a challenge for defenders of Postmortem Opportunity because they cannot fall back on the claim that it is psychologically impossible to change one's fundamental spiritual disposition after death—those who lack faith at death cannot repent and those who are saved at death cannot rebel.

The first thing to see is that there is nothing about the theory of Postmortem Opportunity that requires that it be possible to sin in heaven. Rather, the affirmation that the unevangelized have a Postmortem Opportunity merely invalidates one of the possible answers as to why sin in heaven is impossible—namely, the claim that it is impossible to change one's fundamental spiritual dispositions in the postmortem state. But there are other reasons to assert that it is impossible to sin in heaven. There are two ways to explain the inability of humans to sin in heaven, given the (all too obvious) fact that humans are able to sin prior to death. The first locates the explanation within humans—even if some make a salvific decision upon being given a Postmortem Opportunity, those in heaven are unable to sin; the second locates the explanation in God—we are able to sin, but God doesn't allow it. I prefer the former, for two reasons. First, if humans are able to sin in heaven, and would do so without divine intervention, it seems strained to say that our moral natures are perfected in heaven. Final sanctification, on this account, is simply God doing something in heaven that he did not do in

[30]Augustine, *City of God* 21.17 (*NPNF* 1, 2:466).

this life—namely, stop us from sinning. Second, if God could simply stop us from sinning and his doing so would be compatible with our being in relationship with him, why did he not do so from the beginning, in the Garden of Eden?

It seems better, therefore, to locate the reason for the human inability to sin in heaven in something intrinsic to humans. The trick is doing so while maintaining what Timothy Pawl and Kevin Timpe call "the traditional view of heaven." The traditional view of heaven is the conjunction of the following theses:

1. The redeemed in heaven have freewill, and
2. The redeemed in heaven are no longer capable of sinning.[31]

Pawl and Timpe discuss a variety of different ways of upholding the traditional view of heaven and argue for a view that they think does so most effectively. They say,

> One can be free in heaven but unable to sin in virtue of having a moral character that one has previously freely formed. . . . While an agent must have alternative possibilities open to her at some time in order to be free, the agent need not always have alternative possibilities open to her. She may freely form her character such that she *can't* choose *not* to perform some particular action at a later time, and nevertheless do the latter action freely.[32]

The challenge is affirming Pawl and Timpe's explanation of how humans are both free and do not sin in heaven while also affirming:

3. There are at least some humans (the unevangelized and pseudo-evangelized) who receive a Postmortem Opportunity to repent and have libertarian freedom with respect to that choice.

In other words, while Pawl and Timpe might argue that it is psychologically impossible to change one's fundamental spiritual disposition after death, that explanation is not available to the defender of Postmortem

[31]Timothy Pawl and Kevin Timpe, "Incompatibilism, Sin, and Free Will in Heaven," *Faith and Philosophy* 26, no. 4 (October 2009): 399.
[32]Pawl and Timpe, "Incompatibilism, Sin, and Free Will," 399-400.

Opportunity. What is it that solidifies our freely chosen character if it is not death? Two things: judgment and the apprehension of God's fundamental nature—what is often called the "beatific vision." Judgment is the completion of our journey toward God. The unevangelized and pseudoevangelized, of course, need to hear and respond to the gospel. But judgment day is crucially important even for those who have heard and responded to the gospel. Those who have begun a relationship with Christ in this life and have benefited from the indwelling of the Holy Spirit will have an opportunity to see Christ "as he is" (1 Jn 3:2), or in the words of the apostle Paul, "For now we see only a reflection as in a mirror; then we shall see face to face. Now I know in part; then I shall know fully, even as I am fully known" (1 Cor 13:12). This does *not* imply that beliefs, decisions, and commitments made in this life do not matter, but rather that all of our steps along the journey of salvation lead up to the moment of standing before God. Judgment day for Christians is not a time of shame, but a time of hope and joy. It is the equivalent of a long-awaited wedding day, the moment when the relationship long hoped for and anticipated is culminated.

So while we see who God truly is on judgment day, that does not mean that we experience the beatific vision.[33] The beatific vision—literally: "happy-making sight"—as Thomas Aquinas argues, is not seen with the eyes, but with the intellect.[34] Similarly, C. S. Lewis argues that the attainment of glory is a necessary precondition for the beatific vision.[35] This is important because it is not a minor matter to stand before a perfectly good, holy God. Lewis says, "Some people talk as if

[33]Similarly, while Adam and Eve "walked with God" in the Garden of Eden and Lucifer was with God in heaven, their experience did not involve awareness of God's essence. They did not experience the beatific vision because they had not yet chosen to permit their final sanctification into beings that could experience God's essence.

[34]Thomas Aquinas, *Summa Theologica*, supplement Q. 92, a. 2 (New York: Benzinger Brothers, 1947), 2965.

[35]See the excellent discussion of Lewis's thought on this matter in Matthew Lee, "To Reign in Hell or To Serve in Heaven: C. S. Lewis on the Problem of Hell and the Enjoyment of the Good," in *C. S. Lewis as Philosopher: Truth, Goodness, and Beauty*, ed. David Baggett, Gary Habermas, and Jerry Walls (Downers Grove, IL: IVP Academic, 2008), 161-67.

meeting the gaze of absolute goodness would be fun. They need to think again. They are only playing with religion. Goodness is either the great safety or the great danger—according to the way you react to it."[36] Consequently, judgment day involves our permitting ourselves to be transformed into people who can experience with joy the perception and understanding of God's essence. And those who have freely chosen to be so transformed cannot choose to sin or reject God, despite the fact that they maintain their freedom.

THE "PANDORA'S BOX" OBJECTION

The final theological objection to be discussed in this chapter addresses my invocation of the category of the pseudoevangelized. Arguably, my discussion of the pseudoevangelized is one of the most unique aspects of my account of Postmortem Opportunity; in fact, it is unique among answers to the problem of the destiny of the unevangelized in general. This objection might be called the "Pandora's box" objection,[37] and it seeks to argue that once one creates the category of the pseudo-evangelized, it is difficult to stop it from growing out of control. Recall that the pseudoevangelized are those who have heard a version of the gospel that is inadequate in some way. From the perspective of this objection, the crucial question to be faced is, "Isn't every articulation of the gospel inadequate in some respect?" Perhaps the understanding of God's nature assumed by a presentation of the gospel is skewed? Or maybe the presentation of the gospel makes claims about the Christian life that presents as transcultural a particular culture's ways of responding to the gospel? The opportunities for inaccuracies are probably legion. But, if it might be the case that every presentation of the gospel is inadequate in one way or another, then aren't all people pseudoevangelized? If so, the

[36]C. S. Lewis, *Mere Christianity* (New York: Simon and Schuster, 1996), 38.

[37]To be clear, I am not aware of anybody who has advanced this objection in print. This should not be surprising given that nobody that I know of has really developed the problem of the pseudoevangelized. Rather, this is an objection that has come up in conversation with a number of friends regarding my account of the pseudoevangelized.

very category of the pseudoevangelized opens up Pandora's box and requires the belief that all are pseudoevangelized, at best.

Responding to this objection requires very clearly distinguishing what I am actually claiming for my theory of Postmortem Opportunity, what a theory of Postmortem Opportunity might claim, and what I think is the case. What I claim is that a Postmortem Opportunity is given to anybody who God believes to be in need of it. Moreover, I claim that it is plausible to think that there are some people who fall into the category of pseudoevangelized and that, if so, it is very likely that God would deem them to be in need of a Postmortem Opportunity. But I do not claim that any particular person is actually pseudoevangelized; nor do I claim that there are *any* persons who are pseudoevangelized. This is because neither I nor any other human is in a place to speak to the question of who needs and who doesn't need a Postmortem Opportunity. This isn't to suggest that all Postmortem Opportunity theorists must follow me on this. There certainly could be versions of the theory of Postmortem Opportunity that would happily embrace what might be called "universal pseudoevangelism."[38] In fact, this seems to be the perspective of George Lindbeck. He argues that death itself "be pictured as the point at which every human being is ultimately and expressly confronted by the gospel, by the crucified and risen Lord. It is only then that the final decision is made for or against Christ. . . . All previous decisions, whether for faith or against faith, are preliminary."[39]

Finally, in terms of what I think is the case on this matter, I strongly suspect that there are people in this life who are solidified both for and against God and therefore, even if they are given a Postmortem Opportunity, their spiritual trajectory is set. In other words, I tend to

[38]When I began writing this volume, I was much closer than I currently am to embracing this stance. I do not because of an intensification of two ideas in my thought: the solidification of character and soteric skepticism.

[39]George Lindbeck, *The Nature of Doctrine: Religion and Theology in a Post-liberal Age* (Philadelphia: Westminster, 1984), 59.

believe that universal pseudoevangelism is false. But suppose I am wrong and universal pseudoevangelism is true? Why would that be a problem? It wouldn't be, I suggest, as long as we maintain the conditional "people receive a Postmortem Opportunity if God deems them to need it." If we make sure that we are clear that the recipients of Postmortem Opportunity are not determined by us, but by God, it is difficult to see why it would be a problem if God deemed all to be in need of a Postmortem Opportunity.

CONCLUSION

There are perhaps other theological objections to Postmortem Opportunity out there, but the objections considered in this chapter seem to be the most challenging. However, a different class of objections still remains to be addressed. This kind of objection comes from theories that are similar to Postmortem Opportunity in certain respects, but different in other crucial respects. For example, Inclusivists will accept that those who died without hearing the gospel of Jesus Christ can still be saved, but they argue that, at least for people like George, a Postmortem Opportunity is unnecessary. And Universalists accept that some experience a Postmortem Opportunity, but that it is merely the means by which God brings about universal salvation. The final three chapters consider these important claims.

8

INCLUSIVISM AND POSTMORTEM OPPORTUNITY

Let's begin this chapter by returning to the discussion of the nature of the problem of the destiny of the unevangelized and the taxonomy of views discussed in chapter one. The problem of the destiny of the unevangelized is an inquiry into the theological coherence of God's apparent desire for the universal accessibility of salvation, the apparent requirement that one must hear and respond to the gospel of Jesus Christ to be saved, and the apparent fact that some die without hearing the gospel. In chapter three, I argued that the Restrictivist view is wrong in denying God's desire for universal accessibility and that the Universal Opportunity theorist is wrong in affirming universal accessibility in this life. In this chapter, I take up the Inclusivist's claim that it is possible to be saved without hearing the gospel and responding with explicit faith. While I will end up rejecting this claim, I find Inclusivism to be a much better answer to the problem of the destiny of the unevangelized than either Restrictivism or Universal Opportunity. I also find many of the critiques of Inclusivism to miss the mark rather badly. As such, it is most reasonable to see this chapter as offering an amendment to Inclusivism. While I am relatively sure that this amendment will not be universally embraced by Inclusivists, that does not change the fact that I do not see my position as diametrically opposed to Inclusivism, but rather as building on and extending it. The goal of this chapter is twofold. First, I want to show that Inclusivism is correct in one important sense but is nonetheless insufficient as an explanation of how the unevangelized might be saved. Second, I want to show how the combination of Postmortem Opportunity and Inclusivism is superior to Inclusivism by itself.

THE CASE FOR INCLUSIVISM

John Sanders describes Inclusivism as a wider hope view that affirms "that some of those who never hear the gospel of Christ may nevertheless attain salvation before they die if they respond in faith to the revelation that they do have."[1] In chapter one, following Christopher Morgan, I drew a distinction between General Revelation Inclusivism and World Religions Inclusivism. I will initially focus on the former, but will eventually also address the latter.[2] I see General Revelation Inclusivism as the conjunction of the following theses:

God desires all people to be saved. Contrary to the Restrictivist, who holds that when all things are considered God does not desire the universal accessibility of salvation, the Inclusivist believes that God's desire is that every person he has created enter into a saving relationship with him. Inclusivists point to passages such as 1 Timothy 2:4, 2 Peter 3:9, and Ezekiel 33:11 in defense of their affirmation of God's universal salvific will.

The saving work of Jesus is ontologically necessary for salvation. It is crucial to acknowledge that Inclusivists do not in any sense downplay the importance of the life, death, and resurrection of Jesus for salvation. There is no hint of "other saviors" in Inclusivism. Contrary to Religious Pluralism and Religious Relativism, Inclusivism emphasizes that all who are saved are saved through the saving work of Jesus Christ, even those who have not heard the gospel of Jesus Christ and therefore, do not know the details of how they are being saved. Inclusivists appeal to scriptural evidence like John 14:6-7 and Acts 4:12 in support of this contention.

---

[1]John Sanders, *No Other Name: An Investigation into the Destiny of the Unevangelized* (Grand Rapids, MI: Eerdmans, 1992), 215.

[2]Christopher Morgan, "Inclusivisms and Exclusivisms," in *Faith Comes by Hearing: A Response to Inclusivism*, ed. Christopher W. Morgan and Robert A. Peterson (Downers Grove, IL: IVP Academic, 2008), 32-34.

Some do not hear the gospel of Jesus Christ. The inclusivist position assumes that there are some who are unevangelized, who have not heard the gospel in this life. In other words, the Inclusivist rejects the claim of the Universal Opportunity theorist who claims that God will bring the gospel to all people in this life.

It is possible to be saved without hearing the gospel of Jesus Christ. Inclusivists do not deny the value or importance of preaching the gospel. They merely affirm the possibility that one might be saved without hearing the gospel of Jesus Christ. The salvific work of Jesus is ontologically necessary, but it is not epistemologically necessary. In other words, Inclusivists affirm the salvific value of implicit faith.

Salvation and implicit faith. The distinction between explicit and implicit faith is crucial for Inclusivists. Explicit faith occurs when a person hears the gospel of Jesus Christ and intentionally and consciously embraces it. Inclusivists do not dismiss the value of explicit faith, they only affirm that it is not necessary for salvation. There are a number of closely related components to the Inclusivist's affirmation of the salvific efficacy of implicit faith. The first is what has been called "the Faith Principle." The term was coined by Clark Pinnock as an affirmation of the fact that it is ultimately faith that saves, not the content of one's theological beliefs. He says, "The fact that different kinds of believers are accepted by God proves that the issue for God is not the content of theology but the reality of faith. . . . Theological content differs from age to age in the unfolding of redemption, but the faith principle remains in place."[3] Of course, this is not to say that there is no theological content at all that is required for salvation, but it is not entirely clear what theological content is necessary. J. Gresham Machen perspicuously raised the question of whether humans have the ability to assess whether another person's beliefs constitute faith. He said, "Who can presume to say for certain what is the condition of another

[3]Clark Pinnock, *A Wideness in God's Mercy: The Finality of Jesus Christ in a World of Religions* (Grand Rapids, MI: Zondervan, 1992).

man's soul; who can presume to say whether the other man's attitude toward Christ, which he can express but badly in words, is an attitude of saving faith or not?"[4] In a similar vein, A. H. Strong wrote,

> The patriarchs, though they had no knowledge of a personal Christ, were saved by believing in God so far as God had revealed himself to them; and whoever among the heathen are saved, must in like manner be saved by casting themselves as helpless sinners upon God's plan of mercy, dimly shadowed forth in nature and providence. But such faith, even among the patriarchs and heathen, is implicitly a faith in Christ, and would become explicit and conscious trust and submission, whenever Christ were made known to them.[5]

The second component of the Inclusivist's claim that implicit faith is salvific is closely related to the Faith Principle. I call it the "Degree of Access Principle." This is the principle my students are operating from when they respond with outrage when I threaten to test them on quantum mechanics when what I actually taught in the class was systematic theology. The basic idea of the Degree of Access Principle is that God holds people accountable to the degree and kind of revelation they have been given. Those who have heard the gospel of Jesus Christ are held accountable for their response to Jesus Christ, those who have not heard the gospel but have still seen the character of God through what he has created (Rom 1:19-20) are held accountable for their response to that revelation. Clark Pinnock describes this principle this way: "Since God has not left anyone without witness, people are judged on the basis of the light they have received and how they have responded to the light."[6]

The third component of Inclusivism is a direct answer to the question, How does implicit faith come about? Inclusivists affirm that God's witness is broader than the teaching of the gospel. God reaches out to those who have not heard the gospel in two ways: through

---

[4]J. Gresham Machen, *What Is Faith?* (New York: Macmillan, 1925), 155.
[5]Augustus Strong, *Systematic Theology* (Philadelphia: Judson Press, 1947), 842.
[6]Pinnock, *Wideness in God's Mercy*, 157-58.

general revelation and through his Holy Spirit. In fact, a number of people cite examples of God's witness preceding our evangelism. In his well-known book *Eternity in Their Hearts*, Don Richardson documents a number of cases where missionaries came into contact with people groups who apparently had already responded to God's redemptive work. Richardson likens these cases to Melchizedek, the "priest of God Most High" (Gen 14:18). It is important, however, to realize that the general revelation appealed to by Inclusivists is not something that is accessed on one's own, apart from grace[7]—knowledge of God may be accessible outside special revelation, but it is not accessible outside the context of grace. Moreover, as real and powerful as God's teaching through general revelation is, God did not leave it there, for God also reaches out to those who have not heard the gospel through the Holy Spirit. While not everyone has an opportunity to hear the gospel of Jesus, the Holy Spirit is poured out on all people (Acts 2:17). This Pneumatological Inclusivism affirms that while the Spirit operates within the church, the Spirit is not confined to the church and works beyond the church's reach.[8]

Arguments for Inclusivism. While there is undoubtedly some diversity within Inclusivism, typically Inclusivists appeal to the following kinds of theological and scriptural arguments.

The salvation of premessianic believers. Inclusivists offer the salvation of Old Testament patriarchs and holy pagans[9] as a counterexample to the claim that explicit faith in Jesus Christ is necessary for saving faith.

---

[7]Sanders, *No Other Name*, 235-36.

[8]From my perspective, the Pneumatological Inclusivism of Clark Pinnock and Amos Yong is the most persuasive form of Inclusivism. See Pinnock, *Wideness* and *Flame of Love: A Theology of the Holy Spirit* (Downers Grove, IL: InterVarsity Press, 1996); Amos Yong, *Beyond the Impasse: Toward a Pneumatological Theology of Religion* (Grand Rapids, MI: Baker, 2003); *Discerning the Spirits: A Pentecostal-Charismatic Contribution to Christian Theology of Religions* (Sheffield, UK: Sheffield Academic Press, 2000); and *The Spirit Poured Out on All Flesh: Pentecostalism and the Possibility of Global Theology* (Grand Rapids, MI: Baker, 2005).

[9]The term *holy pagan* comes from Jean Danielou, *Holy Pagans of the Old Testament* (London: Longmans, Green and Company, 1957) and has been popularized by Clark Pinnock. See his *Wideness in God's Mercy*, 161; and *Flame of Love*, 198.

The Old Testament patriarchs like Abraham, while living in covenant relationship with Yahweh, nonetheless lacked any knowledge of Jesus Christ and his redemptive work. Hence John Sanders argues, "If knowledge of Christ is necessary for salvation, then how are we to explain the salvation of the Old Testament believers, whose knowledge was quite limited concerning the Messiah but who were justified by faith in God's Word?"[10] Holy pagans are those such as Enoch, Melchizedek, Abimelech, Jethro, and Job, who (apparently) are not recipients of special revelation, but are nonetheless saved (it seems) because of their obedience and faith. For Inclusivists, the salvation of premessianic believers is not merely a historical oddity. Clark Pinnock argues forcefully that it is a template for how God thinks about the unevangelized in general. He says,

> While everyone will grant that it was possible to respond to God the way Job did in premessianic times, not everyone thinks that the possibility still exists today. This latter hesitation needs to be confronted. Why would it make any difference if Job were born in A.D. 1900 in outer Mongolia? Why would God not deal with him the same way he dealt with him in the Old Testament? A person who is informationally premessianic, whether living in ancient or premodern times, is in exactly the same spiritual condition.[11]

Cornelius. A New Testament parallel to Old Testament premessianic believers is found in the story of Cornelius in Acts 10.[12] Cornelius was a Roman centurion and an uncircumcised Gentile. He and his family are described as "devout and God-fearing." In addition, Cornelius "gave generously to those in need and prayed to God regularly." In response, God sent an angel to Cornelius, who said, "Your prayers and gifts to the poor have come up as a memorial offering before God" (Acts 10:2, 4). The angel then instructed Cornelius, "Send to Joppa for Simon who is

---

[10]Sanders, *No Other Name*, 225.

[11]Pinnock, *Wideness in God's Mercy*, 160.

[12]Tiessen calls Cornelius "the most important individual in the New Testament for the focus of this inquiry" (*Who Can Be Saved? Reassessing Salvation in Christ and World Religions* [Downers Grove, IL: InterVarsity Press, 2004], 175).

called Peter. He will bring you a message through which you and all your household will be saved" (Acts 11:13-14).

Inclusivists argue that Cornelius was already saved before he heard the gospel from Peter because he placed his faith in God, and they point out that Thomas Aquinas and John Calvin shared this opinion.[13] Thomas Aquinas claimed that "he [Cornelius] was not an unbeliever, else his works would not have been acceptable to God, whom none can please without faith."[14] Calvin argues that Cornelius's works are not the means by which he is saved, they are an indication that he has already been illuminated by the Spirit, has responded in faith, and has been sanctified.[15] Therefore, what Peter gave to Cornelius was not salvation, but the "fullness of salvation that comes through a personal relationship with Christ."[16] And what Peter gained from his encounter with Cornelius was a new appreciation for the breadth of God's grace. He says, "I now realize how true it is that God does not show favoritism but accepts from every nation the one who fears him and does what is right" (Acts 10:34-35).

Hebrews 11:6 and the nature of faith. Instead of contradicting the biblical definition of faith, Inclusivists argue that the salvation of premessianic believers and Cornelius is perfectly compatible with the definition of faith presented in Hebrews 11:6: "Without faith it is impossible to please God, because anyone who comes to him must believe that he exists and that he rewards those who earnestly seek him." The message of this passage is that it is not the theological content of faith that saves, it is faith and obedience. Despite knowing nothing about the gospel of Christ, it was by faith that Abraham responded to God: "By faith Abraham, when called to go to a place he would later receive as his inheritance, obeyed and went, even though he did not know where he was going" (Heb 11:8).

[13]Tiessen *Who Can Be Saved?*, 176-78; Sanders, *No Other Name*, 222; Sanders also claims that Luther shares this opinion.

[14]Thomas Aquinas, *Summa Theologica* II-II, q. 10, a. 4, ad. 3 (New York: Benzinger Brothers, 1947), 1216.

[15]John Calvin, *Institutes of the Christian Religion*, 3.17.4; trans. Henry Beveridge (Peabody, MA: Hendrickson, 2008), 530.

[16]Sanders, *No Other Name*, 222.

Similarly, "Job was a person who, provided with some valid information about what is good and true, assimilated it and acted upon it."[17] The conclusion to be drawn here, according to Inclusivists, is that while those who hear the gospel "have the tremendous blessing of knowing that God has raised Jesus from the dead,"[18] it is not knowing about Christ's work that saves, but faith and obedience to the God who sent Jesus to save the world. Pinnock says, "Like Job and Abimelech, there are those who, due to an inner voice, come to a fork in the road and come to God in faith. There is always a way, whatever the path, to come to God. It is always possible to move closer to God than farther away. Those who desire God will be led by his Spirit to closer communion with him."[19]

This argument does not eliminate the role of theological content in salvation, but it does diminish it. Salvation requires some theological content, but it is not clear how much. With respect to salvation, the proper heart disposition is more important than the content of one's theological beliefs. Charles Kraft has made this very point, claiming that the *directional* element of a person's life is more indicative of salvation than the *positional* element.[20] There are many people who are positionally Christians, at least in some sense—they say the right things and by all outward appearances have a relationship with Christ—but in terms of their direction, are heading down completely the wrong path. Perhaps these are people who will protest, "Lord, Lord, did we not prophesy in your name and in your name drive out demons and in your name perform many miracles?" but will hear the terrifying words, "I never knew you. Away from me, you evildoers!" (Mt 7:22-23). On the other hand, Kraft (and other Inclusivists) suggest that there are people who lack knowledge of the gospel of Jesus Christ and, because of that, also lack fundamental theological truths, but

[17]Pinnock, *Wideness in God's Mercy*, 160.

[18]John Sanders, "Inclusivism," in *What About Those Who Have Never Heard? Three Views on the Destiny of the Unevangelized*, ed. John Sanders (Downers Grove, IL: InterVarsity Press, 1995), 39.

[19]Pinnock, *Wideness in God's Mercy*, 161.

[20]Charles Kraft, *Christianity in Culture*, rev. ed. (Maryknoll, NY: Orbis, 2005 [1979]), 187.

who are directionally headed toward relationship with God and, because of that fact, are saved.

Does Scripture teach that "hearing the gospel" is necessary? This final argument is less of a scriptural argument for Inclusivism and more of a way of looking at texts that seem to imply the falsity of Inclusivism. Restrictivists see in Scripture an emphatic refutation of Inclusivism. They appeal to texts like these:

> Acts 4:12: "Salvation is found in no one else, for there is no other name under heaven given to mankind by which we must be saved."
>
> John 14:6: "Jesus answered, 'I am the way and the truth and the life. No one comes to the Father except through me.'"
>
> 1 John 5:12: "Whoever has the Son has life; whoever does not have the Son of God does not have life."

The error Restrictivists make here is assuming that Inclusivists cannot affirm these passages. Inclusivists enthusiastically agree that there is "no other name" that saves; that Jesus is the "way, the truth, and the life"; and that those "without the Son" are not saved. This is because Inclusivists in no way deny the ontological necessity of Jesus, only the epistemological necessity. We are justified by faith, not by knowing that justification is by faith. The bone of contention between Restrictivists and Inclusivists is what it takes to "find salvation," "come to the Father," and "have the Son." In assuming that Inclusivists cannot affirm these verses, Restrictivists beg the question against Inclusivists. To effectively argue against Inclusivism, Restrictivists must not only argue that salvation requires "having the Son," but that the only way to have the son is to respond to the gospel of Jesus Christ with explicit faith. To support this contention they appeal to texts like Romans 10:9-10: "If you declare with your mouth, 'Jesus is Lord,' and believe in your heart that God raised him from the dead, you will be saved. For it is with your heart that you believe and are justified, and it is with your mouth that you profess your faith and are saved."

In response, Inclusivists argue (persuasively, I think) that those who infer the falsity of Inclusivism (or truth of Restrictivism) from this passage are guilty of confusing the paradigmatic picture of salvation presented in Scripture with the mandatory picture. Inclusivists absolutely accept that hearing the gospel of Jesus Christ and responding to that preaching is the paradigmatic path to salvation in the New Testament. What Inclusivists question is whether hearing and responding to the gospel is the *exclusive* means of salvation. In other words, Inclusivists do not question that hearing the gospel and declaring Christ as Lord is *a means* to salvation, what they question is that passages like Romans 10:9 teach that it is the *only means* of being saved. As Sanders points out, the statement "if you confess Christ, you will be saved" does not say anything about the unevangelized that never have an opportunity to confess Christ.[21] In other words, one cannot deduce "if you do not confess Christ, you will not be saved" from "if you confess Christ, you will be saved." Such a deduction commits the fallacy of denying the antecedent.[22] To see this consider the following arguments.

	VALID ARGUMENT		FALLACIOUS ARGUMENT
1	If you confess Christ, you will be saved.	1	If you confess Christ, you will be saved.
2	You confess Christ.	2	You do not confess Christ.
3	Therefore you will be saved.	3	Therefore you will not be saved.

Figure 3

[21]Sanders, *No Other Name*, 67.

[22]Sanders employs this argument, but he errs in seeing it as an example of affirming the consequent—if A then B entails if B then A (*No Other Name*, 67).

To see the error here, consider the following arguments, precisely parallel to the above pair.

	VALID ARGUMENT		FALLACIOUS ARGUMENT
1	If it is raining, the grass will be wet.	1	If it is raining, the grass will be wet.
2	It is raining.	2	It is not raining.
3	Therefore the grass will be wet.	3	Therefore the grass is not wet.

Figure 4

Even though it is not raining, the grass might still be wet if the sprinklers were on or if it was morning and there was a heavy dew. Similarly, it is possible that some who have not confessed Christ are still saved. Abraham, Melchizedek, and Job are obvious examples, and Inclusivists assert that we have reason to hope that the unevangelized who respond to the Holy Spirit's utilization of general revelation is another example.

D. A. Carson has responded to John Sanders version of this argument as follows.

> If all those who confess with their mouth that Jesus is Lord . . . constitute class A, and all those who are saved constitute class B, then if the members of the two classes are the same, it is precisely true to say that if you do not confess Jesus as Lord, . . . you are not saved. In other words, what Sanders has done is *assume* that the two classes do not precisely coincide—which is, of course, nothing more than assuming his conclusion.[23]

[23]D. A. Carson, *The Gagging of God: Christianity Confronts Pluralism* (Grand Rapids, MI: Zondervan, 1996), 312-13; paragraph break removed. He is responding to John Sanders's argument (*No Other Name*, 67). Ronald Nash has a similar argument in *Is Jesus the Only Savior?* (Grand Rapids,

What Carson is really trying to do is modify the major premise in the argument as follows:

> *If and only if* you confess Christ, you will be saved.
>
> You do not confess Christ.
>
> Therefore, you will not be saved.

This revision avoids the fallacy of denying the antecedent, but as a response to Sanders, he is missing the point. This is because Sanders is not even remotely assuming his conclusion in his argument. He is not employing Romans 10:9 as an argument for Inclusivism, he is merely stating that Romans 10:9 taken by itself does nothing to rule out Inclusivism. Moreover, when Carson (and other Restrictivists) add an "if and only if" clause to the major premise, they, not Sanders (and other Inclusivists), are begging the question. Now it might be possible to defend the claim that "if and only if you confess Christ, you will be saved" in other ways, but Sanders's (and my) point is that Romans 10:9 doesn't do the job.

Assessing the arguments for Inclusivism. The above arguments for Inclusivism establish the following three things. First, there is substantial complexity about how salvation was mediated prior to Jesus Christ. Even if Restrictivists are not persuaded by Inclusivists' holy pagans argument, they must acknowledge that dealing with figures like Melchizedek creates complexities for the Restrictivist's picture of salvation. There are ways of dealing with Melchizedek-like cases, of course. Jonathan Edwards suggests that Melchizedek "could have been saved through the traces of original revelation that still remained among his people" since the time of Adam.[24] And Walter Kaiser points

MI: Zondervan, 1994), 144-45. And Robert Peterson cites Carson's argument approvingly in "Inclusivism vs. Exclusivism on Key Biblical Texts" in Morgan and Peterson, *Faith Comes by Hearing*, 197.

[24]Jonathan Edwards, "History of Redemption," in *The Works of Jonathan Edwards*, ed. Harry S. Stout (New Haven, CT: Yale University Press, 1989), 9:179; cited in Tiessen, *Who Can Be Saved?*, 171.

out that Inclusivist's use of Melchizedek as an example of the one who was saved apart from any special revelation are making a big assumption—namely, that God did not reveal himself through direct communication with Melchizedek.[25] The lack of an account of such an encounter in our recorded special revelation does not mean that there was no such encounter. This is, of course, correct. But Kaiser must also admit that he (and like-minded Restrictivists) are also assuming without direct evidence that Melchizedek's faith was based on special revelation. Moreover, this is an assumption that they cannot expect those who do not share their Restrictivist inclinations to accept. The following is their argument:

1. Salvation comes only through special revelation.
2. Melchizedek was saved.
3. Therefore Melchizedek received special revelation.

This is utterly ineffective at blunting the Inclusivist's use of Melchizedek, for the issue at hand is the major premise, which the Restrictivist assumes to be true! So, again, while there are many different avenues of response available to the Restrictivist, it seems difficult to deny that (1) the Bible presents holy pagans like Melchizedek as recipients of salvation and (2) we have no account of special revelation that comfortably explains their salvation in New Testament terms. When one adds to this the notion of God's desire that all hear the gospel and his commitment not to leave himself without a witness, even in a time that precedes the incarnation of Jesus Christ, the arguments for Inclusivism are not easily dismissed.

Second, the Inclusivist's arguments drive home the point that faith is not primarily about theological content, but a matter of one's "directional vector" toward God. Hebrews 11 teaches that it was by faith that

---

[25]Walter Kaiser, "Holy Pagans: Reality or Myth," in Morgan and Peterson, *Faith Comes by Hearing*, 131. Kaiser offers his comments in connection with a response to Don Richardson's *Eternity in Their Hearts*.

Abraham was saved, but it is difficult in the extreme to explain how Abraham's faith included belief in Jesus Christ. Of course, as above, the Restrictivists have options here. For example, Charles Ryrie could affirm, "The basis of salvation in every age is the death of Christ; the requirement for salvation in every age is faith; and the object of faith in every age is God" because his dispensationalism allowed him to say that "the content of faith changed in every dispensation."[26] This sort of response solves the problem in one sense, but makes it way more intractable in another. It helps us see how Abraham could be saved despite his lack of awareness of the gospel, but it would seem to leave a great many, such as late first century denizens of China, with absolutely no hope. Moreover, when does the one dispensation end and when does the next one begin? To highlight this problem, consider a faithful Jewish person living in Alexandria who dies five years after Jesus dies, but because of his isolation never hears of him or his message. Is he judged by the past dispensation or by the new one? Or even worse, suppose he does hear of Jesus, but the presentation was really unclear and shot through with error and falsehood. Such people find themselves in the dispensation of grace and therefore are held accountable to their lack of faith in Jesus Christ, but they lack any messenger (or any reliable messenger) to give them this good news. The question of Romans 10:14-15 (which quotes Isaiah 52:7) is truly their question: "How, then, can they call on the one they have not believed in? And how can they believe in the one of whom they have not heard? And how can they hear without someone preaching to them? And how can anyone preach unless they are sent? As it is written: 'How beautiful are the feet of those who bring good news!'"

Third, the arguments of the Inclusivist force the conclusion that one who responds to the revelation they have been given is doing a morally and theologically praiseworthy thing. Now the Restrictivist might

[26]Charles C. Ryrie, *Dispensationalism Today* (Chicago: Moody, 1965), 123.

simply deny that because of the effects of sin it is impossible for any person to respond to the revelation they have been given without God's grace. But this response misses the point completely, because the Inclusivist can (and should) happily grant that very point. Contrary to the gross (but common) misunderstanding of their position, Inclusivists do not believe that recipients of general revelation are saving themselves through their capacity to reason their way from "what God has created" to "faith in God himself." Rather, Inclusivists believe that God through the Holy Spirit gives grace that enables the recipient of general revelation to respond. The question is not whether salvation requires God's grace, but how broadly is God's grace given? And consequently the Inclusivist's arguments force us to acknowledge that it is a good thing when someone responds to God's grace, however it is given.

The three points above concern General Revelation Inclusivism, but what of World Religions Inclusivism? This question is important, because there are vast numbers of people who are unevangelized in a Christian sense—they have not heard of Jesus—but who are nonetheless faithful adherents of a non-Christian religion. World Religions Inclusivists hold that the various world religions include truth from general revelation and, perhaps, remnants of special revelation and, by virtue of this fact, can be vehicles of salvation. This fact does not deny the ontological necessity of Jesus Christ for salvation, because one is not being saved through Gautama Buddha or Mohammed. Rather, these religious traditions are salvific only because Jesus Christ has made possible the salvation of human beings and only if the teachings of these religions align with the truth of God revealed in Jesus Christ. As such, World Religions Inclusivism should not be confused with a Religious Pluralism, like that espoused by John Hick, which holds that the major religious traditions are equally salvific and that none is privileged in terms of salvific access to God.

While a thorough discussion of this matter is well beyond the scope of this volume, a couple of things must be said to clarify my claims with respect to Inclusivism. I do not believe that non-Christian world religions are intrinsically salvific. I believe this because of my commitment to Christianity and the uniqueness of Jesus Christ. But even apart from that commitment, I hold that the pluralist attempt to find a common salvation in all of the world religions is severely problematic. Not only does doing so ignore the very real differences in how God (or "the ultimate"/"the Real") is understood, it ignores that fact that different religions "face in different directions, ask different questions and look for different kinds of religious fulfillments."[27] This is why S. Mark Heim writes not about religious conceptions of "salvation" but "salvations."[28] Nonetheless, one who claims that the non-Christian world religions are not intrinsically salvific is not committed to the belief that individuals in other religious traditions cannot be saved. On the one hand, my commitment to the exclusivity of salvation through Jesus Christ leads me to believe that while we can learn from other religious traditions and respect them, we will not regard them as salvifically sufficient on their own; on the other hand, my commitment to the universality of God's salvific efforts through the Holy Spirit leads me to hope that God may reach hearts in ways that we might not see as overtly and obviously Christian. As such, it is possible that just as implicit faith might be a response to God's general revelation, to the degree that a religious tradition has preserved that general revelation, it might be said that the religion could direct one toward God.

THE ULTIMATE NECESSITY OF EXPLICIT FAITH

The upshot of the argument in the previous section is that implicit faith is salvific in at least some important sense of that word. The crucial question, however, is this: In precisely what sense is implicit faith

[27]Gerald R. McDermott, *Can Evangelicals Learn from World Religions? Jesus, Revelation, and Religious Traditions* (Downers Grove, IL: InterVarsity Press, 2000), 91.
[28]S. Mark Heim, *Salvations: Truth and Difference in Religion* (Maryknoll, NY: Orbis, 1995), 144-52.

salvific? This question is important because there is an important difference between saying that implicit faith is soteriologically significant and saying that it is soteriologically sufficient. I believe that the preceding arguments are sufficient to establish the former, but not the latter. In other words, I believe that implicit faith is a response to (prevenient) grace and is such that a person might embrace a genuine saving relationship with God if it were offered to them. But I reject the idea that implicit faith by itself is sufficient for God to grant salvation to a person. Even if implicit faith is crucial in defining (or revealing) a person's spiritual directional vector, ultimately salvation requires explicit faith. Consequently, even though in the previous section I argued for the salvific *value* of implicit faith, I will now offer an argument against its salvific *sufficiency*.

The unavoidability of explicit faith. An important question to ask is this: What is the condition that is not only necessary, but sufficient for saving faith? It certainly is not a theological condition, having the correct theological beliefs. Nowhere does Scripture say that even the basic teachings of Christianity are soteriologically necessary. It is difficult to read verses like 1 Corinthians 15:1-6; John 3:16, 18, 36; 5:24; and Acts 16:31 and come away with the idea that it is the content of one's theology that saved. Notice, this does not mean that theology is irrelevant; one is hard pressed to reconcile certain egregious theological errors—such as, "there is no God" or "humans never sin"—with saving faith. But this speaks to the necessity of theological content for salvation, not to its sufficiency. Similarly, while being connected with a church, performing the sacraments, and being a person of virtue and seeking to live in a Christlike manner, are all crucially important for the Christian, they are not what saves a person. They are what a person who is saved does, they are not what salvation is. So what is a sufficient condition for salvation? It is a relational condition. Being in a particular sort of relationship with the God who exists.

The crucial point here is this: the object of faith is the God revealed in Jesus Christ, not a generic ultimate creator. D. A. Carson makes this point powerfully:

> Just as there were many who did not listen to the prophets of old, leaving but a remnant who faithfully obeyed Yahweh's gracious disclosures, so now with the coming of the Son there will be some who think that they honour God while disowning God's Word, his gracious Self-Expression, his own Son. But they are deluded. Now that the Son has come, the person that withholds the honour due the Son similarly dishonours the Father (cf. John 14:6; Acts 4:12).[29]

Some have attempted to obscure this point by shifting the soteriological focus from Christology to either a trinitarian focus or an explicitly pneumatological focus.[30] Both the trinitarian and pneumatological emphases are important—each retrieve aspects of the Christian tradition that have been underrepresented. The problem is describing (and understanding) these moves as shifts. Doing so interjects an aspect of opposition into the expression of the intertrinitarian relationship or between the Spirit and Jesus Christ. While the emphasis on the role of the Holy Spirit is well taken, I suggest that we should understand the work of the Holy Spirit as supportive of the revelatory activity of Jesus Christ, not in opposition to it or as an alternative to it. Stephen Wellum argues this case as follows: "In the canon, the work of the Spirit, as it is progressively disclosed, is never divorced from the work of the Son and bringing people to faith in him. In other words, the Spirit's work is always tied to gospel realities."[31] And even Amos Yong—who is obviously a strong defender of the pneumatological element in salvation—argues that "because the Spirit is the Spirit of Jesus, any desire to bracket the soteriological question [to pneumatological rather than christological concerns] can only be momentary."[32]

---

[29]D. A. Carson, *The Gospel According to John* (Grand Rapids, MI: Eerdmans, 1991), 255.
[30]Yong, *Beyond the Impasse.*
[31]Stephen J. Wellum, "Saving Faith: Implicit or Explicit?" in Morgan and Peterson, *Faith Comes by Hearing*, 171.
[32]Yong, *Beyond the Impasse*, 22.

Consequently, even if implicit faith can be genuinely salvific in the sense that it constitutes a genuine response to God's revelation of himself to those without the benefit of special revelation, one who has genuine implicit faith in God will not reject relationship with Jesus Christ, who is the fullest, clearest expression of God. Or to say the same thing, from the opposite perspective, if one with implicit faith rejects Jesus Christ, their implicit faith was never genuinely salvific. This is, I believe, the clear teaching of John 3:36: "Whoever believes in the Son has eternal life, but whoever rejects the Son will not see life, for God's wrath remains on them."

To illustrate this point consider the following. Suppose that George responded in faith to God's general revelation and, therefore, based on the Faith Principle and the Degree of Access Principle, Inclusivists believe that he is saved. But suppose that everybody who has not heard the gospel, including George, receives a Postmortem Opportunity to see God as he actually is and respond to the gospel of Jesus Christ. But, finally, suppose that when George stands before Jesus on judgment day, he rejects Jesus as being the God in which he has placed his faith. Should Inclusivists still claim that George was saved? Some might respond that it is not possible for someone who has genuinely placed their faith in God to not affirm that when they stand before God, but such a response would miss the point—rather spectacularly, in fact—because the question at hand is whether George's implicit faith is, in fact, genuine faith. And I submit that one who responds to general revelation with implicit faith but fails to respond to Jesus Christ himself with explicit faith, is not saved. What is more, I take this statement to be absolutely uncontroversial, for it is difficult in the extreme to hold that one who has received the best possible revelation of Jesus Christ, from Jesus himself, and rejected it is saved. The only remaining question is whether it is true that those with implicit faith are given an opportunity to make their faith explicit.

Let's state this sequence of thought as clearly and concisely as possible:

1. Implicit faith is salvific in the sense of being a favorable response to God's general revelation and prevenient grace.
2. But a favorable response to God's general revelation is not sufficient by itself for salvation.
3. Consequently, God gives those who have merely implicit faith a Postmortem Opportunity to respond to the gospel with explicit faith and relational commitment.
4. Implicit faith that refuses to become explicit when given the opportunity is not salvific.

The theological takeaway of this argument is that implicit faith is salvific in the sense of being indicative of a positive response to God's grace, but it is not salvific in the sense of being sufficient for salvation. This point is echoed by Clark Pinnock:

> In the case of morally responsible persons confronted with the gospel in this life, they would surely turn to him in explicit faith. If they did not do so, it would prove that they had not been favorably disposed to God prior to that time, since Jesus is the culmination of divine revelation. Pre-Christian faith is valid up to the moment when Christ is preached, but not afterward. When Christ is known, the obligation comes into force to believe on him. The unevangelized are expected to receive the Good News when it reaches them. God's offer becomes an objective obligation at that time, and refusal to accept that offer would be fatal. No hope can be offered to those declining God's offer to them in Christ.[33]

Some Inclusivists might respond that the above argument is actually an argument against Postmortem Opportunity. For if there are some who are saved prior to a Postmortem Opportunity and not saved after it, if would be better to forego the Postmortem Opportunity all together. Such a response ignores the fact that the goal of a Postmortem

[33]Pinnock, *Wideness in God's Mercy*, 168.

Opportunity is not to override genuine faith, but to ascertain whether the prior response to God's revelation was genuine.

This same point may be made in a slightly different way. The goal of salvation is not heaven or eternal life, it is relationship with God himself. Consequently, while there is a value to choosing to do God's will, believing in God, and even having faith, those things by themselves are not what salvation is, they are proximate steps toward salvation or steps that dispose us to choose God when we see him. What must be chosen is God himself, for he is our end and source of happiness. This is why the Inclusivistic attempt to use Hebrews 11:6 as specifying the minimal content of faith, "without faith it is impossible to please God, because anyone who comes to him must believe that he exists and that he rewards those who earnestly seek him," is ultimately unsuccessful. To treat this as a justification of the salvific nature of implicit faith is to miss the entire context of Hebrews—that the implicit faith of the Old Testament expressed in its covenants and priestly institutions "was not an end in itself but a means to an end, i.e., that which anticipated and looked forward to the coming of Christ."[34] The book of Hebrews can be summarized as follows: "If the OT saints persevered by faith, longing for the promises of God to be brought to fulfillment, then how much more should we persevere as those who live in light of what the OT could only anticipate."[35]

Finally, while the Inclusivist's point that faith is not primarily about theological content, but a matter of one's "directional vector" toward God is absolutely correct, it is equally true that an implicit openness to God or a directional vector aimed at God is supremely irrelevant if it does not result in relationship with God. Now it might

[34]Wellum, "Saving Faith," 176.

[35]Wellum, "Saving Faith," 176. A similar point may be made with respect to Acts 2. "To come to Acts 2 and argue that the Spirit is being poured out in such a way that even those who never hear the gospel will be saved, is to completely misunderstand why the Spirit is being poured out in the first place" (Matthew Barrett, "'I Will Pour Out My Spirit on All Flesh.' Are Acts 2 and 10 Proof-Texts for Inclusivism?," *Detroit Baptist Seminary Journal* 17 [2012]: 85-86).

be the case that the Inclusivist's argument is that one whose life has a "God-ward" relational vector will necessarily end up with explicit saving faith. If that is their argument, it hasn't been successfully made and, further, even if it was epistemically certain that a particular person's implicit faith would result in relational commitment to God himself, that fact would not eliminate the need for culmination and commitment. Consider this analogy. A couple is engaged. The bride-to-be desires to be married to her fiancé, she loves him, she is committed to him. Does all of that mean that they are married? No. Does the fact that it is epistemically certain that the bride-to-be will, on the wedding day, pledge herself in marriage to her intended mean that they are married? No. They will be married when they pledge themselves to each other on their wedding day. All of these proximate steps are important and even necessary, but none of the proximate steps entail the final, relational end.

Inclusivism and the pseudoevangelized. The second fundamental problem with understanding implicit faith as sufficient for salvation (or, denying the ultimate necessity of explicit faith) is seen when considering our examples of pseudoevangelism. Inclusivism thrives when discussing the most obvious examples of the unevangelized, our "George" cases. George hasn't heard the gospel, so he is judged by his response to God's general revelation and the leading of the Holy Spirit. But when considering Anna and Sam cases, Inclusivists have little to say that would be different than a Restrictivist—they would probably just adopt some version of the age of accountability or infant baptism argument. Most pressing, however, is the question of how an Inclusivist would handle cases of pseudoevangelism.

Rapunzel is the easiest case for Inclusivists. They might argue that the directional vector of her life at the time of death was indicative of implicit faith. The problem with such a claim is that it is impossible to know what Rapunzel would have done if she would have avoided her fatal car crash. One can speculate, but that is it. Far more difficult for

General Revelation Inclusivists is the case of Kunta Kinte. Kunta has rightly rejected the "gospel" he has been presented and, very likely, he views the Jesus of his white slave owners as more demonic than divine. An Inclusivist who sees some salvific value in other religions, might claim that Kunta's commitment to Islam could be indicative of implicit faith, but it is a stretch for any orthodox Christian inclusivist to claim that Kunta is saved *by virtue of* their non-Christian religious beliefs and *in spite of* explicit rejection of the name of Jesus Christ. Micha is, perhaps, the most difficult case for Inclusivists, because her experiences have left her without faith of any sort. Not only is she not disposed toward faith, it might be possible to say that her ability to respond in faith to anybody has been disabled.

So Inclusivists struggle to explain how the pseudoevangelized, and especially those who are similar to Kunta and Micha, might have an opportunity to be saved. The problem is that we have a strong and justified sense that God would not want Kunta's negative response to the bastardized gospel he heard to be his final answer. Similarly, wouldn't the God who leaves the ninety-nine sheep to seek the lost sheep want to give Micha an opportunity to respond, an opportunity not tainted by the scars of her experience in this life? Now, of course, it is possible that both Kunta and Micha reject Christ's postmortem offer of salvation. But if they do so, it will be because there was nothing that could have brought them to salvation.

COMBINING INCLUSIVISM AND POSTMORTEM EVANGELISM

In the final analysis, it is best to realize that God's soteriological efforts with respect to the unevangelized are multifaceted. First, God reveals his divine nature and power through what he has created. This revelation is salvifically insufficient, by itself, but it does not merely leave us without excuse—it is designed to draw us into relationship with him. Second, working in concert with God's revelation in creation, the Holy Spirit draws all people to God, seeking to convict us of our sin, and make us aware of our need for a Savior. While the Holy Spirit moves paradigmatically, within God's church, there is nothing that stops the Holy Spirit from operating outside the footprint of ecclesiological involvement and speaking to the unevangelized. Finally, God offers those whom he deems to have not had the opportunity to hear the gospel of Jesus Christ in this life a Postmortem Opportunity. In short, I utterly reject the either/or between Inclusivism and Postmortem Opportunity. It is a both/and.

Defending the both/and. This "both/and" claim is controversial. The only figure I am aware of who has defended the combination of Inclusivism and Postmortem Opportunity publicly and at length is Clark Pinnock.[36] While Pinnock argues that "the faith principle is the basis of universal accessibility [of salvation],"[37] he goes on to develop an account of Postmortem Opportunity that he describes as "another way of conceiving universal access to salvation."[38] Pinnock doesn't work out the details of the relationship between his Inclusivism and Postmortem Opportunity, but he clearly sees them both as viable and their conjunction as defensible.

In response, Ronald Nash has articulated an aggressive critique of Pinnock's attempt to combine Inclusivism and Postmortem Opportunity. In fact, he goes so far as to call the combination "logically incompatible."[39] This claim is surprising, for there is nothing *logically* incompatible about the two views.[40] What Nash should have claimed is, given his rigid application of the terms and categories he prefers in this debate, that he cannot see how Inclusivism and Postmortem Opportunity are compatible. Another figure who questions the both/and of Inclusivism and

---

[36]See his *Wideness in God's Mercy*, 149-55. Pinnock also developed his Inclusivist version of Postmortem Opportunity in "Inclusive Finality or Universally Accessible Salvation?" (Evangelical Theological Society Annual Meeting, 1989).

[37]*Wideness in God's Mercy*, 157.

[38]*Wideness in God's Mercy*, 168.

[39]Ronald Nash, *Is Jesus the Only Savior?* (Grand Rapids, MI: Zondervan, 1994), 149.

[40]But not as surprising as Nash identifying Wayne Grudem as a defender of Postmortem Opportunity (*Is Jesus the Only Savior?*, 151).

Postmortem Opportunity is D. A. Carson. To his credit, he realizes that Nash's logical incompatibility claim is a nonstarter.[41] However, he goes on to say, "It is very hard to see why anyone would want to hold both views simultaneously."[42] He offers two rationales for this claim: (1) if implicit faith is salvific, then there is no need of a Postmortem Opportunity, and (2) if people will have a Postmortem Opportunity, then there is no need for them to hear the gospel in this life. The problem with Carson's first claim is that it loses sight of the fact that even if implicit faith is salvific for some, there might be others that would benefit from a Postmortem Opportunity. For example, even if I believed George could be saved via implicit faith, it seems difficult to say that the same benefit could be applied to Anna or Kunta Kinte. Moreover, the truth of Carson's first claim depends on what is meant by "salvific." It is true only if one claims that implicit faith is salvifically *sufficient*. I do not think that implicit faith by itself is salvifically sufficient, so perhaps Carson would simply say that I am not a real Inclusivist, but that ignores the fact that I believe that a person's response of implicit faith to God's leading in this life can be such that when they have a Postmortem Opportunity to repent, they will do so. As such, I affirm that implicit faith is salvifically efficacious, even if it is not salvifically sufficient. It needs to be combined with a Postmortem Opportunity.

Carson's second claim is also false. Those who receive a Postmortem Opportunity are those who God deems to need one, but this doesn't imply that their attempt to understand God in this life or their response to God's revelation of himself via general revelation was irrelevant or unneeded. Consider an analogy: suppose I know that a child in a Sunday school class I am teaching will have an opportunity to hear a presentation of the gospel from the most gifted evangelist of her generation. Does this knowledge make me think that teaching her about

[41]He says, "[Nash's claim] is a little harsh. There is certainly nothing logically contradictory about holding the two views" (*Gagging of God*, 299).
[42]Carson, *Gagging of God*, 300.

God and presenting the gospel to her now is irrelevant? Of course not! As I argued in the previous chapter, even if people have a Postmortem Opportunity that does not in any way undercut our motivation to give the gospel to them in this life, simply because (1) we are called to present the gospel whether it is going to be effective or not and (2) there is no guarantee that those who receive a Postmortem Opportunity to repent will do so. Perhaps Carson is laboring under the assumption that all who receive a Postmortem Opportunity will respond affirmatively, but that is no claim of mine and it ignores the reality of free will.

The Inclusivist's primary objection to what I have argued here will undoubtedly be to my claim that implicit faith is not salvifically sufficient without a Postmortem Opportunity. However, since relationship with God is the ultimate goal of salvation, I don't think I can budge on that matter, but I can acknowledge something that might be true about the effect of implicit faith in this life. Could it be possible that some are so set in their implicit faith that their postmortem decision is a given? Certainly. This idea introduces us to an idea alluded to a number of times already in this volume, namely the idea of the "solidification of faith." The fundamental idea is that consistent choice and commitment in a particular direction produces dispositions to continue in that direction. One might call this the spiritual equivalent of Newton's first law of motion, the law of inertia. Choices create dispositions, ongoing dispositions create habits, and habits create character. It is possible that a person's character is solidified prior to death, and by virtue of this fact, it is certain that when standing before God on judgment day, the direction of that choice is certain.[43] Their ongoing allegiance to God in this life has produced dispositions, habits, and character that renders their commitment to God on judgment day certain. Of course, sadly, the same can be said in the opposite direction. Some choose their own

[43]Notice that the claim "It is possible that one's faith is solidified in this life" is not necessarily the same thing as saying, with John Wesley, "It is possible to be sinless in this life." One who becomes sinless in this life is probably also solidified in their faith, but it seems possible to not be perfectly sinless in this life and still be soteriologically solidified.

selfish desires and refuse to acknowledge any ultimate authority over them. They are then disposed to continue making these choices and ultimately these choices become habitual and part of their character. So, just as it is possible that there are some whose faith is solidified in this life, it is also possible that the lack of faith is solidified in this life. The crucially important point here is this: even if a person's implicit faith is fully solidified in this life, that does not mean that a Postmortem Opportunity is irrelevant.

Postmortem Opportunity and the world religions. Thus far, my comments about Inclusivism have focused on the salvifically efficacious nature of general revelation. But what about the religious traditions of the world? Might it be that an unevangelized person who was a member of a non-Christian religion would be more likely to respond to God's provision of a Postmortem Opportunity by virtue of their religious tradition? I think the answer is yes, but my affirmative answer comes with a slew of qualifications. First, I am not saying that the world religions themselves are vehicles of salvation. I heartily concur with Clark Pinnock when he says, "The idea that world religions ordinarily function as paths to salvation is dangerous nonsense and wishful thinking."[44] Second, while there might be some salvific efficacy in the world religions, it is only to the degree that the religious tradition has faithfully articulated general revelation or faithfully preserved special revelation. Third, I am not claiming that every member of a non-Christian religious tradition will receive a Postmortem Opportunity. It seems quite plausible to me that there are some members of non-Christian religious traditions who can be said to have heard the gospel of Jesus Christ and rejected it and therefore will not be a candidate for a Postmortem Opportunity. But undoubtedly, there are members of other religious traditions who have not heard the gospel—those before the time of Christ, most obviously, but also many, many since that time. I claim

[44]Pinnock, *Wideness in God's Mercy*, 90. This quote is cited approvingly by Tiessen, *Who Can Be Saved?*, 387-88.

only that it is possible that some members of other religious traditions will receive a Postmortem Opportunity and that it is God who ultimately decides who will be a recipient and who will not.

For those members of a non-Christian religion that God deems to be in need of a Postmortem Opportunity, what role does their religious tradition play in their response to God's postmortem offer of salvation? Understanding the possible salvific efficacy of the world religions requires a distinction between the objective and subjective elements of religion. Objectively speaking, the various world religions are incompatible with the message of the gospel of Jesus Christ; nonetheless, a person within a non-Christian religion might approach their religious beliefs and practices in a way that could open their heart to the working of the Holy Spirit. In fact, this same thing may be said of the Spirit's work within Christianity. The Christian religion is not intrinsically or necessarily salvific; rather it is the person and gospel message of Jesus Christ that saves. Christian religious practices are salvific only to the degree that they point us to Jesus Christ and are a response to the grace provided by the Holy Spirit. As such, it is possible to participate in the Christian religion and not know Christ.

To say this is to recognize that when a member of a non-Christian religious tradition embraces relationship with Jesus Christ, there is an element of continuity between their new religious understanding and their past beliefs. As Lesslie Newbigin says, "Even though this conversion involves a radical discontinuity, yet there is very often the strong conviction afterwards that it was the living and true God who was dealing with them in the days of their pre-Christian wrestlings."[45] This is not to say that "faithful practitioners" of non-Christian religions are more likely to respond to a Postmortem Opportunity, if given one. In fact, one could easily draw the opposite conclusion, as does John Barrett: "the most committed practitioners of other religions are often the least

[45]Lesslie Newbigin, *The Finality of Christ* (Eugene, OR: Wipf & Stock, 2009 [1969]), 59.

open to the message of the gospel."[46] At one level, this is uncontroversial since those who are most committed to a set of beliefs are also often the least open to revising them. But it is also possible to imagine an instance where a person was faithfully committed to a value or ideal in a non-Christian religion and that this value or ideal was a faithful expression of God's general revelation. Moreover, upon receiving a Postmortem Opportunity, this person's faithful adherence to the value expressed in their non-Christian tradition would be salvifically efficacious because in Christ they would find an even greater fulfillment of that value. In the final analysis, however, it is probably safe to say that a recipient of a Postmortem Opportunity who finds salvific efficacy in their non-Christian religious tradition would be a person who would not be entirely consistent in following their religious tradition.

The case study of C. S. Lewis's Emeth. I will close this chapter with a discussion of a well-known and much-discussed passage in C. S. Lewis's Narnia Chronicles. I do not discuss Lewis because I believe him to be infallible on doctrine and, therefore, that we should believe whatever he writes on the subject—I consider it at least possible that he is wrong on a few things. Rather, I consider Lewis's account of Emeth because it has been widely interpreted along Inclusivist lines and, as such, is an interesting case study for my combination of inclusivism and Postmortem Opportunity.

Lewis sets *The Last Battle* in the Narnian equivalent of the end times. The nation of Calormen, which worships a wholly evil being, Tash (the functional equivalent of Satan), has taken over Narnia. Among the Calormen soldiers is a young officer named Emeth who describes his religious commitments as follows: "Since I was I boy, I have served Tash and my great desire was to know more of him and, if it might be, to look on his face. But the name of Aslan was hateful to me."[47] Upon being told

---

[46]John K. Barrett, "Does Inclusivist Theology Undermine Evangelism," *Evangelical Quarterly* 70, no. 3 (1998): 237.

[47]C. S. Lewis, *The Last Battle* (New York: Collier Books, 1970 [1956]), 162.

that he could walk through a stable door and see Tash face-to-face, Emeth immediately volunteers. But instead of seeing Tash or even the inside of a stable, he sees a completely different world, an eschatological realm of beauty and happiness. After wandering around in a trance, he is approached by Aslan. Emeth falls at his feet and thinks, "Surely this is the hour of death, for the Lion (who is worthy of all honour) will know that I have served Tash all my days and not him."[48] But Aslan embraces him, saying, "Son, thou art welcome." Aslan goes on to explain that "all the service thou hast done to Tash, I account as service done to me." This is so, Aslan says, not because he and Tash are one, but because "we are opposites."[49] Aslan explains, "For I and he are of such different kinds that no service which is vile can be done to me, and none which is not vile can be done to him."[50] Consequently, one cannot seek Tash out of love and goodness or Aslan out of hatred or a desire for power. As such, despite the fact that Emeth believed that he was seeking Tash his entire life, Aslan informs him that "unless thy desire had been for me thou wouldst not have sought so long and so truly. For all find what they truly seek."

The Inclusivist implications of this story should be apparent. Despite the fact that he has never met Aslan and has even openly rejected the name of Aslan, when Emeth walks through the door, unlike the other creatures (the other Calormen soldier and the dwarves), he can see that he is not in a stable, but in the Narnian equivalent of heaven. The plausible inference is that Emeth's salvation is a result of his implicit faith in Aslan and that, despite appearances, he was actually searching for Aslan, not Tash, his entire life. As such, in this text, Inclusivists see Lewis affirming the salvific sufficiency of implicit faith.

One might merely respond that Emeth is a fictional character and not analogous to any real-world example.[51] But let's set that argument

---

[48]Lewis, *Last Battle*, 162.

[49]Lewis, *Last Battle*, 162-63.

[50]Lewis, *Last Battle*, 163.

[51]This claim is made more likely by the radical dichotomy that Lewis creates between Aslan and Tash. While I am not (even remotely) attempting to downplay the differences between Christian

aside. I will offer two reasons to think that the Emeth example is compatible with Postmortem Opportunity. First, there are extratextual reasons to think that Lewis might have accepted the notion of postmortem repentance. In an April 28, 1960 letter to Audrey Sutherland, Lewis addresses the question of the salvific fate of those before Christ:

> The [New Testament] always speaks of Christ not as one who taught, or demonstrated, the possibility of a glorious after life but as one who first created that possibility—the Pioneer, the First Fruits, the Man who forced the door. This of course links up with 1 Peter 3:20 about preaching to the spirits in prison and explains why our Lord "descended into Hell." . . . The medieval authors delighted to picture what they called the "harrowing of Hell," Christ descending and knocking on those eternal doors and bringing out those whom He chose. I believe in something like this. It would explain how what Christ did can save those who lived long before the Incarnation.[52]

In addition, a closer look at the text of *The Last Battle* itself suggests that the inference of Inclusivism is not as simple as it may appear. Lewis's Emeth example pretty clearly suggests that implicit faith can be salvific in the sense that it can open one's eyes to religious reality, for Emeth sees the world beyond the stable for what it is, he sees the beauty and honor of Aslan, and he finds Aslan because that is who he was truly seeking all his life. But one is hard pressed to say that Emeth has everything he needs from a salvific point of view upon entering the stable, for Lucy describes Emeth's first moments in the stable as follows: "He could see us, and everything else. We tried to talk to him but he was rather like a man in a trance. He kept on saying, 'Tash, Tash, where is Tash? I go to Tash.'"[53] His theological confusion remains, even after entering the stable door. Now, undoubtedly, because of Emeth's love and the genuineness of his search, he sees religious reality better than many

---

and non-Christian conceptions of God, it is difficult to say of non-Christian conceptions of God that they "are of such different kinds that no service which is vile can be done to me, and none which is not vile can be done to [them]."

[52]In *The Collected Letters of C. S. Lewis*, vol. 3, *Narnia, Cambridge, and Joy (1950–1963)*, ed. Walter Hooper (New York: HarperSanFrancisco, 2007), 1148.

[53]Lewis, *Last Battle*, 142-43.

Narnians who have been taught about Aslan from their youth, but in standing before Aslan he must still allow the new picture of religious reality that Aslan presents to override his previous pictures. And crucially, when he stands before Aslan, he responds with faith and love and Aslan responds by breathing on him, taking away his fear, and tells him that they would meet again.[54] So, to expand on Aslan's words: "All find what they truly seek, even if they are unaware of what they have been truly seeking until the end." Emeth undoubtedly embodies the best of the virtues that constitute faith, but none of that suggests that his implicit faith was what saved him or that his postmortem encounter with Aslan was extraneous.

This returns us to the key idea discussed in the previous section—namely, the fact that while implicit faith can be salvific—or, more accurately, the virtues that embody and express implicit faith can be salvific—they must be actualized in a particular choice in order to result in salvation. Paramount among the virtues exemplified by Emeth are intellectual curiosity and a love of truth. Lewis describes Emeth as initially fearful upon meeting Aslan, but he overcame his fear because of his "great desire for wisdom and understanding."[55] Without his desire to know the truth, his fear wins the day and his ignorance remains. So it is not just intellectual curiosity or love or implicit faith that saves, but a willingness and desire to know what is true even if that means overturning what one has always held to be true. If Emeth would have looked at Aslan and, despite his lifetime seeking the truth, rejected him because he did not fit his preconceived notions, then there is no doubt that he would have failed to achieve salvation. This understanding of Emeth fits with what Lewis has said elsewhere:

> There are other people who are slowly becoming Christians though they do not yet call themselves so. There are people who do not accept the full Christian doctrine about Christ but who are so strongly attracted by Him that

[54]Lewis, *Last Battle*, 165.
[55]Lewis, *Last Battle*, 162.

> they are His in a much deeper sense than they themselves understand. There are people in other religions who are being led by God's secret influence to concentrate on those parts of their religion which are in agreement with Christianity, and who thus belong to Christ without knowing it. For example, a Buddhist of good will may be led to concentrate more and more on the Buddhist teaching about mercy and to leave in the background (though he still may say he believed) the Buddhist teaching on certain other points. Many of the good Pagans long before Christ's birth may have been in this position. And as always, of course, there are a great many people who are just confused in mind and have a lot of inconsistent beliefs all jumbled up together.[56]

The key questions regarding Emeth are, When is he saved? And what is it that saves him? Is Emeth saved by virtue of his passionate commitment to Tash? Is he saved by his doing good in the name of Tash? Is he saved by his unwillingness to believe the Shift's syncretistic heresy about "Tashlan?" Is he saved by his desire to see Tash? Is he saved by walking through the stable door seeking submission of self and commitment to a being beyond himself? The thing is that all of these things are crucially important, but none of them by themselves is a sufficient explanation of the salvation of Emeth. It is only the conjunction of these things and his ultimate response when he stands before Aslan that results in the salvation of Emeth. In other words, when asking the question, "What saves Emeth? His implicit faith or his postmortem encounter with Aslan?," the answer must be *both*. Without the implicit faith developed throughout his life, Emeth would not have responded as he did upon meeting Aslan. And whatever implicit faith he developed would have been worthless if, upon meeting Aslan, he rejected him as "not being Tash." Now in the case of Emeth, it may be the case that his implicit faith was solidified before he entered the stable door. But even so, the value of his Postmortem Opportunity is for Emeth to see Aslan and to realize that it is Aslan that he has been following and not Tash. Without that Postmortem Opportunity, Emeth

[56]C. S. Lewis, *Mere Christianity* (New York: Touchstone, 1980 [1943]), 178.

continues in his misunderstanding of who God is and who he is not. And that misunderstanding is definitely not compatible with being in God's presence in heaven.

CONCLUSION

In summary, I accept the Restrictivist's argument for the ultimate necessity of explicit faith and the Inclusivist's argument for the salvific value of implicit faith. The mistake made by both is to reject the possibility of postmortem repentance. Given that assumption, Inclusivists reason from the conjunction of the following, (1) some do not hear the gospel and therefore they are robbed of the opportunity for explicit faith, and (2) God desires all to be saved, to the conclusion that (3) implicit faith is sufficient for salvation. Similarly, again given the assumption that death is the end of salvific opportunity, Restrictivists reason from the conjunction of, (1) some do not hear the gospel and therefore they are robbed of the opportunity for explicit faith, and (2) implicit faith is not salvific, to the conclusion, (3) ultimately God does not desire all to have an opportunity to be saved. The root of the problem in both of these cases is the assumption that death is the end of salvific opportunity. Removing that barrier allows one to see that the arguments for the salvific value of implicit faith are not arguments for their sufficiency and arguments for the necessity of explicit faith do not lend support to the idea that implicit faith is soteriologically useless. Therefore, the weaknesses of Restrictivism are not arguments for Inclusivism and the weaknesses of Inclusivism are not arguments for Restrictivism.

9

WILL ALL BE SAVED?

Any discussion of salvation will eventually have to confront the question of whether all will be saved and, if not, the destiny of those who are not. On the matter of hell, I am resoundingly with C. S. Lewis when he says, "There is no doctrine which I would more willingly remove from Christianity than this, if it lay in my power."[1] Unfortunately, it does not lay in either Lewis's or my power to do so and, therefore, we are left to grapple with this difficult question.

This volume has already discussed and endorsed a number of universalisms. I have argued for universalism with respect to the extent of the atonement, salvific will, and salvific opportunity. The universalism at issue in this chapter, however, is Soteriological Universalism (hereafter, just Universalism)—will all be saved or will some reject God's offer of salvation and spend eternity separated from him in hell?[2] There are a number of important similarities between the theory of Postmortem Opportunity and Universalism. Like Postmortem Opportunity, Universalism accepts unlimited atonement, universal salvific will, and universal accessibility. In addition, and more significantly, the

[1]C. S. Lewis, *The Problem of Pain* (New York: HarperOne, 2001 [1940]), 119-20.

[2]Universalism must be distinguished from what might be called "pluralist Universalism." According to Gregory McDonald, the pluralism of John Hick is Universalist because he "believes that all people will be saved by God through whatever religious system they belong to" (*The Evangelical Universalist* [Eugene, OR: Cascade, 2006], 5). McDonald is right to distinguish religious pluralism from Universalism, but while Hick is pretty clearly a Universalist (there is no mention of hell in his mature thought), his system works against his Universalism. This is because he claims that the only religions that are salvific are those that move one from self-centeredness to others-centeredness and that, therefore, there are religions traditions or ideologies that are not salvific. For more on this see Paul R. Eddy, *John Hick's Pluralist Philosophy of World Religions* (Aldershot, UK: Ashgate, 2002), 106. Also, Robin Parry wrote *The Evangelical Universalist* under the pseudonym Gregory MacDonald. Hereafter, with Parry's permission, I will refer to this book as being written by "MacDonald/Parry."

most plausible version of Universalism is itself a version of Postmortem Opportunity. While there is a Universalistic view that asserts that there are no requirements for salvation and therefore all are saved, such a view is singularly naive and theologically vacuous. It is also doubtful that any theologically thoughtful person has ever actually affirmed it.[3] The most plausible version of Universalism accepts that not all accept Christ in this life and that those who are not saved in this life end up in hell. But the punishment in hell is neither retributive nor eternal and the denizens of hell are provided an open and ongoing Postmortem Opportunity to repent and leave hell.[4]

As such, it is possible to see Universalism as an inference from Postmortem Opportunity. The reasoning here is as follows:

1. God desires all to be saved and will provide a Postmortem Opportunity to those who are not saved in this life.
2. Those who receive a Postmortem Opportunity will eventually be saved.
3. Therefore, eventually all will be saved.

On this view, Postmortem Opportunity is the gateway drug to Universalism. But it is also possible to reverse the implication and make Universalism the gateway drug to Postmortem Opportunity. For example, Keith DeRose believes that there are chances for salvation after death because of the following:

1. There are fairly strong biblical grounds for Universalism.
2. There are strong grounds for Strong Exclusivism—the idea that salvation is exclusively through Jesus Christ.

---

[3]D. P. Walker argues that no one has ever endorsed naive Universalism in his *The Decline of Hell* (Chicago: University of Chicago Press, 1963), 67.

[4]There are some who claim only that people can choose to leave hell, but do not necessarily claim that all will do so. This seems to be the view of Rob Bell in *Love Wins: A Book About Heaven, Hell, and the Fate of Every Person Who Ever Lived* (New York: HarperCollins, 2010). Such views might be called "potential Universalism" since they involve the claim that hell has the potential to be emptied. Universalistic views that claim that hell will be emptied are then best titled "eventual Universalism."

3. The only way to reconcile Strong Exclusivism with Universalism is to allow for Postmortem Opportunity.
4. There are no good reasons to deny the possibility of Postmortem Opportunity.[5]

The task of this chapter is to investigate the biblical and theological evidence for Universalism. If the evidence was strong enough, that would suggest that any version of Postmortem Opportunity should be developed in a Universalist manner, or if it is not Universalist, then the arguments for Universalism would be an objection to my non-Universalist version of Postmortem Opportunity.

EVALUATING SCRIPTURAL ARGUMENTS FOR UNIVERSALISM

It is perhaps folly to attempt to *briefly* consider such an important and complex issue as Universalism. After all, my topic is not Universalism per se, but Postmortem Opportunity. Nonetheless, because when defending the theory of Postmortem Opportunity it is important to ask whether there is a viable non-Universalistic version of Postmortem Opportunity, I need to first consider whether a non-Universalistic theology in general is at all viable.

The arguments for Universalism must be taken seriously. There is a tendency in certain segments of conservative Christianity to ignore the positive arguments for Universalism on the grounds that there are passages that "obviously" teach that some will be in hell forever. This move understands the "God will save all passages" in light of the "hell will be eternally populated passages." This move is understandable—and, as I will argue, not without merit—but one who makes such a move should realize that it is equally possible to read the "eternal hell" passages in light of the "God will save all" passages.[6] The goal is to find a reason to

---

[5]Keith DeRose, "Universalism and the Bible: The *Really* Good News," http://campuspress.yale.edu/keithderose/1129-2/, section 6.

[6]I will argue that while such a move is possible, it is not exegetically preferable.

prioritize one set of passages over the other. In this process, it is important to seek to understand the Universalist texts on their own.

"All" means "all." The first scriptural argument for Universalism are biblical texts that seem to teach that God will save all persons. Let's first set aside texts such as 1 Timothy 2:4, 2 Peter 3:9, and Ezekiel 33:11. As I argued in chapter three, these texts teach "universal salvific will"—that God desires that all people be saved—but these texts do not suggest the truth of Universalism unless they are conjoined with an assertion that God gets whatever he desires. However, there are texts that do not seem to refer merely to God's desires, but to his actions—that he has saved or will save all people. Here are some of the most commonly mentioned:

> John 3:17: "For God did not send his Son into the world to condemn the world, but to save *the world* through him."
>
> Romans 5:18: "Consequently, just as one trespass resulted in condemnation for all people, so also one righteous act resulted in justification and life for *all people*."
>
> Romans 11:32: "For God has bound everyone over to disobedience so that he may have mercy on them *all*."
>
> 1 Corinthians 15:22: "For as in Adam all die, so in Christ *all* will be made alive."
>
> Colossians 1:19-20: "For God was pleased to have all his fullness dwell in him, and through him to reconcile to himself *all things*, whether things on earth or things in heaven, by making peace through his blood, shed on the cross."
>
> 1 Timothy 4:10: "That is why we labor and strive, because we have put our hope in the living God, who is the Savior of *all people*, and especially of those who believe."[7]

It must be admitted that each of these texts, taken by themselves, lends prima facie support to belief in universal salvation. But is a Universalist interpretation the best reading of these passages? Does all always mean all? Of course, often *all* is used in a way that does *not* mean all. When I come home and tell my wife, "All my students flunked!" she doesn't say, "Really, all your students in all of your classes?" Rather, she understands

[7]Others: Is 66:23; Jn 12:32; Acts 3:21; 1 Cor 15:28; 2 Cor 5:19.

that my statement has a contextually determined domain: "all the students in the class in which I gave an exam today." Or, equally likely, she might take into account my penchant for rhetorical statements and interpret my "all my students flunked" as merely saying that "they did worse than I expected." In either case, she will not see my *all* as referring to "all my students."

This is perfectly reasonable, but the Universalist will press the point and argue that while my wife understood that I was only giving an exam in one class, it is not immediately apparent (based on these texts themselves) how the domain of these biblical texts should be limited. Keith DeRose argues, "When the domain is limited, there has to be some fairly clear clue as to what the limited domain is. When 'all' is used in the New Testament, as in 'For all have sinned and fallen short of the glory of God,' and similar passages, the 'all,' I take it, refers to all people."[8] I take DeRose's claim here to be as follows: if the *all* in these texts has a contextually determined domain that actually refers to all of some proper subset of "all people," there should be clear *internal* clues what that restricted domain is. In these cases, he argues that there are no internal clues that restrict the domain:

> (a) there is no such restricted class that clearly presents itself (all the people in this room?), (b) it's incumbent on a speaker to make clear what the class is if he means for it to be specially restricted and no specially restricted class clearly presents itself given current conversational intents and purposes, and (c) the New Testament doesn't specify any such specially restricted class. So, "All have sinned" means that all people have sinned, as almost all would agree.[9]

DeRose raises a salient point, but I think his point is overstated. The proper conclusion of his argument is not that "all means all," but rather that the domain of *all* is not *in this text* explicitly and intentionally limited by the biblical writer. This could mean that "all means all" or that the domain is limited in a way the biblical writer assumed was

[8]DeRose, "Universalism and the Bible," section 3.
[9]DeRose, "Universalism and the Bible," section 3.

really obvious, and was left implicit.[10] There are many instances where *all* is used to mean less than all even if there are no immediate textual clues that the domain is limited. In the case where I informed my wife about how my students did on the exam, *all* meant less than all my students and I merely relied on her assumption that not all of my students took an exam on the same day. In 2 Chronicles 9:23, it says "*All* the kings of the earth sought audience with Solomon to hear the wisdom God had put in his heart"[11] but it is unlikely in the extreme that "all the kings" includes the rulers of the Zhou dynasty in China. So "all the kings" means "all the kings in the world known to tenth century Israel," or the passage might be a deliberate exaggeration to make a point. And when Luke speaks of Paul's visit to the Areopagus in Acts 17:21, he offers the parenthetical comment that "*all* the Athenians and the foreigners who lived there spent their time doing nothing but talking about and listening to the latest ideas." It is supremely difficult to see that *all* really means "all"—how about women, children, and those who were sick? Here *all* probably means "quite a few of the men." And the Pharisees' words about Jesus in John 12:19, "the whole world has gone after him," clearly do not mean "the whole world," since they themselves certainly did not do so.

Herein lies the problem with a straightforward interpretation of these passages. One's opinion of whether the domain referred to by *all* is "actually all" (Rom 3:23, "All have sinned . . .") or "all of some proper subset" (2 Chron 9:23) or even a deliberate exaggeration designed to make a point (Acts 17:21; John 12:19), will depend on assumptions external to the text itself. The point is that one who believes that Scripture teaches that hell will be eternally populated will obviously see these passages differently than one who assumes that God's love is fundamentally incompatible with the eternal separation of some persons

[10]Consequently, I am surprised that DeRose says so confidently, "It's clear that 'all,' at least when used properly, never means anything like that" ("Universalism and the Bible," section 3).

[11]Note also the parallel in 1 Kings 4:34.

from God. Consequently, the fact that these texts can be taken to teach that "all will be saved" is not enough. We need a reason to believe that these passages teach Universalism and we need that reason to be stronger than whatever evidence exists for the belief that hell will be eternally populated.

One possible solution is to acknowledge that the Bible teaches both universal salvation and that those who reject Christ will remain in hell for eternity. This is the solution of M. E. Boring. He argues that the problem arises from the attempt to propositionalize these doctrines, rather than acknowledging that the hell passages and the Universalist passages are images or pictures that both represent God's teaching for the church.[12] While this is a novel suggestion, I concur with Tom Schreiner when he says, "Boring's solution is unpersuasive, for the Pauline threats of punishment do not even work as pictures or images if no threat exists."[13] If we set aside Boring's solution, those who are convinced that Scripture teaches that some will be eternally separated from God are left with trying to explain how all doesn't mean all. There are three general strategies for doing so.[14]

The first strategy is to point out that the immediate context of these verses mitigates their Universalistic implications. For instance, the statement that "the world" will be saved through Christ in John 3:17 is immediately followed by "Whoever believes in him is not condemned, but whoever does not believe stands condemned already because they have not believed in the name of God's one and only Son" (Jn 3:18). Similarly, in 1 Corinthians 15:22—"For as in Adam all die, so in Christ *all* will be made alive"—the *all* must be understood in context of the next verse: "But each in turn: Christ, the first fruits; then, when he

[12]M. Eugene Boring, "The Language of Universal Salvation in Paul," *Journal of Biblical Literature* 105, no. 2 (1986): 269-92, see especially 275.

[13]Thomas R. Schreiner, *Romans*, Baker Exegetical Commentary on the New Testament (Grand Rapids, MI: Baker Academic, 1998), 291.

[14]I am not claiming that each of these strategies address each of the verses listed above; some work for some of the verses, but not for others.

comes, those who belong to him" (1 Cor 15:23). So the *all* is "all of those who belong to him." And while Isaiah 66:23 says, "From one New Moon to another and from one Sabbath to another, *all mankind* will come and bow down before me," this Universalistic tone of this verse is immediately muted in the next verse: "And they will go out and look on the dead bodies of those who rebelled against me; the worms that eat them will not die, the fire that burns them will not be quenched, and they will be loathsome to all mankind" (Is 66:24). So, evidently, "all mankind" that "bowed down to Yahweh" did not include "those who rebelled."

The second strategy is to claim that these passages are best thought of not as saying that all will be saved, but that *the possibility of salvation has been provided to all*, although each person must respond with faith to secure the benefits of Christ's action on the cross. The clearest application of this argument is to 1 Timothy 4:10. As I argued in chapter three, the qualification "especially of those who believe" does not in any way deny that Christ is "the Savior of all people." Rather, the qualification draws attention to the necessity of belief to appropriate Christ's universal saving work and therefore, the "especially of those who believe" undermines the simple inference from Christ's universal atonement to Universalism. Now it would be false to say that this response rules out Universalism. If Christ's death makes possible the salvation of all, it is possible that all will be saved. Dunn makes this point with respect to Romans 11:32, saying "while 'the all' does not necessarily include every single individual (cf. 'all Israel,' 11:26), it certainly does not exclude Universalism."[15] But the point is that these passages are not necessarily indicative of Universalism.

Applying this strategy to other passages is more difficult. Perhaps the most difficult is Romans 5:18-19.[16] The implication of Universalism in the passage is pressed by the parallelism between Adam's trespass,

[15]James D. G. Dunn, *Romans 9–16*, Word Biblical Commentary, vol. 38 (Dallas: Word, 1988), 689.

[16]A pretty good case can be made that Rom 5:18-19 is the strongest Universalist text in Scripture.

which brought condemnation for all, and Christ's redemption, which brings life for all. Of course, it is possible to just say, "Paul cannot be teaching that 'all will be saved' here because of the teaching of other texts such as 1 Thess 1:9." That would be a perfectly reasonable argument, but it is worthwhile to see if there are internal clues that mute the Universalist implications of Romans 5:18-19. A good candidate is found in the preceding verse. Romans 5:17 reads, "For if, by the trespass of the one man, death reigned through that one man, how much more will *those who receive* [root: λαμβάνω] God's abundant provision of grace and of the gift of righteousness reign in life through the one man, Jesus Christ!" God's provision of saving grace through Jesus is given not to all, but to those who receive it.[17] Gregory MacDonald/Robin Parry responds to this argument by saying, "Λαμβάνω here is being used in the passive sense of 'receive' not in the active sense of 'take.'"[18] He goes on to argue: "The reference in v. 17 is not to anything people do to get saved. It refers to God making us recipients of grace and it places no limits on the universal statements in vv. 18-19, for those who receive God's abundant provision of grace could eventually be everyone."[19] This interpretation, however, strongly overinterprets the passivity in Romans 5:17. The passive sense of receive emphasizes the fact that grace is God's gift, but this does not even remotely negate the necessity of a person's response to that grace. That being said, the most effective response to the Universalist's use of Romans 5 is probably to question the argument that *all* always means all.

A third strategy for addressing the "all will be saved" passages is to point out that it is simply false that *all* always and simply means all. In typically pointed and clear fashion, N. T. Wright says, "Frequent

[17]L. Morris, *The Epistle to the Romans* (Grand Rapids, MI: Eerdmans, 1988), 240; H. Ridderbos, *Paul: An Outline of His Theology*, trans. J. R. de Witt (Grand Rapids, MI: Eerdmans, 1975), 340-41; Schreiner, *Romans*, 291; J. Stott, *Romans: God's Good News for the World* (Downers Grove, IL: InterVarsity Press, 1994), 159.

[18]MacDonald/Parry, *The Evangelical Universalist*, 80; transliteration changed to Greek text.

[19]MacDonald/Parry, *The Evangelical Universalist*, 80-81.

appeal is made to Paul's use of the word 'all' (e.g. in Rom 5 and 11, and in 2 Cor 5) with no apparent realization of the different shades of meaning that must be understood in the particular contexts. . . . The word 'all' has several clearly distinct biblical uses (e.g. 'all of some sorts,' 'some of all sorts' etc.), and to ignore this frequently-noted fact is no aid to clear thinking."[20] The universal language in Romans 5:18-19, for instance, is used to make a point that there is no group that is left outside God's saving work. As such, the "all" of Romans 5:18 is, to use F. F. Bruce's words, "All without distinction rather than all without exception."[21] In a context where it was widely assumed that salvation was necessarily limited to some particular subset of humanity, the biblical writers (and Paul in particular) went to great lengths to show that God's salvific plan included Gentile as well as Jew, female as well as male, slave as well as free, poor as well as rich. A good application of this response is to Romans 11:32. Dunn says of this verse, "A Christianity which takes the 'all' seriously cannot operate with any kind of ethnic, national, cultural, or racial particularism or exclusiveness."[22] Similarly, Schreiner argues persuasively that Romans 11:32 should be understood in context of the preceding verses and that Romans 11:30-31 are referring to Jews and Gentiles as groups.[23] And N. T. Wright says of Romans 11:32 that "Paul is drawing to a close his carefully argued case that God's mercy is not for Jews only, nor for Gentiles only, but for all-Jews and Gentiles alike. To assume that this verse must mean 'all men individually' is to take the text right out of the context both of the chapters 9-11."[24]

"Every knee will bow." The second scriptural argument for Universalism are texts that assert that eventually "every knee will bow" to God.

---

[20]N. T. Wright, "Universalism and the World-Wide Community," *Churchman* 89 (July–September 1975): 200.

[21]F. F. Bruce, *The Epistle of Paul to the Romans: An Introduction and Commentary* (Grand Rapids, MI: Eerdmans, 1963), 224. See also, Schreiner, *Romans*, 292.

[22]Dunn, *Romans 9–16*, 689.

[23]Schreiner, *Romans*, 629.

[24]N. T. Wright, "Universalism and the World-Wide Community," 200.

Isaiah 45:22-23:

"Turn to me and be saved,
all you ends of the earth;
for I am God, and there is no other.
By myself I have sworn,
my mouth has uttered in all integrity
a word that will not be revoked:
Before me every knee will bow;
by me every tongue will swear."

Romans 14:11:

"It is written:

'As surely as I live,' says the Lord,
'every knee will bow before me;
every tongue will confess to God.'"

Philippians 2:9-11:

"Therefore God exalted him to the highest place
and gave him the name that is above every name,
that at the name of Jesus every knee should bow,
in heaven and on earth and under the earth,
and every tongue acknowledge that Jesus Christ is Lord,
to the glory of God the Father."[25]

These passages are closely related, as both Romans 14:11 and Philippians 2:10-11 are quotations of Isaiah 45:23. As with the "All will be saved" passages, these texts provide prima facie justification for Universalism. The Universalist uses these texts to establish the major premise in the following argument:

1. All bow a knee.
2. Those who bow a knee are saved.
3. Therefore, all will be saved.

[25]Others: Eph 1:10; Rev 5:13.

One way to refute this argument is to deny the major premise and claim that contrary to the implication of the passages listed above, not all will bow a knee. For instance, one might appeal to the wording of Philippians 2:10a—"that at the name of Jesus every knee *should* bow"—and claim that the point of these passages is that every knee *should* bow, but won't actually do so. There are two rather devastating problems with this argument. First, neither Isaiah 45 nor Romans 14 include any sense of "they *should* bow, but will not." They say that "every knee *will* bow." Second, the "should" in Philippians 2 is aorist subjunctive and should not be understood as "you ought to bow (but might not)" but "you shall bow." A second way of attempting to deny the major premise is to claim that these passages are talking about all kinds of people (one from every tribe), not actually all people. This is more plausible, but is difficult to maintain given the fact that the *all* in Philippians 2 is glossed as "in heaven and on earth and under the earth." The reference to all three levels in ancient cosmology does not imply representatives from each level, but (as John Chrysostom says) "it means the whole world, and angels, and men, and demons."[26]

For these reasons (and undoubtedly others), it is preferable for the non-Universalist to focus on the minor premise and deny that "all who bow a knee are saved." These passages teach that all will be presented with the truth and all will acknowledge that Christ is Lord, but some might bow grudgingly. Thomas Talbott objects to this on the grounds of the verb Paul chose: "confess" (ἐξομολογήσηται: aorist subjunctive of ἐξομολογέω/ὁμολογέω). He argues that "[Paul] chose a verb that throughout the Septuagint implies not only confession, but the offer of praise and thanksgiving as well."[27] He goes on to argue that while a king or queen could force a subject to bow against their will, "praise and thanksgiving can only come from the heart."[28] While the primary

[26]John Chrysostom, *Homilies on Philippians* 7 (*NPNF* 1, 1:13, 216).

[27]Talbott, "Christ Victorious," in *Universal Salvation? The Current Debate*, ed. Robin A. Parry and Christian H. Partridge (Grand Rapids, MI: Eerdmans, 2004), 23.

[28]Talbott, "Christ Victorious," 23.

meaning of ἐξομολογέω/ὁμολογέω is "to declare openly," Lightfoot argues that "its secondary sense 'to offer praise or thanksgiving' has almost entirely supplanted its primary meaning in the LXX."[29] Despite the fact that in the New Testament, the usage of the verb ἐξομολογέω /ὁμολογέω varies widely, sometimes being used as "giving praise" (in Mt 11:25; Lk 10:21; Rom 15:9) and sometimes used as "to declare openly" (in Mt 14:7 and Lk 22:6), James Dunn concurs with Lightfoot's rendering. Speaking about Romans 14:11, he says, "ἐξομολογέω almost certainly is intended in its usual LXX sense, "acknowledge, confess, praise" (as in its only other uses in Paul [15:9 and Phil 2:11]).[30]

Suppose we agree that Paul's use of the word ἐξομολογέω was intended to convey the fact that all will give praise to God? Does this suggest that all will be saved? If one is convinced of Universalism for other reasons, then certainly this reading of Philippians 2:9-11 is preferable, but it doesn't follow that this reading provides decisive evidence for Universalism. First, it could be that at the name of Jesus, all will bow and confess, and the fact that all will do so, itself brings praise to God. In other words, the praise may not be the intent of some people—they might bow and confess grudgingly—but *the fact that* they will still bow and acknowledge Christ as Lord will bring praise and glory to God. Second, it is certainly possible to give praise to somebody, but not be at all happy about it. This Minnesota Vikings fan cannot avoid giving praise to the Green Bay Packers' quarterback, Aaron Rodgers. I'm not at all happy about it and felt an overwhelming desire to delete the sentence as soon as I wrote it, but it is undeniably true that he is a great quarterback and, therefore, integrity demands that I acknowledge it. Finally, even if the word "confess" (ἐξομολογέω) was intended to convey

---

[29] J. B. Lightfoot, *St. Paul's Epistle to the Philippians* (Grand Rapids, MI: Zondervan, 1953 [1913]), 115. The word ἐξομολογήσηται is used 120 times in the Septuagint, primarily as a translation of the Hebrew *yādâh*, praise, confess. See the comments by D. Furst, *The New International Theological Dictionary of the New Testament*, vol. 1, ed. Colin Brown (Grand Rapids, MI: Zondervan, 1975), 344.

[30] Dunn, *Romans 9–16*, 809.

the fact that all will give praise to God, the context of these verses mitigates their use as evidence for Universalism. Isaiah 45 is a statement of the sovereignty of Yahweh over all the nations. They are invited to reject their false gods (Is 45:20-21) and "turn to [Yahweh] and be saved." But Yahweh's promise that "before me every knee will bow; by me every tongue with swear" (Is 45:23) is immediately followed by "All who have raged against him will come to him and be put to shame. But all the descendants of Israel will find deliverance in the LORD and will make their boast in him" (Is 45:24b-25). As Blenkinsopp says, with what I take to be deliberate understatement, "coerced submission to the rule of Yahweh enforced by sanctions falls somewhat short of salvation as we would tend to understand it today."[31]

Similarly, the context of Romans 14:11 also makes a non-Universalistic reading clearly preferable. The purpose of the "weaker and stronger brother" section in Romans 14 is debated,[32] but there can be little disagreement that the immediate context of Romans 14:11 is "do not judge other believers, for we all will stand before God in judgment." Isaiah 45:23 is cited, with the hortatory conclusion: "So then, each of us will give an account of ourselves to God." The "all will have to answer for themselves" context, therefore, makes it difficult to see that Romans 14:11 has in mind a promise of universal salvation.[33]

A final difficulty for the Universalistic reading of these passages revisits a point made earlier, on the "all means all" passages. Either the *all* in these passages truly means all or it does not. If it does, because Philippians 2 frames the *all* as those "in heaven and on earth and under the earth," the *all* very plausibly includes Satan and the demons. But since it is both exegetically and theologically difficult to argue that Satan and the demons will be saved, then Satan and the demons are an

---

[31]Joseph Blenkinsopp, *Isaiah 40–55: A New Translation with Introduction and Commentary*, Anchor Bible (New Haven, CT: Yale University Press, 2002), 262.

[32]C. E. B. Cranfield, *Romans: A Shorter Commentary* (Grand Rapids, MI: Eerdmans, 1985), 335.

[33]Peter T. O'Brien, *The Epistle to the Philippians: A Commentary on the Greek Text*, New International Greek Testament Commentary (Grand Rapids, MI: Eerdmans, 1991), 243.

example of beings who acknowledge the lordship of Christ despite being lost. Consequently, "bowing a knee" to Christ and "confessing" his lordship are not the same thing as worship and they do not necessarily mean that one who does so is saved. One might say one who "bows a knee" and "confesses" will necessarily express the intellectual component of worship, but it is possible that they lack the affective component of worship. All who stand before their Creator and are judged have to acknowledge what is true about God—that he is God, Creator, Redeemer—but they do not have to love it. Consider Satan—he has all the theological head knowledge that one could want. He knows and (grudgingly) acknowledges what is true. His is not an intellectual problem, but an affective problem. He hates God and has chosen to fight him in his futile attempt to keep himself on the throne of his life.

"The gates are open day and night." The final scriptural argument for Universalism (or rather, the last one I will address[34]) are texts that seem to imply that heaven is like a city whose gates are open day and night.

> Isaiah 60:11:
>
> "Your gates will always stand open,
> they will never be shut, day or night,
> so that people may bring you the wealth of the nations—
> their kings led in triumphal procession."
>
> Revelation 21:25-26: "On no day will its gates ever be shut, for there will be no night there. The glory and honor of the nations will be brought into it."

Universalists claim that this depicts the ongoing possibility of entering the city. There are a number of components to this argument. The walls of a city function to mark inside from outside and only the redeemed are allowed to enter these gates. Revelation 22:14 says, "Blessed are those who wash their robes, that they may have the right to the tree of life and may go through the gates into the city." Consequently, those

[34]For other arguments, see the rather splendid volume by MacDonald/Parry, *The Evangelical Universalist*, especially chapters 2–5.

within the walls are the redeemed and those outside are those being punished in hell. Moreover, the purpose of the gates being left open is to allow those who are outside the city to enter. MacDonald/Parry says, "In the oracle of Isaiah 60 on which this vision is based we read that the gates were left open for the purpose of allowing the nations to enter (60:11), and that is the case here too: the open doors are not just a symbol of security but primarily a symbol of the God who excludes no one from his presence forever."[35] And finally, the gates being left open is not just for show for "the nations"—the very same rebellious nations whose judgment is depicted throughout the book of Revelation (Rev 6:15-17; 17:2, 18; 18:3, 9)—enter these gates into their eternal reward.

Evaluating this argument requires understanding two key ideas: (1) What is meant by the metaphor of the "gates being left open?" and (2) Who are "the nations" that enter the gate? Central to answering the first of these questions is acknowledging that metaphors can perform different functions. The fact that the redeemed are described as entering through the gates into the city and the gates are described as being left open does not warrant the conclusion that, as MacDonald/Parry claims, "there is a continuous flow [through the doors] from outside the city."[36] Moreover, if the purpose of the doors being left open was to allow people to pass through them, it is difficult to see how it wouldn't also be possible for there to be a continuous flow of people leaving the city. Therefore, it is better to see the symbol of a city's gates being left open as depicting safety, not a continuous flow of people passing through. A city's gates are shut for one of two reasons: to keep enemies out or to keep inhabitants in. As such, a city whose doors are left open all the time is a city where the inhabitants are unafraid and perfectly content, they have no fear that any enemy will attack, for all enemies have been vanquished, and there is no desire for anything outside the city and therefore no inclination to leave.

---

[35]MacDonald/Parry, *The Evangelical Universalist*, 115.
[36]MacDonald/Parry, *The Evangelical Universalist*, 115.

The reference to "the nations" entering into the heavenly city is a metonym, or a way of referring to the fact that there are representatives from the nations of the earth who have received salvation.[37] It echoes both Revelation 5:9,

> You are worthy to take the scroll
> and to open its seals,
> because you were slain,
> and with your blood you purchased for God
> persons from every tribe and language and people and nation.

and Revelation 7:9: "After this I looked, and there before me was a great multitude that no one could count, from every nation, tribe, people and language, standing before the throne and before the Lamb." In other words, this argument parallels the argument made above on Romans 11:32, where the *all* was "all nations without distinction rather than all without exception." After all, it is possible that "the nation" could have been deceived by the Beast (as in Rev 13:14) even if some individuals within the nation were not. MacDonald/Parry pushes back on this claim, saying that "elsewhere in Revelation the titles 'the nations' and 'the kings of the earth' are always reserved for enemies of Christ and the saints. And we have no grounds for thinking that the referent is any different here. For John to change the referent now without warning nor explanation would only lead to confusion."[38] Here again we have a case of how our background assumptions shape our interpretation. While I grant that this argument explains why MacDonald/Parry (and other Universalists) understand reference to "the nations," I find it surprising that he claims that understanding "the nations" in Revelation 21 as "members from every nation, tribe, people, and language" would be confusing, for even MacDonald/Parry has to acknowledge that this is how this passage was interpreted by the substantial majority of the

---

[37]This is the argument of G. K. Beale, *The Book of Revelation: A Commentary on the Greek Text*, New International Greek Testament Commentary (Grand Rapids, MI: Eerdmans, 1999), 797-98.
[38]MacDonald/Parry, *The Evangelical Universalist*, 116.

Christian tradition, and that they did so without confusion. The "shift in referent" is only confusing if one is trying to see all of the references to "the nations" in Revelation as "the wicked" and reject a non-Universalist understanding of "the nations" in Revelation 21. As such, it is preferable to read the statement that the nations will enter the gates of the heavenly city as depicting the diversity of those who enter the heavenly kingdom.

SCRIPTURAL ARGUMENTS AGAINST UNIVERSALISM

There are two kinds of stances with respect to Scripture and Universalism. The first says, "There is no evidence for Universalism in Scripture; the passages that Universalists appeal to are woefully misinterpreted."[39] The second says, "There are passages that do seem to teach Universalism, but all things considered, Universalism is probably false because the passages that seem to teach that hell will be eternally populated are clearer."[40] My arguments in this chapter should be understood as being robustly in the second category. While I have offered some reasons to believe that the scriptural arguments for Universalism are not necessarily decisive, it would be a stretch to say that they have no merit. In fact, when considering these passages *by themselves*, I would say that there are genuine reasons to accept Universalism. The primary barrier to taking these passages as definitively teaching that all will be saved are the biblical passages that seem to teach that some will eternally resist God's offer of salvation. This section will *briefly* mention these textual arguments.

---

[39]An example of this approach can be found in J. I. Packer, "The Way of Salvation: Part III: The Problems of Universalism," *Bibliotheca Sacra* 130, no. 517 (January–March 1973): 3-11. He summarizes his case as follows: "The arguments for universalism are not cogent. The arguments against it, however, seem to me to be unanswerable" (9).

[40]I accept MacDonald/Parry's challenge that functionally "the tie goes to the universalist." He argues that the problems with developing a theology of hell should cause one to believe that "if a traditional interpretation of a passage and a universalist one reach a hermeneutical stalemate, then reason would lead us to prefer the universalist interpretation" (*The Evangelical Universalist*, 35-36, 131-32). I would say that if the total evidence was split, then we should withhold belief on the question of whether all will be saved and maintain a robust hope for universal salvation.

Many who defend a non-Universalistic account of hell appeal to the passages like Matthew 13:42 and Hebrews 10:26-31 (and many others) that speak of the punishment and suffering of the wicked as sufficient to rebut Universalism. These passages, however, are not as difficult to explain from a Universalistic point of view as traditionalists seem to believe. A Universalist can comfortably affirm these passages and argue that the punishment and suffering experienced by those in hell is remedial, designed to draw them to the place where they bow a knee to God and enter into salvation.[41] The non-Universalist must do better than that. Here are a few attempts at doing better.[42]

2 Thessalonians 1:6-10. Of this passage, Gregory MacDonald/Robin Parry says, "There is only one passage in Paul that, at first sight, really does seem to teach that damnation of sinners is irreversible: 2 Thessalonians 1:6-10."[43]

> God is just: He will pay back trouble to those who trouble you and give relief to you who are troubled, and to us as well. This will happen when the Lord Jesus is revealed from heaven in blazing fire with his powerful angels. He will punish those who do not know God and do not obey the gospel of our Lord Jesus. They will be punished with everlasting destruction and shut out from the presence of the Lord and from the glory of his might on the day he comes to be glorified in his holy people and to be marveled at among all those who have believed. This includes you, because you believed our testimony to you.

The key verse is, of course, 2 Thessalonians 1:9. Those "who do not know God" will not just be punished, they will be punished with "everlasting destruction." If Paul's primary purpose was to teach that Universalism was false, it is difficult to imagine how he could have been any clearer. The Universalist has two arguments against the non-Universalistic import of this passage. First, they argue that the word for "punished" (δίκην) means literally "pay the justice" and should be understood in a

---

[41]For example, see MacDonald/Parry, *The Evangelical Universalist*, 133-35.
[42]Others: Mk 9:43-50; Gal 5:21; Eph 5:5; Jude 6; Rev 14:9-11; 19:3; 20:10-15.
[43]MacDonald/Parry, *The Evangelical Universalist*, 151.

restorative sense.[44] Eventually, the sinner will provide compensation for their sins and that payment deemed by God to be sufficient. Second, the word for everlasting destruction (ὄλεθρον αἰώνιον) does not necessarily mean total destruction, because 1 Corinthians 5:5 uses the word in a way that leads to salvation: "hand this man over to Satan for the *destruction* of the flesh, so that his spirit may be saved on the day of the Lord."[45]

These arguments explain how a Universalist might view this passage in a way that is consistent with their Universalism, but these arguments are not at all convincing. While δίκην perhaps *could* be understood in a restorative sense, there is nothing in the context that suggests that it should so understood, and it is not used in that sense in either of its uses in the New Testament (see also Jude 7). The punishment (or just payment) is one that God inflicts on the unbelievers, not something that the unbelievers do or provide to God. Clearly, the sinner's payment for their sins will be just, but there is no sense that the payment will remove the sinner's sinfulness, but only that they will be destroyed and removed from God's presence.

This raises the question of what is meant by "destruction." The point that 1 Corinthians 5:5 uses this word in a way that does not indicate total destruction is well taken, but ultimately irrelevant. The point of 1 Corinthians 5:5 is that the man's "flesh"—his sinful existence in this life—needs to be destroyed to save his soul. The usage of the word "destruction" in 1 Corinthians 5:5 cannot be used to argue that the meaning of the word "destruction" in 1 Thessalonians 1:9 is less than total because there is a crucial difference in the two contexts—1 Corinthians is referring to a believer and 1 Thessalonians is referring to a unbeliever.[46] The

[44]MacDonald/Parry, *The Evangelical Universalist*, 152-53.

[45]MacDonald/Parry, *The Evangelical Universalist*, 151-53. Universalists like MacDonald/Parry also argue that ὄλεθρον αἰώνιον does not necessarily mean *eternal* destruction because αἰώνιον can mean "in the age to come." I will address the meaning of the word αἰώνιον below.

[46]To his credit, MacDonald/Parry acknowledges this important disanalogy (*The Evangelical Universalist*, 153).

believer's "destruction" is less than total precisely because they are a believer and the unbeliever's "destruction" is total precisely because they are an unbeliever.

Luke 13:22-30. In chapter four, I addressed the objection that this passage taught that a person's salvific fate was sealed at death and found it to be wanting. But I do think that there is a strong argument in this passage for the idea that one's salvific fate is sealed on the day of judgment, and therefore, against Universalism.[47]

> Then Jesus went through the towns and villages, teaching as he made his way to Jerusalem. Someone asked him, "Lord, are only a few people going to be saved?" He said to them, "Make every effort to enter through the narrow door, because many, I tell you, will try to enter and will not be able to. Once the owner of the house gets up and closes the door, you will stand outside knocking and pleading, 'Sir, open the door for us.' But he will answer, 'I don't know you or where you come from.' Then you will say, 'We ate and drank with you, and you taught in our streets.' But he will reply, 'I don't know you or where you come from. Away from me, all you evildoers!' There will be weeping there, and gnashing of teeth, when you see Abraham, Isaac and Jacob and all the prophets in the kingdom of God, but you yourselves thrown out. People will come from east and west and north and south, and will take their places at the feast in the kingdom of God. Indeed there are those who are last who will be first, and first who will be last."

Jesus' answer to the question, "Are only a few people going to be saved?" is to redirect the question away from meaningless speculation about the number of people who will be saved to the personal and practical question of what a person must do to be saved. The reference to the "narrow" door is a statement of difficulty in entering the door and that entrance requires effort, as described powerfully in 1 Corinthians 9:24-27. Many will try and fail to do so (Lk 13:24) and these are people who had an expectation that they would be granted admittance (Lk 13:26). The

[47]One might also appeal to the parable of the rich man and Lazarus (Lk 16:19-31) to make a similar point. I do not because, as I noted in chapter 4, the parable is speaking directly to greed and the misuse of wealth and it is unclear which (if any) of the eschatological details of the parable are intended to be taken literally.

crucial question concerns when the owner of the house closes the door. The common assumption that the door is closed at death is utterly unwarranted. But this passage does clearly highlight a finality—the door will be closed—so it is best to see the closure of the door as occurring on judgment day. This is because that is when it will be revealed whether people have entered through the narrow door or not. The implications of this text for Universalism should be clear. There is a time where the door to salvation will be closed and after it is closed there will be nothing that those who are on the outside can do to enter the house. No previous good acts or supposed relationship will be sufficient. As such, there is no contradiction between Jesus' injunction to "make every effort" now and his assertion that there will be many who "try to enter later," precisely because the effort after the door is closed is fruitless.

Matthew 12:32. In answering the Pharisees' charge that Jesus used demonic power to cast out demons, Jesus responds that the only spirit capable of casting out demons is the Holy Spirit.[48] He then delivers a powerful condemnation of anyone who "speaks against" or "blasphemes" the Holy Spirit: "Anyone who speaks a word against the Son of Man will be forgiven, but anyone who speaks against the Holy Spirit will not be forgiven, either in this age or in the age to come." There are ample debates about what "speaking against the Holy Spirit" is, but for our present purposes we can set those aside. The fundamental relevance of this passage for Universalism is that those who speak against the Holy Spirit *will not be forgiven either in this age or in the age to come*. To avoid the anti-Universalistic implications of this verse, one would have to claim one (or more) of the following: (1) that it is possible that all will be saved, even if some of those will never be forgiven, (2) that there is an age beyond the "age to come" in which some will be forgiven, or (3) that Christ's warning that some will never be forgiven will never occur because no one will ever blaspheme the Holy Spirit. The first of

---

[48]Theodore H. Robinson, *The Gospel of Matthew*, Moffatt New Testament Commentary (London: Hodder and Stoughton, 1928), 113.

these seems ludicrous, given what Scripture repeatedly says about the relationship between forgiveness and salvation, and the third makes it supremely difficult to understand the motivation for Jesus' admonition, so the second is the most plausible recourse for the Universalist.

One suggestion is that "this age" is the pre-Christian age, before the cross, and the "age to come" is the Christian age, after the cross.[49] This would allow for the possibility that some who blaspheme the Holy Spirit might be forgiven in the eschaton, the age after the age to come. However, such a move makes it impossible to understand Mark 10:29-30: "'Truly I tell you,' Jesus replied, 'no one who has left home or brothers or sisters or mother or father or children or fields for me and the gospel will fail to receive a hundred times as much in this present age: homes, brothers, sisters, mothers, children and fields—along with persecutions—and in the age to come eternal life.'" And, similarly, this understanding doesn't sit well with Jesus' explanation of the parable of the weeds in Matthew 13:37-39, which says that "the harvest is the end of the age" (Mt 13:39). More generally, even if it makes sense to talk of various ages in "this life," such an attempt misses the point that it is highly plausible that the phrase "in this age or in the age to come" is an idiomatic way of saying "forever."[50]

"Eternal" punishment. There is an extensive "two ways" tradition in Scripture, especially in the Gospels. The language of "two ways" was familiar to Jewish people in Jesus' time. The language was found in many places in the Old Testament, including Deuteronomy 30:15: "See, I set before you today life and prosperity, death and destruction" and Jeremiah 21:8: "See, I am setting before you the way of life and the way of death." Some of the many examples of the "two ways" tradition in the gospels are (1) the parable of the wheat and the weeds, in which the wheat is harvested and the weeds are burned (Mt 13:24-29, 36-43); (2) the parable of the net that catches the fish (Mt 13:47-50), in which

[49]Others locate the changing of the ages with the destruction of Jerusalem in 70 CE.
[50]Just as the phrase "in heaven, on the earth, and under the earth" means "all of reality."

the good fish are kept and the bad fish are rejected; (3) the parable of the wise and foolish virgins (Mt 25:1-13), in which the wise virgins are prepared and the foolish virgins are shut out of the wedding feast; (4) the story of the sheep and the goats (Mt 25:31-46), in which the "sheep" cared for the "least of these" and the "goats" did not. The problem that these texts pose for Universalists is that they do not seem to simply be articulating ethical expectations—"do good, don't do evil." The context and implication of these statements seems eschatological—these passages assume that there are two ultimate eschatological destinies, one good and one evil.

When Scripture describes the result of those who take the "way of death," the description is some variation of "eternal punishment." Isaiah 66:24 says of those who "rebelled against me" that "the worms that eat them will not die, the fire that burns them will not be quenched, and they will be loathsome to all mankind."[51] Matthew 18:6-9 promises that anyone who "causes one of these little ones—those who believe in me—to stumble" will be "thrown into the eternal fire." In addition, we have already mentioned 2 Thessalonians 1:8-9, where it says that "those who do not know God . . . will be punished with everlasting destruction and shut out from the presence of the Lord." And, finally, perhaps the most important passage is Matthew 25 which has a pair of descriptions of the destination of those who take the way of death.

> Matthew 25:41: "Then he will say to those on his left, 'Depart from me, you who are cursed, into the *eternal* fire prepared for the devil and his angels.'"
>
> Matthew 25:46: "Then they will go away to eternal punishment, but the righteous to *eternal* life."

In each of these passages the meaning of "eternal" (αἰώνιον) when describing "punishment" is obviously of crucial importance. And it is on that word that Universalists pounce. The word literally means "pertaining to the ages or eons," and Universalists can point to numerous

[51]Mk 9:42-48 both cites Is 66:24 and echoes the theme of "unquenchable fire."

biblical examples where the word αἰώνιον is used for a period of time that ends. Another strategy involves arguing that αἰώνιον should be understood qualitatively, not temporally. On this view, "eternal" punishment should be understood as the punishment "characteristic of the age to come."[52] For instance, Universalists point to Romans 16:25-26:

> Now to him who is able to establish you in accordance with my gospel, the message I proclaim about Jesus Christ, in keeping with the revelation of the mystery hidden for *long ages past*, but now revealed and made known through the prophetic writings by the command of the *eternal* God, so that all the Gentiles might come to the obedience that comes from faith.

Here αἰωνίοις is translated once in the sense of "without end" (Rom 16:26) and once as pertaining to an age that will end—and in fact that age did end, since the mystery is "now revealed." So, according to DeRose, there is no problem understanding biblical references to "eternal punishment" as being compatible with Universalism for "not only can the Greek word [αἰωνίοις] mean something that doesn't imply endless duration, but it often does get used with such a meaning."[53]

A number of things may be said about the Universalist's treatment of the concept of eternal punishment in Scripture. Most obviously, it is fallacious to use etymological derivation of a word to determine its meaning—this exegetical fallacy is called the root fallacy.[54] Understanding the meaning of αἰωνίοις as "pertaining to the ages" makes no more sense than trying to understand the word *pineapple* by applying the meaning "pine" and "apple." Rather, meaning should be determined by authorial intention and context. Moreover, there is a very important difference between the usage of the noun αἰών and the adjective αἰωνίος.[55] While the noun may refer to a period of time that has an

---

[52]See David Hill, *Gospel of Matthew*, New Century Bible Commentary (London: Oliphants, 1972), 331.
[53]DeRose, "Universalism and the Bible," section 10.
[54]See the excellent book by D. A. Carson, *Exegetical Fallacies* (Grand Rapids, MI: Baker Academic, 1996), 26-32.
[55]Scot McKnight has argued that "Matthew never uses the adjective αἰωνίος ('eternal') in the sense of 'belonging to this temporally limited age.' . . . In Matthew the adjective αἰωνίος refers to something eternal and temporally unlimited." See his "Eternal Consequences or Eternal

ending, "The NT usage of the adjective . . . is quite consistent in referring to endless or unlimited time."[56] "The only clear exceptions are three passages referring to a past period of long duration. . . . Otherwise the term is used either in the sense 'without beginning or end' . . . or it refers to a future period that has no end."[57] Moreover, not only is the adjective αἰωνίος best understood in this context as "without end," even if one forces the meaning of αἰωνίος as "pertaining to an age," the context demands that the age being referred to is the age to come, which is an age without end.[58] MacDonald/Parry's responds, "True, the age to come is everlasting, but that does not necessitate that the punishment of the age to come lasts for the duration of that age, simply that it occurs during that age and is appropriate for that age."[59] The problem with this argument is that Matthew 25:46 uses the word αἰωνίος to describe both the punishment and reward of the coming age. Given the assumption that Matthew intended to convey the unendingness of heaven, it is difficult to avoid the implication of the unendingness of hell. If MacDonald /Parry wants to understand the punishment as not necessarily unending, but merely "occurring during that age to come" and "being appropriate for that age," why wouldn't the same thing be said of the reward? Moreover, Universalists have to reckon with the fact that the eternal fire into which "those on Jesus' left" are thrown is not prepared for humans who reject God, but "for the devil and his angels" (Mt 25:41).[60] As such,

Consciousness?" in *Through No Fault of Their Own: The Fate of Those Who Have Never Heard*, ed. William V. Crockett and James G. Sigountos (Grand Rapids, MI: Baker, 1991), 153.

[56]Robert L. Thomas, "Jesus' View of Eternal Punishment," *The Master's Seminary Journal* 9, no. 2 (Fall 1998): 158. Thomas says, "In its seventy-four occurrences in the NT, it always has the connotation of something that is unending or without time limitations. Seventy-one of the uses look forward to eternity future, and only three refer back to what mortals would call eternity past (Rom 16:25; 2 Tim 1:9; Titus 1:2)" (158-59).

[57]"*aiōn*"/"*aiōnos*," in *New International Dictionary of New Testament Theology and Exegesis*, ed. Moises Silva, 2nd ed. (Grand Rapids, MI: Zondervan, 2014), 196.

[58]Leon Morris, *The Gospel According to Matthew*, Pillar New Testament Commentary (Grand Rapids, MI: Eerdmans, 1992), 641n79.

[59]MacDonald/Parry, *The Evangelical Universalist*, 148.

[60]Craig S. Keener, *Matthew*, IVP New Testament Commentary Series (Downers Grove, IL: IVP Academic, 1997), 362, and David L. Turner, *Matthew*, Baker Exegetical Commentary on the New Testament (Grand Rapids, MI: Baker, 2008), 609.

it would seem that the unbeliever's punishment would be just as eternal as the devil's.

EVALUATING THEOLOGICAL ARGUMENTS FOR UNIVERSALISM

The previous section was lengthy primarily because it is too easy to dismiss the theological arguments for Universalism on the grounds that "they are not biblical." I do not think they are ultimately successful, but there are serious biblical arguments for Universalism and they should not be just dismissed. There are also serious theological arguments for Universalism. I will consider four. The first three are different ways of making sense of the idea that God's salvific will cannot be frustrated forever and the fourth is the claim that eternal bliss in heaven is incompatible with the existence of an eternal hell.

The question of how God's salvific will can be forever frustrated is obviously a pivotal one. One can of course side step this problem by arguing that God does not have universal salvific will. This approach utterly defangs arguments for Universalism, but comes at the cost of calling into question God's love and goodness. Such an approach, I believe, also does not sit well with Scripture. Consequently, I will be working from the premise that God desires all people to be saved. Universalists acknowledge that God's salvific will can be frustrated for a time. They acknowledge that his desire that all be saved can be thwarted during this life and hence that some people end up in hell. What they reject is that God's salvific will can be frustrated forever. They argue that eventually God will accomplish his salvific will and all will join him in heaven.

Clark Pinnock has described two theological paths to Universalism.[61] The first is the "Augustinian path of sovereign love" whereby God elects every person and provides each person with grace that is irresistible

[61]Clark Pinnock, *A Wideness in God's Mercy: The Finality of Jesus Christ in a World of Religions* (Grand Rapids, MI: Zondervan, 1992), 155-56.

and effective. One taking this path would not have to claim that all are saved in this life, for God can make his grace irresistible whenever he wants to do so. So, presumably, those who hear the gospel in this life are given irresistible grace in this life and those who do not hear or reject the gospel are given irresistible grace at some point in the afterlife, perhaps after an extended stay in hell. Pinnock's second path is the "non-Augustinian path of infinite divine patience." For Universalists who prefer this path, it is not God's power and control that results in all being saved, but the fact that his love and mercy can outlast even the most recalcitrant sinner. I will consider both of these arguments and, after doing so, also consider a third that seeks to question the assumptions of the first two.

Sovereignty Universalism. An example of this sort of approach is found in Karl Barth.[62] This statement itself is controversial, for the debate over Barth's claims regarding Universalism are contentious and probably unresolvable.[63] What Barth clearly rejected was any notion that Universalism could be assumed or that "we could count on it [universal reconciliation] as though we had a claim to it,"[64] for such an assumption would fly in the face of an affirmation of God's freedom in salvation. Nonetheless, it is also probably true that Barth held a Christology that implied Universalism.[65] However Barth's hopeful, christological Universalism is understood, it is clearly on the "sovereignty" path, not the "patience" path. He speaks of God's mercy and grace as a river and the unrepentant heart of a sinner as a dam erected in the

[62]Also Friedrich Schleiermacher, *The Christian Faith*, ed. H. R. Mackintosh and J. S. Stewart (New York: Harper and Row, 1963), 2:539-60, 720-22.

[63]I think that Oliver Crisp is correct when he says, "The scope of human salvation envisioned in the theology of Karl Barth either is a species of Universalism or comprises several distinct, incompatible strands of doctrine that he does not finally resolve." See his *Deviant Calvinism: Broadening Reformed Theology* (Minneapolis: Fortress, 2014), 155.

[64]Karl Barth, *Church Dogmatics: The Doctrine of Reconciliation*, vol. IV/3.1, trans. G. W. Bromiley (Peabody, MA: Hendrickson, 2004 [1961]), 478. Subsequent references will be to this edition.

[65]Eberhard Busch records Barth saying, "I do not believe in universalism, but I do believe in Jesus Christ, reconciler of all." See his *Karl Barth: His Life from Letters and Autobiographical Texts*, trans. John Bowden (Eugene, OR: Wipf & Stock, 2015), 394.

middle of that river, attempting to stop the river from reaching its natural end. While sinners may attempt to place themselves outside of God's election of all in Jesus Christ, Barth says, "But the stream is too strong and the dam too weak for us to be able reasonably to expect anything but the collapse of the dam and the onrush of the waters."[66]

A less controversial example of Sovereignty Universalism is found in Marilyn Adams's *Horrendous Evils and the Goodness of God*.[67] She calls into question the notion that humans have been given the ability to eternally reject God and to experience the separation and misery that goes with that decision. Such a move, Adams suggests, implies that God and humans are moral peers and that the relationship between God and humans should therefore be reciprocal. Adams joins Barth in arguing that this assumption is flawed, and suggests that a better way to think about the relationship between God and humans is with the analogy of a mother and her child. Because the mother loves the child, she will protect that child from dangerous choices. Of course, she wants the child to choose paths that lead to safety and flourishing, but if the child insists on choices that lead to self-destruction, she will prevent the child from doing so. If God prevents us from choosing eternal destruction apart from him by overriding our freedom, his doing so is "no more an insult to our dignity than a mother's changing a diaper is to the baby."[68]

As encouraging as it might be to think of a God who will never allow our freedom to eternally separate us from God, the problems with this view are very real. First, as Gerald McDermott says,

> Karl Barth was right to reject theological abstractions in eschatology that are divorced from the concrete revelation of God in Christ. But when he rests his hopeful Universalism (we may or should hope for the salvation of all) on the knowledge that there is always more grace in God than in us and that God is free to enlarge "the circle of redemption," he embraces his own

---

[66]Karl Barth *Church Dogmatics* IV/3.1, 355-356. A similar argument is made in II/2, 417-419.

[67]Marilyn McCord Adams, *Horrendous Evils and the Goodness of God* (Ithaca, NY: Cornell University Press, 1999).

[68]Adams, *Horrendous Evils*, 157.

sort of abstraction—that God's freedom and election will always prevail over human resistance.[69]

Second, there are good reasons to question the validity of Adams's mother/child analogy. In particular, it seems that God expects more from us in terms of behavior and character development than a mother could ever expect from her child. Even more significantly, it seems that God has chosen to make us colaborers with him in spreading the gospel and informing the world of his love—"They will know me by your love" (cf. Jn 13:35).[70] Moreover, Adams's argument that just as a parent would never allow his or her child to make a choice with disastrous consequences, a loving God would never allow some persons to reject him forever can be turned around and employed to make the opposite point. Those that are damned are damned by their own decision to reject God's gracious offer of salvation. The decision of the damned can only be changed if God overrides their freedom. But doing so would violate their self-determination, which would be something that a perfectly loving God would not and, indeed, could not do,[71] not because it is not within his power to do so, but because it would be a profoundly unloving action. Stopping a child from making a bad decision by kidnapping them or surgically or chemically altering their brain to cease choosing poorly would be "meddling in a way that displayed disrespect for his autonomy as a person"[72] and therefore would be profoundly unloving: "To interfere in this way would remove his autonomy and thus the *meaningfulness* of his freedom and this would be to undermine both his human dignity and the real purpose of the earthly life: autonomous soul-making."[73]

---

[69]Gerald R. McDermott, "Will All Be Saved?" *Themelios* 38, no. 2 (2013): 239.

[70]In chapter 2, I argued that our ability to fulfill the Great Commission has limits and that ultimately, the work of spreading the gospel is God's. This does not, as I see it, undercut the point I just made.

[71]Jonathan Kvanvig, *The Problem of Hell* (New York: Oxford, 1993), 112.

[72]Michael Murray, "Three Versions of Universalism," *Faith and Philosophy* 16, no. 1 (January 1999): 66.

[73]Murray, "Three Versions of Universalism," 66.

Third, if Sovereignty Universalism is true, heaven will be ultimately populated by two classes of people, those who chose salvation and those that did not, but ended up in heaven anyway.[74] Even if there is nothing that distinguishes these two classes of people in terms of appearance or worship and even if the individuals in heaven do not even know which class they are in, God will still know. And the existence of second-class citizens in heaven is nearly impossible to reconcile both with our intuitions about heaven itself and with the concept of eternal happiness in particular.

Finally, the Christian tradition has been nearly universal in affirming that Satan and the demons are not candidates for salvation—largely because it is nearly impossible to find any hint of optimism in Scripture with respect to the eternal destiny of Satan and the demons. This raises the question, How does this fact fit with Sovereignty Universalism? Why can humans be saved, but not fallen angels? Christian theologians have speculated that the difference can be found in the nature of freedom given to humans relative to angels. Based in part on the idea that there is no hint of angels continuing to fall (or be saved), it is possible to speculate that angelic freedom consists in a once-for-all choice for or against God. Furthermore, the once-for-all nature of this choice makes sense given the fact that angels had face-to-face experience with God in heaven. Contrary to humans who walk by faith, not sight (Heb 11:1), angels possessed a clear vision of God. Consequently, any proposal for salvation of Satan and the demons would have to answer the question, What information, experience, or realization could be given to them that they didn't already have before their rebellion? Note also that Matthew 25:41 says, "Depart from me, you who are cursed, into the *eternal* fire prepared for the devil and his angels." The fire is not prepared for humans, but for demonic creatures. Therefore, it seems

[74]I owe this point to Jonathan Kvanvig, "Autonomy, Finality, and the Choice Model of Hell," in *Destiny and Deliberation: Essays in Philosophical Theology* (New York: Oxford University Press, 2011), 15-16. I am not sure, however, he will agree with how I have used this point.

that the fate of unbelievers is the same as that of Satan and the demons. If one wants to argue for the salvation of all persons, it seems that one must also argue for the salvation of Satan and the demons.

Patience Universalism. John Hick states his theological argument for Universalism using an analogy of God as an infinitely wise psychiatrist working to free his human patient from whatever is stopping them from embracing salvation. He says, "We have to suppose, not a human but a divine therapist, working not to a limited deadline but in unlimited time, and ultimately controlling rather than being restricted by the environmental factors. In so far as we can conceive of this, do we not find that it authorizes an unambiguously good prognosis?"[75]

Thomas Talbott has also pressed this line of argument. There are few names in the literature on Universalism that cast a longer shadow than Talbott. His writings are voluminous and his arguments are challenging. Talbott's version of Patience Universalism is based on the claim that it is incoherent to think that anyone could choose hell as a final option. Of course, we choose sin and evil, but this is because we actually believe that it will bring us happiness. When we see matters as they are—when we experience the misery of hell—we will eventually turn to God. But the reason for our return matters: our return must be based on "clear and compelling evidence" that alters our beliefs "in a perfectly rational way."[76] It must not be the case that we turn to God based on threats—"conversion at a sword's point is neither rational nor morally acceptable, nor is it free in any meaningful sense of the word."[77]

Thomas Talbott argues that Universalism can be achieved by God providing the truth to the unrepentant soul: "Once all ignorance and deception and bondage to desire is removed, so that a person is truly 'free' to choose, there can no longer be any motive for choosing eternal

---

[75]John Hick, *Death and Eternal Life* (London: Macmillan, 1976), 254.

[76]Thomas Talbott, "Freedom, Damnation, and the Power to Sin with Impunity," *Religious Studies* 37 (2001): 427.

[77]Jerry L. Walls, "Heaven and Hell," in *The Oxford Handbook of Philosophical Theology*, ed. Thomas P. Flint and Michael C. Rea (New York: Oxford University Press, 2009), 503.

misery for oneself."[78] A very serious initial problem with this perspective concerns the assumption that "true freedom" is incompatible with ignorance. If this is true, it is questionable whether humans are ever truly free. Setting aside that objection, Michael Murray helpfully distinguishes between two senses in which a person can become "fully informed" by God. The first is that their false beliefs are corrected, but the second entails that one's desires have been structured "so they properly reflect the importance of what is known."[79] As Murray argues, it seems clear that one can refuse to embrace relationship with God even if one is fully informed in the first sense—Lucifer is a pretty good example. The problem with this line of argument is this that while God can show a person the truth, it is a real question whether God can remove a person's ignorance, self-deception, and bondage to desire.[80]

This is perhaps the crux of the issue between the Universalist and non-Universalist. Universalists like Talbott seem to have a rather high opinion both of what God can do to transform an individual and of what the experience of suffering in hell can do to change a sinner's mind. But if God is capable of transforming individuals in this way, the very real question arises: Why didn't God just create individuals who were already transformed and place them in a heavenly paradise? Why even create individuals that could sin? Why bother with the difficulties of this life if it is possible to skip past them to eschatological bliss?[81] A second problem with Talbott's claim is related to the first. Following C. S. Lewis, it is unlikely that anyone chooses misery for themselves. Rather, they choose what they deem to be right and best, and when they are miserable, they explain their misery as being the fault of others, or their situation, or perhaps even God. Jerry Walls points out that "a

[78]Thomas Talbott, "The Doctrine of Everlasting Punishment," *Faith and Philosophy* 7 (1990): 37.

[79]Murray, "Three Versions of Universalism," 62.

[80]For more on this question, and particularly on whether it is possible for a person to "freely sin, and hence reject God, without end," see Raymond J. VanArragon, "Is It Possible to Freely Reject God Forever?" in *The Problem of Hell: A Philosophical Anthology*, ed. Joel Buenting (London: Routledge, 2010), 29-43.

[81]Michael Murray also raises this objection. "Three Versions of Universalism," 62-63.

person can so deceive themselves into believing that evil is good, or at least holds sufficient advantage to be gained, that he comes to a point where he consistently and thoroughly prefers evil to good."[82] And even Karl Barth resists the implication that God's nature necessitates eternal patience: "To the man who persistently tries to change the truth into untruth, God does not owe eternal patience and therefore deliverance any more than He does those provisional manifestations."[83]

Ultimately, Talbott's account of Patience Universalism can explain why people might want to leave hell and enter heaven, but it cannot explain why people in hell would want to love and submit to God. What is seems obvious is that after ten thousand years of experiencing the emptiness of their own reign, people in hell will desire a change in their circumstances; but it is implausible to assume that this desire automatically reflects a willingness to embrace Christ as Lord and Savior. And the belief "anything would be better than this" is not an adequate basis for salvation. As C. S. Lewis says, "In the long run the answer to all those who object to the doctrine of hell, is itself a question: 'What are you asking God to do?' To wipe out their past sins and, at all costs, to give them a fresh start, smoothing every difficulty and offering every miraculous help? But He has done so, on Calvary. To forgive them? They will not be forgiven. To leave them alone? Alas, I am afraid that is what He does."[84]

Rejecting the either/or: A third Universalistic option? Before moving on, it is worthwhile to consider whether these two versions of Universalism exhaust the possibilities. Sovereignty Universalism and Patience Universalism each accept an either/or of sorts between divine sovereignty and human freedom. While Sovereignty Universalism says that God's sovereign salvific will can ensure that all will be saved, Patience Universalism rejects that assumption, relying instead on divine

[82]Jerry L. Walls, *Hell: The Logic of Damnation* (Notre Dame: University of Notre Dame Press, 1992), 138.

[83]Barth, *Church Dogmatics* IV/3.1, 477.

[84]Lewis, *The Problem of Pain*, 130.

patience and the infinite amount of time God has to pursue the recalcitrant sinner.

Some will want to reject this either/or and, in so doing, forge a third theological path to Universalism. This seems to be the approach of Swedish theologian Nels Ferré (1908–1971). Ferré acknowledges that there is a contradiction between the affirmation of human freedom and the affirmation that God can guarantee that all will be saved, but he thought that they could both be held as long as one acknowledged that God's methods and logic transcends human logic.[85] Similarly, in a recent and extremely impressive volume titled *The God Who Saves*, David Congdon offers what I take to be the rejection of the sovereignty/freedom either/or—one that is decidedly more developed and nuanced than that of Ferré.[86] His approach starts with a commitment to God's absolute transcendence and, as such, questions one of the fundamental assumptions of both the proponents and opponents of the two other views—namely, the cooperation/competition model of divine and human agency. Congdon argues,

> Once we realize that divine agency operates on a qualitatively different ontological order, we no longer need to worry about a competition between God and the human person, and thus we no longer need to resort to a cooperative account of the divine-human relation. Indeed, both cooperation and competition trade on a fundamentally mythological and metaphysical understanding of God as one causal agent among others in the cosmos. If divine agency does not conflict with any creaturely agency—being of a wholly different order—then a universal divine decision to elect all human beings in Jesus Christ need not compete with the free decision of individual persons.[87]

Neither does the decision to save all undercut divine freedom. The problem with the claim that Universalism obligates God to save all and

[85]Nels Ferré, *The Christian Understanding of God* (New York: Harper, 1958), 22.
[86]David W. Congdon, *The God Who Saves* (Eugene: Cascade, 2016).
[87]Congdon, *The God Who Saves*, 17. Congdon acknowledges that there are various ways of describing the relationship between divine and human agency, "some being more satisfactory than others."

therefore compromises God's freedom is that it begs the question against the Universalist. Congdon says,

> This objection presupposed we already know that God's will is a will to condemn sinners to eternal damnation. . . . If God has determined to send some people to hell, then of course any doctrine that proclaims the salvation of all would be an infringement on God's freedom. There is, of course, a very simple response to this problem, namely, to reject the original premise. Nothing prevents us from saying that God saves all precisely because God *wills* to save all—precisely *as* an exercise of God's sovereign freedom.[88]

Congdon's Universalistic proposal is novel and interesting. His proposal hinges on rethinking our answers to fundamental questions in two different areas: First, theology proper—what sort of being is God? Do traditional understandings of God's freedom compromise his transcendence by making him a "being like other beings" in this world? Is he a God of justice and holiness who might exclude some from his presence or is he a God of boundless mercy who would never do so? Second, theological anthropology—what sorts of beings are humans, how does our freedom operate relative to God's agency, and do we have the capacity to exclude ourselves from God's presence eternally? Congdon's dazzling journey through the intricacies of nineteenth- and twentieth-century theology ends up articulating a theology proper and theological anthropology where Universalism is true by definition. While this is in itself an impressive achievement, one is left with precious few reasons to agree with him. While a theology proper and theological anthropology rethought along Congdon's lines might be theologically compelling to some people, it is less obvious (to me, at least) that the resultant conception of God would elicit love and worship, would be understandable in a meaningful way by human persons without PhDs, and is at all compatible with what is taught in Scripture. In the end, his proposal will be most persuasive to those who are willing to take one more step away from orthodoxy and reconsider the very idea of a conscious afterlife.

---

[88]Congdon, *The God Who Saves*, 14; italics original.

Eternal bliss is incompatible with eternal hell. Universalists argue that the eternal damnation of some is incompatible with the salvation of anyone.[89] Consider the following analogy: suppose my family and I are heading to a destination and there are two planes that can get us there. I am placed on one plane and my family on the other. On my plane, the seats are spacious, the food is amazing, and the person sitting next to me refrains from telling me long stories about her cat. I am in travel bliss. But could I be happy if I found out that my family's situation was not only not blissful, but was profoundly uncomfortable or, worse, that they were genuinely suffering? Despite my enjoyable surroundings and despite my being far from fully sanctified, I am quite sure that I could not. Of course, this is an analogy, so the question is how close this analogy is to the experience of those in heaven who are aware of the suffering of some in hell. Could any person in heaven be truly happy if they knew that simultaneously there were people—and perhaps loved ones—who were suffering horribly? Undoubtedly, a selfish person could ignore the simultaneous and eternal suffering of others, but could a person who was redeemed, sanctified, and Christlike do so?

Eric Reitan argues that this is an argument against what Thomas Talbott calls "moderately conservative theism," which is the combination of the belief that God is perfectly loving and good and the belief that hell exists, held together by the claim that those who are in hell have chosen to be there.[90] I think this is simply false. This is a much more powerful objection to what might be called a "punishment model of hell"—the idea that humans are placed in hell for punishment and that punishment consists of eternal physically painful torture.[91] But this objection just does not have the same force given a "choice model

[89]This phrase comes from the title of Eric Reitan's article, "Eternal Damnation and Blessed Ignorance: Is the Damnation of Some Incompatible with the Salvation of Any?" *Religious Studies* 38, no. 4 (December 2002): 429-50.

[90]Reitan, "Eternal Damnation and Blessed Ignorance," 429-30. The term "moderately conservative theism" is Thomas Talbott's.

[91]Jonathan Kvanvig, *Destiny and Deliberation: Essays on Philosophical Theology* (New York: Oxford University Press, 2011), 5-6.

of hell," and especially one where the suffering in hell is a function of the person's choice to reign in hell rather than serve in heaven (to use Milton's famous phrase). The suffering of people who have chosen a path that results in their suffering elicits a very different emotional response than the suffering of people whose choices did not contribute to their suffering. For example, I do not feel even slightly bad for a person who suffers significant discomfort after choosing to eat a ghost pepper, despite receiving ample warning about what would happen, but I do feel bad for a person who suffers because their "friends" smuggled a ghost pepper into their food. The fact that the suffering in question is chosen or not is of crucial importance, and as such, this argument is less of an argument against non-Universalism (or for Universalism) and more of an argument against a punishment model of hell.

In addition, it is important to notice that the theory of Postmortem Opportunity is itself a strong antidote to this sort of Universalist argument. If there are people who end up in hell that did not have an opportunity for relationship with God or if their opportunity was unclear, partial, or misleading, then their spending an eternity in hell seems problematic. But the claim of the Postmortem Opportunity theorist that God will provide everybody who he knows did not receive an adequate premortem opportunity with one entails that all of those who are in hell have chosen the soteriological ghost pepper with full awareness of the implications of their choices. This doesn't suggest that they will enjoy their eschatological experience, but only that there was nothing that could have been done to encourage a different response.

The debate over Universalism—like many fundamental philosophical debates—is characterized by difficult-to-resolve competing intuitions and assumptions. It seems to me that the Universalist's intuition that it is inconceivable that humans in heaven could be happy if they knew that there were some who are eternally excluded from God's presence is most plausible given the belief that it is inconceivable that humans could be excluded from a perfectly loving God's presence forever. But if it is not inconceivable that some might choose to exclude themselves from God's presence, then the intuition changes. Consequently, the "eternal bliss" argument hinges on the one's sense of the inconceivability of the eternal exclusion of humans from God. If it is not inconceivable that some might be separated from a perfectly loving God forever, then it is not inconceivable that those in heaven might understand why some are excluded.

A final response to this argument highlights another "intuition-level disconnect" between the Universalist and non-Universalist.[92] When pressing this argument, the Universalist assumes that we have a good sense of what we would think and feel if we were in heaven and were contemplating the suffering of persons in hell. I remember trying to imagine what it would be like to be a father back before my first child was born. While some of what I anticipated was correct or at least in the ballpark, my various imaginings about what the specifics of what I would think and feel and do were humorously inadequate and, in retrospect, quite silly. The reality is so much richer and more complicated than I could have ever imagined. I think there is reason to believe that our various attempts to imagine what we will think and feel and do in heaven will be equally inadequate. So, while I feel the weight of the objection that the denizens of heaven cannot be happy as long as some suffer in hell, I think that Stephen Davis's answer is absolutely correct. He says, "I do not know an adequate answer to this question. I expect that if I knew enough about heaven I would know the answer, but I know little about heaven."[93] Consequently, I believe it is possible to grant that it is hard to see how the eternal blessedness of any is compatible with the eternal damnation of some, but still hold that this doesn't justify either "humans will not be happy in heaven" or "hell will eventually be emptied."

---

[92]One might ask why I am talking about intuitions here, rather than arguments. The answer is that I think intuitions come before arguments and our arguments are merely attempts to formalize our intuitions. This does not suggest, of course, that arguments are wholly irrelevant.

[93]Stephen T. Davis, "Universalism, Hell, and the Fate of the Ignorant," *Modern Theology* 6, no. 2 (January 1990): 180.

CONCLUSION

The "intuition-level" disconnects between Universalists and non-Universalists should not be surprising, for something similar happens between competing views in many other debates: between atheists and theists on the existence of gratuitous evil, between internalists and externalists in epistemology, and between Calvinists and Arminians on divine providence. While the scriptural and theological arguments for Universalism certainly have a degree of prima facie plausibility, I ultimately find them to be unpersuasive. They are certainly sufficient to provide one who was already convinced of Universalism with some justification for their theological commitments, but they do not provide one who was not already inclined to accept Universalism with a compelling reason to do so. Moreover, I think that there are sound biblical and theological arguments against Universalism. This leaves me, regretfully, with the belief that it is most likely that there will be persons who reject God's offer of grace and are consigned to hell. What is left to discuss is the relationship between Postmortem Opportunity, Universalism, and hell. That is the task of the final chapter.

10

POSTMORTEM OPPORTUNITY, UNIVERSALISM, AND HELL

It is uncontroversial to say that Universalism is most plausibly thought of as a variety of Postmortem Opportunity. My interest here is with the claim that not only does a commitment to Universalism require Postmortem Opportunity, but whether the requirement is reflexive. If accepting Postmortem Opportunity requires that one accept Universalism, then the scriptural and theological arguments against Universalism are indirectly arguments against Postmortem Opportunity. The underlying argument here is as follows:

1. If Postmortem Opportunity, then Universalism
2. Not-Universalism
3. Therefore, not-Postmortem Opportunity.

The argument form is *modus tollens*: if P then Q, not-Q, therefore not-P. In this chapter, I will seek to refute the major premise in this argument. I will address and respond to two arguments, both of which call into question the viability of a non-Universalist version of Postmortem Opportunity. The first is the claim that no recipient of a Postmortem Opportunity could reject relationship with God and the second is that one who believes in Postmortem Opportunity should also accept that there will be ongoing opportunities to repent in hell. After doing so, I will close this volume with a discussion of what the Postmortem Opportunity theorist might think about the nature of hell.

COULD ANYONE REJECT A POSTMORTEM OPPORTUNITY?

The first argument is simply that nobody could say no to a Postmortem Opportunity. If it is the case that God will give the unevangelized and pseudoevangelized the best possible opportunity to repent, how could anyone reject this offer of salvation? The sense that this objection is damning seems to be common, but ironically, it is rarely made explicit, much less defended. Before engaging this objection, it should be noted that even if this objection was successful, it would not suggest that Universalism was true. That is because the conclusion "All will be saved" does not follow from the claim "All who receive a Postmortem Opportunity are saved." To yield the Universalist conclusion, one must add the premise "All receive a Postmortem Opportunity."[1] Nonetheless, if it is true that all who receive a Postmortem Opportunity are saved, then it is very difficult to explain why a God who desires that all people be saved would not provide a Postmortem Opportunity to all people, even those who reject him in this life. The result would be Universalistic, but not only would this sort of Postmortem Opportunity constitute a second chance, it would utterly undercut the urgency of sharing the gospel in this life. In other words, if this objection is successful, even if Universalism is not necessarily true, it is likely true, and the other objections to Postmortem Opportunity become insuperable.

"Best possible opportunity" argument. There are a couple of ways to press this objection. The first seeks to exploit the claim that the unevangelized/pseudoevangelized will be given the "best possible opportunity" to hear the gospel. One might argue that no one would reject a Postmortem Opportunity as follows:

1. At the Postmortem Opportunity, persons are given the best possible opportunity to respond.

[1]The premise "All who reject Christ in this life" would also work.

2. Some humans fail to respond to this opportunity.

3. If (2), then not (1).

In effect, this argument is that the best possible opportunity necessitates an affirmative response. I think this is false. It does not take seriously enough a number of rather important ideas. The first of these concerns the implications self-determining or libertarian freedom. The nature of libertarian freedom is such that God may provide the best possible opportunity, but it is still within the power of humans with libertarian freedom to reject that opportunity. It doesn't necessitate that some or even any do so, but it requires that it is possible to do so. Now, perhaps, one who objects to Postmortem Opportunity could just argue that humans do not have libertarian freedom, but that would be a difficult case to make and, theologically speaking, makes it exponentially more difficult to explain the existence of evil in God's creation.

Second, we must not forget that the best possible opportunity is still a best possible opportunity to know God *as he is*. Those who assume that it is just obvious that a person being granted a Postmortem Opportunity will be saved have a tendency to assume a picture of God who I call "Baby Jesus" God—that is, they tend to see the Postmortem Opportunity being granted by a gentle, unassuming, perfectly loving deity typified by Baby Jesus. Who could say no to Baby Jesus? This is a caricature, every bit as false as the lightning-throwing, perpetually displeased God of wrath that constitutes the yin to the yang of Baby Jesus. Properly understanding the Postmortem Opportunity on the day of judgment requires an accurate picture of the God offering that opportunity—first, Jesus does not portray a different (nicer, less demanding) God; second, as God, Jesus is the almighty sovereign Creator of the universe, and the first response of those who see him will be utter holy fear and awe. Most importantly, recall that the experience of a Postmortem Opportunity (as articulated in chapter two) includes not only the most persuasive possible picture of God's nature and love (ideal grace), but also an authentic picture of God's holiness and moral/salvific expectations.

A third reason why some might reject even the best possible opportunity for postmortem repentance is the reality of sin and especially what has been called the "noetic effects of sin." The noetic effects of sin not only disable any innate capacity for knowing God—including those faculties or capacities designed by God, such as the *sensus divinitatis*—they also encourage the creation of various idols that we pursue instead of God: self-protection, autonomy, "proof," religious observance, pleasure, or authenticity, to name just a few of the possibilities. These do not just drag us into sin, they are alternatives to God and if pursued habitually, will be chosen instead of God.[2]

"The necessity of epistemic distance" argument. A second kind of argument for the conclusion that no one could say no if given a Postmortem Opportunity focuses not on the "best possible opportunity" but on the experiential immediacy of the experience of God. This objection, in effect, asks the following: "How could you say no to God? He's right there in front of you!" John Chrysostom articulated an objection to Postmortem Opportunity late in the fourth century. He says, "If unbelievers are after death to be saved on their believing, no man shall ever perish," and he cites Philippians 2:10-11 and 1 Corinthians 15:26, saying, "But there is no advantage in that submission, for it comes not of a rightly disposed choice, but of the necessity of things, as one may say, thenceforth taking place."[3] This sort of claim has been enormously influential in the suppression of belief in Postmortem Opportunity and more recently has been influentially articulated by John Hick. In his books *Faith and Knowledge* and *Evil and a God of Love*, Hick articulates a central pillar of his religious epistemology—namely, that creatures cannot be free with respect to their decision to follow

---

[2]For an excellent account of the noetic effects of sin, see Merold Westphal, "Taking St. Paul Seriously: Sin as an Epistemological Category," in *Christian Philosophy*, ed. Thomas P. Flint (Notre Dame: University of Notre Dame Press, 1990), 200-26.

[3]John Chrysostom, *Homily on Matthew* 36.3 (*NPNF* 1, 10:241).

God unless placed at an "epistemic distance" from God. He says, "A quite overwhelmingly unambiguous self-disclosure . . . would be received by a compelling and not a voluntary awareness."[4] On this view, when a person receives a Postmortem Opportunity, the lack of epistemic distance necessitates their response; it is not possible to say no to a Postmortem Opportunity. To be clear, Hick is not merely claiming that it wouldn't be possible for a recipient of a Postmortem Opportunity to maintain reasonable nonbelief of God's existence, for whether or not the old adage "there are no atheists in foxholes" is true, there will certainly be no atheists on judgment day. All standing before God will believe that God exists. Hick's claim goes farther. He claims not only that a Postmortem Opportunity eliminates the freedom of belief in God, but that it eliminates the freedom of salvation: "When we think of a created being thus living face to face with [God] . . . there seems to be an absurdity in the idea of his seeing rebellion as a possibility, and hence in its even constituting a temptation to him."[5]

This is an interesting claim, and if true, constitutes a serious objection to my theory of Postmortem Opportunity. But is it true? Why does freely responding to God's offer of relationship require epistemic distance between us and God? The answer Hick ultimately gives to this question is closely tied up with his commitment to religious pluralism, but I can imagine two kinds of justification for this "freedom requires epistemic distance" claim that do not flow from or entail a commitment to religious pluralism. The first draws on the Platonic dictum "to know the good is to choose the good"—a statement widely and correctly attributed to Socrates, but not actually found word for word in Plato's writings[6]—and the second draws on Thomas Aquinas's view of the beatific vision.

[4]John Hick, *Faith and Knowledge*, 2nd ed. (Ithaca, NY: Cornell University Press, 1966 [1957]), 139.
[5]John Hick, *Evil and the God of Love* (London: Macmillan and Co., 1966), 314.
[6]There are a number of places where the ideas in this dictum can be found, including *Meno* 77b-78c. See Alexander Sesonske and Noel Flemming, eds., *Plato's Meno: Text and Criticism* (Belmont, CA: Wadsworth, 1965), 12-13.

"To know the good is to choose the good." According to Socrates, one who knew the good would choose the good—or, phrased differently, if one does not choose the good, it is out of ignorance; they did not actually know the good. Drawing on this Socratic notion, it is possible to flesh out Hick's epistemic distance argument by claiming that no one who stands before God and clearly sees God's perfection and moral goodness could possibly choose to reject him. Let's express this argument as follows:

1. One who experiences a Postmortem Opportunity will, in God, see perfect goodness.
2. To know the good is to choose the good.
3. Therefore, no one who experiences a Postmortem Opportunity would choose to reject God.

While this is not the place to plumb the depths of Socrates's claim, suffice it to say that there are some very real problems for this argument from a Christian theological perspective. An initial problem with Socrates's dictum is that it entails that all evil is due to ignorance of the good. But such a state of affairs, according to Keith Ward, "seems both to deprive men of real moral responsibility and to leave totally unintelligible the creation of such avoidable ignorance by a perfectly good God."[7] Moreover, the claim that one who sees the good will choose the good ignores some rather prominent biblical examples. Lucifer rebelled against God despite dwelling with him in heaven (Rev 12:3-9) and Adam and Eve rebelled against God in the Garden of Eden (Gen 3). Plato's and Socrates's account also fails to account for the reality of sin and particularly what is called the noetic effects of sin (the effects of sin on the mind). Scripture clearly seems to envision the possibility of seeing the good and choosing not to do it—hence James 4:17: "If anyone, then, knows the good they ought to do and doesn't do it, it is sin for

[7]Keith Ward, "Freedom and the Irenaean Theodicy," *Journal of Theological Studies* 20, no. 1 (April 1969): 252.

them." In this verse (and throughout Scripture) it is assumed that there is an important sense in which people can know the good and not do it. This does not necessarily imply that people choose what they think is bad for them. Rather, people do what they think is good for them, but, sadly, our beliefs about what we think is good for us often do not align with what is actually good for us. In fact, the essence of sin is not just that we do things we shouldn't, it is the choice to create our own standards for right and wrong and to not acknowledge God's moral authority over us. A better picture of the virtues that lead to good choices comes from Aristotle. Knowing the good wasn't enough for Aristotle, he held that it was possible to know the good and not do it. Aristotle held that humans need to *practice* virtue. Virtue needs to be developed over time by the choices one makes. Humans need to "habituate themselves" to virtue in order to truly be virtuous. So this suggests that in the postmortem encounter, even though the unevangelized and pseudoevangelized see God as he is and receive the best possible opportunity to be saved, it is possible for them to reject God's offer of grace if they have lived their lives in a way that practiced selfishness or demanded moral autonomy.

One who would use Socrates's dictum to argue that no one could say no to a Postmortem Opportunity also fails to understand the nature of the encounter with God on judgment day. God's question to the unevangelized will not be, "Do you want to be profoundly happy or profoundly unhappy?" It is undeniably true that we all want to be happy. The more salient question is, "What do you think will make you happy?" Although it is sad to say so, it is likely that many people—and perhaps many who have called themselves Christians their entire life—would chose to be their own god rather than serve for an eternity under the lordship of Jesus Christ—not because they are choosing unhappiness, but precisely because they are choosing their idea of eternal bliss. As such, a far better understanding of the postmortem encounter is given by Milton's famous question: "Do you want to serve in heaven or reign in hell?"

The beatific vision. There is another way of fleshing out Hick's "epistemic distance" argument. It draws not on the idea that seeing the good necessitates choosing the good, but on the idea that those who see God on the day of judgment will experience the beatific vision. Drawing on 1 Corinthians 13:12—"For now we see only a reflection as in a mirror; then we shall see face to face. Now I know in part; then I shall know fully, even as I am fully known"—Thomas Aquinas developed an influential account of the pinnacle of human happiness called "the beatific vision."[8] Ultimate happiness for humans, according to Aquinas, could only be attained when God gives us the gift of a face-to-face experience with him in which we see his essence. But it seems problematic to say that a person who experiences the beatific vision will reject God. As such, this objection to Postmortem Opportunity goes as follows:

1. One who experiences a Postmortem Opportunity will receive the beatific vision.
2. All who experience the beatific vision are perfectly happy and need nothing else.
3. Therefore, no one who experiences a Postmortem Opportunity would chose to reject God.

With Aquinas, I believe that those who receive the beatific vision will be perfectly happy and need nothing else. And, as I suggested in chapter seven, those who receive the beatific vision of God no longer have the capacity to reject God. But, following C. S. Lewis, I hold that the attainment of glory is a necessary precondition for the beatific vision.[9] So one who stands before God on judgment day and receives a Postmortem Opportunity sees God truly, but not fully. They know who God is and

---

[8]Thomas Aquinas, *Summa Theologica*, Supplement, Q. 92, a. 1 (New York: Benzinger Brothers, 1947), 2957-64.

[9]See the excellent discussion of Lewis's thought on this matter in Matthew Lee, "To Reign in Hell or to Serve in Heaven: C. S. Lewis on the Problem of Hell and the Enjoyment of the Good," in *C. S. Lewis as Philosopher: Truth, Goodness, and Beauty*, ed. David Baggett, Gary Habermas, and Jerry Walls (Downers Grove, IL: IVP Academic, 2008), 161-67.

what God expects of them, but they have not received the beatific vision. That is reserved for those who respond affirmatively to God's offer of salvation and enter into glory and eternal relationship with him.

POSTMORTEM OPPORTUNITY AND ONGOING OPPORTUNITIES

I have argued that the unevangelized and pseudoevangelized receive a Postmortem Opportunity to hear the gospel and repent, but in the previous chapter, in response to Patience Universalism, I claimed that God will not provide ongoing opportunities to those who reject their Postmortem Opportunity. One might wonder why. After all, given God's universal salvific will and his special love for the lost, why would he accept no for an answer? Wouldn't the motivation for the provision of a Postmortem Opportunity also be motivation for the provision of ongoing opportunities? Let's call the idea that there will be a time when God treats a person's response to the gospel as final the "finality thesis." While I reject the notion that death is the moment at which one's salvific destiny is sealed, I will argue for the finality and irrevocability of postmortem decision.

There are a couple of reasonable objections to the finality thesis. First, if God did not treat decisions in this life as being the final word, why would the postmortem decision be treated as irrevocable? The answer is that God provided the unevangelized and pseudoevangelized with a Postmortem Opportunity because they did not have a genuine opportunity to respond in this life, but he does not provide ongoing opportunities because after receiving the Postmortem Opportunity, they have not only received a genuine opportunity, they have received the best possible opportunity. The decisions of some—such as George's decision to trust the Creator of the stars—are made with incomplete knowledge. And the decision of others—such as Kunta Kinte's rejection of the God of his white slaveowners—is made with wildly misleading information. But those whom God deems to need a Postmortem

Opportunity are given the information, experience, or perspective necessary to either embrace or reject salvation. The crucial point here is that upon receiving the best possible opportunity to hear the gospel and rejecting it, what additional perspective or information or encouragement could encourage a different decision?

The pushback to this argument is that, by definition, a snap decision on judgment day cannot be the best possible opportunity to respond. But this objection assumes that the postmortem decision would have to be an immediate or snap decision, and that assumption is questionable. There are a pair of reasons for this. First, I think it is reasonable to be strongly agnostic about the experience of time in the afterlife. Even if we bracket metaphysical questions surrounding the nature of time, there still remains an array of phenomenological questions about how we will experience it. For example, time is progressing for me at a much faster rate now than it did when I was a kid. Does that mean that time has sped up? Not at all. It is my perception of the speed with which time is passing that has changed, not time itself. Consequently, even if the passage of time continues into the afterlife, it may still be that our experience of the passage of time in the afterlife and on judgment day in particular will be significantly different than our experience of the passage of time now. Second, recall that in chapter two, I said that there is nothing about the theory of Postmortem Opportunity (or my specific version of it) that requires any particular account of the actual Postmortem Opportunity. I confess that I don't know exactly what it will look like and that is because I don't know what the best possible Postmortem Opportunity to repent will look like. But I don't have any problem saying that God knows and, because he desires all to be saved, that he will provide just such an opportunity. If God knows that a particular person will require X amount of time to respond to his offer of salvation, then I have no problem saying that's what they will be given. Add to this the possibility of the existence of hypertime (an idea alluded to in chapter seven) and there is all the time that a person could want to respond to God's provision of a Postmortem Opportunity.

A second objection to the finality thesis is that, if postmortem choice is possible, what is it that makes an *ongoing* postmortem choice impossible? Is it consistent to allow for postmortem repentance but deny the possibility of ongoing opportunities to repent? Notice that this question is the flip side of a question discussed in chapter seven, whether Postmortem Opportunity entailed the possibility of sin in heaven. Now the question is whether Postmortem Opportunity entails the possibility of repentance in hell. An easy answer to this question is found in embracing Annihilationism: those who end up in hell are destroyed and cease to exist. In fact, Jonathan Kvanvig argues that Annihilationism is the best defense against Universalism. He says, "Unending separation would never, at any point, be final in any modally strong way. Finality only results when union with God is achieved or annihilation occurs."[10] Those who reject God's postmortem revelation are sent to hell where they cease to be. This is possible, but I am interested in seeing whether this question can be answered with a non-Annihilationist view of hell.[11]

One possibility is that one could claim that the persons in hell who have rejected a Postmortem Opportunity are not free in a libertarian sense. Their rejection of their Postmortem Opportunity has solidified their character in a way that they cannot now choose to repent and, as such, their freedom in hell is compatibilist in nature. This answer is possible, but notice that Kevin Timpe and Timothy Pawl's argument that the existence of libertarian freedom is compatible with the inability to sin in heaven can also be applied to the inability to repent in hell. Consequently, one can be free in hell but unable to repent in virtue of having a moral character that one has previously freely formed.

[10]Jonathan Kvanvig, "Autonomy, Finality, and the Choice Model of Hell," in *Destiny and Deliberation: Essays in Philosophical Theology* (New York: Oxford University Press, 2011), 17.

[11]My interest in avoiding Annihilationism is driven primarily by scriptural concerns. As I will argue below, I don't think that the notion of the "destruction of sinners" articulated in Scripture is metaphysical destruction or loss of being.

As Timpe and Pawl argue, "While an agent must have alternative possibilities open to her at some time in order to be free, the agent need not always have alternative possibilities open to her. She may freely form her character such that she *can't* choose *not* to perform some particular action at a later time, and nevertheless do the latter action freely."[12]

These solutions share a common theme, the idea of "solidification of character." But it might be asked, what is it that solidifies a person's character such that they cannot choose to repent in hell or cannot choose to sin in heaven? The traditional answer, "death," is of course, not available to the Postmortem Opportunity theorist. The answer, therefore, must reference the unevangelized person's response to the Postmortem Opportunity itself. The finality of the postmortem decision is a result of the fact that the decision results either in union with God or, since they have rejected the best possible opportunity to repent, the impossibility of being in union with God. Just as one who is in union with God cannot sin, so a person who rejected the best possible opportunity to hear the gospel cannot repent.

POSTMORTEM OPPORTUNITY AND THE NATURE OF HELL

Suppose it is true that not necessarily all are saved. There are some who hear the gospel in this life and reject it, and there are some who do not hear the gospel in this life, are given the best possible Postmortem Opportunity to repent, and they reject it. The theological coherence of this position rests on articulation of a model of hell that is compatible with the ideas already defended in this book: God's love for all people, especially the lost, and the perfect goodness of God. So a final question remains: What understanding of the nature of hell is compatible with an affirmation of Postmortem Opportunity?

---

[12]Timothy Pawl and Kevin Timpe, "Incompatibilism, Sin, and Free Will in Heaven," *Faith and Philosophy* 26, no. 4 (October 2009): 399-400.

The crucial question for any account of hell is, Why does it exist? What is the purpose of hell? Jonathan Kvanvig draws a distinction between two different models of hell or ways of answering the purpose question, the punishment model and the choice model.[13] The purpose of hell on the punishment model, not surprisingly, is retributive punishment. On this view, just as relationship with God constitutes the greatest good, so failure to embrace relationship with God is the most serious sin, and is therefore worthy of the most serious punishment. While this view has, admittedly, been assumed to be true for much of Christian history, it faces debilitating problems. The simple question to be asked of the punishment model of hell is why a perfectly loving God would inflict torture on his creatures forever. The immediate answer is that God is not only a God of love, he is also a God of holiness and justice. And that is, of course, true. But this answer misses the point, because even if it could be explained why God was within his rights in inflicting eternal torture on his creatures, why would a God who was perfectly good *want* to do so? God's holiness demands that he hate sin and that he be separate from sin, but it doesn't demand that he torture the sinner. So the claim that God's holiness and justice requires the eternal torture of sinners is not what is required by holding God's love and holiness in balance, it is what results when one ignores the reality of God's love.

Consequently, given God's love for the lost and given an appropriately scriptural balance between God's love and holiness, the choice model of hell is clearly preferable. On this view, the purpose of hell is not retributive punishment by means of fire and brimstone. After all, even John Calvin thought that the "burning" imagery of hell was metaphorical and not to be taken literally.[14] Rather, hell is self-imposed isolation. Hell is the tragic refuge of those who would rather reign in hell

---

[13]Kvanvig, "Hell," in *Oxford Handbook of Eschatology*, ed. Jerry Walls (New York: Oxford University Press, 2008), 413-26.

[14]John Calvin, *A Harmony of the Gospels: Matthew, Mark, and Luke*, trans. A. W. Morrison (Grand Rapids, MI: Eerdmans, 1972), 1:129. Here Calvin is commenting on Mt 3:12. See also his

than serve in heaven. It is a place where they can be away from God's love and where he will no longer stand at the door and knock (Rev 3:20). This view has been popularized by C. S. Lewis's famous claim that hell is not locked on the outside to keep prisoners in, it is locked on the inside, to keep God out. In the *Problem of Pain*, he says,

> I willingly believe that the damned are, in one sense, successful, rebels to the end; that the doors of hell are locked on the inside. I do not mean that the ghosts may not wish to come out of hell, in the vague fashion wherein an envious man "wishes" to be happy: but they certainly do not will even the first preliminary stages of that self-abandonment through which alone the soul can reach any good. They enjoy forever the horrible freedom they have demanded, and are therefore self-enslaved.[15]

As such, despite being chosen, hell remains a place of enormous suffering. In fact, if it is at all possible to quantify suffering, a case can be made that ongoing, self-imposed suffering is the most severe variety of suffering imaginable. Nonetheless, God's purpose for hell is not to torture those who have rejected him, but to honor their choices.[16] Those who cannot serve in heaven are given what they think they want, a reality in which they are their own God and beholden to none.

This idea is nicely conveyed by a 1960 episode of *Twilight Zone* entitled "A Nice Place to Visit."[17] This episode introduces us to Rocky Valentine, a petty criminal who is shot and killed while committing a crime. He wakes up to find himself in a very nice place, where all of the things that he sought in this life—money, women, and fame—are easily attained. He even has a "guardian angel"—played delightfully by Sebastian Cabot—who helps him secure all the things he prized in his earthly life. While he is initially overjoyed (even if a bit surprised) at his eschatological luck, it doesn't take him too long to realize that the attainment

comments on Mt 25:41 (3:117). This is not to suggest that Calvin embraced a choice model of hell. He did not. Nobody is perfect.

[15]C. S. Lewis, *Problem of Pain* (New York: HarperOne, 1996 [1940]), 130.

[16]Kvanvig, "Hell," 419.

[17]*The Twilight Zone*, episode 28; first aired on April 15, 1960.

of everything that he sought in this life is not very fulfilling. His frustration mounts, and eventually he implores his guardian angel for a change of venue, saying, "I don't belong in heaven! I want to go to the other place!" His guardian angel responds with an evil cackle and says, "Heaven? Whatever gave you the idea you were in heaven, Mr. Valentine? This is the other place!" Rod Serling's voice provides the punchline: "A scared, angry little man who never got a break. Now he has everything he's ever wanted—and he's going to have to live with it for eternity."

The advantages of the choice model of hell are many and profound. First, and most obviously, we are delivered from the insuperable difficulty of reconciling how God's love is compatible with his intentional and eternal torture of persons in hell. The second is less commonly acknowledged, but no less important—namely, the choice model of hell fits much better with an orthodox view of heaven. Kvanvig argues this point as follows:

> The fundamental point to notice here, however, is that the doctrines of heaven and hell are not separable in this way. They are intimately linked, and the account one accepts of one constrains the kind of account one can develop of the other. These points may seem obvious, but they are ignored regularly, especially in discussions of the nature of hell. If we think of hell as a place of punishment, the logical contrast would seem to indicate that heaven is a place of reward. Yet the Christian conception denies that heaven is fundamentally a reward for faithful service; it is, rather, the free and gracious gift of a loving God, unmerited by anything we have done. . . . On the usual position, admission to heaven is explained in terms of God's love, not his justice or fairness, whereas consignment to hell is explained in terms of his justice rather than his love.[18]

So the purpose of hell is to honor the choices of those who will not serve in heaven. Those who end up in hell are those who have chosen it over heaven. But this raises a second crucial question about hell: What is the phenomenology of hell? What is hell like and what will be the experience

---

[18]Kvanvig, "Hell," 420.

of those who choose to go there? One's understanding of the purpose of hell will, of course, constrain one's understanding of the phenomenology of hell. For example, given a choice model of hell, it would be extremely difficult to argue that the phenomenology of hell is fire and burning. The purpose of the references to fire and burning in hell—the most prominent example of which is the "lake of fire" language used in Revelation 19:20; 20:10, 14-15; 21:8—is to convey the reality of suffering in a particularly poignant and culturally relevant way—for that is the way the underworld was depicted in both Egyptian and Greek thought.[19] Scripture also uses other language to describe hell: darkness, separation, isolation; but the most common way to refer to hell is destruction. In Matthew 7:13-14, Jesus draws a contrast between the wide gate that "leads to destruction" and the narrow gate that "leads to life," and in Matthew 10:28 Jesus tells his disciples not to fear those who kill the body but cannot kill the soul; rather "be afraid of the One who can destroy both soul and body in hell." Similarly, Paul warns his readers that those who seek to accumulate earthly riches are pursuing a way of life that leads to "ruin and destruction" (1 Tim 6:9), and he says with great sadness that those who are "enemies of the cross" have "destruction" as their destiny (Phil 3:18-19). And, finally, Peter teaches that the fate of false, greedy teachers will be "destruction" (2 Pet 2:3) and that the day of judgment will see the "destruction of the ungodly" (2 Pet 3:7). But perhaps the most evocative reference to destruction is 2 Thessalonians 1:8-9: " [God] will punish those who do not know God and do not obey the gospel of our Lord Jesus. They will be punished with everlasting destruction and shut out from the presence of the Lord and from the glory of his might."[20]

---

[19]See the Egyptian *Book of the Dead* and Plato, *Phaedo*, 113 (where he is referring to Tartarus). I am not claiming that John used the language of "lake of fire" as an explicit reference to Plato and certainly not in reference to the *Book of the Dead*, only that the language of the underworld or place of the dead being both a place of punishment and having rivers and lakes of fire was a common one in pre-Christian mythologies of hell.

[20]Other passages that seem to refer to destruction of the wicked: Deut 29:20-23; Ps 9:6; 34:16; 37:9-10, 20; Is 1:28-31; 5:24; Dan 2:35; Nahum 1:10; Mal 4:1; Mt 3:10, 12; 1 Cor 3:17; Gal 6:8; 1 Thess 5:3; Jas 4:12; 2 Pet 2:6.

How should these references to destruction be understood? Defenders of Annihilationism argue that the biblical references to "destruction" support the belief that those who are sent to hell cease to be. In other words, they see Scripture articulating a metaphysical understanding of destruction. Arguments in support of this view include the claim that immortality is a gift given to believers, it is not promised to all. Hence John 3:15-16: "that everyone who believes may have eternal life in him. For God so loved the world that he gave his one and only Son, that whoever believes in him shall not perish but have eternal life."[21] In addition, Annihilationists argue that the references to eternal punishment refer to the consequences of that punishment, not its duration. Being "destroyed forever" (Ps 92:7) is not the same as forever being destroyed.

While some references to eternal punishment can be understood as referring to finality, not duration, others are more recalcitrant. For instance, Revelation 14:10-11 and 20:10 refer to sinners being punished "day and night forever and ever."[22] And the references to "unquenchable fire" and the "undying worm" in Mark 9:48 and Isaiah 66:24 convey a stronger sense of ongoing punishment. One would be tempted to ask, "If Scripture desired to teach that punishment was eternal and ongoing, could that notion be conveyed in a way that wasn't capable of being understood as eternal in consequence, not duration?" If Scripture was attempting to distinguish between the theories of Annihilationism and non-Annihilationism, then of course it would be possible, but Scripture does not engage theological questions with that level of abstraction.

Apart from these scriptural arguments, I question whether Scripture intends to convey the idea that sinners truly cease to exist, that their destruction is metaphysical. It seems more plausible to see the references to destruction as being functional, not metaphysical. Those who

---

[21]Other passages that teach this theme: Jn 10:28; 17:2; Rom 2:7; 6:23; 1 Cor 15:42, 50, 54; 1 Jn 5:11.

[22]In response, Annihilationists appeal to Is 34:10, which says that the fire that will consume Edom "will not be quenched night or day; its smoke will rise forever." But here it is likely that "Edom" is used in reference to those outside the covenant; cf. Mal 1:1-5.

choose to reject Christ are "destroyed" but that does not mean they cease to exist. They are destroyed in an analogous manner to a car that has been totaled. It continues to exist, but it no longer functions as it was intended, as a means of transportation. Similarly, humans that reject God continue to exist (metaphysically), they continue to be aware of their existence (consciously), but they can no longer fulfill their intended function of being in an I-Thou relationship with the God who created them and loves them.

This is the notion of hell conveyed by Karl Barth's *das nichtige*—a "nothingness" that stands in unrelenting opposition to God's offer of grace.[23] It also invoked C. S. Lewis's evocative picture of a soul in hell: "For a damned soul is nearly nothing: it is shrunk, shut up in itself. Good beats upon the damned incessantly as sound waves beat on the ears of the deaf, but they cannot receive it. Their fists are clenched, their teeth are clenched, their eyes fast shut. First they will not, in the end they cannot, open their hands for gifts, or their mouths for food, or their eyes to see."[24]

Consequently, those who are given the best possible opportunity to hear the gospel and reject it end up in hell. And persons who enter hell do not cease to be, but they do cease to be human persons. Lewis says, "To enter heaven is to become more human. . . . To enter hell, is to be banished from humanity. What is cast (or casts itself) into hell is not a man: it is remains."[25] And this is because to be human is to be created in God's image and those who finally and irrevocably refuse to image God will, of necessity, cease to be human. N. T. Wright articulates this possibility in a number of his writings. He says,

> If it is possible, as I've suggested, for human beings to choose to live more and more out of tune with the divine intention, to reflect the image of God less and less, there is nothing to stop them finally ceasing to bear that image, and

---

[23]Karl Barth, *Church Dogmatics* III/3 (Peabody, MA: Hendrickson, 2010 [1960]) §50, see especially 349.

[24]C. S. Lewis, *Great Divorce* (London: Geoffrey Bles, 1946), 113-14.

[25]Lewis, *Problem of Pain*, 127-28.

> so to be, as it were, beings who were once human but are not now. Those who persistently refuse to follow Jesus, the true Image of God, will by their own choice become less and less like him, that is, less and less truly human.[26]

These former persons are annihilated in a very real sense, but they do not cease to be.

One might ask what has actually been achieved by my notion of functional annihilation. The first answer is that it is the best interpretation of the biblical data. And that is, of course, not unimportant. But functional annihilation has another advantage. Recall Jonathan Kvanvig's challenge (mentioned above) that "finality only results when union with God is achieved or annihilation occurs."[27] Functional annihilation provides a sense of finality that is every bit as modally strong as metaphysical Annihilationism. Even if beings continue to exist in some sense, they cease to exist as persons, their ability to image God ceases, and (most importantly) their capacity for self-determined choice ends. They have chosen themselves as their god and they can and will chose nothing else.

CONCLUSION

In the final analysis, what does this chapter amount to? Am I claiming that there will be some that will not be in heaven but will instead be eternal denizens of hell? I believe that Satan and the demons will spend eternity in hell, and I believe that all human persons who reject God's gracious offer of salvation will be separated from him eternally. But this does not mean that I claim to know that any particular person will be in hell. While I have considered the arguments for Universalism and found them to be wanting, that does not mean that I know Universalism to be false. This is why the title of this chapter could have been "not *necessarily* Universalism." I have argued that the arguments for

[26]N. T. Wright, *Following Jesus: Biblical Reflections on Discipleship* (Grand Rapids, MI: Eerdmans, 2014 [1995]), 100.

[27]Kvanvig, "Autonomy, Finality, and the Choice Model of Hell," 17.

Universalism are not persuasive and that it is possible to accept Postmortem Opportunity and deny Universalism. Moreover, while I grant that it seems very likely that some will reject God and be separated from him for an eternity, I do not pretend to know who those people will be. This is because—as alluded to a number of times in this volume—I am a soteric skeptic. I do not think that the salvific status of persons is within my ken. As such, there is no person about whom I claim, "They are not saved." My Agnosticism on the salvific status of individuals is universal. Granted, there are some about whom my hope is nearly maximal, and justifiably so (my wife, my mother, and my grandmother) and some about whom I have very little to no hope, and justifiably so (Adolf Hitler, for example). But whatever justification I may or may not have, ultimately I don't know whether any particular person is or will be saved. Moreover, I don't expect to be able to know for such knowing is way beyond my pay grade.

What I do claim is that there will be no person who ends up in hell who did not have a genuine opportunity to embrace relationship with God, whether in this life or due to a Postmortem Opportunity. I believe that this claim is crucially important. Not only does it answer the question of the destiny of the unevangelized, it secures and explains the picture of God desiring to be in relationship with every person that exists and doing everything in his power to secure that relationship, short of eliminating a person's self-determining freedom. The Christian God is truly the God who seeks the lost sheep all the way to the end.

GENERAL INDEX

SCRIPTURE INDEX